Contents

Accounting in a BUSINESS CONTEXT

SECOND EDITION

Aidan Berry and Robin Jarvis

CHAPMAN & HALL

University and Professional Division

London · Glasgow · Weinheim · New York · Tokyo · Melbourne · Madras

Published by Chapman & Hall, 2-6 Boundary Row, London SE1 8HN, UK

Chapman & Hall, 2-6 Boundary Row, London SE1 8HN, UK

Blackie Academic & Professional, Wester Cleddens Road, Bishopbriggs, Glasgow G64 2NZ, UK

Chapman & Hall GmbH, Pappelallee 3, 69469 Weinheim, Germany

Chapman & Hall USA, One Penn Plaza, 41st Floor, New York, NY10119, USA

Chapman & Hall Japan, ITP - Japan, Kyowa Building, 3F, 2-2-1 Hirakawacho, Chiyoda-ku, Tokyo 102, Japan

Chapman & Hall Australia, Thomas Nelson Australia, 102 Dodds Street, South Melbourne, Victoria 3205, Australia

Chapman & Hall India, R. Seshadri, 32 Second Main Road, CIT East, Madras 600 035, India

First edition 1991
Second edition 1994
Reprinted 1995

Printed and bound in Hong Kong

ISBN 0 412 58740 8

A Catalogue record for this book is available from the British Library

Library of Congress Cataloging-in-Publication Data available

Case studies

Series foreword

This book is part of the 'Business in Context' series. The books in this series are written by lecturers all with several years' experience of teaching on undergraduate business studies programmes. When the series first appeared in 1989, the original rationale was to place the various disciplines found in the business studies curriculum firmly in a business context. This is still our aim. Business studies attracted a growing band of students throughout the 1980s, a popularity that has been maintained in the 1990s. If anything, that appeal has broadened, and business studies, as well as a specialism in its own right, is now taken with a range of other subjects, particularly as universities move towards modular degree structures. We feel that the books in this series provide an important focus for the student seeking some meaning in the range of subjects currently offered under the umbrella of business studies.

With the exception of the text *Business in Context*, which takes the series title as its theme, all the original texts in our series took the approach of a particular discipline traditionally associated with business studies and taught widely on business studies and related programmes. These first books in our series examined business from the perspectives of economics, behavioural science, law, mathematics and accounting. The popularity of the series across a range of courses has meant that the second editions of many of the original texts are about to be published and there are plans to extend the series by examining information technology, operations management, human resource management and marketing.

Whereas in traditional texts it is the subject itself that is the focus, our texts make business the focus. All the texts are based upon the same specific model of business illustrated in Figure 1. We have called our model 'Business in Context' and the text of the same name is an expansion and explanation of that model.

The model comprises four distinct levels. At the core are found the activities which make up what we know as business and include innovation, operations and production, purchasing, marketing, personnel and finance and accounting. We see these activities operating irrespective of the type of business involved and they are found in both the manufacturing and service industries as well as in the public and private sectors. The second level of our model is concerned with strategy and management decision-making. It is here that decisions are made which influence the direction of the business activities at our core. The third level of our model is concerned with organizational factors within which business activities and management decisions take place. The organizational issues we examine are structure, size, goals and organizational politics, patterns of ownership and organizational culture. Clear links can be forged between this and other levels of our model, especially between structure and strategy, goals and management decision-making, and how all aspects both contribute to and are influenced by the organizational culture. The fourth level concerns itself with the environment in which businesses operate. The issues here involve social and cultural factors, the role of the state and politics, the role of the economy, and issues relating to both technology and labour. An important feature of this fourth level of our model is that such elements not only operate as opportunities and constraints for business, but also that they are shaped by the three other levels of our model.

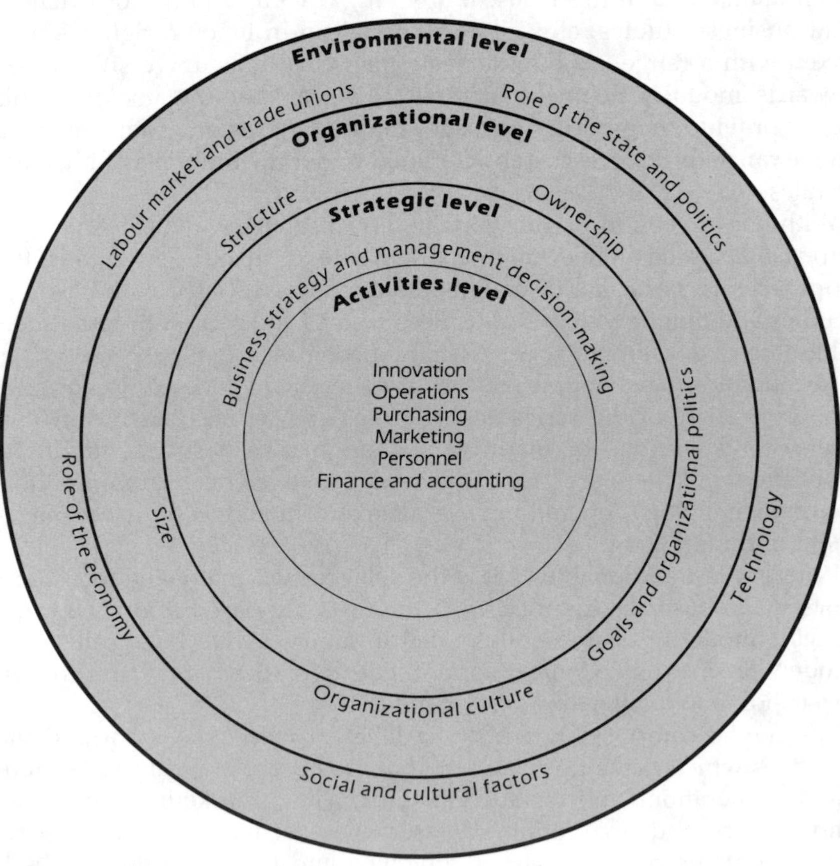

Fig. 1 Business in Context model

This brief description of the 'Business in Context' model illustrates the key features of our series. We see business as dynamic. It is constantly being shaped by and in turn shaping those managerial, organizational and environmental contexts within which it operates. Influences go backwards and forwards across the various levels. Moreover, the aspects identified within each level are in constant interaction with one another. Thus the role of the economy cannot be understood without reference to the role of the state; size and structure are inextricably linked; innovation is inseparable from issues of operations, marketing and finance. The understanding of how this model works is what business studies is all about and forms the basis for our series.

In proposing this model we are proposing a framework for analysis and we hope that it will encourage readers to add to and refine the model and so broaden our understanding of business. Each writer in this series has been encouraged to present a personal interpretation of the model. In this way we hope to build up a more complete picture of business.

Our series therefore aims for a more integrated and realistic approach to business than has hitherto been the case. The issues are complex but the authors' treatments are not. Each book in this series is built around the 'Business in Context' model, and each displays a number of common features that mark out this series. First we aim to present our ideas in a way that students will find easy to understand and we relate those ideas wherever possible to real business situations. Secondly we hope to stimulate further study both by referencing our material and by pointing students towards further reading at the end of each chapter. Thirdly we use the notion of 'key concepts' to highlight the most significant aspects of the subject presented in each chapter. Fourthly we use case studies to illustrate our material and stimulate further discussion. Fifthly we present at the end of each chapter a series of questions, exercises and discussion topics. To sum up, we feel it most important that each book will stimulate thought and further study and assist the student in developing powers of analysis, a critical awareness and ultimately a point of view about business issues.

We have already indicated that the series has been devised with the undergraduate business studies student uppermost in our minds. We also maintain that these books are of value wherever there is a need to understand business issues and may therefore be used across a range of different courses including some BTEC Higher programmes and some postgraduate and professional courses.

David Needle and Eugene McKenna

Preface to the second edition

The second edition of this book has, like its precedecessor, been written specifically with the needs of Business Studies and other non-accounting students in mind. It retains the same approach as the first edition by building from definitions through to a clear understanding of accounting statements and their usefulness and uses in decision making. As was the case in the first edition, the book is broadly based around the needs of users of accounting information.

The approach that has been adopted in both editions is to look initially at a simple cash-based business and then to build from this solid foundation to a more sophisticated model based upon accrual accounting principles. We have retained the worksheet as the vehicle for explaining double entry and were gratified that feedback from lecturers as well as students has confirmed that this approach facilitates the learning and understanding of the principles and interrelationships involved. The text and the case studies have been updated where appropriate to take account of changes in the environment, and we have added some additional exercises to some of the existing chapters. A minor change, but one worthy of note, is that the balance sheet formats have been changed and we have updated the examples to reflect current practice in respect of extraordinary items.

In response to comments received on the first edition, we have included a chapter on financing a business, which introduces the reader to the alternative sources of finance available to different types of business organization. This enables a more complete picture to be given of the balance sheet and the various headings included in that financial statement. In line with recent changes in reporting practice we have included a chapter relating to cash flow statements. We believe that this will assist a student in understanding the importance of both cash flow and profits to a successful business. In the first edition we chose to exclude this area because of the complications of providing an introduction and explanation of what was inherently a flawed statement, i.e. the statement of source and application of funds.

The second half of the book has retained its focus on the needs of internal users, and we have added some further exercises and updated the existing chapters. In addition, following the theme of internal users' needs and taking into account the comments received from

Acknowledgements

The additional chapters and the amendments to the first edition have essentially been derived from the helpful comments and discussions with students and academic colleagues. We therefore wish to express our thanks to our colleagues and students for these constructive contributions.

Finally, we would like to thank our wives, Gill (Berry) and Moira (Jarvis) for their support.

those who have used the first edition, we have included a new chapter on the subject of investment appraisal. This provides readers with a more complete understanding of the planning, control and decision-making processes, which is the theme of the existing chapters, by offering insights into the capital investment decision. Inclusion of this chapter also reflects changing syllabuses on business studies courses and the increasing use of this book on post-graduate management courses and degrees.

We have retained the philosophy of the book which has proved successful for both readers and lecturers using the first edition. We believe that this new edition is an improvement on its predecessor, yet retaining the same approach and style. We hope that it will prove to be more useful and at least as popular as the first edition.

Introduction to accounting 1

This chapter provides an introduction to the users of accounting information, its purpose, uses and limitations. It then analyses its importance and role within a business context at a strategic, organizational and environmental level.

This chapter will introduce you to the role of accounting, its uses and its users. It will also give you an appreciation of the role of accounting both within a business organization and in its external impacts. We shall introduce some ideas about the ways in which accounting assists managers in meeting business objectives through, for example, providing the information necessary to make a decision about buying or renting premises. The impacts of the size and type of organization on accounting will be discussed. For example, in very small organizations such as a window cleaning business the accounting requirements are likely to be less complex than is the case with a larger business such as British Rail. Another factor that both affects and is affected by accounting is the environment. The effects of the environment on accounting can be through the impact of government legislation as happens every time we adopt a new Companies Act or when a new EC Directive on accounting is added to the United Kingdom's statute book. Apart from government action, accounting can be affected at this level by changes in technology. For instance the move towards greater use of flexible manufacturing systems poses a major challenge to accountancy whilst the introduction of information technology has allowed accounting information to be provided more quickly and efficiently, thus enabling different decisions to be taken than would otherwise have been the case. From this brief résumé we can see that the accounting activity interacts with all levels of the 'Business in Context' model as explained in the Series foreword.

In order to understand the role and importance of accounting in the context of business organizations it is first necessary to decide what the word 'accounting' means. If you were to look up the word 'account' in Roget's Thesaurus you would be directed to words such as report and narration. Further investigation would reveal that it is also referred to as commercial arithmetic, double-entry book-keeping etc. These alternatives imply totally different things: a report is something that conveys information for a particular purpose, whereas commercial arithmetic implies a mechanical exercise following agreed rules or principles.

In practice, although accounting is normally seen as a series of figures, which may give the impression that it is only a form of commercial arithmetic, these are, in fact, merely a convenient way of summarizing and reporting information that would be indigestible in narrative form. For example, if you were asked to provide a report giving details of the value of everything you own, it would be simpler to use figures to represent the value rather than words. However, there are certain things that do not lend themselves to summaries in numerical terms. An example may be the value of good health, the value of lead-free petrol, or even the value of a qualification such as a degree, an HND or whatever.

Apart from problems concerned with what can be reported and what should be reported, other problems need to be considered, for example whether it can be reported in a numerical format and whether that is the best format. We also need to consider whom the report is for and what it is to be used for. For instance, you may give totally different accounts of your car's capabilities to a prospective buyer and to a mechanic to whom you had taken it for repairs. So we can see that the question of defining accounting has many facets. We shall look at these issues in more detail later in this chapter. Prior to that, in order to get a better idea of what accounting is generally thought to be about, let us examine some definitions contained in the accounting literature.

A definition that is commonly quoted is that produced by the American Institute of Certified and Public Accountants (AICPA) in 1941:

> Accounting:
> . . .'is the art of recording, classifying, and summarising, in a significant manner and in terms of money, transactions and events which are in part at least, of a financial character, and interpreting the results thereof.'

This definition implies that accounting has a number of components – some technical (such as recording of data), some more analytical (such as interpreting the results) and some that beg further questions (such as 'in a significant manner': significant to whom and for what?).

Let us consider another definition offered by the same professional body:

> Accounting:
> . . . 'is the collection, measurement, recording, classification and communication of economic data relating to an enterprise, for purposes of reporting, decision making and control.'

This gives us a clue to the fact that accounting is closely related to other disciplines (we are recording economic data) and it also gives us some clue as to the uses of accounting information, i.e. for reporting on what has happened and as an aid to decision making and control of the enterprise.

Another part of the same document sees accounting as

> . . . a discipline which provides financial and other information essential to the efficient conduct and evaluation of the activities of any organization.

This suggests that the role of accounting information within an organization is at the very core of running a successful organization. Thus, as we have already noted, accounting can be seen as a multifaceted activity which not only records and classifies information but also provides an input to the decision-making processes of enterprises.

The latter point is brought out more clearly in the later definition provided by the American Accounting Principles Board in 1970 (APE No. 4):

> Accounting is a service activity. Its function is to provide quantitative information, primarily financial in nature, about economic entities that is intended to be useful in making economic decisions, in making reasoned choices among alternative courses of action.

KEY CONCEPT 1.1
Accounting

The important points made in these definitions are that

- accounting is about quantitative information
- the information is likely to be financial
- it should be useful for making decisions

The fact that it is described as a service activity reinforces the point made earlier that in order to understand the usefulness of accounting we need to know who uses it and what they use it for.

For what purpose is it used?

This question can be answered on two levels at least: that of the individual and that of the enterprise. If we take the level of the individual first, accounting information could be used to help them control the level of their expenditure, to assist in planning future levels of expenditure and to help them raise additional finance (e.g. mortgages, hire-purchase etc.) and to decide the best way to spend their money. Thus we see that at the level of the individual, accounting can have three functions, i.e. planning, controlling and decision support.

At the level of the enterprise it is used to control the activities of the organization, to plan future activities, to assist in raising finance and to report upon the activities and success of the enterprise to interested parties.

You will note that the major difference between the two is that in the case of an enterprise, apart from its uses in planning, controlling and decision making which are all internal activities or functions, accounting also has what we could describe as an external function, i.e. that of providing information to people outside the enterprise. The latter function is usually met through the medium of annual accounts or financial reports and is often referred to as financial accounting. The external users may use the information contained in the financial report as part of their decision process or to evaluate what management has done with the money invested in the business. Apart from meeting the needs of external users the system that produces the financial accounting reports also meets some of the needs of internal users, for example, to see the results of plans implemented in the last year. This requires information on the actual outcomes. This can then be evaluated against the projected outcomes, reasons for differences identified and appropriate actions taken. Other needs of management are met through reports based upon information provided by the internal accounting system. The internal accounting system, which may be in addition to the system which underpins the financial reporting system, is often referred to as the management accounting function. The major difference is that management accounting is primarily directed towards providing information of specific use to managers, whereas financial accounting information, which is often less detailed, has many users apart from managers.

Who uses accounting information?

Whether accounting information relates to the activities of an individual or to a business enterprise, its users can be placed in two broad categories:

1 those inside the enterprise – the managers or in the case of a small business the owner;
2 those outside the enterprise, including banks, the government, tax authorities etc.

Internal users

The major internal user is the management of an enterprise. For a small enterprise this is likely to be the owner or a small number of individuals in the case of a partnership. However, many businesses are much larger and these may be owned by numerous individuals or groups of individuals, as is the case with large enterprises such as Woolworths, Marks & Spencers, Sainsburys or British Petroleum. In many cases the major investors are themselves owned by others, as is the case with the major financial institutions. In this situation it is extremely unlikely that the actual owners would or could take an active part in the day-to-day running of the enterprise. Consider the chaos if all the people who bought shares in British Telecom tried to take an active part in the day-to-day running of that business. Instead these owners or shareholders delegate the authority for the day-to-day running to a group of directors and managers.

These directors and managers are involved in the routine decision making and are the equivalent of the owner in a small business in terms of their information needs. These needs are normally met through unpublished reports of various kinds. These reports are generally based on information provided through both the financial and the management accounting systems. The exact nature of the reports will vary from enterprise to enterprise. For example, a department store may require information about the profitability of each of its departments whereas for a factory producing a small number of different products the information required is more likely to be about the profitability of each product.

The form of the report will also vary depending on its purpose. For example, if management wish to control what is going on it will need a report on the past transactions and performance, probably measured against some predetermined standard. For planning purposes, however, a forecast of what is likely to happen in the future will be more important. These different forms of reports and ways of grouping information are normally referred to under the generic heading of management acounting and this form of accounting will be the focus of the second half of this book. At this stage it is worth briefly summarizing the different categories of management accounting reports. To do this we need to make some broad generalizations about the needs of managers and to categorize those needs in some meaningful way. In practice of course there is a certain amount of overlap between the categories but we need not concern ourselves with this at present. The categories will be discussed in greater detail in Chapters 13–19. The broad categories that we have referred to in terms of the needs of managers are as follows.

Stewardship What is often referred to as the stewardship function is in fact simply the need to protect the enterprise's possessions (normally referred to as assets) from theft, fraud etc.

Planning The need to plan activities so that the finance can be raised, marketing and promotional campaigns can be set up and production plans can be made. This is the planning function.

Control The need to control the activities of the enterprise which may include setting sales targets, ensuring that there are enough goods in stock etc. It will also include identifying where targets have and have not been met so that the reasons for the failure to achieve the targets can be identified. This is referred to as the control function.

Decision making The need to make specific decisions (should we produce the item ourselves or buy it in? How much will it cost to produce a particular item? How much money will we need in order to run the enterprise? etc.) This is the decision support function.

A moment's reflection will lead us to the conclusion that the area of management accounting is a vast area in its own right and so, rather than getting deeply involved at this stage, let us first look at the other broad area we identified – the needs of users outside the enterprise, the external users. We shall of course be returning to the needs of internal users in more detail in Chapter 13.

External users

We need to establish who the external users are. Fortunately there have been many reports which have done just that; a good example is *The Corporate Report*, published by the Institute of Chartered Accountants in England and Wales (1975). The list below, taken from *The Corporate Report*, includes most of the accepted users of external financial reports:

> **KEY CONCEPT 1.2**
> ***Financial accounting***
>
> Financial accounting can broadly be thought of as that part of the accounting system that tries to meet the needs of the various external user groups. This it does by means of an annual report which usually takes the form of a balance sheet, profit and loss account and cash flow statement

- the owner/s (shareholders in a company)
- those who lend the enterprise money (e.g. the bankers)
- those who supply the enterprise with goods (suppliers)
- those who buy goods from the enterprise (customers)
- the employees of the enterprise
- the government
- the general public

These groups are normally provided with information by means of published annual reports. This type of accounting is generally referred to as financial accounting. In order to decide to what extent the annual reports meet the needs of the external users and to understand more fully the importance of accounting we shall briefly discuss the needs of the external users listed above.

Owners/Shareholders

As we have said, in the case of a small enterprise the owners are likely to be actively engaged in the day-to-day operations of the enterprise. In these small enterprises therefore the owners' needs will often be met by the management accounting information and reports. As the enterprise grows, however, it is likely that the owners will become divorced from the immediate routine operation and will therefore not have access to the management accounting information, which in any case may be too detailed for their requirements. This is the case in companies quoted on the Stock Exchange. It is also going to be the case in a number of other businesses where the functions of management are carried out by people other than the owners.

In all these cases the owner needs to know:

- whether the enterprise has done as well as it should have done;
- whether the managers have looked after, and made good use of, the resources of the enterprise.

In order to evaluate whether the enterprise has done well and whether resources have been adequately used there is a need to be able to compare the results of one enterprise with the results of others. Information of this type is normally based on past results and under certain conditions it can be provided by financial accounts.

Owners also need to know:

- how the enterprise is going to fare in the future.

Financial accounting is unlikely to provide this information for a variety of reasons, in particular because it is largely if not exclusively based on the past and takes no account of future uncertainties. Past results may be taken into account as one piece of information amongst many when one is trying to predict the future, but in a changing world it is unlikely that past results will be repeated as conditions will have changed.

Although there are limitations on the usefulness of the information contained in annual reports, these are often the only form of report available to an owner who is not involved in the day-to-day activities of the business. Owners therefore have to base their decisions on this information despite its inadequacies. Thus for example a shareholder, who is after all a part owner, may use the accounting information contained in the annual report, by comparing the results of the business with those of another business, to decide on whether to sell his or her shares. In practice the involvement of the shareholder in this process of making comparisons, in the case of a quoted company, is likely to be fairly indirect. This is because most of the information contained in the annual reports will already have been looked at by the owner's professional advisers who may be accountants, stockbrokers or financial analysts. The investor and owner are therefore likely to make the decision based on the professional advice they receive rather than relying upon their own interpretation of the information contained in annual reports. This is not to say that they will rely exclusively on expert information or that they will not use the information provided in the annual reports for their decision. The reality is likely to be a mixture, the balance of which will depend on the degree of financial sophistication of the shareholder or owner, i.e. the less sophisticated they are the more reliance they will have to place on their external advisers.

Lenders

People and organizations only lend money in order to earn a return on that money. They are therefore interested in seeing that an enterprise is making sufficient profit to provide them with their return (usually in the form of interest). This information is normally provided by means of the profit and loss account. They are also interested in ensuring that the enterprise will be able to repay the money it has borrowed; thus they need to ascertain what the enterprise owns and what it owes. This information is normally provided in the balance sheet.

In practice research (Berry *et al.*, 1987 & 1993) has shown that UK bankers use a mixture of different approaches to arrive at the lending decision. The choice of approach has been shown to be related to the size of the enterprise. In the case of smaller enterprises the 'gone concern' or security-based approach, which emphasizes the availability of assets for repayment in the event of the business going bust, predominates and the emphasis is clearly on the balance sheet. However, with very large businesses the approach adopted is more likely to be the 'going concern' approach where the emphasis is more clearly focused on the profitability of the enterprise. The importance of published accounting information in the form of annual reports for this group cannot be overemphasized: nearly 100% of respondents to a recent survey (Berry *et al.*, 1987) said that the reports were very important and always used in making a lending decision.

Suppliers of goods and services

Goods and services can be supplied on the basis either that they are paid for when they are supplied or that they are paid for at some agreed date in the future. In both cases the supplier will be interested to know whether the enterprise is likely to stay in business and whether it is likely to expand or contract. Both these needs relate to the future and as such can never be adequately met by information in the annual report as this relates to the past.

Suppliers of goods who have not been paid immediately will also be interested in assessing the likelihood of getting paid. This need is partially met by the annual report as the balance sheet shows what is owned and what is owed and also gives an indication of the liquidity of the assets. The reason that we are tentative about the use of the balance sheet in this way is that often the information is many months out of date by the time that it is made public, as it is only published annually.

Customers

Like suppliers, customers are interested in an enterprise's ability to survive and therefore to carry on supplying them with goods. For example, if you are assembling cars you need to be sure that the suppliers of your brakes are not going to go bankrupt. The importance of this has increased with the introduction of techniques such as Just-in-time management. The customers in this situation will need to see that the enterprise is profitable, that it owns enough to pay what it owes and that it is likely to remain in business and supply components efficiently and on time. Some of these needs are met at least partially by the profit and loss account and the balance sheet.

The employees

Employees depend on the survival of the enterprise for their wages and therefore are interested in whether the enterprise is likely to survive. In the long term, an enterprise needs to make a profit in order to survive. The profit and loss account may assist the employee in making an assessment of the future viability of the company.

The employee may also be interested in comparing how well the enterprise is doing, compared with other similar enterprises, for the purposes of wage negotiations, although the accounts are only useful for this purpose if certain conditions are met. The accounts can also be used internally for wage negotiations as information about the company's level of profitability and ability to pay can be obtained from them.

The government

The government uses accounting information for a number of purposes the most obvious of which is the levying of taxes. For this purpose it needs to know how much profit has been made. This information is provided in the profit and loss account. The government also uses accounting information to produce industry statistics for the purposes of regulation etc.

It should also be borne in mind that in certain cases these roles are combined with other functions. For example, that of owner (British Coal), customer (defence procurement), or public watchdog (environmental protection boards). Equally it can have any one of these and other roles such as regulatory roles etc. For all these purposes the government uses accounting information.

The general public

The general public may require many different types of information about enterprises in both the public and private sectors. Much of this information is not supplied directly by financial accounts. For example, the public might be interested in the level of pollution resulting from a particular activity. This information is not at present provided by accounting reports; however, accounting reports may be useful in informing the public of the ability of an enterprise to absorb the additional costs of providing pollution controls. On the other hand, certain information provided in financial accounts may be of more direct relevance, e.g. the profitability or otherwise of nationalized industries. The ways in which financial reports are used for presenting both financial information and other information of interest to the public is illustrated in Case Study 1.1 taken from the annual reports of British Coal Corporation and Sainsbury.

CASE STUDY 1.1
British Coal and J. Sainsbury plc

Commentary

Increasing public concern with the environment in the late 1980s and early 1990s has been reflected in the increasing coverage of environmental issues in the annual reports of companies. As you will see from the extracts from the annual report of British Coal Corporation for 1991/2 a whole section was devoted to the environment. This was illustrated with colour photographs which provided a visual representation of the text.

Extract from the annual report of British Coal Corporation, 1991/2

The environment

An important step forward in 1991/2 was the appointment of an Environmental Management Team which has led the way in establishing routine environmental auditing. The team carried out a programme of detailed site audits which compared performance against the standards set by the Corporation's environmental policy, and provided guidance to local environmental auditing teams established in the coalfields. A formal reporting system of basic measures of environmental performance at each site was also introduced towards the end of the year.

This is regarded as only the starting point, allowing specific objectives to be set, and improvements planned and implemented.

British Coal's close relationships with external environmental experts continued to develop. Several university research projects were sponsored to investigate environmental effects such as air pollution in relation to dust, and mining subsidence. Support of Groundwork Trusts has also continued in an effort to improve the environment around older colliery sites.

British Coal officials assisted the House of Commons Select Committee on Welsh Affairs in their investigation into water discharges from abandoned mines.

Mining subsidence The Coal Mining Subsidence Act 1991 came into force on 30 November 1991. The new legislation consolidated the Acts which previously governed coal mining subsidence, gave force of law to various voluntary undertakings on the part of British Coal, and included a number of new provisions.

At the same time the Department of Energy issued a revised version of its leaflet, 'Claimants Rights: A Guide for Householders' reflecting the new legislation. Copies of the new leaflet were enclosed with individual letters to householders, notifying them of future mining operations, sent for the first time in December, 1991. In addition a revised mining search procedure was agreed with the Law Society for the conveyancing of land and property in coalfield areas.

Some 35 claims were settled through the voluntary arbitration scheme for householders which was introduced last year. A further scheme to cover non-domestic properties was being discussed with the Department of Energy and the Chartered Institute of Arbitrators.

During the year 7 868 new claims were received and 10 175 were resolved.

The opencast environment All British Coal Opencast sites are designed with high environmental standards for both site working and land restoration. Before each planning application an Environmental Assessment examines all aspects of site working from visual effect to traffic movement, to ensure that each site operates as a 'good neighbour' in the community.

Eighty per cent of opencast land is restored to agriculture or forestry, in many cases returning to productive use land previously barren through industrial activity. A five-year rehabilitation programme ensures good productivity from the land and a research programme, now twelve years old, enables continuous technical development. Opencast's research farm in South Wales is run on organic lines and has demonstrated that wildlife species on restored land can be many and varied. Some fifty species are used in hedgerow and woodland replanting and the development of new community forests.

New options for land restoration have included major roads, a shopping mall, a regional airport, informal areas of recreational woodland and golf courses. Major nature reserves have been established, and plans drawn up for a one hundred acre reedbed at the East Chevington site, Amble, the largest North of The Wash. At St Aidans in Yorkshire a new nature reserve features specially shaped islands and lakes of varying depth attracting a wide variety of birdlife.

British Coal Opencast's concern for the environment has led to research and sponsorship agreements with such organisations as woodland and county wildlife trusts, and the RSPB, resulting in direct support to protect, for example, hawks, owls, badgers and amphibians. In Scotland the Opencast Region drew up an agreement with Cumnock and Doon Valley District Council aimed at achieving a balance between the needs of industry and the environment. The new Parc Slip Nature Park in South Wales won Opencast a Major Commendation in the Business and Industry Commitment to the Environment Scheme. The Wetlands and Opencast Discovery Centre at the Ebbw Vale Festival of Wales – a joint venture with the Wetlands and Wildlife Trust – is a major attraction.

Coal use and the environment

The Greenhouse Effect While the combustion of all fossil fuels leads to the release of greenhouse gases (principally carbon dioxide), British Coal believes that fuel switching to lower carbon content fuels is a short-term response that will have little or no long-term impact on enhanced global warming. Initial estimates of the environmental impact of global warming have been revised downwards and uncertainty is likely to surround the entire issue for years to come. However, in view of the potential seriousness of global warming, British Coal believes that prudent, 'least regret' measures should be adopted. These measures, which promote major benefits at minimal cost, can be applied to such areas as the improvement of electricity generation and end-use efficiency, and the reduction of emissions from growth areas such as transport.

British Coal's view is that global policies can be adopted that minimise the potential threats without risking major economic dislocation. As part of international initiatives in this area, British Coal is acting as the operating agent for a major International Energy Agency study which will assess power generation technologies with the aim of reducing greenhouse gas emissions from the combustion of all fossil fuels.

Political responses British Coal was closely involved with the Intergovernmental Panel on Climate Change (IPCC) in its preparation of a major background paper for discussion at the UN conference on environment and development (Earth Summit) at Rio de Janeiro.

British Coal also put its views to the House of Lords Select Committee examining EC proposals on European joint carbon and energy taxes. These are that the unilateral implementation of these measures could not be justified under a 'least regret' approach and would cause severe economic dislocation. Neither would it have a significant impact on the transport sector which is the major growth area for CO_2 emissions.

Technical responses British Coal has for many years supported research and development into clean coal technologies. This strategy was endorsed by the findings of the Coal Task Force, a committee set up by the Department of Energy, which made recommendations on future UK coal research. They concluded that the development of clean coal technologies should be continued. Subsequently the Department of Energy set up an Appraisal Working Party to examine in detail options for building and operating a demonstration plant for advanced coal-fired power generation technology.

British Coal, in collaboration with PowerGen, GEC Alsthom, the US Electric Power Research Institute, and the Department of Energy, has demonstrated the feasibility of key aspects of the 'Topping Cycle' technology. The testbed facility, at Grimethorpe in Yorkshire, has now successfully completed its objectives and research into the system is continuing at the Coal Research Establishment near Cheltenham.

British Coal has taken part in a number of specific environmental programmes, including an EC study in relation to proposed limits governing emissions from combustion plant with less than 5MWth input. Research has also been carried out into ways of improving the efficiency and operation of large conventional combustion plant. During the year, the Coal Research Establishment embarked on a major project to examine the build-up of ash deposits in pulverised fuel boilers in collaboration with National Power, PowerGen, Government departments, and other organisations.

The generators are proceeding with plans to install flue gas desulphurisation (FGD) plant on 6 GWe of UK power station capacity. All of this, at Drax and Ratcliffe power stations, is already under construction. Such plant, which can remove 90 per cent of the emissions of sulphur dioxide, offers the best long term solution to SO2 emissions and will enable the UK to comply with European Directives.

The complementary programme to retrofit power stations with low NOx (nitrogen oxide) burners is nearing completion. These burners, which can reduce emissions by over 35%, have now been fitted to 10 GWe of UK coal-fired generating capacity.

Technology transfer British Coal has become increasingly involved in the transfer of technology to less developed countries.

This is an extremely cost effective way of improving the efficiency and environmental impact of global energy use. British Coal is active in a number of projects, including a contract to study energy efficiency and air and water quality in Taiyuan City, the capital of China's Shanxi Province.

Commentary

Although it could be argued that British Coal Corporation is a special case, because of the nature of its business, there is an increasing trend for businesses in general to include additional non-financial information in annual reports. Another example that reflects the increasing awareness of environmental issues is shown by the fact that, in its 1992 Annual Report, J. Sainsbury plc also devoted a section to the environment and the actions it was taking to protect the environment.

Extract from the annual report of J. Sainsbury plc, 1992

The environment – A natural concern

Over the last 15 years we have systematically reviewed our store design to arrive at the concept of a low energy store resulting in annual savings of £10 million. As a consequence of this commitment to energy-saving, we have been granted part-funding by the European Commission for an in-store energy-saving system. Through its use it will be possible, for example, to detect lights or ovens left on accidentally, and to measure any unseasonal use of energy. If the current pilot project is successful, the system will be introduced into all stores to reduce energy consumption by up to 10%, producing projected annual savings of £1.5 million.

We are able to undertake a project of this kind only because we have been installing the necessary computer systems in branches for the past ten years.

Action on CFCs The phasing out of CFCs is one of the biggest challenges facing the food industry today. Sainsbury's is committed to replacing CFCs in refrigeration by the end of 1996. As part of this process, last year we were the first supermarket retailer in Europe to introduce on a large scale an ozone-benign refrigerant in chiller cabinets. In order to ensure that alternatives to CFCs are found as quickly as possible, we have joined forces with retailers in Europe and America to pool information.

A large supermarket can contain up to five miles of refrigerant piping from which it is important to prevent leakages. We have taken a lead with the installation of a leak detection facility in 60 stores containing centralised refrigeration plant systems. A two-year programme is now under way to bring all such stores up to the same standard.

In January we organised a CFC Action Forum for suppliers, distributors and other retailers. The principal speakers included the Environment Minister, David Maclean; Jonathon Porritt; and Joe Farman of the British Antarctic Survey, who first brought the damage to the ozone layer to world attention.

Energy saving in packaging To ensure that our products are packaged in the minimum amount of material necessary, last year we launched a general packaging review. As a consequence we have already identified potential savings of £2.1 million.

These annual savings include 31 tonnes of plastic through the removal of punnets from packs of pitta bread and 119 tonnes through the removal of polystyrene bases from pizza packaging. Additionally, the use of returnable crates, first introduced 30 years ago, now saves about 28 000 tonnes of packaging a year.

During the year customers made greater use of the facilities available at our branches for collecting glass, paper, cans and plastic material for recycling. By working with local authorities we have increased the number of these units to 632.

From this brief survey of the users of accounting information and the uses to which it can be put it is clear that it has effects both within the organization and in the wider environment in which enterprises operate and in which we live. It should also be clear that the environment can use accounting as a tool for enterprise control. Before going on to consider in detail its impact upon the environment and the impact of the environment on accounting we should first consider the limitations of accounting information in order to put its potential impact in context.

Limitations of accounting information

Firstly and perhaps most importantly it has to be stressed that accounting is only one of a number of sources of information available to decision makers. It may be the case that other sources of information are just as important if not more important than the information contained in the accounts. You will have an opportunity to examine this in more detail in the Problems for discussion and analysis at the end of this chapter. However, to give you a flavour of what we are talking about, research with bankers (referred to later) shows that a banker's personal interview with the client is as important as financial information. This is probably because accounting generally only reports on financial items, i.e. those that can be expressed in financial (monetary) terms, whereas the information that bankers are trying to derive from the interview is more qualitative, e.g. an impression of the ability of the applicant to run a successful business. It is also possible that the information which accounting provides is only of secondary importance, as would be the case where new technology has made the precise costing of a product irrelevant because the product is obsolete. The relative importance of various sorts of information is illustrated in Case Study 1.2.

CASE STUDY 1.2
Independent Television Corporation

Commentary

The relative importance of financial and other information varies from one organization to another. Many organizations only quantify and report on their performance in financial terms, others provide the user with a mixture of financial and other performance indicators. The example in this case study, which is taken from the 1992 annual report of the Independent Television Corporation, provides users with a mixture of information about programme hours, staffing and finances.

Extract from the annual report of the Independent Television Corporation, 1992

Independent Television Key Figures (years ending 31 December)

	1991	1992
ITC Licences Extant (nos)		
Terrestrial		
Channel 3 regional	14	15
Channel 3 national breakfast-time	—	1
Channel 4	—	1
Public teletext service	—	1
Commercial additional services	—	1
Cable and satellite*		
Non-domestic satellite	33	45
Licensable programme services	41	51
Local delivery systems (15 years)	9	9
Local delivery transitional (5 years)	49	49
Cable diffusion	45	44
Prescribed diffusion	122	115
Programme hours transmitted (year)		
ITV (in average region)	7490	7490
TV-am	1244	1244
Channel 4	7225	7394
Total	15959	16128

	1991	1992
Staff		
ITC (average number)	254	239
Finance (£m)		
Terrestrial net advertising revenue (1)		
ITV	1344	1411
Channel 4	250	242
S4C	3.5	3
TV-am	74	75
Total	1671.5	1731
Terrestrial sponsorship income	†n/a	9
Total terrestrial qualifying revenue	†n/a	1741
Total satellite and cable programme services qualifying revenue (2)	140	306
ITC rentals and licence fees	21	17
Fourth Channel subscription allocation	313	310
Allocation: Channel 4	255	251
S4C	58	59
Exchequer levy	114	69

Notes
(1) Until the end of 1992 the ITV companies sold airtime on both ITV and the Fourth Channel. The sub-divisions shown are the amounts invoiced to each channel and may not necessarily reflect the share of the terrestrial NAR total which will be earned by each channel when their airtime is sold separately from 1 January 1993.
(2) Advertising revenue, sponsorship, and subscription income for year ended 30 September. Excludes services broadcast wholly outside the UK.

* Including those inherited from the Cable Authority. Licence definitions on page 17.
† Not available

Even given the role of accounting information in relation to other information, we also have to bear in mind that, in general, financial accounting information relates to the past and the decisions that need to be taken relate to the future. Thus, unless the past is a reasonable predictor of the future the information may have limited value for this purpose. In the real world, because of the impact of such things as changes in technology, innovations, changing fashions and inflation the past is unlikely to be a good predictor of the future.

Apart from these problems there is also the question of what is and what is not included in the financial accounts. For instance, some items which, it is generally agreed, should be included in financial reports are often difficult to measure with any accuracy and thus the figures become more subjective. A good example of this problem is an unfinished building. How do we decide on a figure to represent something that is only half complete. Another example is the problem of deciding how long something is going to last, e.g. a motor car clearly loses value the older it gets. We might decide that a car ceases to be useful to the business after four or five years, but this is to some extent an arbitrary decision as there are many older cars that still serve a useful purpose.

In addition to the problem of deciding how long things will last or what stage of completion they have reached, certain items are difficult to quantify in terms of value and are not easily included in financial reports. For example the value of a football club is dependent on its ability to attract supporters; this in turn is dependent on its ability to succeed, which is dependent on the abilities of the players etc. However, although it is doubtful that an exact value could be placed on a player, as this value will vary with the player's fitness, etc., Spurs football club, for instance, include their players in their accounts.

In addition to the questions raised above there are many environmental factors which need to be taken into account but which cannot be adequately included in accounts, although they may be quantifiable in money terms. Examples are the potential market for the product, the impact of European Community (EC) quotas, tariff restrictions and environmental issues. If these were to be included in the annual reports of a business it could lead to a loss of competitive advantage.

Finally we have to deal with the fact that accounting information is expressed in monetary terms and assumes that the monetary unit is stable over time. This is patently not the case and although there has been much discussion on the problems of accounting in times of inflation no agreed solution has yet been found.

We can conclude from the discussion above that, whilst it is clear that accounting provides some information that is useful to decision makers, we must bear in mind:

1 that the information is only a part of that necessary to make 'effective' decisions;
2 that accountancy is as yet an inexact science and depends on a number of judgements, estimates etc.;
3 that the end result of the accounting process can only be as good as the inputs and in times of rising prices some of these inputs are of dubious value;
4 that accounting systems can be counterproductive, e.g. the maximization of a division's profit may not always ensure the maximization of the profit of the enterprise.

Nevertheless, it is clear that accounting is vital to the running of a healthy and prosperous enterprise and arguably it is also an essential prerequisite for a prosperous economy. Before leaving this chapter it would therefore be useful to look at accounting in the wider context of the business and its environment. Using the 'Business in Context' model we shall examine how the accounting function interacts with and is different from other business functions. We shall then examine its contribution to strategic decision making before placing it within the organizational and wider business environments within which it operates.

Accounting as a business function

The accounting department, like the personnel department, operates in theory in an advisory capacity only, providing information for managers to make the decisions. In practice, however, the financial elements controlled by the accounting function and the information it generates are so central to the operation of the enterprise that the influence of accounting is often all pervasive. Although it is essential to the smooth running of the business it does not have as direct an impact as, for example, the buying department or the production line. Its effects are generally more subtle although they may in certain instances be very obvious. For example, if the accounting information indicates that expenses are running at too high a level this may have dramatic repercussions in other functional areas. Training and recruitment budgets may be instantly frozen, producing a significant impact on the work of the personnel department and other operating departments and affecting both staffing and skills levels. Alternatively a decision may be taken to stop expenditure on a current advertising campaign, thus having a direct effect on the work of the marketing department.

Accounting is also unusual in that it can have unintended effects: for example, if sales representatives are judged solely on their sales this may lead them to sell goods to customers who are unlikely to pay in order to achieve the sales targets set. It can also be a very dangerous tool if used in the wrong way; for example, targets could be set to achieve cost savings on a production line with no account taken of the effect on quality or employee safety. Similarly, if it is used by people who do not understand its limitations it can lead to wrong decisions. If, for example, a person was unaware that accounting as generally used takes no account of rising prices, goods could be sold at less than they cost to produce.

The importance of accounting within a business should not be underestimated. It provides the basic information by which managers and owners can judge whether the business is meeting its objectives. Its importance is shown by the high salaries that accountants can command and by the prevalence of accountants on the boards of directors of our major public companies.

Accounting is also different from other business functions in that it is not only a function but also an industry. The accounting industry sells accounting and other advisory services to other businesses and is itself a major employer of graduate labour.

The strategic context

Accounting can be and is used within business to evaluate and shape alternative strategies such as making a component or buying it in from a supplier, thus shaping business plans and activities. At the same time it is itself a function of the type of activity that a business engages in and of the strategies a business adopts. In other words at this level of the 'Business in Context' model the accounting system not only influences business strategies but is itself influenced by the goals, size and structure of the organization. For example the accounting system that would be appropriate for a local builder who does one job at a time and who can clearly identify the amount of time and materials being used on that job would not be appropriate for a manufacturing plant which may use one building and many machines to produce multiple products all at the same time. In the latter case, to be able to identify the materials used and the labour inputs for a specific product would require a much more sophisticated system of accounting. Accounting systems are to a large extent variable and depend on the type of activity or activities in which a business is engaged and on the levels of activity.

The organizational context

Clearly the organization's goals will have a major impact on the accounting system used; for example, to develop an accounting system with the primary purpose of measuring profit would be wholly inappropriate for a charitable organization. Similarly the requirements in terms of accounting reports will be very different in the case of a workers' co-operative, the health service and a profit-oriented company. The co-operative members are more likely to be interested in their pay and their share of the surplus generated than in the enterprise profitability. Shareholders in a company, on the other hand, are likely to be more interested in judging overall profitability and comparing that with alternative investments. In the case of the health service it may be that the owners, i.e. the general public, are primarily interested in the service received rather than its profitability.

Also at this level it should be pointed out that the way in which an organization is structured will have an impact on the type of accounting system that is needed. For example if a brewery operates all of its pubs by putting managers into them it will need an accounting system that allows for the payment of regular salaries and bonuses based upon achieving preset targets. These targets are normally set in terms of barrelage and so it will need to know what the normal barrelage for each pub is; it will also need to know the mark-up on spirits, soft drinks etc, and the approximate mix of sales in order to ensure that its managers are not pocketing the profits. If, however, it sets its organization up so that each pub has a landlord who is a tenant of the brewery, the system required will be different as in this case the landlord is not paid a salary or bonus – his wages instead come from the profits he makes from selling the beers, wines and spirits.

We have already alluded to the effect of the size of the organization on the accounting system. However, it is worth reiterating that, the larger and more disparate the organization is, the greater is the need for organizational controls through a system of accountability which makes managers responsible for the performance of their divisions and which provides reports that can be used by senior managers to evaluate the performance of their subordinates and of the organization as a whole. As we have already mentioned, it is vital that the accounting system is tailored to the needs of the organization; otherwise it will not allow management to control the organization and indeed may have dysfunctional effects. Frequently in the case of a small business little accounting information is available on a day-to-day basis. This may be because the operations are sufficiently simple not to warrant much information but is more likely to be because the owner does not have the skills to produce the information and the costs of hiring in the necessary expertise are perceived as outweighing the potential benefits. It is often the case in small businesses that the only time that accounting reports are produced is at the end of the year to meet the needs of the tax collector and when the bank demands them as a prerequisite to granting a loan or extending an overdraft facility.

The environmental context

Finally, before summarizing the main points covered in this chapter it is worth briefly discussing accounting in the context of the environment which we shall be referring to again in Chapter 3 and elsewhere. In general the environmental aspects of the 'Business in Context' model which interact significantly with accounting are the State, technology and labour. Accounting is also affected by and affects the economy; for example a country such as Brazil suffering from hyperinflation has of necessity to use costs other than original costs in its accounting reports because the value of the monetary unit in which accounting information is expressed is changing so quickly. Going back to the effects of labour, technology etc., we have already discussed the potential uses of accounting information by employees and employee organizations such as trade unions. We have mentioned different forms of organization such as partnerships and companies. In the case of the former there is no requirement for the publication of accounting information whereas for companies not only the form but also the content of their annual reports are laid down by law in the Companies Acts. In addition, for these forms of organization the accounting profession lays down certain rules known as Statements of Standard Accounting Practice (SSAPs) and more recently Financial Reporting Standards (FRS). A similar situation prevails in most Western developed countries although the importance of the legislature *vis-à-vis* professional pronouncements varies from country to country. Similarly the reporting requirements are different in non-capitalist countries where the importance afforded to the profit and loss account is considerably less. Finally no discussion of the impact of the environment is complete without some passing reference to changes in technology. Technology has had a major effect within the accounting function as accounting systems have been computerized. This has allowed accountants to free themselves from the more mundane tasks of recording and allowed them to become more involved in decision support and strategic issues. At another level, however, new technology has imposed and is still imposing challenges on accounting thought. Systems that were appropriate in a labour-intensive environment are found to be lacking in the age of flexible manufacturing systems, Just-in-time management and computer-controlled manufacturing environments.

Summary

In this chapter we have tried to give a flavour of what accounting is and of how it pervades both the internal workings of organizations and the external environment. It can be seen to be at one level a functional area of business and at an external level an important determinant of business survival through its effect on shareholders, lenders, employees etc. We have indicated that there is no perfect accounting report that will meet the needs of all users and that the needs of users vary depending on the purpose to which the report is put. For example in the case of a small business the owner may wish to show a low profit to reduce the potential tax bill but may need to show a high profit in order to convince the banker to lend the business money. We have tried to indicate that accounting will only be useful if it is used correctly and if its limitations are understood. A failing business will still fail even though it has an excellent accounting system; on the other hand, potentially successful businesses have been allowed to go bankrupt because the accounting system did not give the warning signs that it should have done or gave them too late to allow management to take action to rectify the situation.

Before moving on you should work through the review questions and problems to ensure that you have understood the main points of this chapter.

References

Berry, A., Citron, D. and Jarvis, R. (1987) *The Information Needs of Bankers dealing with Large and Small Companies*, Certified Accountants Research Report 7, Certified Accountants Publications, London.

Berry, A., Faulkner, S., Hughes, M. and Jarvis, R. (1993) *Bank Lending: Beyond the Theory*, Chapman & Hall, London.

The Corporate Report ASC (1975) Institute of Chartered Accountants in England and Wales.

Further reading

A fuller discussion of accounting in its wider context can be found in *Financial Accounting*, Chapters 1–3, by J. Arnold, T. Hope and A.J. Southwood (Prentice-Hall, 1985).

Review questions

1 For what purposes is accounting information used?

(a) by the individual,
(b) by the enterprise.

2 Who are the users of accounting information and which accounting reports do they normally use?
3 What are the needs of internal users? Can you identify any other needs of internal users? If so, can you suggest how these would be met?
4 What are the limitations of accounting information?
5 Examples were given for certain of the limitations. Can you give examples of your own?
6 What are the major determinants of a useful accounting system?

Problems for discussion and analysis

1 It was pointed out that accounting information is only a part of the input to the decision-making process. In order to expand your understanding of the role of accounting information, for the situation outlined below

(a) identify the accounting information that would be relevant, and
(b) identify any other information that would be relevant.

Head & Co. is in business making navigation equipment and wishes to diversify into the production of hang gliders. The existing business is based in London but the owners may be willing to move. The owners have little knowledge about the market for hang gliders but feel that there is money to be made in that field.

2 Tack was left some money in his mother's will and decided that he should give up his job and go into business for himself. Whilst the lawyers were still sorting out his mother's estate he started looking round for a suitable business. After a short time he identified a small bacon-curing business that he felt was worth investing in. He was still uncertain how much his mother had left him but thought that it was probably between £40 000 and £50 000. The bacon-curing business was for sale for £100 000 and so assuming that he could finance the remainder he engaged an accountant to check over the books of the existing business and report back to him. As proof of his good faith he deposited with the business agents £1000 which he had in savings.

The report from the accountant confirmed his initial impression that the business was worth investing in and so he paid the accountant's modest fee of £500 in full. At this stage he discussed his plans more fully with his bank manager who was impressed with the professional approach taken by Tack.

The bank manager pointed out that Tack had no business experience and therefore was a high risk from the bank's point of view. However, in view of their long-standing relationship the bank was prepared to take a chance and said that it would lend Tack 40% of the purchase price.

On the basis of this Tack signed a conditional agreement to buy the bacon-curing business. A short time after this he received from the lawyers a letter stating that his inheritance from his mother amounted to only £30 000. He could not raise the additional finance to purchase the bacon-curing business and so withdrew from the agreement, recovered his £1000 deposit and purchased a yacht with the intention of doing charter work to the Caribbean.

You are required to discuss the point at which, in your opinion, the accounting process should begin, giving reasons for your point of view. You should pay particular attention to the dual needs of Tack as an owner and as a manager.

Wealth and the measurement of profit

2

This chapter explains the relationship between wealth and profit measurement. It then introduces some of the alternative measures of wealth available and illustrates the impact the choice of measurement system can have on the resultant profit measure.

In Chapter 1 we established that there are a number of different users of accounting information, each of whom needs different information for different purposes. However, there are some items of information that are required by most users. These relate to what an enterprise owns and what it owes, and to how it has performed or is performing – in other words a measure of performance. The former information, i.e. about what an enterprise owns and what it owes, could be termed the worth of the enterprise or its wealth. This measure of wealth or worth relates to a point in time. The other information required is about the way in which the enterprise performed over a period of time. This performance during a period can be measured as a change in wealth over time. Thus if you increase your wealth you have performed better, in financial terms, than someone whose wealth has decreased over the same period of time. This measurement of changes in wealth over time is referred to in accounting terminology as profit measurement. In this chapter we shall be looking at the ways in which accountants can measure wealth and profit and discussing some of the merits of the alternatives available. We shall also examine in some detail the way in which the choice of a measurement system affects the resultant profit and wealth measures. To do this we need to start by defining profit or wealth as these two ideas are directly linked.

A definition of profit that is widely accepted by accountants is based around the definition of an individual's income put forward by the economist Sir John Hicks (1930) who stated:

> Income is that amount which an individual can consume and still be as well off at the end of the period as he or she was at the start of the period.

This definition can be illustrated diagrammatically as follows:

Figure 2.1

Wealth 0	Wealth 1	Wealth 2
Time T_0	Time T_1	Time T_2
T_0	T_1	T_2
← Profit →	← Profit →	

We can see from Figure 2.1 that we can arrive at the profit for period by measuring wealth at the start of the period, i.e. at time T_0, and subtracting that figure from our measurement at the end of the period, i.e. T_1. Similarly the profit for the second period can be measured by subtracting the wealth at time T_1 from the wealth at the end of period 2, i.e. at time T_2.

It should also be clear from Figure 2.1 that wealth is static and represents a stock at a particular point in time. Thus Wealth 0 is the stock of wealth at time T_0, Wealth 1 is the stock of wealth at time T_1 and Wealth 2 is the stock of wealth at time T_2.

KEY CONCEPT 2.1
Income

A relationship exists between income, or profit, and wealth. The definition above suggests that income can be derived by measuring wealth at two different points in time and the difference between the two figures is the income or profit. An alternative view proposed by other economists suggests that if you first measure income then you can derive wealth. This implies that the relationship is to some extent circular, as depicted below. The different views taken by various economists really relate to how you break into the circle.

income ⇄ wealth

KEY CONCEPT 2.2
Wealth

Wealth is a static measure and represents a stock at a particular point in time. This stock can change over time. Thus the wealth measured at the start of a period will not necessarily be equal to the wealth measured at the end of the period. The difference between the two is the profit or loss for that period of time.

If we look at the way in which profit is depicted in Figure 2.1, it is apparent that profit is a flow over time, i.e. to measure the profit earned over a period of time it is necessary to measure the stock of wealth at the start and end of that period.

> *Profit* represents the difference between the wealth at the start and at the end of the period. Unlike wealth which is essentially a static measure, profit is a measure of flow which summarizes activity over a period.
>
> **KEY CONCEPT 2.3**
> ***Profit***

To summarize, we have shown that we can express the profit for the first period, i.e. from time T_0 to time T_1, as

$$\text{profit period 1} = \text{Wealth 1} - \text{Wealth 0}$$

Similarly we can express the profit for the second period, i.e. the period between time T_1 and time T_2 as

$$\text{profit period 2} = \text{Wealth 2} - \text{Wealth 1}$$

We have also established that the profit is derived by measuring the wealth of an individual, or an enterprise, at two points in time. This, on the face of it, is reasonably straightforward but let us now look in more detail at what we are trying to measure and how we are to measure it.

We shall start by examining the case of an individual because this will be simpler and more in line with your own experience. The underlying arguments and principles are just the same for an enterprise but the degree of complexity involved increases in the case of an enterprise especially large multinational companies. Let us suppose that we asked an individual to measure his wealth, i.e. the sum of his possessions less what he owes.

Example 2.1

Alex came up with the following lists of items owned and told us that he owed nothing.

At the start of the year T_0	At the end of the year T_1
A new Ford Escort	A one-year-old Escort
Three new suits	The same three suits
Five shirts	The same five shirts
Four sweatshirts	Five sweatshirts
£400 cash	£500 cash

Whilst the lists above may accurately reflect what Alex owns and what he owes we cannot easily see whether he is better or worse off at the end of the year than he was at the start. We could perhaps say with the benefit of our own knowledge of the world that he must be worse off because everything is one year older; this, however, assumes that the value of his possessions decreases with time. In many cases that is a reasonable assumption but clearly there are some cases where their value increases: for example, would our attitudes change if the car was a 1906 Bentley. Leaving that question aside for a moment, you will have noticed that once we started to discuss the measurement of wealth we also started talking of the more abstract concept of value.

This raises two questions, one of which relates to value which we shall discuss in more detail later whilst the other relates to the way in which we assign value. In the case of the lists of possessions above the easiest item to deal with in terms of value is the cash. This is because it has already had a value assigned to it with which we are all familiar, i.e. a monetary value. On the face of it, therefore, it seems that if we assigned a monetary value to each of the items in the list we would have solved part of our problem at least. In fact it is not as easy as that. We all know that the value of money is not stable; we only have to listen to our grandparents or even our parents talking about what money used to buy to realize that the value of money has decreased over time.

If we leave the problem of the changing value of money aside and we use money as a measure of value, then we have no problem with the value of the cash in the bank, but what of the other items? What is the value of the car for example? Is it worth less because it is one year older, and if so how much less? The same line of argument can be applied to the suits and shirts, but in the case of the sweatshirts we do not even know whether they are the same sweatshirts; clearly there must be at least one that has been acquired during the year as he has five at the end compared with four at the beginning. We also have yet to establish whether the age is important for the purposes of arriving at a value. In order to be able to decide on that question we need first to look at the possibilities available to us.

Although numerous alternatives are put forward many are combinations of those dealt with here. We shall limit our discussion to the most commonly quoted possibilities. For convenience, and in order to help understanding, we shall first deal with those that relate to cost and then discuss those that are based on some concept of value. We start with original cost, then look at historic cost and finally discuss replacement cost. Before doing that, however, it is worth looking at Case Study 2.1 which shows the values that would be obtained for both wealth and profit using a hybrid method known as current cost accounting. The definitions of the terms will be explained where appropriate later in this chapter. The important point to note at this stage is the relationship between wealth and profit and the way in which a change in the measurement of one affects the other. This will be explored in more detail, using an example called Alex, later.

KEY CONCEPT 2.4
Original cost

The cost of the item at the time of the transaction between the buyer and seller.

Original cost

The original cost of an item is the cost at the time of the transaction between the buyer and the seller. It should be noted that we have made a number of assumptions about there being a willing buyer and willing seller which do not need to concern us at this point. Leaving those problems aside, on the face of it this seems to be a fairly easy figure to arrive at. It is in fact not so easy. Consider the case of this book. Is the original cost the price you paid in the bookshop? Or is it the price the bookshop paid the publisher? Or do we go back even further to the cost to the publisher? Or further still to the cost to the authors? Each of these is a possible measure of the original cost, but the question is which is the right cost. The answer is that the cost is the cost to the individual or enterprise on which you are reporting. This cost is normally referred to as the historic cost.

KEY CONCEPT 2.5
Historic cost

The cost incurred by the individual or enterprise in acquiring an item measured at the time of the originating transaction.

Historic cost

Historic cost is the cost incurred by the individual or enterprise in acquiring an item measured at the time of the originating transaction. It is extremely important as it underpins most current accounting practice. We can see that the historic cost of the book to you will be different from the historic cost to the bookshop. This of course is what keeps the bookshop in business. But let us take our example a stage further. Let us assume that, for whatever reason, at the end of the year you decide you no longer need this book; you therefore decide to sell it. In this situation you will probably find that the book is no longer worth what you paid for it and therefore the historic cost is no longer a fair representation of the book's worth or of your wealth. In order to tackle this problem, when measuring your wealth at the end of the year you could write the historic cost down to some lower figure to represent the amount of use you have had from the book. Accounting follows a similar process and the resulting figure is known as the written-down cost. It can be described as the historic cost after an adjustment for usage.

CASE STUDY 2.1
British Gas plc

Commentary

The debate about the most appropriate method of arriving at a figure for the capital of the business has gone on for many years. In the 1980s all quoted companies were required to report using an alternative valuation base, known as current cost accounting. This was in addition to the normal report using historic cost as the basis for accounting. Although most companies did not continue this practice into the 1990s, some examples of this alternative basis of accounting can be found in the annual reports of the public utilities that were privatized in this period. The example below is from the 1992 annual report of British Gas plc.

Extracts from the annual report of British Gas plc, 1992

Current cost balance sheets

	Notes	Group As at 31 December 1992 £m	Group As at 31 December 1991 £m
Fixed assets			
Intangible assets	10	638	787
Tangible assets	11	24 132	22 257
Investments	12	139	63
		24 909	23 107
Current assets			
Stocks	14	593	579
Debtors (amounts falling due within one year)		2 451	2 536
Debtors (amounts falling due after more than one year)		556	334
	15	3 007	2 870
Investments	16	536	1 126
Cash at bank and in hand		46	28
		4 182	4 603
Creditors (amounts falling due within one year)	17	(4 235)	(4 370)
Net current assets/(liabilities)		(53)	233
Total assets less current liabilities		24 856	23 340
Creditors (amounts falling due after more than one year)	18	(3 761)	(2 992)
Provisions for liabilities and charges	19	(738)	(260)
		20 357	20 088
Capital and reserves			
Called up share capital	20	1 078	1 065
Share premium account		87	34
Current cost reserve		16 962	16 584
Profit and loss account		1 799	2 081
Associated undertakings		7	—
	21	18 855	18 699
British Gas shareholders' interest		19 933	19 764
Minority shareholders' interest		424	324
		20 357	20 088

Group current cost profit and loss account

	Notes	Year ended 31 December 1992 £m	Nine months ended 31 December 1991(i) £m	Year ended 31 December 1991 £m
Turnover	1	10 254	6 794	10 485
Cost of sales		(5 099)	(3 475)	(5 297)
Gross profit		5 155	3 319	5 188
Distribution costs		(2 397)	(1 723)	(2 289)
Administrative expenses		(1 329)	(945)	(1 226)
Current cost operating profit	1 and 2	1 429	651	1 673
Share of profits less losses of associated undertakings		7	—	—
Gearing adjustment		41	27	39
Net interest	4	(311)	(182)	(243)
Current cost profit before exceptional charges and taxation		1 166	496	1 469
Exceptional charges	5	(320)	—	—
Current cost profit before taxation		846	496	1 469
Taxation	6	(371)	(227)	(556)
Current cost profit after taxation		475	269	913
Minority shareholders' interest		(2)	10	8
Current cost profit attributable to British Gas shareholders		473	279	921
Dividends	7	(613)	(437)(ii)	
Transfer from reserves	21	(140)	(158)	
Current cost earnings per ordinary share – basic	8	11.0p	6.5p	21.6p
Current cost earnings per ordinary share – before exceptional charges	8	17.0p	6.5p	21.6p

(i) Nine months ended 31 December 1991 information represents the statutory comparison whilst the year ended 31 December 1991 information is supplementary (see Principal accounting policies – change in accounting reference date, page 5).
(ii) On a notional basis the dividend for the year ended 31 December 1991 would have been 13.4p per ordinary share (£571m). As a result of the change in accounting reference date from 31 March to 31 December in 1991, the 1992 dividend is not directly comparable with 1991.

The adjustment for usage is commonly referred to as depreciation, and there are a number of ways of arriving at a figure for it, which we shall deal with in Chapter 8.

The problem with historic cost and written-down historic cost is that with the value of money and goods changing over time it is only likely to be a fair representation of value at a particular point in time, i.e. at the point of the original transaction. At any other point it will only be a fair representation of value by chance unless the world is static, i.e. with no innovation etc. Clearly this is not the case and so we should look for alternative measures. One such alternative to the original or historic cost of an item is its replacement cost. This is certainly more up to date and allows for the changes that will take place in a non-static world.

KEY CONCEPT 2.6
Replacement cost

The amount that would have to be paid at today's prices to purchase an item similar to the existing item.

Replacement cost

The replacement cost of an item is the amount that would have to be paid at today's prices to purchase an item similar to the existing item. It is often very relevant as those of us who have had cars written off will know. In those cases the amount that the insurance company pays you often bears no relationship to what it would cost to replace your car, because yours was better than average or had just had a new engine put in. The problem that arises in using replacement cost is firstly that you have to want to replace the item. You may not want to replace a textbook that you used at school as it would no longer be of use to you. Even if we assume that you do want to replace the item, you may find that it is difficult to identify the replacement cost. Think of a specialist item such as Windsor Castle!

It may be that even if you could replace an item with an exact replica you may not wish to do so. For example you may wish to obtain a newer version or one with extra functions. The most obvious example of this kind is the replacement of computer equipment, which is constantly expanding in power whilst its size and its price are generally decreasing. This leads us to the same problem that we had with historic cost in that the replacement cost of a computer does not take into account the age of the machine that we actually own. The solution is the same as for historic cost: estimate the effect of usage and arrive at a written-down replacement cost.

As we can see there are distinct problems in using either historic cost or replacement cost. In a number of situations these are unlikely to be useful measures of value or wealth. Historic cost is unlikely to be useful when prices change, whatever the reason for that change. Replacement cost, on the other hand, whilst overcoming that problem by using up-to-date costs is itself irrelevant if there is no intention of replacing the item with an exact replica.

Before reading the next section on alternative measures based on value rather than cost it is worth spending a few minutes thinking of the situations in which historic cost and replacement cost are appropriate and those situations when they are unlikely to be suitable. This is important, because any measure is only useful if it is the appropriate measure to do the job in hand.

For example, whilst the acceleration of a car may be important in certain circumstances it is irrelevant for an emergency stop. Similarly the historic cost or replacement cost of a motor car is unlikely to be useful if we wish to sell the car as the selling price will be governed by other factors. The alternatives to these cost-based measures are measures which are related to value. However, as we shall see, value-based measures also have their own set of problems.

KEY CONCEPT 2.7
Economic value

Economic value is, or would be, an ideal measure of value and wealth.

The value of the expected earnings from using the item in question discounted at an appropriate rate to give a present-day value.

Economic value

The economic value of an item is the value of the expected earnings from using the item discounted at an appropriate rate to give a present-day value. The problem is not in defining the measure but in actually estimating future earnings as this implies a knowledge of what is going to happen; problems of foreseeing technological change, fashion changes and such like make the estimation of future earnings problematic. Even if we assume that this can be done, we are then left with the question of finding an appropriate rate at which to discount the estimated future earnings. The problem here is that each individual may wish to use a different rate depending on his or her circumstances. For example, a millionaire may not worry very much if money is available in a year rather than immediately but if you have no money to buy your next meal the situation is entirely different. We should not totally discount the possibility of using this measure because of these problems since with the use of mathematical techniques relating to probability it is still a useful tool in decision making. In fact it is the basis underlying techniques such as net present value which is often used in investment appraisal decisions and which we shall discuss in more detail later.

KEY CONCEPT 2.8
Net realizable value

The net realizable value is an alternative measure of value to economic value.

The amount that is likely to be obtained by selling an item, less any costs incurred in selling.

Net realizable value

The net realizable value is the amount that is likely to be obtained by selling an item, less any costs incurred in selling. On the face of it such a measure should be easily obtainable but in practice the amount for which an item can be sold will vary with the circumstances of the sale. The problems of arriving at the net realizable value are apparent in the second-hand car market where there is a trade price and a range of retail prices. Another good example is the house market, where independent valuations can differ by as much as £40 000 on a property worth between £110 000 and £150 000. Apart from the problem of arriving at a value, other factors will affect the net realizable value. For example, if you are hard up you may be prepared to accept less than the market value in order to get a quick sale. The value in the latter situation is known as the *forced sale value*, and is the most likely value where circumstances are unfavourable to the seller. If, on the other hand, the market conditions are neutral between buyer and seller, then the net realizable value is likely to be the *open market value*.

It should be clear from the above that plenty of alternative measures are available, each of which has its own problems. If you remember, the starting point for this discussion was that we wished to establish whether Alex was better off at the end of the period than he was at the start. Had he made a profit? The problem is not one of finding a concept of profit, as there are plenty within the economics literature apart from the one that we have already referred to which was provided by Hicks (see, for example, Fisher's (1930) income concept and that of Friedman (1957)). The problem is in fact one of measurement as most of these concepts rely either on a measurement of future income streams or on the measurement of wealth.

We have already pointed out that to measure future income streams is extremely difficult in the real world because of the effects of uncertainty. This then leaves us with the alternative of measuring wealth and leads us to the question of finding the most appropriate measure. As we have seen, all the measures put forward so far have inherent problems, and it may be that the solution lies in combining one or more of these measures to obtain the best measure. For the purposes of this introductory text it is probably unnecessary to probe this area in greater depth but some references are given at the end of the chapter which will provide further background for those interested in pursuing the topic. Before leaving this area completely let us reconsider the example based on the wealth of Alex and assign some values to see what effect the choice of measure will have.

Description		*Year T_0*	
	Replacement cost	*Historic cost*	*Net realizable value*
Ford Escort	4850	4850	4400
Suits	240	210	30
Shirts	75	75	10
Sweatshirts	50	50	20
Cash	400	400	400

If you study the figures carefully you will notice that the only figure common to all three columns is the cash figure. Apart from the cost of the suits the replacement cost and the historic cost are also identical. In reality this will always be the case at the time when the goods are bought, but it is unlikely to be so at any other time. In this example the fact that the replacement cost of the suits is different from the historic cost indicates that some, or all, of these suits were bought when the price of suits was lower than it was at the start of the year in question. In other words, the point in time at which we are measuring is different from the date of acquisition and, as we said, in these circumstances the replacement cost is likely to differ from the historic cost.

You should also have noticed that the net realizable value is lower than the historic cost and replacement cost, even though some of the items were clearly new at the start of the year. Once again this is obviously going to be the case in most situations, because personal goods that are being resold are effectively second-hand goods, even though they may not have been used. The situation for a business enterprise is not necessarily the same because sometimes the goods are bought not for use but for resale, e.g. by a retailer or wholesaler. In these cases the net realizable value of the goods bought for resale should be higher than the cost – otherwise the retailer would not stay in business very long.

Let us now look at Alex's situation at the end of the year and assign some values to the items owned at that time. We shall then be in a position to measure the profit or increase in wealth and to use this as a basis for discussion of some of the problems of measurement which we referred to earlier.

Description		*Year T_1*	
	Replacement cost	*Historic cost*	*Net realizable value*
Ford Escort	3195	4850	3000
Suits	270	210	27
Shirts	80	75	5
Sweatshirts	50	50	15
Cash	500	500	500

You will notice that the figures have changed in all cases except under historic cost, where they are the same as at the start of the year, except for the cash. This highlights one of the problems with this measure, in that it only tells us what an item costs and gives no clue to what it is worth.

It is also worth looking more closely at the car. As you can see the replacement cost is lower than at the start of the year. This is because the car we are replacing at the end of the year is a one-year-old model, rather than a new model. You will also see that the replacement cost is higher than the net realizable value. This is because costs would be incurred in selling the car and the amount that you would get would be reduced by these costs.

Let us now look at what we get in terms of our measures of wealth and profit, starting with historic cost.

Description	*Year T_0*	*Year T_1*
Ford Escort	4850	4850
Suits	210	210
Shirts	75	75
Sweatshirts	50	50
Cash	400	500
	5585	5685

We can now measure the profit under historic cost as we have a figure for wealth at the start and end of the year. Thus using the formula

wealth 1 − wealth 0 = profit

we get

£5685 − £5585 = £100

Let us look at what would happen if we used replacement cost rather than historic cost.

Description	*Year T_0*	*Year T_1*
Ford Escort	4850	3195
Suits	240	270
Shirts	75	85
Sweatshirts	50	50
Cash	400	500
	5615	4100

We can now measure the profit under replacement cost as we have a figure for wealth at the start and end of the year. Thus using the formula

wealth 1 − wealth 0 = profit

we get

£4100 − £5615 = £1515 loss

In other words, according to the replacement cost figures we are £1515 worse off at the end of the year than we were at the start.

Finally let us see what the situation would be if we were using the net realizable value to arrive at our measures of wealth.

Description	*Year T_0*	*Year T_1*
Ford Escort	4400	3000
Suits	30	27
Shirts	10	5
Sweatshirts	20	15
Cash	400	500
	4860	3547

We can now measure the profit under net realizable value as we have a figure for wealth at the start and end of the year. Thus using the formula

wealth 1 − wealth 0 = profit

we get

$$£3547 - £4860 = £1313 \text{ loss}$$

Once again, using net realizable value as the basis of measuring wealth we find that Alex is worse off at the end of the year than he was at the start.

You may well be wondering at this point which is the correct answer, and this takes us back to the question of who is to use the information and for what purpose it is to be used. Clearly this varies from case to case; however, it is more important, at the present time, that you understand that differences arise depending on the valuation method adopted. You may feel that as Alex is clearly worse off at the end of the first year than he was at the start (he no longer has a brand new car) replacement cost or net realizable value are the better alternatives. However, you must bear in mind that we are trying to measure the amount that can be spent whilst maintaining wealth and that there is therefore a hidden assumption that Alex wants to maintain the wealth he had at the start.

This may not in fact be the case because of changes in circumstances. He may for example have been banned from driving, which would mean that he does not want to replace his car. The net realizable value model would be more useful now as he would probably want to sell the car. However, although he has lost his driving licence he will still need to go out even if only to buy food. He is going to need to wear some clothes, and so to value these on the assumption that they are going to be sold is not a defensible position.

Conclusion

We have seen that there are a number of alternative ways of measuring a person's wealth and that each has its own problems. One of the most commonly cited problems with both replacement cost and net realizable value is that they are subjective, which is true in many cases. This is one reason why accounts are still prepared using historic costs even though, as we have seen with the simple example of Alex, this can lead to irrelevant information being produced and wrong decisions being taken. Another reason that is often cited for retaining historic cost in the accounts is that it is a system which is based on what was actually spent and owners of enterprises need to know what money has been spent on. But to what extent can the advantage of historic cost make up for its deficiencies as a measure of wealth and therefore as the basis of the profit measure? This question is and has been the subject of much debate and that debate will continue for many years to come. For our purposes we only need to be aware of the problems associated with using each of the alternatives because they may well lead to different decisions being made. The fact that these alternatives are not just theoretical views with no practical significance is illustrated in Case

Study 2.2 which draws attention to the alternatives used by British Petroleum in 1992 and their effect on profit.

CASE STUDY 2.2
British Petroleum plc

Commentary

The fact that there are a number of alternative ways of arriving at a value for the balance sheet and their effect on the profit figures is amply illustrated in the extract from the annual report of British Petroleum for 1992. This shows the profits for the last five years on a replacement cost basis. You can see that in 1992 the profit on a replacement cost basis was £1884 m., compared to a loss of £458 m. using historic cost as the basis of valuation.

It is also worth noting that British Petroleum plc also provides a second set of figures, 'adjusted for the average UK retail price index'. These figures not only take into account the change in the price of the specific items owned by British Petroleum but also take account of the effects of inflation on the unit of measurement. In this case the unit of measure is the pound sterling. It is quite striking that what appears to be a substantial increase in turnover over the five-year period is really very small when the figures are adjusted by the retail price index.

Extracts from the annual report of British Petroleum plc, 1992

Information on price changes

The following information is given as an indication to shareholders of the effect of changes in the general level of prices in the UK over the past five years. The figures show the main elements of the financial results and the BP share price, in both money of the year and as adjusted by the average UK retail price index for each year.

As reported

			£ million		
	1988	*1989*	*1990*	*1991*	*1992*
Turnover	24 706	29 056	33 039	32 613	33 250
Replacement cost operating profit	2 314	2 423	2 725	2 371	1 884
Replacement cost profit before exceptional items and discontinued operations	937	890	1 039	928	536
Historical cost profit (loss)	1 210	2 134	1 688	415	(458)
Earnings (loss) per ordinary share:					
On profit (loss) for the year	20.0p	39.0p	31.5p	7.7p	(8.5)p
On replacement cost profit before exceptional items and discontinued operations	15.5p	16.3p	19.4p	17.2p	9.9p
Dividends per ordinary share	13.50p	14.90p	16.05p	16.80p	10.50p
Ordinary share price					
High	295p	341p	376p	357p	296p
Daily average	257p	293p	335p	329p	240p
Low	233p	249p	304p	276p	184p

Adjusted for the average UK retail price index of:

	106.9	115.2	126.1	133.5	138.5
			£ million		
Turnover	32 009	34 933	36 288	33 834	33 250
Replacement cost operating profit	2 998	2 913	2 993	2 460	1 884
Replacement cost profit before exceptional items and discontinued operations	1 214	1 070	1 141	963	536
Historical cost profit (loss)	1 568	2 566	1 854	431	(458)
Earnings (loss) per ordinary share:					
On profit (loss) for the year	25.9p	46.9p	34.6p	8.0p	(8.5)p
On replacement cost profit before exceptional items and discontinued operations	20.1p	19.6p	21.3p	17.8p	9.9p
Dividends per ordinary share	17.49p	17.91p	17.63p	17.43p	10.50p
Ordinary share price					
High	382p	410p	413p	370p	296p
Daily average	333p	352p	368p	341p	240p
Low	302p	299p	334p	286p	184p

Summary

We have looked at a definition of wealth and of profit which is commonly used and indeed underpins current accounting practice and we have found that there are problems in actually measuring wealth. We have looked at four alternative measures: historic cost, replacement cost, net realizable value and economic value. We have shown by way of a simple example that each of the first three produces a different answer and in the course of our discussion we have pointed to some of the problems and assumptions underlying each alternative. At the present time there is no generally accepted right answer, and in fact the most commonly used system is that based on historic cost (although it should be noted that Philips, the electronics giant, has used replacement costs for a number of years). Finally it should also be pointed out that change is likely to be slow in coming as the present system, based on historic cost, is familiar to all and has, it is said, worked well in the past, although it is unclear what criteria are being used to back up this claim.

References

Fisher, I. (1930) *The Theory of Interest*, Macmillan.

Friedman, M. (1957) *A Theory of the Consumption Function*, Princeton University Press.

Hicks, Sir John (1946) *Value and Capital*, Clarendon Press, Oxford.

Further reading

For those who wish to examine the economic value approach, a good exposition can be found in *A New Introduction to Financial Accounting*, by R.G. May, G.G. Mueller and T.H. Williams (Prentice Hall, 1980).

Review questions

1 Profit is normally seen as a flow over time whereas wealth can be described as a stock at a point in time. Explain in your own words the difference between a stock and a flow.
2 There are a number of different ways in which we can measure wealth. List the alternatives discussed in the chapter together with any drawbacks or problems that were identified with their use.
3 In certain situations we said that written-down cost could be used as an alternative. Explain in your own words the difference between cost and written-down cost and suggest when the latter would be more appropriate.
4 What effects, if any, do rapid changes in technology have on the appropriateness of each of the alternative ways of assigning a cost or a value to an item.

Problems for discussion and analysis

1 Under certain circumstances only one of the alternative methods of valuation is the most appropriate. Giving brief reasons for your choice, suggest the most appropriate value to be placed on each item in the following.

Jean owns a shop which used to sell clothes but she has now decided that given the location she would make more money running a restaurant at the same premises. She has obtained planning permission for the change of use and has bought some of the equipment needed but has not yet started trading. She has made a list of the items that the business owns which is reproduced below:

(a) freehold shop
(b) hanging display rail for clothes
(c) a two year old car which is essential for the business
(d) new restaurant tables and chairs
(e) cash till
(f) quantity of fashion garments that were not sold in the closing down sale.

You may find that you need more information or have to make some assumptions. This is normal but you should state any assumptions that you are making.

2 In the example of Alex in the text, no allowance was made for the fact that an item had been in use for some time. Whilst it is intuitively obvious that the utility of most things declines over time, it is more difficult to identify the extent of that decline over a given period. In addition, even if we could identify the decline in utility and the utility remaining we still have to assign some monetary amount to both parts. We said in the chapter that this was done by arriving at a written-down cost or value. For each of the following examples suggest, with reasons, the best method for arriving at the written-down cost or value.

(a) A machine which will produce 10 000 items and will then need to be replaced. Production each year is to be matched to sales and estimates of sales are 1000 units in year 1, 2500 units in year 2. Sales in the years after that cannot be forecast with any accuracy.
(b) A leasehold property on a five year non-renewable lease.
(c) A company car.
(d) A microcomputer.
(e) Computer software.

3 Two brothers decided to go into business buying and selling beds. Details of their transactions are set out in the case study below.

They initially bought 400 beds at £100 each and a delivery van for £6000. At the end of six months they had sold 300 of the 400 beds for £150 each. Unfortunately during that time the bed manufacturer had increased the price to £120 each and was their only source of supply. To make matters worse a discount store had opened in the area and it was selling the same beds at £140 each. The brothers found that on average over the six months they had incurred costs for advertising, petrol etc. which amounted to £10 for each bed sold.

On the basis of the information above, calculate what the brothers' wealth was at the start and end of the six months and what profit had been made.

4 Having calculated the profit for the first six months discuss whether the profit figure is a useful benchmark for measuring the performance of the business, and also whether it is useful as a guide to future profitability.

3 The measurement of wealth

This chapter explores the concepts of wealth in more detail and relates them to the balance sheet, which can be viewed as a surrogate wealth measure. The elements of the balance sheet are defined and the interrelationships and interdependency of assets, liabilities and owners' equity are explained.

In Chapter 1 we discussed the objectives of accounting reports and the influences of users on financial reporting. We also discussed the limitations of accounting information and the role of accounting in business, its effect on business and some of the factors which influence accounting. In Chapter 2 we examined some possible approaches to income measurement from the point of view both of the economist and of the accountant. We shall now look more specifically at the ways in which accountants measure wealth and income.

We suggested that the problem facing accountants is that of finding an appropriate basis for the measurement of wealth. There is also the additional problem that with the complexity involved in the real world a system that only measures wealth and derives income from it will not be able to cope with the complexity of present-day enterprises. Consider a large retailing group such as Sainsbury: should they have to carry out a valuation of all their premises, vehicles, stocks etc. on one day of the year? The costs of such an operation would make it prohibitively expensive, even if it was logistically possible. For companies such as Hanson Trust, where operations are carried out on a world-wide basis, these logistical problems would be even greater. Such a system would also lead to problems because management or the owners would not be able to make decisions on a day-to-day basis as they would only have information at hand once a year. Because of these problems with annual valuation systems we need to find separate ways of measuring wealth and income.

The measurement of income will be dealt with in detail in Chapter 4. In this chapter we concentrate on the problem of the measurement of wealth and the way in which accounting approaches that problem. We shall look in some detail at the use of the balance sheet as the measure of wealth, at its component parts such as assets and liabilities, and finally at the format in which the balance sheet is presented and the way in which that is influenced by the type of organization, the environment and the needs of the users.

The measurement of wealth

In the case of an individual, we have said that wealth can be found by simply listing the items you own, assuming of course that you do not owe anybody money as this will clearly reduce your wealth. To some extent the same can be said for an enterprise, although the level of complexity will, of course, be greater. The way in which this is done for an enterprise is similar to that for an individual but the resulting statement is called a *balance sheet*. You should note that the balance sheet relates to a position at a point in time. It is because of this that the analogy with a snapshot is often found in accounting textbooks.

KEY CONCEPT 3.1
The balance sheet

The balance sheet is a statement, at one point in time, which shows all the items (assets) owned by the enterprise and all the amounts owed by the enterprise (liabilities).

The definition is not intended to be comprehensive – it merely provides us with a basic idea of what we are referring to. Before looking at the balance sheet in more detail it is important to appreciate that, although an enterprise does not exist in the same way as a person, for accounting and for some legal purposes an enterprise is presumed to exist in its own right. It is therefore treated as a separate entity from the person or persons who own or operate it. In broad terms it is possible to account for any unit which has a separate and distinct existence. It may be that this is a hotel, for example, or a group of hotels or a more complex organization such as Forte. This idea of a separate entity is often referred to in accounting literature as the *business entity* principle. It applies equally to organizations that are not commonly referred to as businesses such as charitable organizations, clubs and societies. The question of whether the entity should be accounted for separately is related not only to the legal situation but also to the question of whether it can be seen to have a separate existence.

KEY CONCEPT 3.2
The business entity principle

The business entity principle states that transactions, assets and liabilities that relate to the enterprise are accounted for separately. It applies to all types of enterprise irrespective of the fact that the enterprise may not be recognized as a separate legal or taxable entity.

Whilst the application of this principle and the reasons for it are fairly self-evident when we are looking at large public companies such as ICI or Shell, they are less clear with smaller enterprises such as the corner newsagents or a second-hand car business. If, for example, you decided to set yourself up as a car dealer, for accounting purposes the cars purchased as a car dealer and the money earned as a result of that activity would be treated separately from your own personal car and money. This allows the tax authority to tax you separately on the profits from your business and it also helps you to arrive at the value of your business should you wish at some stage to sell it or take in a partner. The important point to remember is that for each business entity it is possible to account separately and therefore to draw up a balance sheet at a point in time. We shall now examine these balance sheets in more detail.

Importance of balance sheets

The purpose of a balance sheet is to communicate information about the financial position of an enterprise at a particular point in time. It summarizes information contained in the accounting records in a clear and intelligible form. If the items contained in it are summarized and classified in an appropriate manner it can give information about the financial strength of the enterprise and indicate the relative *liquidity* of the assets. It should also give information about the liabilities of the enterprise, i.e. what the enterprise owes and when these amounts will fall due. The combination of this information can assist the user in evaluating the financial position of the enterprise. It should be remembered, however, that financial statements are only one part of the information needed by users and thus the importance of this accounting statement should not be over-emphasized.

KEY CONCEPT 3.3
Liquidity

Liquidity refers to the ease with which assets can be converted to cash in the normal course of business.

In the vast majority of cases enterprises draw up a balance sheet at least once a year. It could be done more frequently of course, or indeed less frequently, although convention dictates that a normal accounting period is a year and tax laws and other legislation are set up on that basis. It should also be remembered that because the balance sheet represents the position at one point in time its usefulness is limited as the situation may have changed since the last balance sheet was drawn up. For example, you may draw up a balance sheet every December and so if you looked at the balance sheet in October it would be ten months out of date. It may be helpful to extend our earlier analogy and picture a business as a movie and a balance sheet as a still from that movie. Clearly in the case of a movie the still does not give a complete picture and the same can be said for the balance sheet.

We need to know what balance sheets contain. We have already said that they are similar to an individual's own measurement of wealth. Therefore if you think how you would measure your own wealth you will realize that you need to make a list of what you own (assets) and take away from that what you owe (liabilities). For an enterprise this listing of assets and liabilities at a particular point in time is the enterprise's balance sheet.

Given this information about the contents of a balance sheet, let us look in more detail at what is meant by assets and liabilities. We shall consider assets by looking at what constitutes an asset and how assets are classified into subcategories.

Assets

Although we can find many definitions of assets, some of these are less useful than others. Most contain some of the vital elements of a useful description, but a clear working definition is needed. For our purposes we have taken that provided by Lall (1968), whose definition is given in Key Concept 3.4. This definition is not dissimilar to that adopted by the accountancy profession and included in international accounting standards. We shall now examine its various components in order to make the nature of an asset somewhat clearer.

KEY CONCEPT 3.4
Definition of an asset

Embodiments of present or future economic benefits or service potentials measurable in terms of monetary units, accruing to an enterprise as a result of economic events, the enjoyment of which by the enterprise is secured by the law.

Future benefits, service potentials

The clear implication in the terms 'future benefits' and 'service potentials' is that, in order to be an asset, there must be some clear expectation that some benefit will be derived by the enterprise either now or in the future. This implies that the item must have some specific *usefulness to the enterprise*. An item that has no specific usefulness for the enterprise is therefore not an asset. This is particularly important in times of rapidly changing technology as it suggests that the question of what is and what is not an asset can only be decided on the basis of its usefulness to the enterprise. For example, it is fairly obvious that a gold mine full of unmined gold is an asset for a mining business. However, there will come a point when all the gold has been removed and all that is left is a hole in the ground. The hole in the ground is no longer useful to the mining enterprise and it ceases to be an asset.

However, for a different type of enterprise, e.g. a rubbish disposal business, a hole in the ground is useful. We can therefore conclude that in order to be classified as an asset an item must be useful to the enterprise itself.

Measurable in monetary units

In certain circumstances enterprises may gain future benefits from items which may be impossible or difficult to measure in monetary units. For example, a producer of jams may be able to advertise that they are jam makers 'By Appointment'. The fact that they have a Royal Appointment may well increase their profits and thus being 'By Appointment' is of benefit to the business. The problem facing accountants is how, having decided that there is a future benefit, that benefit is to be measured in monetary terms. In this particular example it would be almost impossible to isolate the effect that the Royal Appointment has in monetary terms and therefore we do not include it in the balance sheet as an asset even though the business is clearly getting a benefit from it. Other examples of items which are clearly of benefit but which are not included for accounting purposes are a good location, a highly motivated workforce or a reputation for excellent service. You will remember from Chapter 1 that we discussed this problem in the context of the limitations of accounting information.

Legal ownership

Many definitions of assets imply that in order to be an asset something must be owned. In reality most assets *are* owned, but the assertion that ownership is a precondition for the recognition of an asset by an enterprise is not strictly true. For example, a rental agreement for a house that entitles you to occupy the house at a rent of £20 a week obviously confers a benefit if the market rental is, say, £90 a week and thus may be seen as an asset. On the other hand the fact that an individual or enterprise owns an item does not necessarily mean that there is any future benefit to be obtained. For example an old motor car that has failed the MOT test may cease to be an asset, and in fact unless it can be driven to the breaker's yard it may become a liability.

Accruing to an enterprise

Whilst it may seem patently obvious that the benefits should *accrue* to the enterprise, i.e. be received by the enterprise at some point in time, it is vital in many cases to be able to separate out the assets of the enterprise from those of the owner for reasons referred to earlier. For example, the factory building is likely to be an enterprise asset as the benefits from its use are likely to accrue to the enterprise. However, if the enterprise is a corner shop with residential accommodation, it is somewhat less clear which part of the building is an asset of the business and which is not. In practice it may well be that some of the goods held for resale are actually physically stored in part of the residential accommodation. There is unfortunately no general rule which can be applied and each case must be considered on its merits. The process of distinguishing between the assets of the owner and those of the business is merely an application of the business entity principle referred to earlier. In simple terms this principle states that the business should be viewed as separate from the owner and therefore accounted for separately.

Fixed and current assets

For accounting purposes assets are normally separated as far as possible into subcategories. The reasoning behind this is that accounting statements should provide information that is useful in making economic decisions. These decisions, it is suggested, can be made more precisely if some indication is given regarding the nature of the assets of the enterprise. The categories most frequently used are fixed and current assets.

Fixed assets

Although the term fixed assets is used frequently in accounting literature there is no precise definition of what constitutes a fixed asset. One possible definition of a fixed asset is as follows.

> A fixed asset is an asset that is retained for use in the business and is not for resale in the normal course of business.

This definition suggests that the distinction relates to the use to which the asset is put. However, the conventional distinction between fixed and current assets requires a further element relating to time and implies some degree of permanency. For example, it is generally accepted that factory buildings are fixed assets as they are retained for use, are not resold and will last for a long period of time. It is the latter element relating to time that is missing from the above definition. If we simply used the definition above, office stationery would meet the criteria of a fixed asset. It is quite clear, however, that office stationery is unlikely to be even semi-permanent and is essentially a different type of asset from the factory building previously discussed. This may lead us to a definition that includes some reference to the life of an asset.

A definition that relates solely to the life of an asset, however, is not sufficient on its own. For example a fixed asset could be defined as an asset that will last for a considerable period of time. This definition is deficient because it says nothing about the use of the asset within the business. Thus, for example, a washing machine would be classified as a fixed asset using this definition. However, there are clear differences between the way in which the washing machines should be treated in the books of a launderette and in the books of an electrical retailer even though the life of the washing machine does not change merely as a result of its being owned by a different business. This leads us to the conclusion that there are two elements involved in deciding what is and what is not a fixed asset, i.e. the *use* to which the asset will be put and the *life* of the asset within the business. This provides us with a working definition of a fixed asset.

KEY CONCEPT 3.5
Fixed assets

An asset that is acquired for the purposes of use within the business and is likely to be used by the business for a considerable period of time.

Current assets

As with fixed assets, the definition of a current asset is not as clear as might be expected. Some accounting textbooks suggest that current assets are those assets known as circulating assets, i.e. those which are part of the operating cycle. This does not really help as we need to know what an operating cycle is or what circulating assets are.

The operating cycle

It is perhaps easier to understand the term operating cycle if we look at one or two examples. In the case of a shop selling clothes the operating cycle may consist of buying garments and selling them for cash. In the case of an assembly business the operating cycle may involve more processes such an buying two or more components, assembling them, then selling them and then collecting the cash. Thus the operating cycle has no fixed time period but depends on the nature of the business and may in fact extend over a number of years. This would be the case with property development, shipbuilding and other heavy construction industries. The fact the operating cycles are of different lengths is not vital as in general terms those assets that are part of the operating cycle are similar and are likely to be items such as stock, cash in the bank etc.

The realization period

Other accounting texts suggest that what distinguishes current assets from other assets is whether or not they will be realized in the form of cash in the current accounting period. By convention accounting periods are normally one year. If we applied this test strictly we would find that in certain cases such as our shipbuilder referred to above something that is part of the operating cycle will not in fact be realized in the form of cash within a year.

In practice it is suggested that the classification is based on both these principles. For our purposes, therefore, a useful working definition is that given in Key Concept 3.6 which combines these two properties and therefore overcomes the problems inherent in using either on its own.

> A current asset is one which is either part of the operating cycle of the enterprise or is likely to be realized in the form of cash within one year.
>
> **KEY CONCEPT 3.6**
> ***Current asset***

By looking at the definitions of fixed and current assets it should be clear that it is possible to think of some assets that a business might own that do not easily fit within either category. An example of such an asset is a trademark or a patent on a product or process that has been developed by the enterprise itself. A number of ways of dealing with this problem have been suggested. However, the American solution of coining the title *indeterminate assets* for those assets not easily classified as fixed or current overcomes most of the main problems and is sufficient for our purposes at this stage.

Having looked at what constitutes an asset and at the way in which assets are divided into subcategories on the balance sheet, we can now turn to the other part of the balance sheet – what is owed or, to use accounting terminology, the liabilities.

Liabilities

As with the general term assets a useful working definition of liabilities must contain a number of components. A suitable definition is that put forward by Bull (1984) in Key Concept 3.7.

> The existing obligations of the business to provide money, goods or services to an agent or entity outside the business at some time in the future.
>
> **KEY CONCEPT 3.7**
> ***Liabilities***

The definition implies that the liability must exist at the present time. It also implies that the date by which that liability must be paid is known. A more simple definition which is adequate for our purposes is:

> Liabilities are what the business owes.

An alternative way of looking at them is to view them as claims on the assets of the business.

Current liabilities

Given that we have used a simple definition for liabilities we can also use a simple definition of current liabilities (Key Concept 3.8). This definition is in fact in line with the heading under which current liabilities are shown in the published accounts of companies. The most common example of a current liability is a bank overdraft which in theory at least may have to be repaid to the bank on demand. Another example is where goods are bought on credit terms and the supplier has not been paid at the balance sheet date.

KEY CONCEPT 3.8
Current liabilities

Those liabilities falling due for payment within one year.

Other liabilities

Clearly there are other types of liability which do not have to be repaid in full in one year; an everyday example of this type of liability is a mortgage on a house. In the case of a business, however, this type of liability may take a number of forms such as a bank loan repayable in three years or five years etc. Liabilities of this sort are longer-term liabilities and are normally put under the heading:

Amounts falling due after more than one year.

Owners' equity

The owners' equity or share of the capital of the business can be viewed in a number of ways. In a sense it is a liability of the business in so far as it is a claim on the assets. However, it differs from other liabilities in that other liabilities have definite dates by which they are to be paid and are fixed in amount. The owners' equity, on the other hand, is normally left in the business as long as it is required. Another way of viewing the owners' equity is as a residual claim on the assets of the business after all the other liabilities have been settled. In general, however, the owners' equity is normally shown under two headings, i.e. that which is put into the business and that which is earned by the business and left in the business. The latter category we shall refer to as *retained profits*. In the case of an individual this is analogous with wealth, whereas when the owner is a business it is often referred to as capital. As we showed in Chapter 2, the amount of this wealth or capital is dependent on the measure used, i.e. replacement cost, net realizable value etc. It is therefore better to view owners' equity as a residual claim rather than as capital or wealth as those expressions imply that an absolute measure of owners' equity is possible.

> Owners' equity is in one sense a claim on the assets of the enterprise. It is different from other liabilities in that the amount cannot necessarily be determined accurately. It can be viewed as a residual claim on the assets of the enterprise.
>
> **KEY CONCEPT 3.9**
> ***Owners' equity***

The balance sheet

As we have already indicated, the balance sheet of an enterprise can be viewed as a statement of assets and liabilities at a particular point in time. Because the business is an artificial entity, by definition all its assets belong to someone else. This idea is summed up fairly simply in the balance sheet equation:

$$\text{assets} = \text{liabilities}$$

The equation describes the balance sheet in its simplest form and must always hold true. However, it uses a very loose definition of liabilities and can be further refined to highlight the differences between pure liabilities and owners' equity as follows:

$$\text{assets} = \text{liabilities} + \text{owners' equity}$$

This equation can be rewritten to highlight the fact that owners' equity is a residual claim on the assets:

$$\text{Assets} - \text{liabilities} = \text{owners' equity}$$

Simple balance sheets

To illustrate the equation above a simple balance sheet can be constructed using the information contained in Example 3.1.

Example 3.1 Keelsafe, Part 1

Harry Keel had just been made redundant and he decided to start up a small business making safety harnesses which he called Keelsafe Safety Harnesses. For this purpose he purchased

One industrial sewing machine for	£550
A quantity of heavy duty webbing material for	£300
A quantity of sewing materials costing	£100
A second-hand typewriter for	£ 50
A supply of office stationery and letterheads	£ 50
One cutting machine for	£400

The remaining £50 of his redundancy money was put into a business bank account.

Part 1

At this stage we could draw up a list of assets of the business as follows.

Assets	£
Sewing machine	550
Webbing	300
Sewing materials	100
Typewriter	50
Stationery	50
Cutting machine	400
Cash in bank	50
	1500

We could also identify the owner's equity in the business as being £1500, i.e. the amount he put in. Thus the other side of the balance sheet and indeed the accounting equation would be

Owner's equity	£1500
	1500

Before moving on, it is worth thinking about how we obtained the figure for owner's equity; all we did was to list what Harry's business owned and then, as it did not owe anything to anybody but Harry, the owner, we made the balance sheet balance by recording the amount the business owed to Harry, the owner's equity.

Let us take this example a bit further.

Example 3.1 Keelsafe, Part 2

As the business was just starting Harry decided that until the business got off the ground he would operate from home and use the garage to manufacture the safety harnesses and the front room of his house as an office. His house had originally cost him £20 000 in 1979.

Part 2

This additional information, on the face of it, presents us with a problem as we do not know how much of the £20 000 relates to the garage and to the front room. We know that the business uses some of the house and that the house is an asset; the question is whether it is an asset of Harry himself or of the business and if it is the latter how should we record it and at what amount. To answer this question we need to go back to our definition of an asset as:

> Embodiments of present or future economic benefits or service potentials measurable in terms or monetary units, accruing to an enterprise as a result of economic events, the enjoyment of which by the enterprise is secured by the law

Bearing in mind the business entity principle, we can see from the definition that the garage is not an asset of the business as the business is viewed as a separate entity from the owner. It is Harry Keel himself who owns both the house and the garage, and he also retains the legal right to enjoy the benefits from their use. Thus the garage is not an asset of the business as the business has no legal right to use the garage; it therefore does not need to be included in the balance sheet of the business. A similar argument can be applied to the front room which is being used as an office.

Example 3.1 Keelsafe, Part 3

When Harry starts to make up the harnesses he realizes that he needs to buy some fasteners. He therefore approaches a supplier and finds that enough fasteners to fit all the harnesses he can make up with his existing materials will cost him £300. As he has used up all his redundancy money he approaches his bank who agree to make a loan of £500 to his business which he has called Keelsafe Safety Harnesses. He borrows the £500, puts it in the business bank account and then buys the fasteners with a cheque drawn on that account.

Part 3

We shall look first at this transaction and then draw up a new balance sheet. The reason we have to draw up a new balance sheet is that we are now at a different point in time and you will remember that a balance sheet shows the position at one point in time only.

The actual transaction on its own can be looked at in two stages.

Stage 1

The first stage is that we borrow the money from the bank. This has two effects: we increase the business assets as the business will get a future benefit from the use of that money, and we also increase the business liabilities as the business now owes the bank £500. This viewed on its own can be depicted as:

	assets	=		liabilities
Cash in bank	+£500	=	Loan	+£500

Stage 2

If we now look at the second stage where some of the money in the bank is used to buy the fasteners, we can extend Stage 1 and depict this as

	assets	=		liabilities
Cash in bank	£500	=	Loan	£500
Cash in bank	−£300			
Fasteners	+£300			

We can see that all that has happened is that we have exchanged one asset for another and the totals on either side of the equation have remained the same.

Before going on to draw up a new balance sheet you should note the important principle that we have just illustrated. The principle is that there are two sides to every transaction. At the first stage the two sides of the transaction were an increase in assets with a corresponding increase in liabilities, whereas at the second stage there was a decrease in one asset with a corresponding increase in another asset. This principle is often referred to as the principle of duality, which is essentially a grand-sounding title for the principle that all transactions have two sides.

KEY CONCEPT 3.10
The principle of duality

The principle of duality is the basis of the double-entry book-keeping system on which accounting is based. It states that

Every transaction has two opposite and equal sides

Having established this principle we can now draw up the new balance sheet of Keelsafe Safety Harnesses. Unlike the previous balance sheet this time we classify the assets into fixed and current assets and group these together to make the balance sheet more meaningful. Another way in which we can make the balance sheet more meaningful is to order the assets in descending order of liquidity, i.e. the more difficult the item is to turn into cash the less liquid it is. Thus the sewing machine as a fixed asset is seen to be less liquid than the stocks of fasteners etc. Similarly these are shown as less liquid than the cash at the bank.

You will also note that each of the groups of assets is subtotalled and the subtotal is shown separately. The total of all the assets is then shown. It is double underlined to indicate that it is a final total. It is conventional to use single underlining for subtotals and double underlining to denote final totals.

Having classified and listed the assets of Keelsafe we then show the amounts owed by the business subclassified into the amount the business owes to Harry (the owner's equity) and the amount it owes to others.

Balance sheet of Keelsafe Safety Harnesses as at 31 May 1993

	£	£
Fixed assets		
One sewing machine		550
One cutting machine		400
Typewriter		50
		1000
Current assets		
Office stationery	50	
Webbing material	300	
Sewing materials	100	
Fasteners	300	
Cash at bank	250	1000
		2000

	£	£
Financed by		
Owner's equity	1500	1500
Bank loan		500
		2000

The balance sheet has been rearranged to emphasize the differences between the various types of assets and Harry Keel's residual claim on the assets after the other liabilities have been paid. It should be noted that the balance sheet is headed with the name of the business and the date at which the balance sheet is drawn up.

It is worthwhile, before you proceed any further, to re-examine the definitions of fixed and current assets and ensure that you understand why the items above have been classified as they have.

Having done that we can now proceed to examine the determinants of the format of balance sheets and the ways in which they can be used, together with their limitations. First, however, it is worth looking at Case Study 3.1, the balance sheet of W.H. Smith Ltd, and reading the commentary that follows it.

CASE STUDY 3.1
W.H. Smith Ltd.

Balance Sheets
As at 30 May 1992

	Note	*1992* £m	*1991* £m
Fixed assets			
Tangible fixed assets	12	—	—
Investments	13	300.9	258.0
		300.9	**258.0**
Current assets			
Stocks		—	—
Debtors	14	271.5	73.9
Assets in the course of disposal		—	—
Cash at bank and in hand		—	—
		271.5	73.9
Pension prepayment	15	—	—
Creditors: amounts falling due within one year	16	(95.0)	(49.1)
Net current assets		**176.5**	**24.8**
Total assets less current liabilities		**477.4**	**282.8**
Creditors: amounts falling due after more than one year	17	(3.1)	(41.1)
Provisions for liabilities and charges	19	—	—
Minority interests		—	—
Total net assets		**474.3**	**241.7**

	Note	1992 £m	1991 £m
Called up share capital	20	135.8	101.5
Share premium account	21	205.0	30.9
Revaluation reserve	21	58.1	58.1
Other capital reserve	21	33.4	33.4
Profit and loss account	21	42.0	17.8
Total capital and reserves		**474.3**	**241.7**

Commentary
As you will see the balance sheet classifies the assets between fixed assets and current assets. It then lists the amounts owing currently to arrive at a figure of net current assets. This is followed by the other liabilities leaving a balance sheet total of net assets, i.e. assets minus liabilities. This is then balanced on the other side of the balance sheet by the owners' equity. This balance sheet is therefore a variation on the equation

assets − liabilities = owners' equity

The meaning of the various subheadings and classifications will be discussed in later chapters.

Determinants of the format of the balance sheet

We shall examine the purpose of the balance sheet and its limitations. We shall also consider some of the influences affecting the way in which it is presented and the extent to which this is determined by the type of organization and the users of the statements.

Purpose and limitations

The balance sheet is in essence a list of the assets and liabilities of the enterprise or organization at a point in time. The fact that it represents the position at one point in time is itself a limitation as it is only relevant at that point in time. At any other time, as we have seen in the case of Keelsafe, a new balance sheet has to be drawn up. This means that in order for the balance sheet to be useful it should be as up to date as possible, and that its utility diminishes the more out of date it becomes. Similarly, in order that it is an accurate measure of the assets and liabilities the values of those assets and liabilities should be as up to date as possible, and herein lies another limitation.

As we saw in Chapter 2 there are a number of ways in which assets can be valued, some of which are more subjective than others. The right value to choose depends on the purpose for which the balance sheet is to be used. For example, if we want to know how much each item cost, then the original, or historic, cost would be appropriate. If, on the other hand, we wanted to know how much each item could be sold for, then the net realizable value may be appropriate. Alternatively if we wanted to know how much the business as a whole was worth it is likely that neither of the afore-mentioned would be appropriate. Partly because of the difficulties involved in choosing an appropriate valuation and partly by convention, accountants have traditionally used the historic cost as the basis of valuation of assets in the balance sheet.

Clearly in certain cases this has led to assets being stated at a figure which bears little if any relation to their current value. The most obvious example of this in recent years has been the changes in prices and values of land and buildings. Because of this one often sees land and buildings shown in published accounts at a valuation rather than at cost.

An allied problem to the changes in the prices of specific assets is the fact that the unit of measurement, i.e. in our case the pound, does not itself represent a constant value over time. For example you cannot buy as many goods with a pound today as you could ten years ago. This once again limits the usefulness of the information contained in the balance sheet.

Influences on the format of the balance sheet

We shall consider the Business in Context model and use it to examine the various influences on the balance sheet. We shall examine the various influences on the balance sheet under the headings of strategic, organizational and environmental factors. Finally we shall look at the needs of users. No discussion of accounting statements would be complete without some reference to their needs.

The strategic context

As we have already shown in some of the examples that we have used, the activity in which the organization is involved can have dramatic effects on the classification of an asset (remember the case of the car dealer compared with the manufacturing business). Similarly we have illustrated in the example about gold mines that what might not be an asset for one business would be an asset of another business undertaking a different activity. Apart from these cases, which are to some extent reasonably clear cut, the activity can have dramatic effects on the difficulty or otherwise of drawing up a balance sheet. Consider for example the problems of a football club trying to account for star players, or of a high technology business trying to decide whether the cost of the patent on a new product is going to yield any future benefit when the state of the art is changing so rapidly.

There are also issues relating to the ways in which a business is perceived and the ways in which management would wish the business to be perceived. For example research (Carsberg *et al.*, 1985) has shown that management, especially the management of smaller organizations, perceive that bankers are interested in the amount of assets available as security for a loan or overdraft. There is therefore a temptation to try to enhance the value of assets perhaps by revaluing the land and building prior to applying for a loan. Similarly in a number of cases where a business is in trouble the assets have been revalued in order to bolster the image of the business and to promote the impression of it having 'a sound asset base'.

The organizational context

One of the prime determinants of the content and format of the balance sheet is the type of organizational structure involved. For example an incorporated business, i.e. a company, is subject to certain rules and regulations imposed by the state, whereas a partnership or sole proprietorship has no such restrictions. A company has to produce annual accounts and file a copy of these at Companies House, whereas in the case of a partnership there is no such requirement. Similarly a business that is part of a larger organization may well have to comply with the rules and format of accounts that suit that organization as a whole.

The need to comply with the organizational needs may also be affected by who owns the business. For example a company operating in the UK which is owned by an American company would have to comply with UK regulations but would also report to the US parent company in a format that complies with US regulations. If we contrast this with a business that is owned by two partners, there are no restrictions or rules imposed on this type of organization and the partners can decide for themselves what format the balance sheet should take and indeed how often it should be drawn up.

Another factor affecting the format of the balance sheet will be the size of the organization. In the example used we have assumed a very small operation and so all the assets could be individually listed. In the case of a larger more complex organization there will be a need for assets to be summarized under broad headings; otherwise the level of detail would be such that the user of the statement would find it extremely difficult or impossible to get an overall picture.

Finally, we should mention the influence of organizational goals although they are to some extent interconnected with the type of organization. Consider for example an organization set up for charitable purposes (which may or may not be incorporated): of what relevance to that organization is a classification such as 'owners' equity'? Similarly, if you looked at the accounts of your local authority you would not expect to see a heading for owners' equity or retained profits.

The environmental context

At the environmental level the most pervasive influence on the form and content of the balance sheet is the State, through the medium of legislation. As we have already indicated, the format and content of balance sheets as well as the way in which they are drawn up is different in some respects in the UK and in the USA. Even within the

UK there are different rules about the format and level of sophistication depending on whether the organization is a charity, a local authority, a company registered under the Companies Acts or a co-operative registered under the Provident and Friendly Societies Act. Even within these categories there can be different rules: for example a small company may produce abridged accounts for filing with the Registrar of Companies. A public company, on the other hand, also has to comply with the rules and regulations laid down by the Stock Exchange. Additionally there are other rules relating to content, laid down for companies by the professional accounting bodies, which are known as Statements of Standard Accounting Practice and Financial Reporting Standards (FRS). Whilst it is important to appreciate that these differences exist, the details of the differences are not relevant for the purposes of this text.

Users of accounts

As we discussed in Chapter 1, there are a number of different users who may have conflicting needs for information. To some extent the rules and regulations laid down by the State could be said to encompass some of these needs. However, those rules only lay down a minimum requirement. For example, whilst the Companies Acts require that loans and overdrafts should be shown, research shows that bankers would like to see details of the repayment dates of those loans in the accounts. On the other hand, the owners of the company may not wish to have that information made public. A similar conflict arises between the needs of managers, who may wish to know what it would cost to replace an asset rather than be presented with a statement which shows them what the asset cost when they bought it, and the needs of the owners, who may wish to know what management has spent their money on and how much each item cost.

Conclusion

In this chapter we have defined the nature, purpose and content of balance sheets and have highlighted some of the problems in drawing up such a statement. We have also introduced you to the wider context in which accounting reports can be viewed. It is important before proceeding further that you make sure that you understand the definitions involved and can apply them to real problems. As you have seen, a balance sheet can take many forms and clearly in a book of this nature there is no necessity to cover all of these. For simplicity, therefore, we shall use one format throughout the book and this is the one given below, together with an explanation for the choice of format. It is important that you understand the reasons for the choice of the suggested format as this will aid you in interpreting accounting information at a later stage.

Suggested balance sheet format

Balance sheet of 'Simple' as at 31 December 19X1

	£	£
Fixed assets		
Land and buildings		200
Machinery		100
Motor vehicles		50
		350
Current assets		
Stocks of raw materials	200	
Stocks of finished goods	110	
Cash in hand	20	
	330	
Creditors: amounts falling due within one year		
Bank overdraft	190	
	190	
Net current assets		140
Total assets less current liabilities		490
Creditors: amounts falling due after more than one year		
Bank loan		150
		340
Financed by		
Owners' equity		100
Retained profits		240
		340

As numerous formats are available and these, to some extent at least, are dependent on the type of organization, we have used a format which we consider to be appropriate to an introductory level text. If you wish to look at other formats you will find these referred to in the additional reading at the end of the chapter. Before following a different format, you should ensure that you understand the reasons behind the alternative format and you should consider whether the information given is as clear as in the format suggested above.

Reasons for choosing the format above

The balance sheet is headed with the name of the organization and the date to which the balance sheet relates. As has already been explained, a balance sheet relates to one point in time and that date needs to be clearly stated in the heading.

Within the balance sheet itself we commence with the 'Fixed assets' which are shown in descending order of permanence and liquidity. For example, the land and buildings will probably outlast the motor vehicles. They will also take longer to sell if we wished to sell them as we would first have to empty them whereas the motor vehicles could be sold almost immediately.

The 'Current assets' are also shown in descending order of liquidity. For example, in order to turn the raw materials into cash we first have to go through a manufacturing process to get them ready for resale and then sell them, whereas in the case of the stock of finished goods the manufacturing process has already taken place. Note also that all the current assets are added together and a total is given.

A similar rationale applies to the 'Creditors: amounts falling due within a year' as to current assets and once again these are totalled. You will find that 'Creditors: amounts falling due within a year' are often referred to as the 'current liabilities'. We shall use these terms interchangeably in this text.

The next heading is 'Net current assets' and this is arrived at by subtracting the total of the current liabilities from the total of the current assets. If this figure is positive it indicates that, assuming a one-year period, then we should realize enough from selling our current assets to pay the liabilities due within one year. Obviously things in reality are not so clear-cut, as we may need to pay large amounts almost immediately, whereas some of our current assets may take a relatively long time to turn into cash. Also there are certain types of business where the figure could in fact be negative. If it is negative then the term 'net current liabilities' is used.

The next sub-heading on the top half of our balance sheet is the total of all the assets less the current liabilities. This is then reduced by any amounts owing that do not have to be repaid within a year, referred to as 'Creditors: amounts falling due after more than one year'. The resultant figure represents the amount of the business belonging to the owners; this is the figure to which the other half of the balance sheet should total. You will see that this total is different from the previous totals, in as much as it is double underlined. This is simply a way of differentiating a sub-total from the final total.

The other half of the balance sheet shows the way in which the assets are financed by the owners' capital. It is again sub-divided, insofar as the amounts due to the owners are separately classified between those that the owner contributed to the business and those that the business generated as a result of trading, i.e. the retained profits.

Summary

In this chapter we have seen that a balance sheet is an attempt to show the financial position at one point in time. We have also introduced the idea that a business is viewed for accounting purposes as a separate entity from its owner (the business entity principle). From this starting point we have gone on to define assets, liabilities and owner's equity and to look at the balance sheet equation. Before moving on to the next chapter you should ensure that you have understood what is contained in this chapter by working through the review questions and the problems and case studies given below. As with previous chapters the answers to the review questions are all within the text.

References

Bull, R.J. (1984) *Accounting in Business*, 5th Edn, Butterworths, p. 22.

Carsberg, B.V. *et al.* (1985) *Small Company Financial Reporting*, Prentice Hall International, London.

Lall, R.M. (1968) 'An enquiry into the nature of assets', *The New York Certified Public Accountant*, November, pp. 793–7.

Further reading

Students who wish to examine the regulatory framework for companies in more detail are referred to *Form and Context of Company Accounts*, Cooper & Lybrand (Financial Training Publications, 1986).

Review questions

1 What are the essential elements of a useful definition of an asset?
2 What are the deficiencies, if any, in the following definition of an asset?

   Assets are the things a business owns.

3 What are the essential elements of a useful definition of a fixed asset?
4 Explain in your own words the difference between fixed assets and current assets and why it is important to classify assets into subgroups.
5 Explain in your own words what a liability is and the differences between liabilities and owners' equity.
6 What is the purpose of a balance sheet and what information does it contain?

Problems for discussion and analysis

1 Prepare a balance sheet from the following information and comment on the position of the business as shown by that balance sheet.

	£
Stock of goods held for resale	6 500
Freehold land and building	34 000
Mortgage on land and building	29 000

	£
Cash in tills	500
Fixtures and fittings	7 600
Office furniture	2 300
Bank overdraft	20 700
Delivery van	3 200
Owners' equity	?

2 In each of the following situations identify whether the item should be included in the balance sheet of Transom Trading at 31 December 1991, and if so at what amount and under which heading. Transom Trading is a retailer of motor spares and accessories. In all cases reasons for your decision must be given.

(a) A freehold shop bought in August 1991 for £88 000.
(b) A mortgage of £30 000 taken out to buy the shop in August 1991.
(c) Goods on the shelves at the end of the day on 31 December 1991. These goods had a resale value of £12 000 and had been purchased by Transom Trading for £8000.
(d) Delivery van, costing £6000, which Transom Trading ordered on 20 December 1991 but which was finally delivered and paid for on 2 January 1992.
(e) Shop fittings which were worth £3000 and had been bought at an auction by Transom Trading for only £1500 prior to opening the shop in August 1991.
(f) A Ford Fiesta costing £3500 which the owner of Transom Trading had bought in November 1991 for his wife to use. He had found that the Ford Granada Estate which he had bought second-hand in September for £4000 was being used exclusively for collecting and delivering goods for Transom Trading and not as a family car as originally intended.
(g) One cash register which was rented from Equipment Supplies at an annual rental of £200.
(h) One cash register which Transom Trading had bought in November 1991 for £600.
(i) A bank overdraft which amounted to £6500 on 31 December 1991.
(j) A supply of seat belts which the owner of Transom Trading had bought for £600 in September from a market trader in good faith and which were subsequently found to be defective.

3 Using the information in Problem 2 above calculate the owner's equity and draw up the balance sheet of Transom Trading as at 31 December 1991.

4 Fred owns a garage and has tried to get everything together ready for the business accounts to be drawn up. He has drawn up the list of items below. You are required to identify with reasons the balance sheet heading under which each item should be classified, and the amount at which it should be included.

(a) A motor car bought for resale at a cost of £3500; the retail price was £5000.
(b) Various loose tools for car repairs which cost £700.
(c) Two hydraulic jacks which had each cost £120.
(d) Freehold premises which had cost £40 000.
(e) The cost (£600) of digging and finishing a pit for repairs.
(f) Spare parts held as a general stock, originally costing £790.
(g) Spare parts bought from the previous owner when the garage was bought. At that time the value was agreed at £600 but it was subsequently discovered that only £200 of these spares were of any use.
(h) Breakdown truck which cost £3000 for the basic truck and £600 to have the crane fitted.
(i) A customer's car worth £1500 which was being held because the customer had not paid an outstanding bill of £300.
(j) Fred's own car which cost £4000. This is used mainly for business but Fred also uses it in the evenings and at weekends for the family.
(k) Customer goodwill which Fred reckons he has built up. He thinks that this would be worth at least £7000 if he sold the garage tomorrow.
(l) A bank loan for £1500 repayable within three months.
(m) A 20 year mortgage on the property amounting to £24 000 which has not been fully repaid. The amount still outstanding is £18 000.

The profit and loss account 4

In this chapter the attention is turned to the measurement of profit and the use of a profit and loss account as the mechanism by which profit can be measured. The components of the profit and loss account, revenue and expenses are defined and contrasted with assets and liabilities in order to illustrate the important differences between the components of the balance sheet and those of the profit and loss account.

We have already seen that we can measure profit by measuring wealth at two points in time. We have also shown that the way in which wealth is measured in accounting terms can be roughly equated with balance sheets, and we have looked at some of the issues arising from the alternative choices in respect of assigning monetary values to wealth measurement.

In this chapter we shall be concerned with an alternative way of measuring profit, using a profit and loss account. Our starting point and approach is very similar to that taken in the previous chapter. We look at what a profit and loss account is, why it is important, why it is produced and what it contains. We then consider some determinants of the content of a profit and loss account and some of the issues that have to be dealt with when drawing up a profit and loss account.

Importance of profit and loss accounts

Unlike a balance sheet which communicates information about a point in time, the profit and loss account relates to a period of time. It summarizes certain transactions taking place over that period. In terms of published reports the period is normally one year, although most businesses of any size produce profit and loss accounts more regularly, usually quarterly and often monthly. These monthly or quarterly accounts are normally for internal consumption only, although often banks request copies or make the production of such accounts a condition of lending money. The reason that the banks require these accounts on a regular basis is that they need to monitor the health of the business they are lending to. They want to be confident that the managers of the business are aware of what is happening and taking action to rectify the situation if the business is making losses.

As far as owners and managers are concerned, if they want the business to flourish, there is little point in finding out at the end of the year that the price at which goods or services were sold did not cover what it cost to buy those goods. By that stage it is too late to do anything about it. If a problem is identified at the end of the first month, however, it can be dealt with immediately by putting up prices, buying at a lower price or whatever is appropriate to the particular business.

Clearly the profit and loss account is a very important statement as it tells you whether a business is profitable or not. We have all heard the expression 'what is the bottom line?'. The bottom line referred to is the amount of profit made by a project or business. By comparing that profit with how much wealth is needed to produce it, you can decide whether to invest in a business. Other factors which also need to be taken into account are the risks involved and your own judgement of future prospects in order to decide whether the return as measured by the profit and loss account is adequate. Therefore, it can be argued that the profit and loss account provides some of the basic financial information for a rational decision to be made. We should remember, however, that although most of us think of business as being primarily motivated by profits, this is not always the case. Many small businesses make profits which are unsatisfactory from the point of view of a rational economic assessment, but the owners' motivation may not be profit. They may simply hate working for any boss, or they may value leisure more than additional profits.

Having talked about why a profit and loss account is important let us now look at what it is and what it contains. We have said that it is a statement covering a period of time, normally one year, and that its purpose is to measure profit, i.e. the increase in wealth. It does this by summarizing the revenue for that period and deducting from that the expenses incurred in earning that revenue. The process is therefore simple, but to be able to do it we need to look at the definition of revenue and expenses.

Revenue

Let us take a fairly standard definition of revenue and look at it in some detail so that we understand what it means (Key Concept 4.1). As is usual with definitions, this one seems on the face of it fairly complex. This is because it is trying to cover all eventualities. In most cases revenue is so obvious that it hits you between the eyes. For example, we would all agree that in a greengrocer's the revenue is going to be the amount that the fruit and vegetables were sold for, and in most cases that amount will all be in cash in the till. However, if we complicate it a bit more and suppose that our greengrocer supplies fruit and vegetables to a couple of local restaurants who settle their bill every month, we find that in order to define revenue we have to include not only cash sales but also the other sales for which we have not been paid. The latter amounts are referred to as 'receivables' by American textbooks or as 'debtors' in the UK. These debtors of course are shown in our balance sheet as assets because we shall get a future benefit from them. We shall discuss the treatment of debtors in more detail in Chapter 7.

KEY CONCEPT 4.1
Revenue

Revenue is the gross inflow of cash, receivables or other consideration arising in the course of the ordinary activities of the enterprise from the sale of goods, from the rendering of services, and from the use by others of enterprise resources, yielding interest, royalties and dividends.

Let us develop our example of the greengrocer a bit further to illustrate other parts of the definition. Let us assume that, as well as supplying the local restaurants who pay monthly, he also supplies his accountant, but instead of the accountant paying cash the arrangement is that the accountant does the accounts for nothing instead of charging the normal fee of £520 per year. These goods are effectively being sold to the accountant; all that has happened is that instead of the accountant paying the greengrocer £10 per week and then the greengrocer paying the accountant £520 at the end of the year they have simply agreed to exchange goods for services. These services are an example of what is referred to in the definition as 'other consideration'.

At this stage we should have a fair idea of what revenue is: it relates to goods and services sold. However, we need to be careful to ensure that we only include in revenue sales that are part of our normal business activity. To illustrate, let us assume that the greengrocer sells one of his two shops: should this be seen as revenue or is it different from selling fruit and vegetables? Clearly the answer is that it is different, because without a shop the business will cease to exist, whereas one cauliflower more or less does not threaten the existence of the business. Thus we need to differentiate normal sales of goods and services from the amounts arising from the sale of what is essentially the fabric of the business. The latter amounts will be dealt with separately and we explore their treatment in more detail in Chapter 8.

Finally before leaving our greengrocer illustration let us assume that, having sold one of the shops, the greengrocer decides to invest the money in some shares or in a building society until such time as a new shop can be found. In this situation the money invested, which is effectively surplus to immediate requirements, will generate additional revenue in the form of interest or dividends. This is a form of revenue which is different from our main source of revenue. It would, in this case, be shown separately but included in the total revenue for the period. In certain cases, however, the interest may be the major source of revenue – if, for example, the main activity of a business is lending money. Similarly dividends may be the main source of revenue for an investment trust.

So we can see that, although broadly speaking revenue is synonymous in many cases with sales, the actual revenue of a business is dependent on the type of business and the particular activity giving rise to the revenue. In the example we have used we have seen that in its simplest form revenue was equal to cash sales. However, for some business activities the distinctions are not so clear and this leads to problems in deciding what revenue relates to a particular period. This of course would not be a problem if accounting periods were the same as the period of a business cycle. For example if a housebuilder takes 18 months to build and sell a house there is no problem in finding the revenue for the 18 months. Unfortunately, the normal accounting period is 12 months and, as we have pointed out earlier, management and others need information on a more regular basis than that. What then is the revenue of our housebuilder for the first six months, or for the first year? This leads us to the question of when revenue arises and when it should be recognized. To help in answering this we adopt a principle known as the realization principle.

KEY CONCEPT 4.2
The realization principle

The realization principle states that revenue should only be recognized

(a) when the earning process is substantially complete and
(b) when the receipt of payment for the goods and services is reasonably certain.

The realization principle

The realization principle is defined in Key Concept 4.2. You may have noticed that, unlike our definitions which tend to be fairly precise and all inclusive, this principle is carefully worded to avoid too much precision. It is meant to provide some basic criteria which can be applied to the particular circumstances. The final decision on whether revenue is recognized is in practice often a matter of judgement rather than fact. Before looking at an example, let us first look at the wording used in the realization principle. Firstly you will see that it talks of process, which implies a period rather than a point in time. It also talks of 'substantially complete', which leaves the question of what is 'substantial': is it two-thirds or 90% or what? The principle also talks of payment being reasonably certain. Once again this leaves room for the exercise of judgement and raises the question of what is 'reasonable certainty' in an uncertain world.

Obviously if we sell goods to a reputable customer of long standing we are going to be reasonably certain that we shall be paid. If on the other hand we sell goods to a shady character then we may be a lot less confident that we shall be paid. Rather than looking at numerous examples of this type let us start by looking in general terms at a production and selling process and examining the possible points at which we could recognize revenue in accordance with the realization principle.

Point 1 Inputs
↓
Point 2 Production
↓
Point 3 Finished goods
↓
Point 4 Sale of goods
↓
Point 5 Receipt of cash

Clearly it is unlikely that revenue would ever be recognized at point 1 but as we shall see all the other points could be appropriate in different circumstances. If we start at the end of the process, i.e. point 5, on the face of it this seems to be a safe place to recognize revenue as the earnings process is likely to be complete and payment is certain because the cash has been received. In many cases point 5 is the appropriate point – as for example in the case of our greengrocer. However, he also had some other sales which were paid for monthly in arrears, so those may have to be recognized at point 4 as at that point the earning process is complete and payment is reasonably certain. On the other hand, if we take our builder and use either of these points we would get a situation where there was no revenue for the first 17 months but a lot in the eighteenth month. Of course in practice even in the case of our builder, if there was a contract to build the house for someone then cash would have been paid on account. The point we are making here is that point 4 and point 5 are not necessarily appropriate in all cases.

One could argue that for a shipbuilder points 4 and 5 are inappropriate as cash is received throughout a contract and the point of sale is in fact before the production process starts. In this case, as a ship takes a number of years to build, it is also inappropriate to choose point 3 as this would lead to all the revenue arising in one year. Therefore it may in fact be that point 2 is appropriate if the earning process is 'substantially' complete and, as is likely, payments on account have been received. A similar argument applies to the cases of a property developer or a building subcontractor.

From the discussion above it should be obvious that each case needs to be judged on its merits. You may for example like to think about when the appropriate time for revenue recognition would be for the following businesses.

1 a local newsagent;
2 a supplier of components to Ford Motors;
3 a gold-mine where all output is bought by the government at a fixed price;
4 an aircraft manufacturer.

If you have applied the realization principle you should have had little problem with the first example but the others are more problematic and are discussed more fully at the end of the chapter. If you feel unsure of your own solutions you may wish to refer to that discussion before proceeding any further.

The problem of when to recognize revenue is very important because the profit and loss account is based upon the revenue for a period and the expenses for that period. Before going on to discuss expenses we should first discuss how we establish which expenses to include. This is done by means of the matching principle (Key Concept 4.3).

KEY CONCEPT 4.3
The matching principle

We must match the revenue earned during a period with the expenses incurred in earning that revenue.

We can therefore see that the realization principle is of prime importance as it defines the revenue with which the expenses have to be matched. If we include additional revenue then we must also include expenses incurred in earning that additional revenue. On the face of it this matching is fairly straightforward. However, there are a number of areas where problems arise. These may be to do with timing (as we discuss later) or a combination of timing and uncertainty, as we illustrate in Case Study 4.1.

CASE STUDY 4.1
BP annual report 1992

Extract from Accounting Policies Statement

Exploration expenditure

Exploration expenditure is accounted in accordance with the successful efforts method. Exploration expenditure is initially classified as an intangible fixed asset. When proved reserves of oil and gas or commercially exploitable reserves of minerals or coal are determinded the relevant expenditure is transferred to tangible production assets. All exploration expenditure determined as unsuccessful is charged against income. Exploration leasehold acquisition costs are amortized over the estimated period of exploration.

Exploration costs incurred under production sharing contracts are classified as loans within fixed asset investments. Provisions are initially made against these loans in accordance with the successful efforts method. On the determination of proved oil and gas reserves in contract areas provisions against expenditures, which are recoverable under contracts from future production, are written back to income.

Commentary

This extract from the Accounting Policies Statement illustrates the problems of matching in conditions of uncertainty. In this case BP, like many other oil companies, has to decide how it should treat the expenditure on exploring new oil fields etc. The problem is really whether an asset exists, i.e. is there a future benefit to be obtained, and is that benefit reasonably certain? Clearly we can assume that BP only spends money on exploration if there is a chance of a future benefit but, taking into account the uncertainty of that benefit, BP exercises prudence where there is some doubt of the eventual outcome. The concept of prudence is explored in more detail later in this book (Chapter 6). At this stage the reader should be aware that in reality life is not as simple as it would appear and hard and fast rules are often inappropriate. Thus some judgement needs to be exercised, as we illustrated when discussing the realization principle.

Expenses

An expense is defined in Key Concept 4.4. Whilst the definition is fairly straightforward it leads us on to having to define what a cost is. As you will see later there are numerous ways of arriving at a cost. However, for our present purposes we can say that a cost means a money sacrifice or the incurring of a liability in pursuit of the business objectives.

Some examples of costs are:

- wages, which normally involve a money sacrifice;
- use of electricity, which normally involves incurring a liability to pay at the end of a quarter;
- purchase of a machine, which will normally incur a money sacrifice or a liability;
- purchase of goods for resale, which will normally incur a money sacrifice or a liability.

KEY CONCEPT 4.4
An expense

An expense is an expired cost, i.e. a cost from which all benefit has been extracted during an accounting period.

Although all the examples can clearly be seen to fit our definition of costs they are not necessarily expenses of the period. For example the machinery is likely to last more than one period and so it cannot be seen as an expired cost. Similarly the goods bought for resale may not be sold during the period and they therefore cannot be seen as an expense of the period for two reasons. Firstly the benefit has not expired as we shall be able to sell those goods at some time in the future. Secondly they cannot be matched against the revenue earned during the period. There are other situations where the point at which a cost is incurred and the point at which the benefit arises do not coincide. We shall discuss these in more detail shortly.

Before we do that it is worth emphasizing once again that we are dealing with a separate business entity and only costs relating to the business objectives can ever become expenses. This is very important as in many cases, especially with small businesses, the owner and the business are to all intents and purposes the same, but we are drawing up accounts for the business only. Thus if we find that a bill has been paid to buy a new double bed for a newsagent's business this cost is not an expense of the business because it relates to the owner personally, not the business. Such items often go through a business bank account but need to be separated out and shown as withdrawals of the owner's capital rather than business expenses.

These withdrawals are often referred to in the accounting literature as drawings. We could provide numerous examples of these, some of which are less obvious than others. For example, is the tax and insurance of the car a business expense if the car is also used for family transportation? The guiding principle in making a judgement is whether or not the cost has been incurred in pursuit of the objectives of the business.

We shall return to the discussion of drawings later, but let us now consider some possible situations in which we have to decide whether a cost which is clearly a business cost is an expense of the period. There are three possible situations that we need to discuss. These are where:

- costs of this year are expenses of this year;
- costs of earlier years are expenses of this year;
- costs of this year are expenses of subsequent years.

Costs of this year are expenses of this year

This is the most normal situation and is also the simplest to deal with. It occurs when an item or service is acquired during a year and consumed during that same year.

Note that no reference is made to whether the item acquired has been paid for. It may be that it has still not been paid for even though it has been acquired and used. A common example is telephone calls which are only paid for at the end of the quarter. The question of the timing of payment is not relevant to the process of matching expenses and revenues.

Costs of earlier years are expenses of this year

These can be divided into those that are wholly used up in the current period and those that are partly used up in the current period.

Wholly expenses of this year

The most obvious example of this is the stock of goods in a shop at the end of the year. The cost of buying those goods has been incurred in the year just ended but at the year end the benefit has not expired; they are therefore assets at the year end. However, in the next year they will be sold and thus will become expenses of the next year. The process that has occurred can be illustrated as follows.

If we buy goods in November 19X1 but do not sell them until January 19X2 and we have a year end in December 19X1 then the goods are an asset at that date, i.e. 31 December 19X1, as the benefit is not used up. The cost, however, has been incurred in that year. In 19X2 the goods are sold and therefore the benefit is used up and there is an expense for the year ended December 19X2, although the cost was incurred in the previous year. This can be seen diagrammatically as follows:

1.1.X1 ⟷	31.12.X1	⟷ 31.12.X2
Cost incurred	Asset at	Goods sold
Goods bought	year end	Expense

A similar situation arises when services are paid for in advance and are not fully used up at the end of the accounting period. For example, if the rent is payable quarterly in advance on 31 March, 30 June, 30 September and 31 December and the enterprise has a year end on 31 December, then the cost will be incurred in year 1 for the quarter to 31 March, year 2. However, the benefit will be used up in the first quarter of year 2 and thus the expense belongs to year 2.

These expenses are normally referred to as 'prepaid expenses' and frequently arise in respect of rent and water rates. For an individual the most obvious examples of this type of expense are annual subscriptions to clubs and societies, car insurance, road fund licence etc.

Other situations, for a business, where a cost may relate to more than one period arise frequently. For example, it we assume that the car insurance of the business was payable on 1 July 19X1, then half of that cost would be used up and become an expense for 19X1 and half would be used up and be an expense of 19X2. The crucial test is whether the benefit has been used up at the year end. If not there is a future benefit and we therefore have an asset.

All these examples refer to costs incurred in the past which are expenses of the current year. Another category that needs to be considered is where costs have been incurred in the past and only part of the benefit is used up in the current year.

Partly expenses of current year

An everyday example of this is any consumer durable, e.g. a car, washing machine, television etc. In all these cases the costs are incurred at a point in time but the benefits are expected to accrue over a number of years. In a business enterprise the equivalent of our consumer durables are fixed assets such as machinery, office equipment etc. The allocation of the cost of these items to subsequent accounting periods is called depreciation and this will be dealt with in more detail in Chapter 8.

Costs incurred this year which are expenses of later years

Just as some of the costs incurred in previous years are expenses of the current accounting period, costs incurred in the current period may be expenses of future periods.

Examples that spring to mind are car tax, insurance, rates etc. The due date for payment of these is unlikely to concide with the end of the accounting period, nor would we want them too as this would lead to an uneven cash flow. Other examples are goods held in stock at the year end and fixed assets bought during the year.

If we take our previous example of our annual car tax we can see that, if we pay for that in the current year 19X2 on 1 July, then part of that cost will relate to next year 19X3.

1.1.X2 ←——→ 31.12.X2 ←——→ 31.12.X3
↓ ↓
Tax paid Tax paid
←—— Expense period ——→

Having looked at revenues and expenses we now need to recap on how these fit together in the profit and loss account before looking at a simple numerical example.

The profit and loss account

The purpose of this statement is to measure the profit or loss for the period. It does this by summarizing the revenues for the period, matching the expenses incurred in earning those revenues and subtracting the expenses from the revenues to arrive at the profit or loss. This could be depicted as:

$$R - E = P$$

or

$$\text{revenue} - \text{expenses} = \text{profit}$$

Before going on to examine what the profit figure could be used for let us see how this fits with the measurement of wealth described in Chapter 3.

In Chapter 3 we said that profit is the difference between wealth at the start and end of the year, i.e.:

$$\text{wealth 1} - \text{wealth 0} = \text{profit } P_1$$

or

$$W_1 - W_0 = P_1$$

The alternative way of measuring profit was to take expenses from revenue. We also said in Chapter 3 that wealth in accounting terms was measured by assets minus liabilities. The resultant figure, i.e. the residual, was referred to as the owners' equity. Thus we said that at time T_0 the owners' equity is:

$$\text{assets at } T_0 - \text{liabilities at } T_0 = \text{owners' equity at } T_0$$

If we add to the owners' equity at T_0 the profit for the period T_0 to T_1, then the resultant figure will be our wealth at T_1 which will equal our assets minus liabilities at T_1, i.e.

$$\text{assets at } T_1 - \text{liabilities at } T_1 = \text{owners' equity at } T_0 + \text{profit } P_1$$

or

$$A_1 - L_1 = O_0 \pm (R - E)_1$$

This shows us that there is a relationship between the profit and loss account and the balances sheet; the nature of that relationship will become clearer in Chapter 5. However, let us now look at an example of a profit and loss account and then consider what it is used for, its format and its limitations. In Case Study 4.2 we use the transactions of Blakes Enterprises, a paint shop, and see what should go into the profit and loss account for the year to 31 December 1989.

CASE STUDY 4.2
Blakes enterprises

Blakes Enterprises is a new retail paint outlet set up at the start of the year. Its transactions for 1989, its first year, are summarized below.

Dates	*Description*	*Amount*
1 January	Purchase of freehold shop	£60 000
1 January	Rates for the year	£ 2 000
1 April	Van purchased	£ 8 000
1 April	Van – tax and insurance for a year	£ 600
1 July	Purchase of washing machine	£ 300
Various	Wages to shop assistant for year	£ 6 000
Various	Goods bought and resold	£18 000
Various	Goods bought but unsold	£ 4 000
Various	Cash from sales	£45 000
Various	Motor expenses and petrol	£ 1 200
Various	Money withdrawn by Blakes	£ 6 000

Purchase of freehold The benefit arising from this cost has clearly not expired during the period although some part of the benefit may have been used up. At this stage we shall not try to measure the part used up but we should bear in mind that at a later stage we shall need to make such allocations.

Rates for the year This is clearly a cost and an expense of the year in question and should be included in the profit and loss account.

Purchase of van As with the freehold shop the benefit is likely to be available over many periods and we should theoretically allocate to the profit and loss account for the year the amount of the benefit used up. This allocation is done by means of a depreciation charge which we deal with later in the book. At this stage therefore we shall merely note the idea that an allocation should be made.

Van – tax and insurance This was paid for in advance on 1 April for a full year. At the end of our accounting period, i.e. 31 December, we shall have used nine months' insurance and tax, i.e. nine-twelfths of the total. The expense for the period therefore is 9/12 × £600, i.e. £450. The remaining £150 relates to the next year and is an asset at the end of the year as the business will receive some future benefit. This and similar items are discussed in more detail in Chapter 7.

Purchase of washing machine We know that Blake's Enterprises is a retail shop selling paint. It is therefore highly unlikely that the washing machine was bought for use by the business although it has been paid for out of the business bank account. This is not, therefore, an expense of the business, nor is it an asset of the business as the business will not get any future benefit. It is, in effect, a withdrawal of capital by the owner and should be treated as drawings.

Wages for year This is clearly a business expense as the wages are paid to the shop assistant and the benefit has been used up. From the information we have, the whole £6000 relates to the accounting period, and therefore the expense charged to the profit and loss should be £6000.

Goods bought and resold These goods have been sold to customers. We therefore no longer own them and are therefore not entitled to any future benefit. Thus the whole of the £18 000 is an expired benefit and as such should be charged as an expense in the current year's profit and loss account.

Goods bought but unsold These goods are still held by the business at the end of the year. The benefit from the goods is still to come in the form of cash when they are sold. Goods held in stock are therefore an asset rather than expense of the period we are dealing with. Note that the test being applied is whether there is a future benefit or whether the benefit is past. If the former is the case there is an asset; if it is the latter situation then there is an expense.

Cash from sales This is the revenue of the business for the year and as far as we can tell it is the only revenue. The full amount of £45 000 should be shown as sales revenue in the profit and loss account.

Motor expenses and petrol Once again the benefit from these has expired. The whole of the £1200 should therefore be charged as an expense to the current year's profit and loss account.

Money withdrawn by Blake Given the present information we cannot categorically say whether this is a business expense or not. If it is in effect wages for Blake's work it could be argued that it is a genuine business expense. If, on the other hand, it has simply been withdrawn because Blake has decided to buy a new boat for personal use then it is clearly drawings. For the present we classify it as drawings.

We can now draw up the profit and loss account of Blakes Enterprises for the year ended 31 December 1989.

Profit and loss account of Blakes Enterprises for the year ended 31 December 1989

	£	£
Sales revenue		45 000
Cost of the goods sold		18 000
Gross profit		27 000
Rates	2 000	
Van tax and insurance	450	
Wages	6 000	
Motor expenses	1 200	9 650
Net profit		17 350

You will notice that we have shown a gross profit and a net profit. Gross profit can be defined as sales less cost of goods sold; net profit can broadly be defined as gross profit less operating costs, administrative costs and other charges.

The reason for showing a gross profit is to enable Blake to see that the business is doing as well as it should. Most retail businesses know what percentage of the selling price is profit and what is cost; Blake for example has costs of 40% of the selling price and would expect a gross profit margin of 60% of the selling price. If next year the gross profit margin was only 50% Blake would want to know why. The answer must lie either with the sales figure, i.e. the price has been reduced or all sales have not been included, or with the cost of goods: the price from the supplier may have risen or the amount sold has been incorrectly calculated.

The net profit figure, as can be seen from the definition above, can be affected by numerous expenses. It is the figure often referred to as the bottom line. You may see sets of accounts in which the owners' drawings are deducted from this figure to arrive at a figure of profit retained in the business. The reason for not taking drawings off the net profit figure is similar to the argument for a gross profit in so far as a business will normally incur similar expenses year to year, i.e. Blake will probably need a shop assistant next year, will have to pay rates etc. These amounts will be reasonably constant and the net profit as a percentage of sales should therefore be reasonably constant. The owners' drawings, on the other hand, may fluctuate widely from year to year and therefore to include these in the calculation of net profit would mean that the net profit would fluctuate widely as well. This would make any analysis of the performance of the business more difficult than if the drawings are taken after the net profit has been determined.

Determinants of the format of the profit and loss account and its uses

Unlike the balance sheet which represents the position at a point in time, the profit and loss account tries to represent a series of transactions over a period of time. Let us look first of all at what determines the format of the profit and loss account as this also, to some extent, determines its usefulness and its limitations. For this we shall follow a similar format to Chapter 3 in that we shall look at the strategic context, the organizational context and the environmental context.

The strategic context

To a limited extent the type of business activity will determine the presentation and context of the profit and loss account. For example, in the case of a retail business such as Blakes Enterprises a gross profit figure may be useful, but in a service business such as for example a hotel, which is highly labour intensive, the revenue earned may bear little if any relationship to inputs of physical goods. Thus the type of activity has an effect on what is being reported and how it should be reported. Similarly the objective of the preparers of information often has an effect on the profit and loss account. If for example the accounts are being prepared for tax purposes the owner may wish to reduce profit, or defer it to the next year if at all possible. On the other hand, if the accounts are to be used to borrow money, then a healthy profit may be what is required to be portrayed. Whilst we should not give the impression that the profit can be manipulated at will, it is clear from our discussion that there are a number of areas of judgement which allow slightly different results to be obtained from the same basic data. The extent to which manipulation is practised is often limited by the fact that there are a number of conflicting requirements which mean that manipulation of the profit one way for one purpose is detrimental for another purpose. It should also be borne in mind that the profit and loss account can only be as good as the information on which it is based. Thus for a fish and chip shop whose owner only records every second sale through the till, the accounts will only record those transactions that go through the till.

The organizational context

As with the balance sheet a prime determinant of the content and format of the profit and loss account is the type of organizational structure involved. The content and format of the profit and loss account for a company is determined by the relevant Companies Acts and in addition is subject to regulations imposed by the professional accounting bodies. The latter regulations are contained in Statements of Standard Accounting Practice and the Financial Reporting Standards. Another important determinant is ownership: a company may have to produce accounts that comply with both UK and US regulations, for example, if it is owned by a US parent.

For other types of organization such as sole proprietorships and partnerships there are virutally no regulations covering format. Because the profit and loss account is being prepared for owners who are also managers, it is normally the case that for these organizations the level of detail in the profit and loss account is greater. The reason for this is that the annual report, as well as being a report on performance, acts as a basis for management decisions about the organization.

The size and complexity of an organization is often a determinant of the level of detail contained in accounts prepared for external consumption. These accounts for external consumption are only one form of account as regular profit and loss accounts are normally prepared for internal use by the managers of any organization and these internal reports will generally be more detailed than the reports produced for external users.

Finally it is important to remind ourselves that the type of organization and the organizational goals may make a profit and loss account less relevant and in some cases irrelevant. Should charitable organizations make profits, or is the prime interest how any surplus monies have been used to further the aims of the charity? Clearly different statements are appropriate to the needs and aims of different organizations.

The environmental context

As we have stated in Chapter 3 there are a number of environmental influences on the format and content of the published accounts, including the profit and loss account. In some countries a particular influence that is more relevant to the profit and loss account than the balance sheet is the taxation legislation. In some European countries, such as Germany, unless an amount is in the profit and loss account it is not allowable for tax purposes. (This is not the case in the UK.) This can lead to charging in the current year 'expenses' from which there is still a future benefit to be obtained, in order to minimize the tax bill for the year.

Users of accounts

The users of accounts often have different requirements from each other. As we have said, owner managers would normally require more detailed information. The tax authorities often require specific information to decide whether a particular expense is allowable for tax purposes. Apart from these influences there is also confidentiality: a business does not necessarily want its competitors, or indeed its customers, to know how much profit it is making.

Summary

In this chapter we have identified what revenue is and explained two important principles, i.e. the realization principle and the matching principle. We have also looked at the question of what constitutes a business expense and seen that:

1 expenses are not necessarily the same as costs;
2 all costs must relate to the business before they can even be considered as expenses.

We have also pointed out that the definitions both of assets and of expenses relate to benefits to the business. The important difference is that assets give future benefits whereas expenses relate to benefits used up in the accounting period. This leads us to a series of questions relating to assets and expenses which may assist in the correct classification of items. These questions may be summarized in the form of a decision tree:

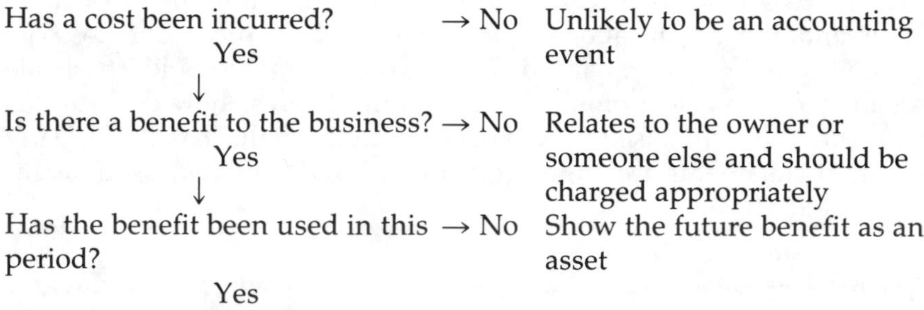

Charge as an expense

Discussion of recognition of revenue for examples in the chapter

1 A local newsagent: The business is likely to be mainly cash based so point 5 is probably most appropriate although this will depend upon how many customers buy their newspapers etc. on account.

2 Supplier of components: Clearly point 5 is too late as even at point 4 the earnings process is complete and payment is reasonably certain. However, it could be argued that if the component supplier has a fixed contract with Ford an earlier point, such as the point at which the goods are ready to be delivered, may be appropriate. This may well become closer to the 'norm' if more large firms adopt Just-in-time principles as these lead to dedicated stocks being held by their suppliers rather than by them.

3 A gold mine: A similar argument as for the component supplier could be applied here as the earnings process is substantially complete at the point of production and payment is certain as the government buys all output.

4 An aircraft manufacturer: Your answer here will depend on the assumptions you have made. If for example you assumed that the aircraft manufacturer is making to order then your judgement of certainty of payment would be different than if you assumed that it produced aircraft and then tried to sell them. Similarly if you thought of an aircraft producer as producing Boeing 747s you may have thought of the production process as spreading over a number of years, in which case point 2 may have been your judgment. If on the other hand you thought of the manufacture of light aircraft such as Piper Cubs, you may have assumed a shorter production cycle, in which case point 2 would not be appropriate.

Further reading

Readers interested in pursuing the question of when revenue should be recognized may refer to an interesting discussion in J.H. Myers: 'The critical event and the recognition of net profit', *The Accounting Review*, October 1959, pp. 528–32.

Review questions

1 In your own words define revenue.
2 At what point should revenue be recognized?
3 In your own words define an expense.
4 How does an expense differ from a cost?
5 'Expenses are always the same as costs for a period.' Discuss the truth of this statement using examples to illustrate your argument.
6 What is the purpose of a profit and loss account and who would use it?
7 Describe the difference between an expense and an asset.
8 In what circumstances would it be inappropriate to recognize a cost as either an expense or an asset?

Problems for discussion and analysis

1 In each of the following situations, discuss whether the item would be included in the profit and loss account for the year to 31 December 1993 and at what amount. The business is that of a builder and builder's merchant.

(a) Sales of general building materials by the builder's merchant to third parties amounted to £26 000 of which £24 000 was received in cash by 31 December 1993 and the remainder was received in January 1994.
(b) Three house conversions were started and completed during the year at a price of £24 000 each. These amounts were received in full by 31 December 1993.
(c) One office conversion which had been 60% complete at the end of 1992 was completed in 1993 at a price of £40 000. Invoices on account amounting to £24 000 had been sent out in 1992.
(d) The building materials sold to third parties during the year had cost £14 000 of which all but £1000 had been paid for by December 1993.
(e) The building materials used on the three houses referred to in (b) had cost £18 000 and had all been paid for by December 1993.
(f) Wages paid in respect of the houses mentioned in (b) amounted to £20 000 for the year.

(g) The costs relating to the office mentioned in (c) were as follows:

Wages paid in 1992	£8000
Wages paid in 1993	£6000
Materials used in 1992	£8000
Materials used in 1993	£7000

(h) The storemen's wages in the yard amounted to £8000 for the year.

(i) The owner who worked full time in the business paid himself a salary of £9000 and also withdrew £1000 in cash from the business to pay a pressing personal debt.

(j) The motor expenses paid in the year were broken down as follows:

Annual road tax on three vans paid 1 April	£300*
Annual insurance on vans paid 1 April	£480*
Repairs and petrol for vans	£600
Annual road tax on owner's car paid 1 June	£100*
Annual road tax on owner's wife's car paid 1 June	£100
Annual insurance on owner's car paid 1 June	£120*
Annual insurance on owner's wife's car paid 1 June	£120*
Repairs and petrol for the two cars	£800

* The charge for road tax had gone up by £20 per vehicle in the previous year and insurance premiums had risen by 20%. All these charges are paid annually in advance.

(k) The following bills were also paid during the year:

Electricity (payable at end of each quarter)	1 February	£54
	1 May	£45
	1 August	£45
	1 November	£60
Rent for 1 year to 1 April 1994	1 April 1993	£400*
TV licence to 1 April 1994	1 April 1993	£60*

* The rent had remained the same as in 1992 but the TV licence had gone up from £50 to £60.

2 Based on your decisions, draw up a profit and loss account for 1993 using the information above.

3 There are two partners in AB & Co., an electrical retailer. They have each withdrawn £5000 in cash from the business during the year. B has also taken from the business for personal use a washing machine which cost £200 and which had a selling price of £280. A has been paid wages of £12 000 and B has been paid £6000 in wages. Discuss how each of the above should be dealt with in the accounts giving reasons for your decisions.

Introduction to the worksheet 5

This chapter uses the worksheet as the vehicle to explain and explore the interrelationships between profit and loss and balance sheet items. The concept of duality, which is central to all double-entry recording systems, is introduced, explained and its use illustrated through the worksheet.

In Chapter 3 we discussed the question of how we measure what a business is worth at a particular point in time by using the balance sheet, whilst in Chapter 4 we discussed the measurement of the profit for a period of time through the use of the profit and loss account. We also indicated that the profit could be measured either using the profit and loss account or from the increase in wealth over a period of time. Because of the complexity of most business organizations and the number of transactions involved we need to have a system from which the details for inclusion in the balance sheet and profit and loss account can be drawn. This system also needs to have some built-in checks and balances to ensure as far as possible that transactions are not omitted and to allow us to trace back to the original source any errors that are identified. To cope with these and other demands a form of recording known as double-entry book-keeping was developed. This system is based on a rule known as *the principle of duality* (see Key Concept 3.10). This principle was discussed in some detail in Chapter 3, and it was further exemplified in our discussion of the balance sheet equation which we defined as:

assets = liabilities + owners' equity

We also showed that the owners' equity was increased by the profits made by the business, and we defined profit as:

profit = revenue − expenses

We can therefore see that if the balance sheet at the start of the period is stated as:

$$\text{assets at } T_0 = \text{liabilities at } T_0 + \text{owners' equity at } T_0$$

then the balance sheet at the end of the period can be depicted as:

$$\text{assets at } T_1 = \text{liabilities at } T_1 + \text{owners' equity at } T_0 + (\text{revenue} - \text{expenses})$$

From these equations it should be clear that there is a relationship between assets, liabilities, owners' equity, revenue and expenses and that with every transaction recorded we must ensure that there are two sides in order that the equation remains true. This may seem complicated but it will become much clearer when you see how the double-entry system of recording works.

KEY CONCEPT 5.1
Application of the principle of duality

Applying the duality principle to our equation we find that, if we increase our assets, we must have

either increased our liabilities
or made a profit
or increased our owners' equity

In other words, the principle of duality when applied to the balance sheet equation holds that both sides of the equation must always be equal.

We shall deal with fairly simple examples to illustrate the principles, which are the same no matter how complex the business. It is normally the number of transactions that is the problem rather than the complexity, and most large businesses and indeed some fairly small businesses have to have very sophisticated recording systems to deal with the thousands of transactions that take place during a year. This is of course one of the major uses, if not the major use, of computers in business today. Computers not only provide a vehicle for recording the accounting transactions but the more sophisticated systems will also analyse the data and produce reports such as balance sheets, profit and loss accounts and other reports tailormade to the particular needs of the users or managers of the business. For our purposes, however, we do not need to introduce a high level of sophistication to understand the principles involved and we can set up a perfectly adequate double-entry book-keeping system using a spreadsheet approach in the same way as computer packages such as Lotus 1-2-3 use a spreadsheet. We shall refer to our manually produced spreadsheet as a worksheet and we shall use the worksheet to illustrate the basics of double-entry book-keeping.

The worksheet is set out in the form of the balance sheet equation with columns headed as appropriate. We shall use the following simple data to illustrate the worksheet.

Example 5.1

Beetle started up a small business and the first transactions were as follows:

1 to open a business bank account and deposit £5000 of Beetle's own money;
2 to buy a van for £2000;
3 to buy some goods for resale for £3000 cash;
4 to get a bank loan of £6000;
5 to buy some machinery for manufacturing for £4000 cash.

Each of these transactions has been entered on the worksheet (version 1) and you should look at that whilst reading the description of what has been done.

Before looking at the transactions in detail let us briefly discuss the way in which the worksheet has been set up. You will notice that there is a column in which the transaction is identified and described. This identification and description in our case has been done via the item number and the transaction taking place. You could include a fuller description, however: the date, the invoice number, the name of the suppliers involved or whatever is appropriate.

After the column containing the description there are columns for each asset purchased and these are separated from the liabilities and owner's equity. Thus we have in effect across the top of our worksheet the balance sheet equation:

assets = owner's equity + liabilities

Having made that very important point let us now examine each of the transactions in turn and see how they have been entered into our double-entry worksheet.

To make things easier the transactions are repeated and are followed by the worksheet and then by descriptions of how they are entered on the worksheet:

1 to open a business bank account and deposit £5000 of Beetle's own money.
2 to buy a van for £2000.
3 to buy some goods for resale for £3000 cash.
4 to get a bank loan of £6000.
5 to buy some machinery for manufacturing for £4000 cash.

Beetle worksheet version 1

	Assets				= Equity + Liabilities	
	Cash	*Van*	*Stock*	*Machine*	*Equity*	*Loans*
Item 1	5000				5000	
Item 2	−2000	2000				
Item 3	−3000		3000			
Item 4	6000					6000
Item 5	−4000			4000		
Balance	2000	2000	3000	4000	5000	6000

Item 1
In the case of this transaction Beetle expects to get a future benefit; therefore we have an asset. So we have opened a column for cash and entered the amount paid into the bank account. On the other side of our worksheet we have opened a column entitled Owner's equity and have entered in that column the amount that the owner has put into the business, in effect the amount that the business owes the owner. Before moving on to the next item it should be noted that if we were to total up our worksheet we would have the figures for the balance sheet at that point in time, and this is true at every stage as long as all transactions up to the balance sheet date have been recorded.

Item 2
For this transaction we have opened another column in which we have recorded the van as an asset as it will give a future benefit and we have also deducted the amount we paid for the van from the cash column. The worksheet if totalled now would still balance and would correctly record that the business owns a van which cost £2000 and has £3000 in the bank.

Item 3
Next we used some of our cash to purchase a stock of goods for resale. We therefore need to record that our asset cash is reduced by £3000 and that we have a new asset 'Stock' which cost us £3000. You should remember that we have classified the stock as an asset because we have assumed that we will get a future benefit from it.

Item 4
In this transaction we borrowed some money and put it in our bank. The amount in the bank is therefore increased by the amount of the loan (£6000) and on the other side of the worksheet we open a column in which we record the fact that the business has a liability, i.e. it owes somebody money (in this case £6000). Once again if we were to total up our worksheet at this point we would find that it balanced.

Item 5
This transaction involves using one asset, our cash, to purchase another, machinery. Once again the machinery can be viewed as an asset of the business as the business is going to get some future benefit. So all that is needed is to open a column for our new asset and show that it cost £4000 and reduce the amount we have in our bank by the same amount.

From the worksheet above it should be obvious that every transaction involves two entries. For example when the owner pays in the money an entry is made in the Cash column and one is made in the Owner's equity column. It should also be apparent that if all the columns are totalled the worksheet will always balance. If either of these points is not clear to you it is important that you look again at what has been done so that you understand both these points before moving on.

You may have noticed that in the worksheet all the transactions are ones that only affect the balance sheet. In order to provide a clearer understanding of the way in which the worksheet is used and how profit and loss account transactions are recorded we shall extend our example by a few more transactions.

Example 5.1 – further information

6 Beetle hired a machine operator who worked on the goods previously bought (see item 3) and who was paid £500.
7 Beetle sold the finished goods for £5000.

Dealing first with item 6, we can see that when Beetle paid the wages there was an expectation that there would be a future benefit because the cost of the goods held had increased by the amount spent on changing them from their original form to their final form. We could either record these wages as an asset in their own right or add them to the cost of the goods bought and call that finished stock. We shall take the latter course in this example. Thus the entry we need to make is to open a column for 'Finished goods', reduce the cash by £500, and record the £500 spent in the Finished goods column.

However, we have said that the cost of the finished goods is the cost of the raw materials plus the wages and at present we have only dealt with the wages. To deal with the raw materials we need to reduce the stock column by £3000 and add that amount to the Finished goods column.

Turning now to item 7, clearly we have some sales revenue here so we can open a new column which we will title 'Profit and loss account' and in this we enter sales of £5000. We also need to enter the increase in cash of £5000 in the cash column.

If at this stage we were to draw up a balance sheet it would balance and show us that a profit of £5000 had been made. However, that would be incorrect because we have not applied the matching principle, i.e. we have not shown any expenses incurred in producing the sales of £5000. We can try to identify these expenses directly, as we know they consist of the cost of the raw materials and the wages, i.e. the amount in the Finished goods column. An alternative would be to look at each of our assets and ask ourselves the question: is there a future benefit to be obtained or has the benefit expired? If there is a future benefit then we have an asset; if the benefit has already passed then we have an expense. If we did this in this case, we would have to come to the conclusion that, as we had sold the goods represented by the figure of £3500 in the Finished goods column and had received the benefit from selling them in the form of £5000 in cash, then these are clearly not an asset any longer and should be charged as an expense of the period. We thus have to make a further adjustment to our worksheet which we will call item 7a. Our new worksheet will now be as follows.

Beetle's worksheet version 2

	Assets					= Equity + Liabilities		
	Cash	*Van*	*Stock*	*Machine*	*Finished goods*	*Equity*	*Loans*	*Profit and loss*
1	5000					5000		
2	−2000	2000						
3	−3000		3000					
4	6000						6000	
5	−4000			4000				
	2000	2000	3000	4000		5000	6000	
6	−500				500			
6			−3000		3000			
7	5000							5000
7a					−3500			−3500
	6500	2000	0	4000	0	5000	6000	1500

Before leaving this simple example let us extract from the worksheet a balance sheet at the end of the period in question and a profit and loss account for the period.

Balance sheet of Beetle at the end of the period

	£
Fixed assets	
Van	2 000
Machine	4 000
	6 000
Current assets	
Cash	6 500
	12 500
Financed by	
Owner's equity	5 000
Profit	1 500
	6 500
Loans	6 000
	12 500

A careful study of the figures in the balance sheet and a comparison with the last line of the worksheet will make it clear that the balance sheet is in fact the bottom line of the worksheet after appropriate classifications have been made.

Profit and loss account of Beetle for the period

Sales revenue	5000
Cost of goods sold	3500
Profit for the period	£1500

You will notice that the profit and loss account is simply a summary of the profit and loss column in the worksheet.

If we consider what we have done in the example we can see that the system of double entry is merely a convenient way of recording transactions in a logical manner. The system is not complex – all it requires is an understanding of addition and subtraction together with the knowledge that the equation must always be in balance. It also requires the application of our definitions to classify a particular transaction correctly and so if you have had problems in understanding why a transaction is dealt with in a particular way you should return to Chapters 3 and 4 and reread the definitions.

Before going on to try an example yourselves it is worth spending some time reflecting on what we have just said by reference to the last example. If we look at any of the columns we can see that there is simply addition and subtraction taking place; a good example is the cash column where we make additions as money comes into the business and make deductions as money is spent. Another feature of the system that is not so obvious is that if we make mistakes there is an automatic check because in the end the worksheet will not balance. If this turns out to be the case we have two ways of finding the error: we can either do a line by line check to ensure that each of our lines has balanced or we can total the columns at various stages to see where the error is likely to be. For example, if we had an error in the worksheet we have just done we could look at the totals after entering item 4 or item 5 or whatever. Quite often the error is reasonably obvious as the amount involved gives us a clue. The easy way to illustrate this is to put some deliberate errors into the context of the worksheet we have just completed.

Single entry error

Let us assume that we forgot the basic rule that each transaction has two sides and when we paid the wages we simply deducted the £500 from the cash column. Our worksheet would appear as follows.

Beetle's worksheet version 3

	Assets					=	Equity + Liabilities	
	Cash	*Van*	*Stock*	*Machine*	*Finished goods*	*Equity*	*Loans*	*Profit and loss*
	2000	2000	3000	4000		5000	6000	
6	−500							
6			−3000		3000			
7	5000							5000
7a					−3000			−3000
	6500	2000	0	4000	0	5000	6000	2000

You will notice that because we did not record the other side of the wages transaction the amount charged to the profit and loss account in respect of the goods we sold is only £3000 and the profit is increased to £2000. If we now add up the two sides of our worksheet we find that the assets side totals £12 500, i.e. £6500 + £2000 + £4000, whereas the other side totals £13 000 i.e. £5000 + £6000 + £2000. The difference between the two is £500 which, of course, should direct us to the wages as the likely cause of the problem.

Incorrect double entry

Another common cause of errors is incorrect double entry. In this case two sides are recorded but they do not leave the equation in balance. Let us assume for example that we had got the entry for the wages correct but that we had incorrectly classified the £5000 Beetle obtained from selling the goods as an increase in cash and an increase in finished goods rather than as sales revenue. The resultant worksheet would then be as follows.

Beetle's worksheet version 4

	Assets					= Equity + Liabilities		
	Cash	*Van*	*Stock*	*Machine*	*Finished goods*	*Equity*	*Loans*	*Profit and loss*
	2000	2000	3000	4000		5000	6000	
6	−500				500			
6			−3000		3000			
7	5000				5000			
	6500	2000	0	4000	8500	5000	6000	0

You will notice that we no longer have a cost of goods sold which is of course logically consistent because, as a result of our error, we no longer have any goods sold. What we have instead is a worksheet that has assets that total £21 000 while the other side totals £11 000. The difference in this case is £10 000 which is twice the amount involved in the error.

Addition, subtraction and transposition errors

Another common cause of errors is that we have simply failed to add or subtract correctly. The only way round this problem is to recheck all our totals and all our addition and subtraction. We can reduce the size of that task by balancing our worksheet on a regular basis so that we know where the error is likely to be. A similar problem is a transposition error where, for example, we recorded the total of our cash column as £5600 instead of £6500, i.e. we transposed the order of the 6 and the 5.

This is a common error and happens to all of us. In this case we can identify that it may be a transposition error because the difference of £900 is divisible by 9. This will always be the case if we simply transpose two figures, e.g. 45 as 54, 97 as 79 etc. Notice that the difference is divisible by 9 but it does not necessarily have the number 9 in the difference. The difference between 97 and 79 is 18 which is divisible by 9.

Before moving on we suggest that you draw up your own worksheet for the following set of transactions and compare them with the answer given at the end of the chapter. If your answer varies from the one given try to identify what you have done, e.g. classified an item as the purchase of an asset. When you have done this you can then compare your explanation with our explanation of that item. Your entries do not necessarily have to be identical with ours as there are many different ways of setting up the worksheet and of arriving at the correct answer to show the position at the end of the month. We can illustrate this by reference to the example based on Mary's business which is set out below.

Example 5.2

Mary decided to start a business selling second-hand cars. She had saved up some money of her own but this was not enough to start and so she had obtained an interest-free loan from her parents. The transactions of the business for the first month were as follows. All transactions were cash transactions.

Day 1 Opened a business bank account and paid in £500 of her own money.

Day 2 Paid into the bank £2000 that she had borrowed from her parents for use by the business.

Day 3 Found a suitable showroom and paid a fortnight's rent of £100.

Day 4 Went to the car auction and bought the following cars for cash.
1980 Ford Fiesta for £1000
1977 Ford Escort for £500
1975 Volkswagen Beetle for £300

Day 5 Bought some office furniture for £120.

Day 6 Employed a teenager who was on the dole to clean cars for her at the rate of £10 per car and paid out £30.

Day 8 Placed adverts for all three cars in the local paper. The cost of advertising was £20 per day for each car. She decided that all three should be advertised for two days, and so the total cost was £120.

Day 9 Sold the Ford Fiesta for £1500 cash.

Day 10 Sold the Ford Escort for £700 cash.

Day 11 Returned to the car auction and bought a Sunbeam Horizon for £1500.

Day 12 Employed her teenage friend to clean the Horizon for £10.

Day 15 Re-advertised the Volkswagen for three days at £20 per day, total cost £60.
Day 17 Advertised the Horizon using a special block advert which cost £75 in total.
Day 18 Paid rent of showroom for the next fortnight amounting to £100.
Day 19 Was offered £400 for the Volkswagen.
Day 20 Accepted the offer for the Volkswagen. Was paid £400.
Day 22 Sold the Horizon for £1800.
Day 23 Went to the car auction and bought a Vauxhall Cavalier for £2300.
Day 24 Had the Cavalier professionally valeted at a cost of £40.
Day 25 Advertised the Cavalier using the special block advert at a cost of £75.
Day 26 Decided that as things were going so well she would repay her parents £200.
Day 27 Took the Cavalier on a test drive with a customer and seized the engine.
Day 29 Had the Cavalier repaired at a cost of £300.
Day 30 Sold the Cavalier for £2700.
Day 31 Paid electricity bill of £40 for the month.

To illustrate the different treatments possible let us consider the transaction on day 3 where Mary paid a fortnight's rent in advance. The question arises whether this is an expense or an asset. Let us consider the alternatives.

On day 3 it is reasonably clear that we have an asset in that we will get a future benefit in the form of the use of the showroom for two weeks. On the other hand, if we are recording the transaction for the first time at the end of the month we can then argue that the transaction is an expense because at that point in time the benefit has expired. Thus, we could record on day 3 the payment and an asset and then re-evaluate all our assets at the end of the month as we have done on our worksheet. Conversely we could wait until the end of the month and just record an expense. We would recommend at this stage that you adopt the former treatment for two reasons: firstly it ensures that you re-evaluate all your assets at the end of the month, and secondly shortcuts often cause more problems than they are worth if you are unfamiliar with the area.

Another transaction that should be mentioned is the adverts on day 8 and other days. In these cases a similar dilemma to that already identified with the rent exists. However, there is another problem in that, whereas with the rent we knew that there was going to be a future benefit, in these cases it is far from certain that there will be a future benefit. In other words we do not know when we place the advert whether anyone will reply to it and, even if they do, whether they will buy the car. In these cases we apply a principle known as 'prudence' which says that unless you are reasonably certain of the future benefit then you should not recognize an asset. This is similar to the rule for the recognition of revenue which we discussed in Chapter 4. Prudence, however, goes somewhat further as it encourages us to state assets at low values rather than recognizing an uncertain increase in value, and it suggests that if we think that there is a reasonable chance of a loss we should recognize that loss immediately rather than waiting until it arises.

As you are probably beginning to recognize, accounting is not just about recording; it is also about exercising judgement within a framework of broad and often very general principles. The important factor to remember as you work through the example above is that you are making judgements and applying the definitions set out in the previous two chapters, and you need to be aware of what you are doing and why you are doing it. You should now attempt to produce your own worksheet and extract a profit and loss account and balance sheet.

If your worksheet is correct the balances on the bottom line of your worksheet should be those in the balance sheet set out below. The profit and loss account follows the balance sheet and is merely a summary of the profit and loss column on the worksheet.

Balance sheet of Mary's business at the end of the month

	£
Fixed assets	
Furniture	120
Current assets	
Cash	2730
	2850
Financed by	
Owner's equity	500
Profit for the month	550
	1050
Loan	1800
	2850

Profit and loss of Mary's business for month 1

	£	£
Sales revenue		7100
Cost of cars sold		5600
Gross profit		1500
Expenses		
Rent	200	
Cleaning	80	
Advertising	330	
Repairs	300	
Electricity	40	950
Net profit		550

Even if you find that your answer is correct, before proceeding to the next chapter you should read the explanations for the treatment of the transactions on days 3, 6, 18, 19, 26, 27 and 29 as these are of particular interest and will assist you in the future. If your answer disagrees with ours the full worksheet and explanations are given at the end of this chapter after the review questions and problems.

Summary

This chapter has introduced you to the worksheet and recalled the concept of duality which states that for accounting purposes there are two sides to every transaction. We have also shown the importance of asking ourselves some basic questions: what exactly is an asset, an expense etc? Hopefully we have also illustrated that simply by referring back to the definitions contained in Chapters 3 and 4 most if not all the problems you are likely to encounter can be solved.

We have also provided, by means of the worksheet, a simple vehicle for recording, checking and extracting a balance sheet and profit and loss account. We have shown that the basis of accounting is very simple as long as you follow the basic principles, and for those times when you do lapse the system used on the worksheet should provide you with a simple and effective check. Finally we have introduced you to the idea that accounting is not a science, that it involves elements of judgement, and we have provided you with the 'prudence' concept as a useful tool to assist in arriving at your judgement.

Review questions

1 Describe in your own words what is meant by the concept of duality.

2 In each of the following cases describe the two entries required on the worksheet.
   (a) The owner pays £500 into the business bank account.
   (b) A desk is bought for £100 for the business, paid for from the bank account.
   (c) The business buys goods for £200.
   (d) The rent of the premises of £50 for the first week is paid.
   (e) A potential customer makes an offer for the goods of £250.
   (f) The wages of the employee amounting to £60 are paid.
   (g) The firm receives another offer of £350 for the goods, accepts this offer and is paid immediately.

3 In situations where doubt exists as to whether a transaction has resulted in an asset or expense what questions should be posed?

4 If some doubt still remains how should a choice be made? Explain any principles involved.

Problems for discussion and analysis

1 In each of the following situations discuss the potential effect on the business and suggest possible ways in which those effects could be reflected on the worksheet.

(a) The owner starts up a new business and pays £1000 into the business bank account. In addition it is decided that the owner's car will be used exclusively for the business. The car was purchased last year at a cost of £5000 but a similar one year old car could be bought for £4500.

(b) Goods previously bought by the business for £500 were sold to a customer for £800. However, prior to taking delivery of the goods the customer changed his mind and decided that he did not want the goods after all.

(c) Another batch of goods which had been bought for £400 and sold for £600 was subsequently found to be faulty. The options available are as follows:

- (i) Give the customer a rebate on the purchase price of £100.
- (ii) Refund the full selling price to the customer and reclaim the goods.

If this course of action is followed a further £140 will need to be spent to rectify the faults.

2 Leech has recently gone into business selling office chairs. Details of her transactions for the first month are given below.

Day 1 Opened a bank account and paid in £5000 of her own money. Transferred the ownership of her car to the business at an agreed price of £2000.
Rented an office/showroom at a rental of £120 per month and paid one month's rent.
Bought a desk, typewriter, answer-phone and sundry office equipment at a cost of £800.

Day 2 Bought 100 chairs at a price of £35 per chair and paid for them immediately.

Day 3 Received delivery of the chairs.

Day 5 Placed advert in trade paper offering the chairs for sale on the following terms.

Single chairs	£50 per chair including delivery
Ten or more chairs	£45 per chair including delivery

The advert cost £200 and was paid for immediately.

Day 8 Received separate orders for 12 chairs at £50 each together with accompanying cheques.

Day 9 Paid the cheques into the bank and despatched the chairs. The delivery costs were £72 in total and were paid straightaway.

Day 11 Received six orders for ten chairs each at a cost of £45 per chair together with six cheques for £450.

Banked the cheques and despatched the orders. The delivery charges were £50 for each order making a total of £300 which was paid immediately.

Day 14 Leech paid herself two weeks' wages from the business, amounting to £150 in total.

Day 16 Bought another 20 chairs for £35 each and paid for them immediately.

Day 21 Paid £150 for car repairs.

Day 23 Received an order for 20 chairs at £45 each; banked the cheque and arranged delivery for £40 which was paid for immediately.

Day 24 Placed a further advert in the trade paper at a cost of £200 which was paid for immediately.

Day 27 Received one order for 15 chairs at a price of £50 each (this order totalled £750) and another order for seven chairs at a price of £50 each (a total of £350). The cheques were banked and the chairs were despatched at a total cost of £100 which was paid immediately.

Day 28 Drew another £150 from the bank for her own wages. Sold the remaining six chairs at a price of £250 for all six to a customer who walked into the showroom. The customer paid the £250 in cash and this money was banked. No delivery costs were incurred as the customer took the chairs away.
Paid the telephone bill of £30 and the electricity bill, £40.

(a) In each situation where there are two possible treatments discuss the arguments in favour of and against each alternative.
(b) Based on the outcome of your discussions draw up a worksheet and enter the above transactions.
(c) Extract a balance sheet at the end of the month and a profit and loss account for the month.
(d) Discuss the performance of the business for the period as revealed by the accounts you have prepared, paying particular attention to its cash position and its profitability.

Answer to example 5.2

Worksheet of Mary's business

	Assets				=	Equity + Liabilities		
	Cash	*Cars*	*Rent*	*Furniture*		*Equity*	*Loans*	*Profit and loss*
Day 1	500					500		
Day 2	2000						2000	
Day 3	--100		100					

	Assets				= Equity + Liabilities		
	Cash	*Cars*	*Rent*	*Furniture*	*Equity*	*Loans*	*Profit and loss*
Day 4	−1800	1800					
Day 5	−120			120			
Day 6	−30						−30
Day 8	−120						−120
Day 9	1500						1500
Day 9*		−1000					−1000
Day 10	700						700
Day 10*		−500					−500
Day 11	−1500	1500					
Day 12	−10						−10
Day 15	−60						−60
Day 17	−75						−75
Day 18	−100		100				
Day 20	400						400
Day 20*		−300					−300
Day 22	1800						1800
Day 22*		−1500					−1500
Day 23	−2300	2300					
Day 24	−40						−40
Day 25	−75						−75
Day 26	−200					−200	
Day 29	−300						−300
Day 30	2700						2700
Day 30*		−2300					−2300
Day 31	−40						−40
Balance	2730	0	200	120	500	1800	750
Day 31†			−200				−200
Balance	2730	0	0	120	500	1800	550

* You will notice that every time we sold a car we immediately transferred the cost of that car from our Cars column to the profit and loss as an expense. This transfer was carried out because, having sold the car, we no longer expected a future benefit and therefore we no longer had an asset. An alternative treatment would be to do this exercise at the end of the month.

† When we complete our worksheet it is important to review our assets and ask ourselves the question: are these still assets? If (as in this case) the answer is no, then we need to transfer their cost to the profit and loss account as an expense of the period.

Transaction summary

We have set out below the transactions that took place together with the treatment of those transactions on the worksheet and, where appropriate, explanations of that treatment and acceptable alternatives. If there are any items that you still do not understand you should try to examine them in terms of the basic definitions referred to in Chapters 3 and 4.

Day 1 Opened a business bank account and paid in £500 of her own money.

Here we have created a business asset in the form of cash and have also opened an account to show the owner's stake in the business under the heading of owner's equity.

Day 2 Paid into the bank £2000 that she had borrowed from her parents for use by the business.

Once again the business has acquired an asset as it will get a future benefit from the cash. It has also acquired an obligation to pay somebody some money and as such has a liability for the amount borrowed.

Day 3 Found a suitable showroom and paid a fortnight's rent of £100.

We have already discussed this transaction in the main body of the chapter. Our treatment has been to reduce our asset cash in the bank and to record an asset of the prepaid rent from which we will derive a benefit in the future.

Day 4 Went to the car auction and bought the following cars for cash.

1980 Ford Fiesta for £1000
1977 Ford Escort for £500
1975 Volkswagen Beetle for £300

Clearly by paying out £1800 we have reduced our cash at the bank and so that is one side of the entry. The other side is to record the cars as an asset as we shall get a future benefit from these.

Day 5 Bought some office furniture for £120

This is exactly the same as the previous transaction. We have merely exchanged one asset, cash, for another, furniture.

Day 6 Employed a teenager who was on the dole to clean cars for her at the rate of £10 per car and paid out £30.

In this case one side of the transaction is clear inasmuch as the cash has clearly been reduced by £30. The question that then arises is whether there is an asset or an expense. We have shown the cost of the car cleaning as an expense because we are uncertain that any future benefit will arise from this particular expenditure. The fact that a car is cleaned does not add any intrinsic value and in fact it is probably necessary to clean all the cars in the showroom regularly because customers expect to buy clean cars.

Day 8 Placed adverts for all three cars in the local paper. The cost of advertising was £20 per day for each car. She decided that all three should be advertised for two days, and so the total cost was £120.

You should refer back to the text for a detailed discussion of the reasons for our treatment of this item. What we have done is to apply the prudence principle, treated the item as an expense and charged the item to the profit and loss account at the same time as we reduced our cash by £120.

Day 9 Sold the Ford Fiesta for £1500 cash.

Clearly we have another £1500 in our bank and so we increase our cash column. We also have a sale which accords with our definition of revenue and so we bring that revenue into the profit and loss column.

Day 9*

Here we have reduced our assets by the cost of the car we sold and charged that cost, i.e. the cost of the expired benefit to the profit and loss column.

Day 10 Sold the Ford Escort for £700 cash.

See the explanations for day 9 above. If you have got these wrong make sure you understand why, and then correct your worksheet for all similar items before reading on.

Day 11 Returned to the car auction and bought a Sunbeam Horizon for £1500.

This is in essence the same as the transaction on day 4. If you have made an error you should reread that explanation and check that your treatment of the transaction on day 23 is correct before moving on.

Day 12 Employed her teenage friend to clean the Horizon for £10.

This is in essence the same as the transaction on day 6. If you have made an error you should reread that explanation and check that your treatment of the transaction on day 24 is correct before moving on.

Day 15 Re-advertised the Volkswagen for three days at £20 per day, total cost £60.

See the explanation for day 8 above.

Day 17 Advertised the Horizon using a special block advert which cost £75 in total.

See the explanation for day 8 above.

Day 18 Paid rent of showroom for the next fortnight amounting to £100.

This is in essence the same situation as day 3. The entry should therefore be the same. At this stage you could also reduce the rent column by the rent for the first two weeks and charge this to the profit and loss column as the benefit has now expired. We have not done this because we wished to illustrate the importance of the final review before a balance sheet and profit and loss account are finally drawn up.

Day 19 Was offered £400 for the Volkswagen.

There is no need to record this as the transaction is not substantially complete at this stage and so we would not recognize revenue. If you have shown a sale at this stage reread the definition of revenue given in Chapter 4.

Day 20 Accepted the offer for the Volkswagen. Was paid £400.

Now we have a sale and revenue can be recognized as in day 9 above.

Day 22 Sold the Horizon for £1800.

Once again we have a sale and revenue can be recognized.

Day 23 Went to the car auction and bought a Vauxhall Cavalier for £2300.

See day 4 for explanation of the treatment.

Day 24 Had the Cavalier professionally valeted at a cost of £40.

This is the same as the cleaning. The fact that it was done professionally does not alter the argument set out in respect of day 6 above.

Day 25 Advertised the Cavalier using the special block advert at a cost of £75.

This should be treated in the same way as previous adverts for the same reasons.

Day 26 Decided that as things were going so well she would repay her parents £200.

This is a different transaction from any of the ones we have dealt with so far. Those dealt with expenditure of cash for either a past or a future benefit. In this case we have reduced our cash in order to pay back an amount that the business owes, i.e. we have used some cash to reduce our liability. Thus we reduce the amount shown as owing in the loan column by the £200 and we reduce the amount of cash we have by £200.

Day 27 Took the Cavalier on a test drive with a customer and seized the engine.

Although an economic event has happened we cannot account for it as at this stage the effect of that event cannot be adequately expressed in monetary terms.

Day 29 Had Cavalier repaired at a cost of £300.

We are now in a position to account for the event as we know the effect in monetary terms. However, we are left with the question of whether the expenditure is going to provide a future benefit or whether it is an expense. We need to ask ourselves whether the expenditure added to the asset. If it has then there is no problem in recognizing the transaction as one which creates an asset. If, however, the expenditure merely restores the asset to the state that it was in previously, then it is doubtful that it relates to an asset and applying the prudence principle we would be safer to charge it to the profit and loss account as an expense, which is what we have done. In essence this is a shorthand way of recording two events. The first is that the engine blew up, so reducing the future benefit we could expect from the asset. If we knew the extent of this reduction we could have charged that as a past benefit. If we had done that then the repairs could legitimately be viewed as enhancing the future benefit to be obtained in respect of the reduced asset. This whole process is in fact shortcut because we do not know what the loss in value of future benefits was; we are therefore in effect using the cost of repairs as a surrogate for that loss in value.

Day 30 Sold the Cavalier for £2700.

See previous transactions of this type on days 9, 10 etc.

Day 31 Paid electricity bill of £40 for the month.

Here we have a reduction of the cash in respect of the use of electricity over the past month. The benefit has clearly expired and we therefore have an expense.

6 Stocks and work in progress

This chapter takes the reader away from the assumptions adopted in the earlier chapters whereby all transactions took place during the year and all goods bought were sold. The problems of arriving at a figure for the cost or value of stock are examined, together with the effects of valuation decisions on profits and on the balance sheet.

In all the examples we have looked at to date we have made some simplifying assumptions in relation to the goods purchased which we refer to as the stock of the business. The first assumption was that no stocks were held at the end of the period. The use of this assumption meant that we had no problem in identifying what stock had been sold or what it cost. It also meant that the question of whether the goods held in stock at the end of the period were still worth what we had paid for them did not arise. We also only dealt with single-product businesses which had fairly straightforward processes for converting the goods purchased into saleable commodities. Finally our examples only dealt with start-ups, i.e. businesses in their first year. This meant that the question of how to deal with the stock held at the beginning of the year did not need to be considered.

Clearly the real world is more complex than this. Businesses are generally more complex. They may have multiple processes or multiple stock lines or both. In this chapter, therefore, we shall be relaxing all these assumptions and discussing the effects on the balance sheet and profit and loss account. We shall also be considering:

- the nature of stocks in different types of business;
- the problems arising with more complex businesses, in particular those of work in progress and finished goods;
- the determination of the cost of stock sold during a period;
- the accounting entries needed to record stock on the worksheet;

- the issue of valuation and how a change in the basis of valuation will affect the balance sheet and profit and loss account.

In reality, stock is very important because there is often a high level of resources invested in the stock of a business. In many businesses this has led to a reappraisal of the way in which they operate and the adoption of techniques such as Just-in-time management which can lead to savings in the costs of holding high levels of stocks. Often the reason that businesses held high levels of stocks was that these were felt to be necessary in order to meet customer demand and to ensure that the production process was not held up. The costs involved in holding high levels of stocks were twofold: first there was the obvious cost that in order to hold stock you need space and space costs money; there was also the less obvious cost associated with having to borrow money or find some other form of finance to buy and maintain the stock levels.

The adoption of Just-in-time techniques led to a reappraisal of the production process and demand cycle in order that the level of stocks was reduced to a minimum. A side effect of this is that many of the large manufacturing firms who have adopted the technique have had to take a closer look at their suppliers to ensure that they have the capability to provide supplies regularly and on time. It has in some cases led to a situation where stocks previously held by the manufacturer are now being held by the components supplier, so shifting the cost of holding stock.

So far we have discussed stock and work in progress without really defining these terms. Rather than attempting to find one generic definition it is probably easier to look at what comprises stock and work in progress as this will lead to a better understanding of the terms. Stock can be said to comprise the following.

- Goods purchased for resale. For example, packets of cereal are purchased by a supermarket to be sold to their customers; cars are purchased by motor dealers to resell to their customers.
- Raw materials purchased for incorporation into the product or products being manufactured or assembled for sale, e.g. wood purchased by a furniture manufacturer or steel purchased by a car manufacturer.
- Consumable goods, which are bought not for resale but for use within the business operation. These could consist of supplies of oil for machine maintenance, supplies of stationery or cleaning materials.

You may have noticed from the examples used that the stocks are related to the type of business. For example, cars owned by a furniture manufacturer will not be classified as stock because they are held for use in the business and not for resale. You may also have noticed that the last category mentioned is different from the others as it is not held for resale. It is in fact another form of current asset which is only called stock because it is a stock of items which are held by the business and we have no more suitable term.

KEY CONCEPT 6.1
Stock

Stock comprises goods purchased for resale or goods purchased for conversion into goods for resale, or consumable stores. The distinguishing feature of stock is the intention to resell the item in some form or to use it in a relatively short period of time.

Having looked at some of the ideas that give an indication of what comprises stock let us now look at work in progress and finished goods. These are both merely different types of stock – the difference lies in the fact that they have normally gone through some production or assembly process.

In general all these forms of stock and work in progress fall within the definition of current assets which we adopted in Chapter 3. That definition was 'a current asset is one which is either part of the operating cycle of the enterprise or is likely to be used up or realized in the form of cash within one year'. You will notice if you consider the examples given that in some cases the goods will be realized within the year, as in the case of the cereals for the supermarket, and in some cases the reason something is classified as stock is because it is part of the operating cycle of the business, as in the case of the building contractor. You will also probably have noticed that the nature of the business is a major determinant of what is classified as stock or work in progress. We shall now explore this aspect of stock and the question of stock valuation in more detail.

KEY CONCEPT 6.2
Work in progress

Work in progress is the term applied to products and services that are at an intermediate stage of completion; for example, if you envisage an assembly line for microcomputers, at any point in time there will be some partially assembled machines somewhere on that production line. An even more obvious example, which we can observed merely by walking round any town centre, is partially completed buildings which are work in progress for some building contractor. A less obvious but equally valid example of work in progress is the time spent to date by an architect on a half-finished drawing.

Finished goods

Finished goods are goods that have been through the complete production or assembly cycle and are ready for resale to the customer. Examples are cars for Ford, computers for Apple or IBM, and videos for Amstrad.

The nature of the business and stock valuation

It is fairly obvious that the nature of the business has an impact on the type of stock held. We would expect the type of stock held by a greengrocer to be different from that of a company like British Petroleum. What may be less obvious is the way in which the nature of the business affects the question of stock valuation. To illustrate this let us first look at a retailer and a manufacturer and then compare the latter with a provider of services, such as a firm of solicitors.

In the case of a retailing business the stocks held are those goods purchased for resale; because of the nature of the business there is generally little if any change between the goods bought by the business and the goods it sells. Its operating cycle could be seen as

Purchases → Stock → Sales
(input) (output)

If we can establish what the goods cost we can arrive fairly easily at a valuation of stock, because the operating cycle is very simple.

If we now examine the situation of a manufacturing company we find that in order to manufacture goods we need an input of raw materials, of labour and of other items such as the nuts and bolts needed to assemble a car or paint to protect and colour it. These inputs can and often do occur at multiple points in the production process. However, for our purposes a slightly simplified version of the manufacturing process, such as that given below, will suffice to illustrate the points being made.

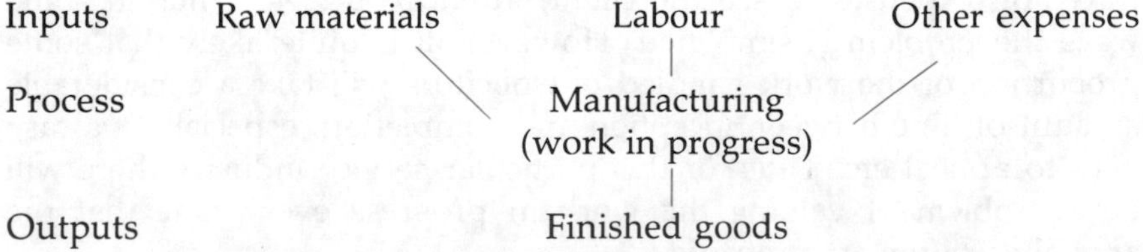

A more detailed illustration of the business as a series of inputs and outputs can be found in Chapters 1 and 6 of the companion volume Business in Context in this series (Needle, 1989).

A business with a process similar to that described is likely, at any point in time, to have a stock of raw materials, a stock of goods in the process of completion, its work in progress, and a stock of finished goods. This can be illustrated by a simple diagram such as Figure 6.1.

In the case of the raw materials the question of stock valuation is similar to that faced by a retailer. For the other categories, however, the question of valuation is often more complex. Do we include the cost of labour in the value of partially completed goods and, if so,

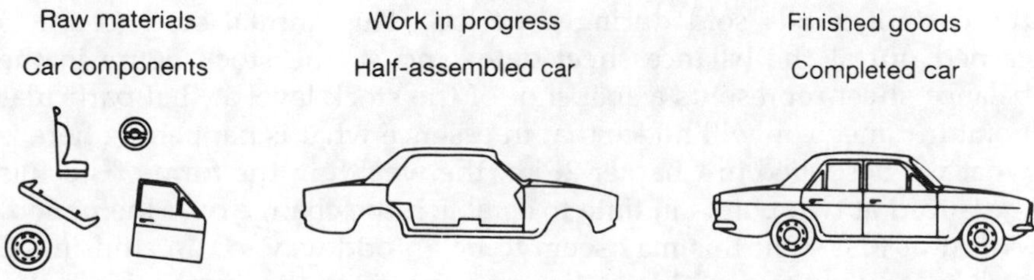

Figure 6.1

which labour? One possible answer would be to include labour involved in the production process and exclude other labour. This is easy in theory but in practice it is not so clear cut. For example, are the foreman and production manager involved in the production process and, if so, what part of their labour cost is attributable to a particular product? The whole question of what should and should not be included is vital as it has a direct effect on profit. In some industries where pricing is on a 'cost plus' basis it could be the difference between survival and bankruptcy. If, for example, we quoted a selling price that did not cover all our costs we could end up entering into a contract which could lead to the downfall of the business. Indeed some commentators have suggested that the Rolls Royce collapse in 1972 was caused by their being tied into an unprofitable contract.

The discussion so far has emphasized the manufacturing sector. What of the service sector? In this sector the question of stock valuation can be very straightforward as in the case of a newspaper vendor or more complex as in the case of solicitors, architects and accountants. If we consider the case of a firm of solicitors, the inputs will not be raw materials but will be in the form of labour and expenses such as travelling expenses to see the client, attend court etc. Thus in some ways the problem is simplified. However, it is quite likely that some proportion of the work handled by solicitors will take a considerable amount of time between inception and completion, especially if a case goes to appeal etc. Thus for this particular service industry there will be a problem of valuing the work in progress every time that the annual accounts are prepared.

The determination of the cost of goods sold

In previous chapters we assumed that all goods bought in the period were sold in the period and that we could clearly identify the actual goods we sold during the period. In practice even in fairly simple businesses it is doubtful whether it would be possible to identify the goods actually sold and, even if it were possible, we would need to consider the question of whether doing so was cost effective. Because of the difficulties involved in recording every item sold and the question of the cost effectiveness of such an exercise some smaller businesses have little if any formal stock records. Instead they rely on keeping accurate records of purchases and the annual stock count to establish the cost of goods sold during a period. This annual stock count is carried out at the balance sheet date, and so the stock figure in the balance sheet represents a snapshot of the stock level at that particular point in time. You will notice that in essence what is happening here is what we described in Chapter 2, i.e. the wealth in the form of stock is measured at two points in time to establish the change over the period. Whilst at first sight this may seem to be an odd way to run a business, it is in fact quite sensible when you consider the impossible job a confectionery manufacturer would have in trying to keep track of every

Mars bar, KitKat, or Milky Way made. In fact if you talk to owners of small businesses you may be quite surprised at how accurately they can value their stock simply by looking at what they have in the shop and on the shelves of their storerooms.

What we have just said should not be taken to imply that all retailers have poor stock records. In fact some of the major retail chains have very sophisticated stock record systems that operate at the point of sale: every time the cashier enters the sale of a tin of baked beans the stock records for that store are automatically updated via a computer link from the tills to the stock recording system. (Theft by staff or 'shrinkage' can also be measured precisely.) However, whilst such an investment may be necessary and cost effective for large multiples it is at present outside the grasp of smaller retailers and is probably more sophisticated than they need.

Clearly, for a business that has accurate and detailed stock records, arriving at the value of stock and the cost of goods sold is reasonably simple. Therefore let us look at the situation where detailed stock movement records are not kept and see how we can arrive at the cost of the goods sold and the cost of those still in stock at the end of the year. In these cases we need to count the stock at the start of the year and at the end of the year. From these two figures and the figure for goods purchased during the year we can derive the cost of the goods sold during the year. In other words if we add the purchases to the stock of goods we had at the start of the year that will tell us the total of the goods we have held during the year. If we then subtract what we have left at the end of the year the resultant figure must be the cost of the goods we have sold during the year, assuming of course that we have allowed for any taken by the owner for personal use etc. This relationship, which is perhaps difficult to describe, can be more easily understood if it is shown in the form of an equation:

Opening stock + Purchases − Closing stock = Cost of goods sold

The information to solve the equation can be derived as follows:

Opening stock	from the balance sheet at the start of the year
Purchases	from the supplier's invoices
Closing stock	from a physical stock count at the end of the year.

The importance of determining stock level is examined in Key Concept 6.3.

KEY CONCEPT 6.3
The importance of determining stock levels

Because the cost of goods sold is calculated by combining the purchases with the stock figures, the opening and closing stock levels are vital in determining the cost of goods sold. They therefore have a dual role in the balance sheet in determining wealth and, through the cost of goods sold, in determining profit.

Let us look at a simple example to illustrate the process referred to in the equation above and see how it is entered on the worksheet.

Example 6.1

The summarized transactions of Tento during the year were as follows.

Sales	£20 000
Purchases	£12 000
Other expenses	£ 6 000

The stocks at the end of the period had been counted and were valued at £7000. The balance sheet of Tento at the start of the period was as follows.

	£
Fixed assets	
Premises	20 000
Current assets	
	5 000
Stocks	11 000
Cash	36 000
Owners' equity	36 000
	36 000

Solution 6.1

We start by entering the opening balances on our worksheet which will now appear as follows.

Worksheet of Tento version 1

	Assets			=	Equity	+	Liabilities
	Cash	*Stock*	*Premises*		*Equity*		*Profit and loss*
Balances	11 000	5 000	20 000		36 000		

If we now enter the transactions for the year and draw up a preliminary total our worksheet will look like this:

Worksheet of Tento version 2

	Assets			=	Equity	+	Liabilities
	Cash	*Stock*	*Premises*		*Equity*		*Profit and loss*
Balances	11 000	5 000	20 000		36 000		
Sales	20 000						20 000
Purchases	−12 000	12 000					
Expenses	−6 000						−6 000
Subtotal	13 000	17 000	20 000		36 000		14 000

The worksheet at this stage shows that we have a stock of goods of £17 000 whereas we know from our stock count that what we actually have is £7000. In other words the asset at the end of the year, i.e. the part that will provide a future benefit, is only £7000. Using our equation we can establish that the cost of goods sold during the year was £10 000. This is of course an expense because the benefit is in the past.

The figure of £10 000 was arrived at as follows.

Opening stock	+	Purchases	−	Closing stock	=	Cost of goods sold
£5 000	+	£12 000	−	£7 000	=	£10 000

Having found that the cost of goods sold is £10 000, we can now enter this on our worksheet and draw up our balance at the end of the year. This is done as follows.

Worksheet of Tento version 3

	Assets			=	Equity +	Liabilities
	Cash	*Stock*	*Premises*		*Equity*	*Profit and loss*
Balances	11 000	5 000	36 000			
Sales	20 000					20 000
Purchases	−12 000	12 000				
Expenses	−6 000					−6 000
Subtotal	13 000	17 000	20 000		36 000	14 000
Cost of sales		−10 000				−10 000
Balance	13 000	7 000	20 000		36 000	4 000

We would show the calculation included in the worksheet above on a profit and loss account as follows.

Profit and loss of Tento for the year

	£	£
Sales		20 000
Opening stock	5 000	
Purchases	12 000	
	17 000	
Less: Closing stock	7 000	
Cost of sales		10 000
Gross profit		10 000
Other expenses		6 000
Net profit		4 000

An alternative simplified presentation would be as follows.

Profit and loss of Tento for the year

	£
Sales	20 000
Cost of sales	10 000
Gross profit	10 000
Other expenses	6 000
Net profit	4 000

The latter format which does not show how the cost of goods sold is calculated is closer to what you are likely to see in the published accounts of quoted companies.

Before we move on to the area of valuation it should be noted that, because of the relationship between the balance sheet and the profit and loss account, an error in the opening stock figure, the purchases figure or the closing stock figure will not only change the profit but it will also change our balance sheet.

Valuation of stock

In general, if prices of goods stayed constant over time, tastes did not change and there were no changes in technology, then we would have no problem with stock valuation. However, the real world fortunately is not like that; this has the advantage that civilization can progress but it creates some problems for accountants (a small price to pay you might think!). The question of how changes in prices can affect stock valuation is wide ranging and is allied to the question of how the cost of stock is arrived at. We shall therefore first consider the effects of changes in taste and technology; then we shall look at how cost is arrived at before finally considering the effects of price changes.

Changes in technology and taste

We have grouped technology and taste together because although the causes are different the effects on stock valuation are the same. Let us consider the effect of changes in technology, of which there are hundreds of everyday examples such as the use of microcomputers instead of mainframe machines and the advances in microcomputer technology. A fairly dramatic example of this effect was the introduction of the Sinclair QL, a microcomputer which retailed at £399. This undoubtedly made a number of other machines seem heavily over-priced. In turn, when other manufacturers had caught up with the technology, the QL was over-priced and Sinclair had to reduce the retail price to £199. For the purposes of our illustration let us assume that we are a retailer who has a stock of ten QLs bought (before the price reduction took effect) at a cost of £300 per machine. If we valued our closing stock on the basis of the cost our asset would be shown as £3000.

However, we said in Chapter 3 that an asset is the right to a future benefit. In the retailer's situation the future benefit that can be obtained is only £199 per machine, the new retail price. Thus in this case the cost does not reflect the future benefit that the retailer is likely to get. A fairer reflection would be the amount the QL could be sold for. However, even the £199 is probably overstating the benefit as there will undoubtedly be some costs incurred in selling the QLs. If for example these costs were estimated to be £10 per machine, then the amount of the future benefit would in fact be £189. This is referred to as the net realizable value of the goods.

> Net realizable value is defined as the estimated proceeds from the sale of items less the costs of selling these items.
>
> **KEY CONCEPT 6.4**
> ***Net realizable value***

A similar effect would have arisen if the goods could only be sold either at a reduced price or for scrap because of changes in people's tastes. In each of these cases the cost is not relevant to the future benefit and a better valuation would be the net realizable value. This leads us to the idea that we should compare the cost of an item with what we can get for it and, if the latter figure is lower, use that figure to value our stock. Expressed in more formal terms this is the valuation rule included as Key Concept 6.5 below.

You may well wonder why, if the net realizable value is higher than the cost, that higher value is not used. The reason for this is that the attainment of the higher value is uncertain as tastes etc. may change; thus we apply the prudence principle in these cases. This concept has to be used in conjunction with the realization principle which we discussed in some detail near the start of Chapter 4.

Having established the general rule for stock valuation and seen the reasons for the rule, the next question that we need to address is how to establish the cost that is referred to in the rule.

> Stock should be valued at the lower of cost and net realizable value.
>
> **KEY CONCEPT 6.5**
> ***The valuation rule***

> Profits are not anticipated and revenue is not recognized until its realization is reasonably certain. Provision is made for all potential losses.
>
> **KEY CONCEPT 6.6**
> ***The prudence concept***

Establishing the cost of stocks

As we have already indicated, the more complex the process involved the more difficult it is to establish the cost of the stock. The problem is what we should and what we should not include. The debate on this subject has been going on for some considerable time in the literature relating to management accounting and will be explored in more detail later when we discuss the alternative methods that could be used to arrive at cost. Fortunately, for our purposes at present we need only be aware in fairly general terms what the alternative methods are, as the choice between the methods has to some extent been made for us through custom and practice and the rules laid down for companies in Statement of Standard Accounting Practice 9 (SSAP 9). This deals with the question of stocks and work in progress. Before looking at what that standard lays down let us briefly consider the alternatives. These are best considered by means of a simple example.

Example 6.2

Let us assume that a business produces spanners. Each spanner requires £0.30 of steel, and takes 15 min labour to produce. The business employs ten people to make spanners and they each produce 140 spanners per week and are paid £70 each per week. We also assume that we have a foreman overseeing our workers who is paid £100 per week and that at the end of the year we have one week's production, i.e. 1400 spanners, in stock. The question that we have to answer is what is the cost of the 1400 spanners we have in stock at the end of the year.

Solution 6.2

One solution might be to establish how much it would cost to produce one extra spanner.

Clearly one spanner would cost £0.30 for materials and we would need to pay a worker for 15 min to produce it. This would cost £0.50, i.e. £70 per week divided by the number of spanners produced which was 140. Thus the marginal cost of producing one spanner is £0.80. If we then applied this cost to our stock we would value our stock at 1400 × £0.80 = £1120. This would be the cost using a marginal cost basis.

On the other hand it could legitimately be argued that the cost of producing 1400 spanners, i.e. a week's production, is made up as follows:

	£
Steel 1400 × £0.30	420
Direct labour, ten staff at £70	700
Foreman's wages	100
Total cost	£1 220

The latter method of arriving at the cost is known as absorption costing.

You will note that the difference between the two is £100, i.e. the foreman's wages are not included on a marginal cost basis.

As we have said, to some extent the choice between the two has been made for us by the requirements of SSAP 9 which states that cost is

> ... that expenditure which has been incurred in the normal course of business in bringing the product or service to its present location or condition. (Para. 17)

It further states that

> . . . this expenditure should include, in addition to cost of purchase, such costs of conversion as are appropriate to that location and condition.
> (Para. 17)

The costs of conversion referred to include direct costs (similar to our labour and materials in the example above), production overheads (such as our foreman's wages) and any other overheads that are attributable to bringing the stock to its present location and condition. An example of these would be the cost to Ford of transporting engines from its production plant to the assembly line factory.

In all the examples we shall deal with we shall adopt a method of arriving at cost which will include all the costs which are obviously attributable to the stock, work in progress or finished goods. This can be done on the worksheet as illustrated in the following example.

Example 6.3

Bertie had his own business which assembled bicycles from a number of components. This involved the following processes:

Process 1 Assembling of frames, saddles and handlebars
Process 2 Adding wheels to the partially completed frames

The first process takes 1 hour and costs £5 in wages, whilst the second process takes less time and costs £3 in wages. Thus to assemble a complete bicycle costs £8 for labour. The frames, saddles and handlebars are bought from one supplier for £40 per set, and the wheels come from a different supplier and cost £20 per set.

We shall assume for simplicity that it is the first year of the business and that Bertie has started with £10 000 of his own money. During the year Bertie bought 500 frame sets at a total cost of £20 000 and 600 pairs of wheels at a total cost of £12 000. He paid wages of £3200. He sold 350 bicycles for £140 each, making a total of £49 000 in revenue. His only other expenses were the rent of a showroom which cost him £5000 for the year.

At the end of the year he had in stock 50 completed cycles, 100 untouched frame sets and 200 pairs of wheels.

If we summarize the information we have been given in total and enter it on our worksheet we can then deal with the closing stock and the cost of goods sold.

Summary of the information:

Cash at start	£10 000
Owner's equity	£10 000
Frame sets bought	£20 000
Wheels bought	£12 000
Wages paid	£ 3 200
Other expenses	£ 5 000
Sales revenue	£49 000

Our worksheet would now appear as follows.

Bertie's worksheet version 1

	Assets				= Equity + Liabilities	
	Cash	*Frames*	*Wheels*	*Wages*	*Equity*	*Profit and loss*
Balance	10 000				10 000	
Frames	−20 000	20 000				
Wheels	−12 000		12 000			
Wages	−3 200			3 200		
Rent	−5 000					−5 000
Sales	49 000					49 000
Subtotal	18 800	20 000	12 000	3 200	10 000	44 000

You will notice that the rent of the showroom has been included as an expense. This is a selling expense and therefore could not be classified as an overhead attributable to bringing the goods to their present state and condition if we were valuing stock.

Turning now to the wages, we were told that each bicycle cost £8 for labour and that he has sold 350 bicycles. The labour in respect of the bikes sold is therefore 350 × £8 = £2800. The completed bicycles in stock cost 50 × £8 for labour. If we do similar calculations for the frames and the wheels we find that the cost of goods sold should be as follows:

Frames 350 × £40	= £14 000
Wheels 350 × £20	= £ 7 000
Wages 350 × £ 8	= £ 2 800

The amounts to be included in our stock of finished goods are

Frames 50 × £40	= £2 000
Wheels 50 × £20	= £1 000
Wages 50 × £ 8	= £ 400

If we now wish to put this on the worksheet we shall first need to open a column for our finished goods and then enter the above information. Our worksheet will be as follows.

Bertie's worksheet version 2

	Assets				=	Equity	
	Cash	*Frames*	*Wheels*	*Wages*	*Finished goods*	*Equity*	*Profit and loss*
Balance	10 000					10 000	
Frames	−20 000	20 000					
Wheels	−12 000		12 000				
Wages	−3 200			3 200			
Rent	−5 000						−5 000
Sales	49 000						49 000
	18 800	20 000	12 000	3 200		10 000	44 000

	Assets				=	Equity	
	Cash	*Frames*	*Wheels*	*Wages*	*Finished goods*	*Equity*	*Profit and loss*
Frames		−14 000					−14 000
Wheels			−7 000				−7000
Wages				−2 800			−2 800
Frames		−2 000			2 000		
Wheels			−1 000		1 000		
Wages				−400	400		
	18 800	4 000	4 000	0	3 400	10 000	30 200

We shall briefly examine what we have just entered on our worksheet. We have dealt initially with the cost of the goods sold and have transferred the costs of the raw materials, frames and wheels, together with the labour costs associated with the assembly process, to the profit and loss column as an expense of the period. You will note that here we have employed the matching principle and matched the costs of assembling 350 bicycles with the revenue earned from selling 350 bicycles. We have then dealt with the bicycles which we have assembled but not sold, our finished goods, and transferred the costs associated with those bicycles to a finished goods column. Now if we look at our final balances we find that what is left in stock is 100 frames at £40, 200 pairs of wheels at £20 and finished goods which have cost £3400 to get to their present state and condition.

Another way of looking at what is happening in Bertie's business is to see it as a flow through a factory which is represented by the accounting system. Thus the inputs are the frames, wheels and labour. These together form the work in progress, which then becomes finished goods ready for resale. The worksheet would therefore look something like this.

	Raw materials →			WIP →	Finished →	Sales
	Frames	*Wheels*	*Wages*	*Work in progress*	*Finished goods*	*Profit and loss*
Balance						
Frames	20 000					
Wheels		12 000				
Wages			3 200			
Rent						−5 000
Sales						49 000
Balance	20 000	12 000	3 200			44 000
Frames	−16 000			16 000		
Wheels		−8 000		8 000		
Wages			−3 200	3 200		
Finished goods				−27 200	27 200	
Cost of goods sold		4 000			−23 800	−23 800
	4 000		0	0	3 400	20 200

Having dealt with the question of what is included in cost, the last area which we have to consider is the effect of price changes on the cost of goods sold and the closing stock.

Before moving on you might like to try to identify what would have happened had the 50 bicycles been partially completed, in other words only process one had been completed. You may assume that there were no other changes in costs. A worksheet showing that situation is included at the end of the chapter for you to compare your answer with.

Effects of price changes

Although we have considered the effect of downward movements in price under the heading of changes in technology we also need to consider the effect of increases in the input price of our stocks, i.e. increases in the prices we pay to our suppliers. As we have already indicated there would be no real problem if all sales could be identified with the actual goods sold. In practice, however, a builder's merchant for instance has a pile of bricks and sells them in any order depending on the ease of access. We cannot therefore work out whether a particular brick sold was bought by the builder's merchant when the price of bricks was 30p or whether it was bought after the price had gone up to 33p. It is not feasible or cost effective to trace each brick through the process. We therefore have to find some system that will give a reasonable approximation of the cost of the goods we have sold and of the cost of the stock remaining. There are of course numerous possibilities at various levels of complexity. For our purposes we shall concentrate on three which exemplify the problem and illustrate that solutions tend to be arbitrary.

In order to illustrate the differences between the methods let us take some fairly simple data.

Example 6.4

Barbara started the year with some goods in stock and bought additional goods as required during the year. The price of the goods she bought rose steadily during the year. The summarized data for her transactions are as follows.

	Units	*Cost per unit*
Goods in stock at the start of the year	400	£1.00
Purchases, quarter 1	500	£1.10
Purchases, quarter 2	400	£1.20
Purchases, quarter 3	400	£1.25
Purchases, quarter 4	300	£1.40

Goods sold during the year 1800 units for a total of £2400

Using the data above we shall illustrate how the adoption of different valuation rules affects not only the stock value at the end of the year but also how it affects the cost of sales and therefore the profit. We shall start by considering a method of valuation called first in, first out (FIFO).

First in, first out

The FIFO method is based on the artificial assumption that the first goods bought are the first sold. This means that in effect the stock held at the end of the period is assumed to be that purchased most recently. It is probably the most common basis of stock valuation in the UK and there are many situations when it is clearly the obvious choice. This would be the case for any industry or business dealing in consumables. It should be pointed out that, surprisingly, the choice of method for arriving at the cost of stock generally has little if anything to do with actual stock movements.

In our example this method would mean that all the opening stock together with that purchased in the first three quarters would be assumed to have been sold together with 100 units bought in the fourth quarter. This would leave a closing stock of 200 units which were bought in the fourth quarter.

FIFO					
Opening stock	400	£1.00	£400.00	Sales	£2 400.00
Quarter 1	500	£1.10	£550.00		
Quarter 2	400	£1.20	£480.00		
Quarter 3	400	£1.25	£500.00		
Quarter 4	100	£1.40	£140.00		
Cost of goods sold			£2 070.00		£2 070.00
Closing stock	200	£1.40	£280.00	Profit	£330.00

Last in, first out

The last in, first out (LIFO) method is based on the assumption that the last goods bought are the first sold. It therefore charges the latest price from suppliers against the revenue, and leaves the closing stock at a value based on outdated prices. In industries where prices are rising steadily this is more likely to give a profit figure that can be maintained in the future. It is similar in its effect on the profit and loss account to what would occur if we had used replacement cost accounting.

In our example this method would mean that all the stock purchased in the year together with 200 units of the opening stock would be assumed to have been sold. This would leave a closing stock of 200 units which were in stock at the start of the year. These would be included at the original price and thus the balance sheet value is deliberately understated.

LIFO					
Quarter 4	300	£1.40	£420.00	Sales	£2 400.00
Quarter 3	400	£1.25	£500.00		
Quarter 2	400	£1.20	£480.00		
Quarter 1	500	£1.10	£550.00		
Opening stock	200	£1.00	£200.00		
			£2 150.00		£2 150.00
Closing stock	200	£1.00	£200.00	Profit	£250.00

Average cost

The average cost method is basically a compromise between the two methods we have already discussed. It makes no assumptions about the way in which goods flow through the business and is probably more neutral than either of the previous methods.

For the purposes of arriving at the profit and loss charges all that is needed is to work out the average cost per unit of stock and multiply that by the number of units sold. Similarly the closing stock is arrived at by taking the number of units left in stock multiplied by the average cost per unit. This leads to a profit and stock figure which is between the two identified under FIFO and LIFO and which is calculated as shown below.

Average cost					
Opening stock	400	£1.00	£400.00	Sales	£2 400.00
Quarter 1	500	£1.10	£550.00		
Quarter 2	400	£1.20	£480.00		
Quarter 3	400	£1.25	£500.00		
Quarter 4	300	£1.40	£420.00		
	2 000		£2 350.00		
Average cost	1	£1.175			
Cost of goods sold	1 800	£1.175	£2 115.00		£2 115.00
Closing stock	200	£1.175	£235.00	Profit	£285.00

Some of the issues drawn out in the discussion in this chapter are illustrated in extracts from published accounts given in Case Study 6.1.

CASE STUDY 6.1
Amstrad and Bass plc

Extracts from Amstrad Annual Report 1991/2

Accounting Policies

Stock and work in progress Stock and work in progress are stated at the lower of cost and net realizable value. Cost is represented by materials and direct labour, together with an appropriate element of production overhead. Provision has been made for obsolete and slow-moving stock.

Notes to the accounts

Stocks

	1992	1991
	£000	£000
Raw materials and consumables	4750	12680
Finished goods and goods for resale	73046	163248
	77796	175928

Commentary

The accounting policy note tells us that the cost is arrived at using an absorption costing basis, i.e. bringing in appropriate production overheads. It also tells the user that provision has been made in respect of obsolete and slow-moving stock, which, given the high technology goods in which Amstrad deals, may well have a major effect on the value of stocks. The note to the accounts indicates that Amstrad classify their stocks into two broad categories. The first includes components and consumable stores, while the second is goods ready for sale.

Extracts from Bass Plc Annual Report 1992

Accounting Policies

Stocks The basis of valuation is as follows:

i) Raw materials, bought in goods, bottles, pallets and consumable stores at the lower of cost and net realizable value on a first in first out basis.
ii) Work in progress and finished goods at at the lower of cost, which includes an appropriate element of production overhead costs, and net realizable value.

Costs include all expenditure incurred in bringing each product to its present condition and location. Net realizable value is based on estimated selling prices less further costs expected to be incurred in bringing the stocks to completion and disposal.

Notes to the accounts

Stocks

	1992	1991
	£m	£m
Raw materials	39	32
Work in progress	60	53
Finished goods	113	112
Consumable stores	37	40
	249	237

The replacement cost of stock approximates to the value at which they are stated in the accounts.

Commentary

Here we have a good example example of the different types of stock held from raw materials to finished goods with consumable stores separately classified. The accounting policy statement also gives more details of the method of arriving at the cost of the stock i.e. using the FIFO method. In addition the note to the accounts also informs the user of the accounts that the value is a reasonable approximation of the replacement cost of the stocks.

Summary

In this chapter the businesses we have considered have been trading for some time. We have shown how we establish the cost of goods sold during a period and the closing stock. We have also looked at what constitutes cost when dealing with stock and have introduced the ideas of marginal and absorption costing. In the latter part of the chapter we have seen that changes in technology can lead to stock being sold at less than cost and that changes in prices affect both the balance sheet and the profit and loss account. Finally we have considered three possible methods for arriving at the cost of goods sold during a period and at the closing stock figure. It can be seen that some of the issues faced in accounting for stock are often a direct result of the management strategies adopted. For example, Just-in-time will affect the amount of stock held. Other factors at the organizational level that will have an impact are the size of the organization (Tesco is likely to hold a wider range of goods than the corner shop) and the organizational structure: a particular factory may manufacture just one component or a number of components. We have also discussed factors at the environmental level such as changes in technology and the economy. Other factors may be the effect of quotas, such as the EC rules on local content etc.

References

Needle, D. (1989) *Business in Context*, Van Nostrand Reinhold.
Statement of Standard Accounting Practice 9 (SSAP 9) (1988) *Stocks and Work in Progress*, Accounting Standards Committee.
Statement of Standard Accounting Practice 2 (SSAP 2) (1971) *Disclosure of Accounting Policies*, Accounting Standards Committee.

Further reading

Article on Just-in-time: Robert A. McIllhattan (1987) 'The JIT philosophy', *Management Accounting*, September 7, pp. 20–6.

Answer to Example 6.3

	Cash	*Frames*	*Wheels*	*Wages*	*Work in progress*	*Equity*	*Profit and loss*
Balance	10 000					10 000	
Frames	−20 000	20 000					
Wheels	−12 000		12 000				
Wages	− 3 200			3 200			
Rent	− 5 000						− 5 000
Sales	49 000						49 000
	18 800	20 000	12 000	3 200		10 000	44 000

	Cash	*Frames*	*Wheels*	*Wages*	*Work in progress*	*Equity*	*Profit and loss*
Balance	18 800	20 000	12 000	3 200		10 000	44 000
Frames		−14 000					−14 000
Wheels			−7 000				− 7 000
Wages				−2 800			− 2 800
Frames		− 2 000			2 000		
Wheels			−1 000		1 000		
Wages				−250	250		
Balance	18 800	4 000	4 000	150	3 250	10 000	20 200
Wages				−150			− 150
	18 800	4 000	4 000	0	3 250	10 000	20 050

You will notice in this case that the wages column ends with a balance of £150 still in it. Given our assumptions this cannot be attributed either to the cost of the bicycles or to the work in progress; nor is it an asset at the end of the year as there is no identifiable future benefit. It is therefore treated in the same way as the showroom rent, i.e. as a period expense, and charged to the profit and loss account.

Review questions

1 What main categories of stock are likely to be held by a manufacturing business?
2 In arriving at a figure for stock in a business that manufactures and assembles furniture, what questions would need to be considered?
3 What would be the effect on the profit if goods costing £6000 were excluded from the opening stock figure?
4 What are the effects of omitting goods costing £500 from the year end stock figure?
5 Why is it necessary to value stock at the lower of cost and net realizable value?
6 Explain in your own words the difference between absorption costing and marginal costing.
7 Which of the following costs would be appropriate to include in a marginal costing system?

Director's salary
Foreman's wages
Machine operators' wages
Cost of raw materials

8 Of the costs above which would be appropriate to include in arriving at cost under an absorption costing system?
9 Name three methods of stock valuation and describe the differences between them and the effects of those differences.
10 Think of examples of types of business where one method of stock valuation would be more appropriate than the others.

Problems for discussion and analysis

1 In the situation described in the following example discuss which costs, if any, should be included in the stock valuation, and at what point in time they should be included.

Hank is in business manufacturing sails. The sail material is purchased in 100 m lengths and these are delivered to the storeman who sorts the materials according to quality and width. The material is then issued to the cutting room where five people are employed, one of whom is the cutting room supervisor. After cutting, the material is passed through to the machining room where the sails are sewn up and the hanks etc. are put on. The machining room has seven staff employed full time including a supervisor. From the machining room the sails go through to the packaging department where they are folded, inserted in sail bags and either sent to the despatch department or put into stock. The packaging department and the despatch department each employ one member of staff working on a part-time basis. The whole operation is under the control of a production manager who also has responsibility for quality control.

2 Discuss the ways in which your answer to problem 1 would be affected by the use of a marginal cost basis of stock valuation.

3 Simon has recently gone into business making meat pies. Details of his transactions for the first month are given below.

Day 1 Opened a bank account and paid in £20 000 of his own money.
Purchased an oven to make pies at a cost of £10 000.
Paid rent for production space for the first month of £200.

Day 2 Bought the following supplies for cash:
1100 lb of flour at 60p per lb.
1100 lb of meat at £1 per lb.

Day 3 Withdrew £1000 to pay a pressing personal debt.

Day 3 to 31
Made 4000 pies and sold 3900 pies.
Each pie takes 4 oz of flour and 4 oz of meat and was sold for £1.
At the end of the month he still had in stock the expected 100 lb of flour, 100 lb of meat and 100 finished meat pies.

Day 31 Paid himself £1600 wages for the month. He estimates that half his time is spent on production and the rest on selling and administration.
Paid production overheads of £120 for the month.
Paid administration expenses of £50 for the month.

(a) Draw up a worksheet, balance sheet and profit and loss account for Simon's business.

(b) Comment on the performance of the business.

4 Using the information in the example below, discuss the accounting treatment of each transaction and the possible value of the stock at the end of the month.

Stern has recently gone into business assembling hang gliders. Details of the transactions for the first month are given below.

Day 1 Opened a bank account for the business and paid in £50 000 of his own money.
Purchased assembly machinery for £40 000 cash.
Rented factory space at a rental of £200 per month and paid one month's rent in advance.

Day 2 Bought 1000 m of tubing for the hang glider frames at a price of £250 per 100 m and paid the £2500 in cash.

Day 3 Purchased 150 sets of material for sails for £20 per set and paid the £3000 immediately. Each hang glider takes one set of sails.

Day 8 Received an order for 20 hang gliders at £400 each together with a cheque for £8000.

Day 9 Banked the cheque and commenced manufacture of the hang gliders.

Day 14 Completed manufacture of the 20 hang gliders and despatched the completed order to the customer, paying the delivery charges of £200 immediately.

At this stage it was possible to do some preliminary calculations relating to the manufacture of each hang glider. These calculations showed that each hang glider required the following:

Labour	Sail machining	30 min per unit
	Frame assembly	2 h per unit
	Final assembly	30 min per unit
Materials	Metal tubing	4 m per unit
	Sails	one set per unit

Day 15 Received an order for another 200 hang gliders at a price of £250 each. Payment is to be made on a cash-on-delivery basis.

Day 16 Commenced work on the new order.

Day 26 Purchased another 100 sets of sails and paid for them in cash. The price had gone up to £22.00 per set, making a total of £2200.

Day 30 Paid wages of £320 for the month based on four 40 h weeks at £2 per hour.

Day 31 Established the position at the end of the month as follows:

Completed hang gliders ready for delivery	20
Manufactured frames	10

Stocks of materials were as follows:

Steel tubing in stock	800 m
Sets of sails in stock	210 sets

5 Draw up a worksheet and enter the transactions outlined in the example above.
6 Draw up a balance sheet and profit and loss account for Stern.
7 Comment on the situation as revealed by the balance sheet and profit and loss account of Stern.
8 Spain has recently gone into business manufacturing office chairs. Details of the transactions for the first month are given below.

Day 1	1 Opened a bank account and paid in £10 000 of own money. Purchased machinery to make the chairs at a cost of £4000 paid for immediately. Rented factory space at a rental of £200 per month and paid one month's rent in advance. Bought office equipment at a cost of £400.
Day 2	Bought 1000 m of steel tubing at a price of £50 per 100 m and paid for this immediately.
Day 3	Purchased 250 packs of end fittings for £125, together with a quantity of screws costing £40. Both of these purchases were paid for immediately.
Day 4	Purchased 150 sets of ready-cut seat bases and backrests at a price of £5 per set, and paid for them.
Day 5	Bought upholstery materials and cloth for seat covers for £400.
Day 8	Received an order for 20 chairs at £50 each together with accompanying cheque.
Day 9	Paid the cheque into the bank and commenced manufacture of the chairs.
Day 14	Completed manufacture of the chairs for order and despatched these to the customer, paying £40 total delivery charges.

At this stage it was possible to do some preliminary calculations relating to the manufacture of the chairs. These showed that each chair required the following:

Labour	manufacturing, 2 h per frame upholstering seats and backrests, $\frac{1}{2}$ h per set assembling chairs, $\frac{1}{2}$ h per chair
Materials per chair	4 m of metal tubing one pack of end fittings one set of seat/backrest quantity of upholstery materials etc.

Day 15	Received an order for another 200 chairs at a price of £50 each. Payment was to be on a cash-on-delivery basis.
Day 15	Commenced work on the new order.
Day 26	Purchased and paid for another hundred sets of seats and backrests. However, the price per set had gone up to £6.
Day 30	Paid himself wages for the month of £320 calculated on the basis of £80 per week for a 40 h week.

The position at the end of the month was established as follows.

Completed chairs ready for delivery	20
Manufactured frames	10

In addition there was in stock
800 m of steel tubing
210 packs of end fitting
210 seat and backrest sets
half the screws and upholstery materials

Draw up a worksheet for Spain and enter the above transactions.

9 Draw up a balance sheet at the end of the month and a profit and loss account for the month for Spain.

10 Discuss the performance of Spain's business for the period.

7 Debtors, creditors, accruals and prepayments

The progression from a simple cash-based business is taken one stage further in this chapter, where sales on credit and purchases on credit are discussed. The matching principle is explained and the treatment of amounts due to the business and owed by the business are explored in some detail.

In all the examples we have dealt with so far, and indeed in all our discussions, we have always assumed that all transactions are on a cash basis. As we pointed out in Chapter 3, this is unlikely to be the case. Therefore we need to consider how we deal with the situation where a business buys goods from its suppliers on credit terms and also supplies goods to customers on credit terms. We need to consider how to deal with the situation where a business has to pay for goods or services in advance, for example insurances, or when it pays after receiving the goods or services, as would be the case with most raw materials and with services such as electricity, telephones etc.

As these transactions directly affect both the balance sheet and the profit and loss account, we need a system that deals with them in an appropriate way to ensure that expenses are matched with revenue and that the balance sheet reflects the position at the balance sheet date. In other words the system must ensure that the balance sheet shows the assets held at the balance sheet date and the amounts owed at that date. The profit and loss account must also record the actual sales for the period and the expenses related to those sales. Not to do so would contravene the matching and realization principles and the accounts would merely reflect the timing of cash receipts and payments rather than the economic substance of the transactions that the business has engaged in during the period. Such a system of accounting is known as accrual accounting. In this chapter we shall examine situations in which the economic substance of the transaction does not occur at the same time as the cash flow and the way in which accrual accounting deals with these situations. In particular we shall look at how it deals with debtors, prepayments and bad debts, and at creditors and accruals.

Debtors and prepayments

In American accounting literature, debtors are often referred to as 'amounts receivable'. You may find initially that the American term is easier to remember as it is more descriptive than the term debtors. As we say in Key Concept 7.1, debtors arise when a business has sold goods for which payment is not received at the point of sale. In this situation we need to recognize the revenue from the sales even though the cash has not yet been received. If, however, we simply entered the sales on the worksheet the accounts would not balance as there would only be one side to the entry. This is in conflict with the principle of duality. We cannot use the cash account for the other side of the transaction as no cash has been received. However, we do have an asset, as we have a right to a future benefit in the form of cash. The way in which accrual accounting solves the problem is to open a column, or account, for this asset which we call 'debtors'. Normally debtors pay within a year and therefore you will generally find debtors classified under current assets.

KEY CONCEPT 7.1
Debtors

Debtors arise when a business sells goods or services to a third party on credit terms, i.e. when goods or services are sold on the understanding that payment will be received at a later date.

Prepayments

Prepayments, as the name implies, are payments in advance. They often arise in respect of such services as insurance, road tax etc. The payments must relate to the use of such services by the business and not by the owner in a personal capacity, a distinction sometimes difficult to establish in the case of small businesses. The proportion of the payment that relates to benefits still unexpired at the year end will be shown as a current asset in the balance sheet of the business. Prepayments therefore differ from debtors in that they relate to payments made by the business rather than to revenue earned from sales. Also, the future benefit will be in a form other than cash receipts.

We can now look at an example of debtors and prepayments.

Example 7.1

We assume a business, Pitco, has the following transactions for the period from 1 January to 31 March.

Sales for cash	£6000
Sales on credit	£4000
Cash received from credit sales	£3000
Rent for the quarter, paid 1 January	£ 500
Insurance, year to 31 December, paid 1 January	£1200

We can see that the revenue consists of the sales for cash and the sales on credit. Of the latter we can also see that there is still £1000 which has not been received, i.e. £4000 less the £3000 received. This £1000 should be shown as a debtor at 31 March. As far as the payments are concerned, the rent is clearly an expense of the quarter as all the benefit from using the premises for the quarter has expired. The insurance premiums paid are for the whole year and so we have to decide what benefit has been used up and what is a future benefit. In this case we have used up three out of the 12 months' benefit and so we have an expense of £300 and a prepayment of £900.

If we put the above information onto a worksheet this will appear as follows.

Pitco worksheet version 1

	Assets			= Equity + Liabilities	
	Cash	*Debtors*	*Prepaids*	*Owner's equity*	*Profit and loss*
Cash sales	6000				6000
Credit sales		4000			4000
Cash from sales	3000	−3000			
Rent	−500				−500
Insurance	−1200		900		−300
Balance	7300	1000	900	0	9200

You will note that in our worksheet we have shown the credit sales in the profit and loss and recorded at the same time an asset of £4000. This asset was subsequently reduced by the cash received of £3000. You may also have noticed that we charged the rent straightaway as an expense and split the insurance premium paid between the prepaid column and the expenses.

An alternative approach would have been to enter both the rent and the insurance as prepayments when they were paid on 1 January and then to consider at 31 March whether they were still assets. This we would do by answering the question: has the benefit been used up? If we had adopted that approach our worksheet would appear as follows.

Pitco worksheet version 2

	Assets			= Equity + Liabilities	
	Cash	*Debtors*	*Prepaids*	*Owner's equity*	*Profit and loss*
Cash sales	6 000				6 000
Credit sales		4 000			4 000
Cash from sales	3 000	−3 000			
Rent	−500		500		
Insurance	−1 200		1 200		
Balance	7 300	1 000	1 700	0	10 000
Rent expense			−500		−500
Insurance expense			−300		−300
Final balance	7 300	1 000	900	0	9 200

As you can see, the end result is the same. The advantage that this presentation has is that it shows clearly what we have done, which always helps in case an error is made. The choice of which presentation to use is personal but we recommend that you use the latter and that you get into the habit of reviewing all the balances, i.e. whether they are still assets or liabilities, before finally extracting a balance sheet and profit and loss account. The advantages of this approach will become more obvious as we proceed through this chapter and the next.

KEY CONCEPT 7.2
Prepayments

The key question that must be considered is whether the benefit has been used up or whether there is still some future benefit to be obtained. If there is a future benefit accruing to the business we have an asset; if there is no future benefit we have an expense, which must be matched with revenue.

Bad debts

Before leaving the question of debtors and prepayments let us consider how we would deal with a situation where, when we come to the end of the quarter and review the balances, we find that some of the amounts owed by customers are not likely to be collectable.

Example 7.1 continued

Of the £1000 Pitco is showing as debtors it is only likely to receive £800 because a customer who owed £200 has left the country and is very unlikely to pay up. In this situation the £200 is not an asset as any future benefit expired when our customer skipped the country.

The first question that arises is whether it was a genuine sale. In other words, at the time of making the sale were we reasonably certain that we would receive payment. If the answer is yes, then we have correctly recognized the revenue and the debtor. What needs to be done now is to deal with the situation that has arisen as a result of later events. This is done by reducing the amount shown as debtors by £200 and charging the £200 as an expense of the period. The worksheet would now appear as follows.

Pitco worksheet version 3

	Assets			= Equity + Liabilities	
	Cash	*Debtors*	*Prepaids*	*Owner's equity*	*Profit and loss*
Cash sales	6 000				6 000
Credit sales		4 000			4 000
Cash from sales	3 000	−3 000			
Rent	−500		500		
Insurance	−1 200		1 200		
Balance	7 300	1 000	1 700	0	10 000
Rent expense			−500		−500
Insurance expense			−300		−300
Bad debts		−200			−200
Final balance	7 300	800	900	0	9 000

It should be noted that the bottom line now represents assets which have a future benefit at least equal to the amount shown.

An example of the problems caused by uncertainty over whether a debt is collectable or not is shown in Case Study 7.1.

CASE STUDY 7.1
Barclays plc

Commentary

The note to the accounts of Barclays plc for 1992 shows an amount owed to Barclays by customers and in respect of finance leases of £88 071m and a provision for bad and doubtful debts against this of £3613m. The breakdown of this provision is shown later in the note where it is revealed that it is split into three types of risk, namely specific and general credit risks and country specific risks. The last part of the note gives the breakdown of the charge for the year.

Extract from the annual report of Barclays plc

Notes to the accounts

16 Advances and other accounts

	1992	*1991*
Advances and other accounts comprise	£m	£m
Lendings to customers	82 902	80 352
Finance lease receivables	5 169	5 075
	88 071	85 427
Less: provisions	3 613	2 686
	84 458	82 741

Placings with banks (over 30 days)	10 885	9 225
Other accounts	5 574	5 378
	100 917	97 344

Lendings and finance lease receivables, by geographical area		
United Kingdom	64 102	63 832
Other European Community	8 722	7 684
North America	10 229	9 568
Rest of the World	5 018	4 343
	88 071	85 427

Assets acquired in the year for letting under finance leases amount to £1067m (1991 £1616m).

Other accounts include £1860m (1991 £2130m) accrued interest, £586m (1991 £556m) equipment leased to customers under operating leases, which is net of accumulated depreciation charges of £259m (1991 £225m), the shareholders' interest in the long-term assurance fund of £289m (1991 £244m), purchased mortgage servicing rights of £372m (1991 £258m) and London Metal Exchange warrants £537m (1991 £255m).

	1992	*1991*
Movements in provisions for bad and doubtful debts	£m	£m
Provisions at beginning of year	2 686	2 335
Charge for the year, net of recoveries of £60m (1991 £50m)	2 534	1 547
Amounts written off, net of recoveries	(1 849)	(1 208)
Changes in Group structure	(14)	(27)
Exchange and other adjustments	256	39
Provisions at end of year	3 613	2 686
Provisions at 31st December		
Specific – credit risks	2 247	1 615
General – credit risks	690	468
	2 937	2 083
Specific – country risk	676	603
	3 613	2 686

The charge for the year in respect of bad and doubtful debts comprises:

	1992	*1991*
Specific provisions – credit risks:	£m	£m
United Kingdom	1 960	1 309
Other European Community	145	63
North America	183	266
Rest of the World	40	41
	2 328	1 679

Opening general provisions, net of exchange and other adjustments	(464)	(389)
	1 864	1 290
New general provisions – credit risks	690	468
	2 554	1 758
Specific provisions – country risk	(20)	(211)
	2 534	1 547

Having looked at how debtors and prepayments are dealt with, we can now consider how to deal with the situation in which we receive goods or services before paying for them.

Creditors and accruals

When an established business buys goods it rarely pays cash. In fact it is normally only when a business is just starting, or in exceptional cases, that trade credit is not given. The question we have to address is how a business would deal with goods supplied on credit when it may have used them or sold them before it has to pay the supplier. However, before we deal with that question we need to explain the difference between creditors and accruals.

Creditors arise when goods or services are supplied to an enterprise for which an invoice is subsequently received and for which no payment has been made at the date of receipt of the goods or services. As we have already said, most established businesses will receive most of their raw materials and components on the basis that payment is due within a certain time period after delivery. At the date at which we draw up a balance sheet, therefore, we need to acknowledge that there are amounts owing (liabilities) in respect of these supplies. These are normally referred to as 'creditors' in the UK or as 'amounts payable' in the USA.

Accruals

Accruals are in some ways similar to creditors in that they relate to amounts due for goods or services already supplied to the enterprise. They differ not because of the nature of the transaction but because, at the time of drawing up the balance sheet, the amounts involved are not known with certainty. This is usually due to the fact that the invoice for the goods has not been received. A common example of a situation where this arises is telephone bills which are always issued in arrears; other examples are electricity and gas bills. These are also generally received after the end of the quarter to which they relate. In these situations, therefore, all we can do is to estimate what we think is owed for the service the business has used during the period. This estimate may be based on the last quarter or the previous year or on some other basis which the business considers more accurate. An example may help to clarify the treatment of creditors and accruals and the differences between the two.

KEY CONCEPT 7.3
Creditors and accruals

Creditors are amounts owing at a point in time, the amounts of which are known.

Accruals are amounts owing at a point in time, the amounts of which are not known with any certainty.

Example 7.2

For the year to 31 December 19X1 Archie & Co. had the following transactions:

1 Paid £6000 of Archie's own money into a business bank account together with £5000 borrowed from a friend.
2 Bought 1000 items from a supplier for £12 per unit.
3 Paid the electricity bills for lighting and heating for three quarters, amounting to £1500.
4 Paid supplier £9000 for items purchased.

If we enter the above transactions on a worksheet and explain how they are dealt with, we can then deal with the other transactions of Archie's business. Our worksheet for the first transactions will look like this:

Archie's worksheet version 1

	Assets		=	Equity + Liabilities		
	Bank	*Stock*	*Equity*	*Profit and loss*	*Loan*	*Creditors*
Item 1	6 000		6 000			
	5 000				5 000	
Item 2		12 000				12 000
Item 3	−1 500			−1 500		
Item 4	−9 000					−9 000
Balance	500	12 000	6 000	−1 500	5 000	3 000

Let us examine each of the transactions in turn.

Item 1

By now we are all familiar with transactions of this type which create an asset and a corresponding liability in the form of money owing either to the owner or to some third party.

Item 2
This is slightly different from the previous examples which have dealt with the purchase of stock. Up to now we have assumed that the stock was paid for when we received it. In this case, however, we are only told that during the year we bought items for £12 000. We have no idea, at present, how much we have actually paid out in respect of these items or how much is still owing. Therefore we show that we are owing money for all the items and open up a column for our creditors and show £12 000 in that column.

Item 3
Once again this is a familiar item as we receive a bill which is paid for in cash. However, it should be borne in mind that we have in fact only paid for three quarters whereas we have consumed a year's supply of electricity. We therefore need to make some provision for the other quarter. A safe estimate could be that the fourth quarter's bill would be the same as the other quarters, i.e. approximately £500. It may of course turn out to be more or less. We are not attempting 100% accuracy, however, we just need to give a reasonable picture of the situation.

Item 4
We now know that, of the £12 000 we owe to suppliers, £9000 was paid in the year. We therefore need to reduce our cash by that amount and reduce the creditors by the same amount.

Let us now return to the question of the electricity bill. We said that we need to make an accrual which we estimated to be £500. Let us see how this affects our worksheet using the balances from the worksheet above.

Archie's worksheet version 2

	Assets		=	Equity + Liabilities			
	Bank	*Stock*	*Equity*	*Profit and loss*	*Loan*	*Creditors*	*Accruals*
Item 1	6 000		6 000				
	5 000				5 000		
Item 2		12 000				12 000	
Item 3	−1 500			−1 500			
Item 4	−9 000					−9 000	
Balance	500	12 000	6 000	−1 500	5 000	3 000	
Accrual				−500			500
	500	12 000	6 000	−2 000	5 000	3 000	500

As we can see, an additional column is opened for the accrual, with a corresponding entry in the profit and loss account. The balance sheet still balances and it now gives a truer picture of the goods we own and the amounts we owe.

Before leaving the subject of debtors and creditors here are some more transactions for Archie & Co. which you should try to work through yourself and then compare your answer with the answer shown below.

Example 7.2 continued

Archie & Co's other transactions in the year to 31 December 19X1 were as follows.

Item 5 Paid loan interest of £300 in respect of the half year to 30 June 19X1.
Item 6 Sold 800 items at £50 per item, all on credit.
Item 7 Received £34 000 from customers in respect of sales.
Item 8 Paid £1500 rent for five quarters as rent of the premises is due quarterly in advance.

Note for the purposes of presentation our answer combines the debtors and prepayments in one column and the creditors and accruals in one column.

Archie's worksheet version 3

	Assets		=		Equity + Liabilities		
	Bank	*Stock*	*Debtors and prepaids*	*Equity*	*Profit and loss*	*Loan*	*Creditors and accruals*
Balance	500	12 000		6 000	−1 500	5 000	3 000
Accrual					−500		500
Balance	500	12 000	0	6 000	−2 000	5 000	3 500
Item 5	−300				−300		
Item 6			40 000		40 000		
Item 7	34 000		−34 000				
Item 8	−1 500		1 500				
Balance	32 700	12 000	7 500	6 000	37 700	5 000	3 500

If we now review the position at the year end as shown on our worksheet we find that the asset 'prepaids' is no longer going to give us a future benefit of £1500 as four quarters' rent relate to the year just gone and therefore the benefit has been used. We also find that the interest paid is only for the first half of the year and yet we have had the benefit of the loan for the full year; we therefore need to make a provision or accrual for a further £300. We should also realize that our stock figure represents 1000 items at £12 each and that, of those, 800 items were sold; therefore our cost of sales should be £9600. Our worksheet will now be as follows.

Archie's worksheet version 4

	Assets		=		Equity + Liabilities		
	Bank	*Stock*	*Debtors and prepaids*	*Equity*	*Profit and loss*	*Loan*	*Creditors and accruals*
Balance	32 700	12 000	7 500	6 000	37 700	5 000	3 500
Rent			−1 200		−1 200		
Interest					−300		300
Cost of sales		−9 600			−9 600		
Balance	32 700	2 400	6 300	6 000	26 600	5 000	3 800

We can now extract the balance sheet and the profit and loss account for the first year of Archie's business.

Profit and loss account for Archie & Co.
for the year ended 31 December 19X1

	£	£
Sales		40 000
Cost of goods sold		9 600
Gross profit		30 400
Electricity	2 000	
Loan interest	600	
Rent	1 200	3 800
Net profit for the year		26 600

Balance sheet of Archie & Co. at 31 December 19X1

	£	£
Current assets	2 400	
Stocks	6 000	
Debtors	300	
Prepayments	32 700	
Cash at bank	41 400	
Current liabilities		
Creditors	3 000	
Accruals	800	
	3 800	
Net current assets		37 600
		37 600
Financed by		
Owner's equity		6 000
Profit for year		26 600
		32 600
Loan		5 000
		37 600

Having now established how to deal with debtors, creditors, accruals and prepayments, let us examine what happens in the second year of Archie's business.

Example 7.2 continued

For the year to 31 December 19X2 Archie & Co's transactions were as follows.

1 Bought 1000 items on credit at £12 per item.
2 Paid suppliers £14 000.
3 Paid electricity bill of £2300 for last year and three quarters of 19X2.
4 Paid loan interest of £600.
5 Sold 1000 items on credit terms at £50 per item.
6 Received £46 000 from customers.
7 Paid rent of £1200.

We should briefly discuss some of these items before we enter them on a worksheet.

Let us consider the payments to suppliers and the payment for electricity. In neither of these cases do we know exactly which parts of the payments relate to this year and which to last year. In the former case it does not really matter and in the latter case it is reasonable to assume that £500 relates to last year and £1800 to the first three quarters of this year. As with last year we have to make an estimate of the amount due in respect of the last quarter. Based on the same quarter of the previous year we would estimate £500 but this is clearly too low as, based on the three quarters this year, electricity is now costing £600 a quarter. Therefore a reasonable estimate would be £600.

The loan interest is similar to the situation just dealt with except that in this case there is more certainty that £300 relates to the previous year and £300 to this year. Therefore we need to make an adjustment in respect of the £300 we still owe for the current year.

As far as the cost of sales is concerned there is no real problem as prices have remained constant and we have bought and sold 1000 items in the year.

The situation with debtors is the same as for creditors. We cannot identify the individual payments, but in this particular example it does not make any difference.

Finally, the annual rent is £1200, payable in advance. As the first quarter was paid for last year, this payment relates to three quarters of the current year and one quarter of next year.

After entering these transactions the worksheet should look something like the one below. It is possible to take some shortcuts and get the same answer but you should bear in mind that such shortcuts can lead to errors.

Archie's worksheet 19X2 version 1

	Assets			=	Equity + Liabilities		
	Bank	*Stock*	*Debtors and prepaids*	*Equity*	*Profit and loss*	*Loan*	*Creditors and accruals*
Balance	32 700	2 400	6 300	6 000	26 600	5 000	3 800
Item 1		12 000					12 000
Item 2	−14 000						−14 000
Item 3	−2 300				−1 800		−500
Item 4	−600				−300		−300
Item 5			50 000		50 000		
Item 6	46 000		−46 000				
Item 7	−1 200		300		−900		
Balance	60 600	14 400	10 600	6 000	73 600	5 000	1 000
Cost of sales		−12 000			−12 000		
Rent			−300		−300		
Electricity					−600		600
Interest					−300		300
Balance	60 600	2 400	10 300	6 000	60 400	5 000	1 900

The balance sheet at the end of 19X2 and the profit and loss account for that year can now be extracted and these are shown below.

Balance sheet of Archie & Co. at 31 December 19X2

	£	£
Current assets		
Stock	2 400	
Debtors	10 000	
Prepayments	300	
Cash at bank	60 600	
	73 300	
Current liabilities		
Creditors	1 000	
Accruals	900	
	1 900	
Net current assets		71 400
		71 400
		£
Financed by		
Owner's equity		6 000
Profit for year		33 800
Profit from 19X1		26 600
		66 400
Loan		5 000
		71 400

Profit and loss account of Archie & Co.
for the year ended 31 December 19X2

	£	£
Sales		50 000
Cost of goods sold		12 000
Gross profit		38 000
Electricity	2 400	
Loan interest	600	
Rent	1 200	4 200
Net profit for the year		33 800

Summary

In this chapter we have dealt with the question of how accruals accounting deals with the problem that, if accounts were prepared on the basis of cash flows, the matching principle would be contravened. We have shown how sales on credit are included as revenue and how the amounts not received at the end of the year are dealt with as debtors and shown as current assets as they will provide the business with a future benefit. We have also examined the way in which payments in advance can be dealt with in order that expenses are matched against revenue. In addition we have shown how accrual accounting allows bad debts, where the future benefit has expired, to be dealt with. From the point of view of goods supplied to the business we have seen how creditors are dealt with and how accruals arise. The principle that is common to all these items is that the accounts should comply with the matching principle. The balance sheet should record the rights to future benefits and what the business owes at a particular point in time.

Review questions

1 In your own words describe what a creditor is and when creditors arise.
2 Explain the difference between creditors and accruals.
3 Why are debtors and prepayments classified as current assets?
4 When do prepayments arise and how do they differ from accruals?
5 Explain the matching principle.
6 Why is it necessary to identify debtors and creditors?
7 How do debtors affect the profit and loss account?

Problems for discussion and analysis

1 In each of the following situations describe the way that the transaction would be dealt with in the accounts of the business and

identify, where appropriate, the effect on the balance sheet and profit and loss account.

(a) Purchase of stock of raw materials on credit terms.
(b) Purchase of production machines for cash.
(c) Receipts from customers in respect of credit sales.
(d) Repayment of a loan.
(e) Payment in respect of research expenditure.
(f) Sale of goods on credit.
(g) Payment to supplier in respect of goods already delivered.
(h) Payment of wages to clerical workers.
(i) Payment of wages to production workers.
(j) Payment of loan interest.
(k) Payment of an electricity bill from last year.
(l) Payment of rent quarterly in advance.
(m) Withdrawal of cash from the business by the owner.
(n) Receipt of cash from the owner.
(o) Withdrawal of stock for personal use by the owner.
(p) A customer going into liquidation owing money.

2 On 1 May 19X1 Barbara paid £3000 into a business bank account as capital for her new business which she called Barbies Bikes. The transactions during May were as follows.

May 3 Bought van for £800 cash.
6 Bought goods on credit from Drake for £700.
8 Paid rent of £120 for the quarter.
14 Bought goods on credit from Gander for £300.
16 Made cash sales of £200.
18 Made credit sales of £400 to Bills Bikes.
21 Paid the garage account of £20 for petrol and oil.
23 Sold more goods on credit to Swans for £600.
24 Paid Drake £682 after taking advantage of a 2.5% discount for prompt payment.
30 Received £360 from the liquidator of Bills Bikes and was advised that no more would be forthcoming.
31 Paid monthly salary to shop assistant of £400.
Received back from Swans goods with an invoice price of £80 which they had not ordered.

Other information: No stock count was done at the end of the month but all goods were sold at a price based on the cost price plus one-third.

(a) Discuss how each transaction should be treated.
(b) Discuss what if any accruals and prepayments are or should be involved.
(c) Draw up a worksheet, balance sheet and profit and loss account.

Fixed assets and depreciation 8

Just as the previous chapters extended the simple cash-based system to take into account current assets and current liabilities, this chapter takes the model one stage further and explores assets with longer lives. The problems in arriving at the true cost of these fixed assets is discussed together with the issues of matching the benefits used up in an accounting period with the revenue earned. Various alternative methods of doing this via depreciation are explored and their limitations illustrated.

In Chapter 3 we discussed the definitions of assets and of fixed and current assets. We defined an asset in accordance with the definition suggested by R. M. Lall reproduced below. The distinction that we made in earlier chapters between assets and expenses is that an asset relates to present or future benefits whereas an expense relates to past or expired benefits. Thus we have stocks of goods held at the year end shown as an asset and the cost of the stocks sold during the year charged as an expense. Similarly some of the assets we hold change form during a period or from one period to the next. For example, debtors become cash, or they become expenses when a debt becomes uncollectable. This applies to all assets in the long run but in the case of fixed assets it takes longer to use up the future benefits than it does with current assets. We defined fixed assets in Chapter 3.

KEY CONCEPT 3.4
An asset

Embodiments of present or future economic benefits or service potentials measurable in monetary units, accruing to an enterprise as a result of economic events, the enjoyment of which by the enterprise is secured by law.

KEY CONCEPT 3.5
A fixed asset

An asset that is acquired for the purposes of use within the business and is likely to be used by the business for a considerable period of time.

The fact that these assets neither change form nor get used up in a short period poses some problems for accountants. These problems are in some ways similar to those we identified when discussing stock valuation. In that case we found that there was a problem in allocating costs such as the wages of the foreman and in deciding which part of that cost should be allocated to the costs of the goods sold during the period, i.e. the expired benefit. There was also the question of how much should be allocated to the stock held at the end of the period. (This was shown as an asset as there was a future benefit to be derived.) The problem can be looked at from a more general angle. From the point of view of the balance sheet (which tells us what we own at a particular point in time) we have to try to identify the amount of the future benefit left at the end of each year. On the other hand, from the perspective of the profit and loss account, we need to measure the amount of the future benefit used up during the year so that we can match this expense with the revenue earned in that period. Whichever way we choose to look at the problem, we are still left with the issue of how to measure the future benefit to be derived from the use of the asset. This is because the balance sheet and profit and loss account are linked. It was argued in Chapter 2 that accounting largely adopted a definition of profit based on Sir John Hick's definition of income.

KEY CONCEPT 8.1
Income

Income is that amount which an individual can consume and still be as well off at the end of the period as he or she was at the start of the period.

This we said could be illustrated diagrammatically as

$$\begin{array}{ccc} \text{Wealth at } T^0 & \text{Wealth at } T^1 & \text{Wealth at } T^2 \\ T^0 & T^1 & T^2 \\ \leftarrow \quad \text{Profit} & \rightarrow \quad \leftarrow & \text{Profit} \quad \rightarrow \end{array}$$

We can see from the diagram that wealth at T^0 plus the profit for the period will give us wealth at T^1. Thus we can either measure the wealth in the form of future benefits at the end of each period, which brings with it the problems of valuation (as discussed in Chapter 2), or we can try to measure the profit by matching the revenue with the benefits used up during the period, which brings its own attendant problems (as we found with stock and cost allocation in Chapter 6).

We look first at the idea of measuring future benefits with specific regard to fixed assets. Theoretically this may be possible. For example, we could measure the benefits to be derived from selling the products which our fixed assets help us to produce. In a world in which there is uncertainty, however, this process is far from straightforward. For example, what effects do technological advances have on the market for our products? How does that affect the future benefits to be derived from the use of our asset? What is the effect of competition? It may affect our market share. What is the effect of a change in production technology? It may allow competitors with newer equipment to produce the same product at a cheaper price.

In fact, it is extremely difficult to measure the future benefit in the long term as we do not know what changes the future will bring, and therefore we cannot estimate their effects. Traditionally accounting has solved this conundrum by the simple expedient of valuing assets at cost unless there is reasonable certainty that this value is incorrect, either because it is lower, as would be the case if changes in technology made the fixed assets obsolete, or because it is clearly considerably higher. This situation generally only applies to land and perhaps to buildings (although some would argue with the latter proposition especially in a recession). The approach to profit measurement via asset valuation in terms of future benefits is in general avoided by accounting, which leaves us with the alternative approach, i.e. measuring expired benefits and matching these with revenues. The problem with this system is that if you were able to tell how much benefit had expired you would then be able to work out what the unexpired or future benefit was. This, we have just argued, is extremely difficult to do in reality because of the problems of uncertainty.

Accountants handle the difficulty by trying to take some cognizance of the fall in value of the fixed assets. This is done by means of a depreciation charge, which is a way of spreading the original cost of a fixed asset over its useful life and thereby charging the profit and loss account with some amount relating to the use of the asset.

This approach does not, in itself, solve the problem of how to deal with uncertainty as the useful life of a fixed asset is itself uncertain. Other issues also arise: (1) How does a fixed asset differ from a current asset? (2) What is the cost of a fixed asset? (3) How should we spread the cost over the useful life? We need to examine each of these issues if we are to understand what the profit and loss and balance sheet figures mean.

Difference between fixed and current assets

We have already defined fixed and current assets in Chapter 3. If you look at the definitions you will see that the difference is in the main related to the intention and the nature of the business. In simple terms a car is not a fixed asset in the case of a motor dealer because it is not the intention of the dealer to use it within the business for a considerable period of time. The problem with a definition that relies on the intentions of the business is that these change from time to time as the nature of the business changes or the product changes. This may mean that an asset that was classified as a current asset may be re-classified and become subject to depreciation. As these problems rarely arise we can safely ignore them in this book.

The cost of a fixed asset

On the face of it the question of what an asset costs should present few if any difficulties. This is true in some cases, but in a great many cases the answer is less clear. To illustrate the point let us look at the situation in which an individual buys a house. If we were to read the legal contract between the seller and the buyer we would find within that contract an agreed price. We could therefore argue that the cost is that agreed price, but were you to talk to someone who has recently purchased a house you would find that there were other costs associated with buying that house such as solicitors' fees, surveyors' fees etc. The question is whether these should be treated as part of the cost of the asset or whether they are expenses. In this particular situation the way in which an accountant might answer the question is to argue that the amounts involved are not material compared with the cost of the house. This is not really a very satisfactory solution as it merely avoids the question instead of answering it. Accounting does not, in fact, provide an answer to the problem. There are some broad guidelines which accountants use, however. We shall examine some possible examples and identify the basis of the decision.

KEY CONCEPT 8.2
Materiality

Broadly, an item can be said to be material if its non-disclosure would lead to the accounts being misleading in some way.

Before doing that, however, we need to explain the idea of materiality. This is a concept often used in the accounting literature and, like a number of other concepts such as prudence, it provides a rule of thumb approach to assist in making judgements. For example, the cost of a car is likely to be material in the case of a small retailer, but in the case of ICI the effect on the fixed assets would be negligible as they are measured in millions of pounds. Thus materiality is a relative measure and all aspects of the situation need to be looked at before a decision is made. Having introduced the idea of materiality we can now move on to try to establish the guidelines we referred to above through a series of examples.

Example 8.1

A delivery van is purchased by a retailer of office stationery for £7600. The price includes number plates and one year's road fund licence.

Discussion

It is clear that in this example we have a fixed asset. The question is only how much the fixed asset cost. Included in the £7600 is the cost of number plates and one year's road fund licence. The road fund licence could hardly be described as a fixed asset as it only lasts for one year, whereas the number plates are clearly part of the cost of the fixed asset in that they will remain with the van over its useful life.

Example 8.2

Let us now assume that, as the retailer did not have the cash to buy the van outright, it was purchased on hire purchase. The hire purchase contract allowed the retailer to put down a deposit of £3400 and then make 24 monthly payments of £200. Thus the total cost of buying the same van would be £8200 compared with the cash price of £7600.

Discussion

The fact that the retailer has decided to finance the purchase in a different way has, on the face of it, added to the cost of purchasing the van. However, this is somewhat misleading as the cost of the van is in fact the same. What has happened in this case is that the retailer has incurred an additional cost which does not relate to the van itself. This additional cost relates to the cost of borrowing money, which is effectively what hire purchase is. If the retailer had borrowed money by a bank loan and then paid cash for the van the cost of the van would have been the cash price and the interest on the loan would be dealt with separately. Thus in the case of hire purchase all that needs to be done is to identify the part of the payments that are interest charges and deal with those in the same way as we would deal with interest on loans. In this particular example the interest is £600. The £600 interest would of course be charged to the profit and loss account as an expense over the 24 months it takes to pay the hire-purchase company.

Example 8.3

A manufacturer bought a second-hand machine for £8000, which had cost £15 000 new. The cost of transporting the machine to the factory was £500 and the costs of installation were £400. When it was installed it was found that it was not working properly and it had to be repaired which cost £300. At the same time a modification was carried out at a cost of £500 to improve the output of the machine. After two months' production the machine broke down again and was repaired at a cost of £200.

Discussion

The starting point is the basic cost of the machine which was £8000. The fact that it had cost £15 000 when it was new is not relevant. What we need to bring into the accounts of our manufacturer is the cost to that business, not the original cost to the seller. With the other costs, though, the decisions are less clear cut. For example, should the cost of transport be included? One answer would be to argue that in order to obtain the future benefits from the asset we needed to incur this cost and so this is in fact a payment for those future benefits. If we followed this line of argument we could then include the costs of installation, the initial repairs and the modifications. This would seem reasonable as long as we are happy that the future benefits are likely to exceed the costs incurred to date. This is clearly a question of judgement because of the uncertainty surrounding the estimation of future benefits.

You will have noticed that we referred specifically to the initial repairs rather than all the repairs. The reason for this is that in the first case it could be argued that the reason the business was able to buy the machine cheaply was because it was not working properly. In the second instance, however, the argument is less clear cut, as the repairs might simply be due to normal wear and tear and should therefore be judged as part of the cost of running the machine in much the same way as we would view the cost of car repairs as a part of the costs of running a car.

We can see from these examples that there is no easy solution to the problem of what should and should not be included in the cost of fixed assets. Each case is judged upon its merits and a decision is made about whether the cost should be included in the expenses for the year or added to the cost of the asset. The broad rule of thumb that can be used to assist in these decisions is: has there been an enhancement of the potential future benefits? If there has, then the cost should be added to the asset. If, however, the effect is simply to restore the status quo, as is the case with car repairs, then it is more reasonable to treat those costs as expenses of the period in which they arise. This approach conforms to the prudence concept which we have referred to earlier.

The useful life of fixed assets

In our introduction we mentioned the useful life of the asset and how we spread the cost over the useful life. This raises a number of issues: How do we judge the useful life? What cost do we spread over the useful life? How do we spread it? The last point will be dealt with below in our discussion of depreciation, but it is worth examining the other two first. The first point is how we judge the useful life. The answer is that all we can hope for is an approximation of the useful life. The reason we can only approximate comes back to the question of uncertainty in respect of the future. Similarly if we try to arrive at the cost that we wish to spread over the useful life we could argue that we should take into account anything that we shall be able to sell our asset for when it is no longer viable to use in our business. This amount, the residual value, is only a guess because of the uncertainty involved. In reality it is quite likely that such issues are sidestepped and that assets are classified into broad groups which are then assumed to have a useful life based upon either past practice or the norm for the industry. All too often one can visit factories where a vital machine in the production process has no book value in the accounts because the estimate of the useful life was incorrect.

Having made it clear that there is no magic formula for arriving at either the cost or the useful life, let us now examine the way in which we spread the cost over the useful life. This is done by means of depreciation.

Depreciation

We have suggested some reasons for charging depreciation which we shall discuss more fully shortly. What we have not done is to define depreciation precisely. (Instead we have tried to give a flavour of what depreciation is.) However, no discussion of depreciation would be complete without at least looking at the definition provided in the accounting standard on the subject, SSAP 12. This Standard defines depreciation (see Key Concept 8.3).

This definition is, in fact, difficult to comply with because it assumes that we shall be able to take into account changes in technology and the market. This might be possible in the short term but is much more difficult in the long term. As fixed assets are essentially long-term assets the requirement to take these changes in technology and the market into account is, in practice, difficult to comply with. Whilst we could spend some considerable time analysing the definition it is more important that we consider the question of why we depreciate assets and what depreciation can and cannot be expected to achieve.

> **KEY CONCEPT 8.3**
> ***Depreciation***
>
> ...the measure of the wearing out, consumption or other reduction in the useful economic life of a fixed asset whether arising from use, effluxion of time or obsolescence through technology or market changes.

Why depreciate?

One reason already mentioned for why we depreciate is to match the revenue earned in a period with the expense connected with earning that revenue. In essence the argument for matching the cost of goods sold with the sales or of matching expenses with sales is the one being applied here. The major difference is that those other items are ascertainable with a reasonable degree of accuracy, whereas depreciation is only an estimate and subject to all sorts of inaccuracies.

A second and more contentious reason for providing for depreciation is in order to maintain the capacity of a business to continue its production. Clearly if a machine comes to the end of its useful life the business will need another machine if it is to carry on producing the goods. This, of course, assumes that it would wish to replace the machine, which in itself has underlying assumptions about the product still being produced, the technology in terms of production processes being the same etc. This question is directly related to our original problem in Chapter 2 of measuring wealth or the state of being well-off. Such a measure depends on how you define wealth and whether that changes. For example, a car may be seen as an asset until such time as we run out of petrol reserves; at that stage we may not want to include a car in our measurement of wealth. Therefore to have retained profits in order to ensure we always had a car would not have been appropriate.

This second reason for providing for depreciation is also contentious because in fact all accounting depreciation does is to spread the original cost and maintain the original capital. In fact operating capacity is not maintained through depreciation, as no account is taken of changes in prices, in technology, or in consumer demand. Neither is any account taken of changes in the size of the business. This may have implications in terms of economies of scale. We cannot guarantee that we shall have enough money left in the business as a result of our depreciation charges to replace an existing machine with one of equal capacity should we so wish. Having made the point that there is no guarantee that the changes will equal the requirements for replacement because of changes in those requirements and the environment, let us look at how depreciation would maintain capital if the requirements and the environment did not change.

We will start by looking at an example to see what happens if we ignore depreciation and then how it is dealt with in terms of the accounts.

Example 8.4

Toni buys a van for £4000 and sets up as an ice cream seller. In addition to the van £1000 cash is put into the business which is subsequently used to buy stocks of ice cream.

At the end of the first year the sales have been £6000 and the total expenses including the cost of ice creams, van repairs and running costs were £3000; all the stock has been sold and so all the money is in cash. Thus the business has £4000 in cash – the original £1000 plus the money from sales of £6000 less the expenses paid of £3000.

Toni therefore withdraws £3000 on the assumption that the business is still as well off as it was at the start. That is, the business had at the start of the year a van plus £1000 in cash; it still has the van and so there only needs to be £1000 left in for the status quo to be maintained. Let us assume for convenience that the situation is repeated for the next three years.

Under these assumptions the profit and loss accounts and balance sheets of the business would be as follows:

Profit and loss accounts of Toni's business

	Year 1	*Year 2*	*Year 3*	*Year 4*
Sales revenue	6 000	6 000	6 000	6 000
Cost of sales	3 000	3 000	3 000	3 000
Profit	3 000	3 000	3 000	3 000
Withdrawal	3 000	3 000	3 000	3 000
Retained profit	0	0	0	0

Balance sheets of Toni's business

	Year 1	*Year 2*	*Year 3*	*Year 4*
Fixed assets				
Van	4 000	4 000	4 000	4 000
Current assets				
Cash	1 000	1 000	1 000	1 000
	5 000	5 000	5 000	5 000
Owner's equity	5 000	5 000	5 000	5 000
	5 000	5 000	5 000	5 000

If we assume that the van would last four years we can see that in fact the balance sheet at the end of year 4, assuming it reflects future benefits, should be as follows.

	£
Fixed assets	
Van	Nil
Current assets	
Cash	1000
	1000
Owner's equity	1000
	1000

As we can see, there is not enough money left in the business to replace the van and in this situation the business cannot continue. If we compare our results with our definition of profit in Chapter 2 it is clear that our profit measure must have been wrong as Toni is not as well off at the end of year 4 as at the beginning of year 1.

The problem has been that the profit has been overstated because no allowance has been made for the fact that the van has a finite useful life which is being eroded each year. If we assume that the cost should be spread evenly over the four years and call this expense depreciation, then our profit and loss accounts would appear as follows.

Revised profit and loss accounts of Toni's business

	Year 1	*Year 2*	*Year 3*	*Year 4*
Sales revenue	6 000	6 000	6 000	6 000
Cost of sales	3 000	3 000	3 000	3 000
Gross profit	3 000	3 000	3 000	3 000
Depreciation	1 000	1 000	1 000	1 000
Net profit	2 000	2 000	2 000	2 000
Withdrawal	2 000	2 000	2 000	2 000
Retained profit	0	0	0	0

As can be seen, the net profit has been reduced by £1000 for the depreciation each year and Toni has withdrawn only £2000 each year. The balance sheets would now be as follows.

Revised balance sheets of Toni's business

	Year 1	*Year 2*	*Year 3*	*Year 4*
Fixed assets				
Van	4 000	4 000	4 000	4 000
Depreciation	1 000	2 000	3 000	4 000
Net book value	3 000	2 000	1 000	0
Current assets				
Cash	2 000	3 000	4 000	5 000
	5 000	5 000	5 000	5 000
Owner's equity	5 000	5 000	5 000	5 000
	5 000	5 000	5 000	5 000

As we have seen, the effect of charging depreciation in the profit and loss account was to reduce the net profit which in turn led to a reduction in the amount available to be withdrawn each year. The reduced withdrawal has led to the cash balance increasing each year by £1000 until at the end of year 4 there is £5000 in the bank and Toni is in a position to replace the van, assuming of course that the price of vans has not changed. If you compare the two sets of balance sheets there is another change – the fixed asset reduces each year by the amount of the depreciation charge. These two effects should not be mixed up. The increase in cash is as a result of withdrawing less, *not* as a result of providing for depreciation. The latter does not in itself affect the cash balance, as is obvious if we work through year 1 of this example on a worksheet.

Worksheet showing year 1 of Toni's business

	Cash	*Van*	*Equity*	*Profit and loss*	*Depreciation*
Start	1 000	4 000	5 000		
Sales	6 000			6 000	
Expenses	−3 000			−3 000	

	Cash	Van	Equity	Profit and loss	Depreciation
Depreciation				−1 000	1 000
Withdrawal	−2 000			−2 000	
Balance	2 000	4 000	5 000	0	1 000

As you can see, the depreciation charge does not affect the cash column in any way.

An alternative way of dealing with depreciation on a worksheet is to reduce the asset column by the depreciation. If we did this our worksheet would appear as shown below. However, we recommend that wherever possible the worksheet should include a separate column for depreciation as this adds to the clarity and allows one to identify roughly how far through its useful life the asset is at the end of the year. In our example we can see that it cost £4000 and £1000 depreciation has been charged and so we know that we are a quarter of the way through its estimated useful life.

Alternative worksheet of Toni's business for year 1

	Cash	Van	Equity	Profit and loss
Start	1000	4000	5000	
Sales	6000			6000
Expenses	−3000			−3000
Depreciation		−1000		−1000
Withdrawal	−2000			−2000
Balance	2000	3000	5000	0

In this example we have assumed that the cost should be spread evenly over the life of the asset. This is known as straight line depreciation and is one of a number of alternative methods that can be used as the basis for providing depreciation. Each of these alternatives will give a different figure for the depreciation each year and as a result the 'written-down value', often also referred to as the 'net book value', will change. This is illustrated in more detail after our discussion of the most common methods of depreciation. Before going on to that discussion you need to understand what 'written-down value' means.

KEY CONCEPT 8.4
Written-down value

This is normally the cost of the fixed asset less the total depreciation to date. In certain cases, usually with freehold buildings, the asset may be revalued. In these cases the written-down value is the valuation less the total depreciation to date.

Methods of depreciation

As we have said there are a number of alternative methods of depreciation, the choice of the appropriate method, at least theoretically, depending on the nature of the asset being depreciated. In practice, however, the only methods in common usage are the straight line method and the reducing balance method, and the former is used by the vast majority of businesses. The reason for this is probably purely to do with simplicity of calculation. In this regard it would be useful for you to look at the accounting policies statements in published accounts to try to ascertain the reasons underlying the choice of depreciation method. As we shall see in the discussion below a case can be made for using different methods for different assets or classes of assets. In reality, it may be the fact that assets are put into broad categories that leads to the predominance of straight line depreciation which we shall now discuss more fully.

The straight line method

We have already seen that this is a very simple method which probably explains why so many companies use it. The assumption, with regard to asset life, that underlies the choice of this method is that the asset usage is equal for all periods of its useful life. The way in which the depreciation charge is calculated is to take the cost of the asset less the estimate of any residual value at the end of the asset life and divide it by the useful life of the asset. Thus an asset which cost £130 and which has an estimated life of four years and an estimated scrap value of £10 would be depreciated by £30 per year. This was arrived at by using the formula

$$\frac{\text{cost} - \text{residual value}}{\text{useful life}}$$

In our case this works out as follows:

$$\frac{£130 - £10}{4} = £30 \text{ per annum}$$

Reducing balance method

The reducing balance method assumes that the asset declines more in the earlier years of the asset life than in the later years. In fact it is likely that in most cases the cost of repairs will rise as the asset becomes older and so this method when combined with the cost of repairs is more likely to produce a more even cost of using an asset over its full life. It is less frequently used than the straight line method probably because it is slightly more difficult to calculate, although with the increasing use of computers this should not really cause any problems. The method applies a pre-calculated percentage to the written down value, or net book value, to ascertain the charge for the year. In order to arrive at the percentage we use the following formula:

$$\text{rate of depreciation} = 1 - \sqrt[\text{useful life}]{\frac{\text{scrap value}}{\text{cost of asset}}}$$

Comparison of the two methods

We consider a business that has an asset which has an estimated useful life of three years, cost £15 000 and has an estimated scrap, or residual, value of £3000.

For the straight line method we need to depreciate at £4000 a year, i.e.

$$\frac{15\,000 - 3000}{3} = £4000 \text{ per annum}$$

For the reducing balance method we first need to find the rate of depreciation to apply. In this case it will be 41.5% which we arrive at by using the formula below.

$$\text{rate of depreciation} = 1 - \sqrt[3]{\frac{£3000}{£15\,000}}$$

$$= 0.415 \text{ or } 41.5\%$$

This rate is now applied to the net book value, i.e. the cost less depreciation to date.

Year	*Straight line method*			*Reducing balance method*		
	Balance sheet		P & L	Balance sheet		P & L
	Cost	15 000		Cost	15 000	
1	Depreciation	4 000	4 000	Depreciation	6 225	6 225
	Net book value	11 000		Net book value	8 775	
	Cost	15 000		Cost	15 000	
2	Depreciation	8 000	4 000	Depreciation	9 865	3 640
	Net book value	7 000		Net book value	5 135	
	Cost	15 000		Cost	15 000	
3	Depreciation	12 000	4 000	Depreciation	12 000	2 135
	Net book value	3 000		Net book value	3 000	

As can be seen from the example the charge to the profit and loss account in each year and the accumulated depreciation in the balance sheet are quite different with the two methods, although the methods charge, in total, the same amount and come to the same residual value.

Under the straight line method the charge to the profit and loss is £4000 each year and so the accumulated depreciation rises at £4000 a year.

Under the reducing balance method the charge to the profit and loss is based on 41.5% of the balance at the end of the previous year. Thus in year 1 it is 41.5% of £15 000, in year 2 it is 41.5% of £8775 and in year 3 it is 41.5% of £5135.

As we have said, both methods achieve the same result in the end as with both methods the asset is written down to its residual value at the end of year 3. It is the incidence of the charge to the profit and loss account which varies, not the total charged. Whilst in theory the choice of depreciation method should be governed by the nature of the asset and the way in which the benefit is used up, in practice little, if any, attention seems to be paid to this. However, it is worth spending some time understanding when each method would be appropriate. We have said that the straight line method implies that the benefit from the use of the fixed asset is used up in an even pattern over its useful life. This suggests that it is time which is the determining factor governing the life of the asset rather than the amount of use to which it is put. Thus if we take the case of a building it is unlikely that the amount of use it gets will materially affect its lifespan and so straight line depreciation would be appropriate. On the other hand, if we think about the way in which a car engine, for example, wears out this is more likely to relate to usage, i.e. the more miles the car does the more wear and tear on the engine. In such a case the straight line method is unlikely to be the most appropriate method, but we do not have a commonly accepted method that relates directly to usage.

The reducing balance method, however, has characteristics that make it a possible alternative to a direct measure related to usage in that it charges the most benefit used to the early years, as would be the case if the asset were used up by the mileage alone or by the number of hours a machine was run etc. It is of course only an approximation. It is probably not worth while from a cost–benefit point of view, however, to measure the number of hours a machine is run for and calculate a precise figure as the total life of the machine and so on are all subject to estimation errors.

We can therefore argue that where the life of the asset relates to time then the straight line method is likely to be more appropriate, but in the situation where the asset is used up through hours run, or mileage or any other measure relating to usage, then the reducing balance method may well give a better approximation of the benefit used up in a period. (see Case Study 8.1).

CASE STUDY 8.1
Straight line and reducing balance methods

We have said that the vast majority of companies use the straight line method of depreciation and a good example of the rates that are applied to different classes of assets is provided by the following extract from the accounting policies statement of Merrydown plc.

Extract from the annual report of Merrydown

Tangible fixed assets & intangible fixed assets other than goodwill

Interests in freehold land and buildings including investment properties and primary vats are stated at cost or valuation. Full valuations are made by independent professionally qualified valuers at least every five years. The bases of valuation, as considered appropriate by the valuer, are open market value for existing use or depreciated replacement cost. The cost of other tangible fixed assets is their purchase cost, together with any incidental expenses of acquisition. Depreciation is calculated so as to write off the cost, or valuation, of tangible fixed assets (excluding land and investment properties) on a straight line basis over the expected useful economic lives of the assets concerned. The principal annual rates used for this purpose are:

	%
Freehold buildings	2
Primary vats	5
Other plant and equipment	5–7$\frac{1}{2}$
Office equipment and motor vehicles	10–25

No depreciation is provided on investment properties, they are subject to annual valuation by the directors with the assistance of independent professional advice and as stated above they are independently valued at least every five years.

Commentary

In the case of other plant and equipment apart from vats the rates used vary slightly depending on the type of equipment. These variations are more marked in the case of office equipment and motor vehicles where the range is from 10% to 25%.

An alternative to the straight line method is the reducing balance method or one that relates to usage. An example of the latter is used by British Petroleum for certain assets, as is indicated by the following extract from the BP annual report 1992.

Extract from the annual report of BP, 1992

Depreciation

Oil, minerals and coal production assets are depreciated using a unit-of-production method based upon estimated recoverable reserves. Other tangible fixed assets are depreciation on the straight line method over their estimated useful lives. Where liabilities exist for dismantling and abandonment, these costs are accrued on a unit-of-production basis.

Commentary

Here we have a mix of methods being used. The first is based on actual usage measured against an estimate of the total capacity of the asset, in this case a deposit of coal or an oil field. The remainder of the assets are depreciated on the straight line method. In this case the rates are not explicitly stated in the Accounting Policy Statement from which the above extract is taken.

Sale of fixed assets

Before leaving the discussion of fixed assets and depreciation we should examine the situation that arises when we sell a fixed asset. It should be obvious from our discussion above that the net book value of the asset, i.e. the cost less depreciation to date, is unlikely to bear any resemblance to the market price of that asset. This means that when an asset is sold the selling price will either be less than or exceed the net book value and a paper loss or profit will arise. If for example we sold the asset used in our previous example at the end of year 2 for £6000, then under the straight line method there would be a paper loss of £1000 (net book value of £7000 compared with the £6000 we sold it for). However, if we had been using the reducing balance method we would show a 'paper profit' of £865, i.e. the net book value of £5135 compared with the sale proceeds of £6000. We have referred to these as paper profits and losses because what they really are is the difference between our estimate of the future benefit being used up and the actual benefit used up. In other words, they are a measure of the error in our estimates. We shall now look at the way in which these are treated using the worksheet to illustrate the effect on the profit and loss account.

Example 8.5

A business bought an asset for £15 000. It estimated the useful life as three years and the scrap or residual value as £3000. The business uses straight line depreciation. For the purposes of illustration we shall assume that its sales are £14 000 a year and the total expenses are £9000 each year for both years 1 and 2. We shall also assume that at the end of year 2 it sold the fixed asset for £6000.

Solution

We can calculate the depreciation charge as £4000 a year for each of the two years.

Worksheet

Year 1	*Cash*	*Asset*	*Disposal*	*Equity*	*Profit and loss*	*Depreciation*
Asset	−15 000	15 000				
Sales	14 000				14 000	
Expenses	−9 000				−9 000	
Depreciation					−4 000	4 000
Balance	−10 000	15 000		0	1 000	4 000
Year 2						
Sales	14 000				14 000	
Expenses	−9 000				−9 000	
Depreciation					−4 000	4 000
Balance	−5 000	15 000		0	2 000	8 000
Asset		−15 000	15 000			
Depreciation			−8 000			−8 000
Sale proceeds	6 000		−6 000			
	1 000	0	1 000	0	2 000	0
Loss on sale			−1 000		−1 000	
Final balance	1 000	0	0	0	1 000	0

You will notice when you look at the worksheet that the full depreciation is charged in both years 1 and 2. The reason for this is that the asset was used for the full year in both years. If it had been used for less than a full year then we should have had to apportion the charge.

At the end of year 2, having used the asset for the full year, we decide to sell the asset. As you can see this involves a number of entries on our worksheet which we shall examine in turn.

For clarity we have opened a separate column in our worksheet which we have called a 'Disposal' column. An alternative way would have been to deal with all the entries in the fixed asset column but that is more difficult to follow. First, as we have sold the asset we need to transfer the cost and any associated depreciation to a disposal column. We receive some cash in exchange for the asset and so we show the cash in our cash column and in our disposal column. This leaves us with a balance on our disposal column of £1000 which is the amount of the paper loss that we have made. This paper loss is transferred to the profit and loss account.

Our worksheet once again shows the correct position as we have no asset or depreciation associated with our asset and our profit to date is reduced to £1000 because of the underestimate or paper loss in respect of the use of the asset for the two years.

The alternative way of dealing with the disposal on a worksheet is as follows.

Note

The worksheet given below starts from the balances at the end of year 2 after the depreciation for the year has been charged but before the disposal of the asset has been dealt with. The major difference is that instead of opening a new account to deal with the disposal all the entries are put through the existing columns or accounts.

Worksheet – alternative presentation

	Cash	*Asset*	*Equity*	*Profit and loss*	*Depreciation*
Balance (Year 2)	−5 000	15 000	0	2 000	8 000
Depreciation		−8 000			−8 000
Sale proceeds	6 000	−6 000			
	1 000	1 000	0	2 000	0
Loss on sale		−1 000		−1 000	
Final balance	1 000	0	0	1 000	0

Some find this format easier to follow and work with. The choice of which way the entries are put on the worksheet is in fact irrelevant. It is the principle involved that is important and you may choose the method with which you feel most comfortable.

In published accounts of companies there is a requirement to show the fixed assets, additions and disposals, and movements in respect of depreciation in full. An example of such disclosure is given in Case Study 8.2.

CASE STUDY 8.2
Writing back depreciation on sale of an asset

Extract from the 1989 Annual Report of The Body Shop International Plc

Notes on the Accounts continued

28 February 1989
11 Tangible Fixed Assets continued

	Freehold property £000	*Short-term leasehold property* £000	*Plant and equipment* £000	*Total* £000
Cost				
At 1 October 1987	85	2 956	2 242	5 283
Additions	444	7 112	2 866	10 422
Disposals	—	(1)	(80)	(81)
At 28 February 1989	529	10 067	5 028	15 624
Accumulated depreciation				
At 1 October 1987	8	345	1 035	1 388
Disposals	—	—	(47)	(47)
Charge for the period	18	353	982	1 353
At 28 February 1989	26	698	1 970	2 694
Net book value				
At 28 February 1989	503	9 369	3 058	12 930
At 30 September 1987	77	2 611	1 207	3 895

Additions to leasehold property in the period include £4.786 million in respect of the new warehouse currently under construction. No depreciation has been provided for in the period in respect of this amount.

Commentary

The extract gives information about the various categories of assets including their cost and any additions and disposals during the year to arrive at the balance at the end of the year. This is similar to what we do on our worksheets in this chapter. You should also note that where an asset is disposed of any depreciation charged on that asset is taken out of the accumulated depreciation in the same way as we have illustrated. This was the case in respect of £47 000 relating to the £80 000 of plant and machinery disposed of in the period.

Summary

In this chapter we have re-introduced the definition of assets and of fixed assets and we have examined some of the problems associated with arriving at the cost of a fixed asset and estimating the useful life and the residual value. We have also considered the nature of depreciation, why it is charged to the profit and loss account, and the way in which it is treated in a balance sheet. We have seen that there are two methods of depreciation in common usage and we have examined the differences between these and the effects on the profit and loss account and the balance sheet. Finally we have discussed and illustrated the way in which a sale of a fixed asset is dealt with via the worksheet.

References

Statement of Standard Accounting Practice 12 (SSAP 12) (1987) *Accounting for Depreciation*, Accounting Standards Committee.

Further reading

A full discussion on depreciation is contained in *Depreciation: Depreciating Assets by* W.T. Baxter (Gee, 1981).

Review questions

1 What is the purpose of depreciation?
2 Why is it unlikely that depreciation will provide for replacement of the fixed asset?
3 What factors need to be taken into account in determining the useful life of an asset?
4 On what basis do we decide what should and should not be included in the cost of a fixed asset?
5 Describe what is meant by the net book value and the written down value of an asset.
6 What are the assumptions underlying the two main methods of depreciation?
7 An expense has been defined as a past or expired benefit. In what way does depreciation differ from other expenses?
8 In the chapter we described the profit or loss arising on the disposal of a fixed asset as a paper profit or loss. Explain how this profit differs from that arising on the sale of stock.

Problems for discussion

1 In each of the following situations discuss the most appropriate method of depreciation giving reasons for your choice.

Land and buildings: The land was purchased for £300 000 and £400 000 was spent on the erection of the factory and office accommodation.

Motor vehicles: The business owns a fleet of cars and delivery vans all of which were bought new. The owners have decided to trade in the vehicles for new models after four years or 60 000 miles, whichever is sooner. The anticipated mileage figures are 12 000 miles per annum for the cars and 20 000 miles per annum for the vans.

Plant and machinery: The plant and machinery owned by the business can be broadly classified into three types as follows.

Type 1: Highly specialist machinery used for supplying roller bearings to Manicmotors Ltd. The contract for supply is for five years, after which it may be renewed at the option of Manicmotors. The renewal would be on an annual basis. The machinery is so specialist that it cannot be used for any other purpose. It has an expected useful life of ten years and the residual value is likely to be negligible.

Type 2: Semi-specialist machinery which is expected to be productive for ten years and have a residual value of 10% of its original cost. However, other firms operating similar machines have found that after the first three years it becomes increasingly more costly in terms of repairs and maintenance to keep machinery of this type productive.

Type 3: General purpose machinery which has an estimated useful life of 80 000 running hours. Based on present levels of production the usage is 8000 hours a year but as from next year this is expected to rise to 12 000 hours a year if the sales forecasts are correct.

2 Using a worksheet draw up the balance sheet and profit and loss account for the business whose transactions are set out below:

Month 1 Bert put in £9000 of his own money and transferred his own car into the name of the business. At the time of the transfer it would have cost £6000 to buy a new model of the same car but as the car was one year old its second-hand value was only £4000.
The business then bought a machine for £4000 paying for this in cash, and at the same time bought a second machine on credit terms. The credit terms were a deposit of £1000 which was paid in cash and two equal instalments of £900 payable at the start of months 4 and 7 respectively. The cash price of the machine was £2500.

Month 2 Bought raw materials for £3000 and paid cash and made cash sales of £3000.

Month 3 Paid rent in arrears for the three months, amounting to £600 in cash.
Paid wages of £1500 for the three months to date.
Made cash sales of £4000 and purchased more raw materials, again for cash, amounting to £8000.

Month 4 Paid instalment on machine of £900 in cash and made cash sales of £4000.

Months 5–7	Bought raw materials for cash for £2000 and made cash sales of £5000, paid wages for three months of £1500, the rent for three months, £600, and the second and final instalment on the machine of £900.
Months 6–12	Made cash sales of £14 000, bought raw materials for cash for £6000, paid wages for six months of £3000 and paid rent for three months of £600.

At the end of the year he has raw materials in stock which cost £2000. He calculates that the car will last two more years after which he thinks he will be able to sell it for £400. The machines have useful lives estimated at three years and will then be sold for £100 each. Since Bert is not very good with figures he opts for straight line depreciation on all the fixed assets.

9 Financing and business Structures

To date, the chapters have largely been concerned with what an organization does with an asset once it has been acquired. In this chapter we turn our attention to how the business raises the money to acquire its assets. The various types of finance available to different types of organizations are discussed, as are the effects of the finance mix on the returns to the owners.

In this chapter, we shall consider the different forms of finance a business uses and the effects of the organizational structure upon the sources of finance available. We shall also consider the financing structure of an organization and its effect on financial risk. For these purposes, it is necessary to differentiate between business risk and financial risk.

Broadly speaking, business risk applies equally to all firms in an industry, with some variations relating to size and diversity – i.e. it is industry specific rather than firm specific. Financial risk is more firm specific; it relates to the financial structure of a business, i.e. the way in which it finances its assets.

Before commencing our discussion of the different types of finance, it is important to appreciate that the choice of appropriate finance can be vital to the long-term success of a business. Ideally, the type of finance should match the purpose for which it is to be used. For example, using what is essentially short-term finance for the purchase of a building merely creates problems when the financier has to be repaid. The building is still needed and therefore replacement finance has to be found. Similarly, taking out a loan repayable over 20 years to buy an asset that is only going to be needed for a few years would leave the business in the position of having to pay interest on money it no longer needs. These are, of course, extreme examples, but they do serve to illustrate the point that the finance must be matched with the purpose for which it is to be used.

> The finance used and the period of that finance should be matched to the period for which it is required and the purpose for which it is to be used.
>
> **KEY CONCEPT 9.1**
> ***Type of finance***

Although any attempt to classify different types of finance is problematic, it is useful to look at some broad categories and a division based upon the period of finance is the one we have chosen to use. In considering the various forms of finance we shall endeavour to follow a pattern of providing a general description of the source of finance, discussing its uses, limitations, costs and availability.

Short-term finance

Conventionally, short-term finance is seen as finance for a period less than a year. It should be used to finance short-term capital requirements such as working capital requirements, i.e. financing stock and debtors. A number of sources of finance are available, the most common being trade credit, bank overdraft and factoring.

Trade credit

We have already come across trade credit in Chapter 7 which dealt with debtors and creditors. Normally a supplier will allow business customers a period of time after goods have been delivered before payment is required. The period of time and the amount of credit a business gets from its suppliers is dependent upon a number of factors. These include the 'normal' terms of trade of that industry, the creditworthiness of the business and its importance to the supplier. Thus, for example, a small clothing retailer is likely to get less favourable terms than a major group such as Marks and Spencer.

In general, trade credit, which is widely used as a source of finance, provides short-term finance. This is normally used to finance, or partially finance, debtors and stock. As such, its importance varies from industry to industry. For example, manufacturing industries, where there is greater investment in stock and work in progress, are more likely to rely on trade credit than service industries. Within an industry there may also be variations. For example, a restaurant is less likely to rely on trade credit than a public house, where a lot of money is tied up in stocks. In fact within the licensed trade many publicans rely quite heavily on trade credit and this reliance makes them vulnerable if that credit is not managed effectively. Effective management in a small business setting requires a balance to be struck between taking advantage of trade credit and not being perceived as a slow payer. If too long a period is taken to pay, the supplier may impose less favourable terms next time. The temptation to extend the repayment date can lead to the withdrawal of any period of credit, which means that all supplies have either to be paid for in advance or on a cash on delivery basis. Ultimately, too heavy a reliance on trade credit can leave a business vulnerable to the supplier petitioning for bankruptcy or liquidation. Although suppliers are generally reluctant to take such steps, if they believe that they are more likely to recover their money by such a course of action that is what they will do.

Trade credit is often thought of as cost-free credit, which is not strictly true, as quite often suppliers allow a small discount for early payment. Therefore taking the full period to pay has an opportunity cost in the form of the discount forgone. This opportunity cost has to be weighed against the availability of funds within the business or the cost of raising additional funds. Unlike other forms of short-term finance there is generally no requirement for security.

KEY CONCEPT 9.2
Trade credit

Trade credit is a form of short-term finance. It has few costs and security is not required.

Factoring

If a business makes sales on credit, it will have to collect payment from its debtors at some stage. Up until that point, it will have to finance those debtors, either through trade credit, an overdraft, or its own capital. The costs of this finance can be very high and many small businesses will be hard up against their limits in terms of their overdraft and the amount and period of trade credit taken. In order to release the money tied up in debtors the business can approach a factoring company. These are finance companies which specialize in providing a service for the collection of payments from debtors.

Essentially, the way the system works is that the factoring organization assesses the firm's debtors, in terms of risk and collectability. It then agrees to collect the money due on behalf of the business concerned. Once an agreement is reached, the factoring company pays the business in respect of the invoices for the month virtually straight away. It is then the factoring organization's responsibility to collect from the debtors as soon as possible. In this form of finance the security provided by the business is in the form of the debts being collected. The factoring company charges for the service in the form of interest based on the finance provided and by a fee for managing the collection of the debts. This form of finance is therefore more expensive than trade credit but can be useful as it allows the business to concentrate on production and sales and improves the cash flow. Factoring, however is not available to all industries. In some cases this is because it is inappropriate – e.g. most retailing operations – and in others the factoring companies are reluctant to be involved because of a lack of clear legal definitions.

> Factoring provides short-term finance. Costs include an interest charge and a debt management charge. The finance is secured on the debtors.
>
> **KEY CONCEPT 9.3**
> ***Factoring***

Bank overdrafts

Banks provide short-term finance for working capital, either in the form of short-term loans or, more commonly, in the form of an overdraft. The difference is that a loan is for a fixed period of time and interest is charged on the full amount of the loan, less any agreed repayments, for that period. An overdraft, by contrast, is a facility that can be used as and when required and interest is only charged when it is used. Thus, if a business knows that it needs money for a fixed period of time then a bank loan may be appropriate. On the other hand, if the finance is only required to meet occasional short-term cash flow needs then an overdraft would be more suitable. We shall discuss loans in more detail under the heading of medium-term finance.

Although many businesses use overdrafts as a semi-permanent source of finance this is not how the banks would like to see this form of finance used. Bank managers like to see a business bank account, on which an overdraft facility has been provided, 'swinging' between having money in the bank account and using the overdraft. They do not see an overdraft as a form of permanent working capital.

A bank overdraft carries with it a charge in the form of interest and often a fee for setting up the facility. The latter, which is a one-off charge, has become more common in recent years. As far as the interest is concerned, the rate of interest charged is related to the risk involved and the market rates of interest for that size of business. In general, the more risk is involved, the higher the rate of interest. Due to the fact that they operate in a volatile market, small firms tend to be charged higher rates of interest than large firms.

In addition, banks will normally require security, which can take various forms. In the case of a small business the security could be a charge on the assets of the business. In many cases, however, the property is already subject to a charge as it is mortgaged. In these situations the bank may take a second charge on the property or on the owner's home or homes if more than one person is involved. Alternatively, or in addition, the bank may require personal guarantees from the owner, or in the case of a limited company, the directors.

For larger companies, the security may be a fixed charge on certain assets, or a floating charge on all the assets. In the case of very large companies the risk involved is lower and the competition between the providers of finance is greater. Because of this competition, for large companies overdrafts tend to be cheaper and more accessible; security is also less of a factor.

KEY CONCEPT 9.4
Bank overdrafts

Bank overdrafts provide finance only when it is needed. Costs include interest and often a set-up charge. In general, some form of security will be required.

Medium-term finance

There are a number of sources of medium-term finance that can be used by a business. We shall limit our discussion to medium-term loans, leases and hire purchase.

Loans

As we pointed out, an alternative to overdraft finance for short-term finance requirements is bank loans. In general, loans should only be used when finance is required for a known period of time. Ideally that period should relate to the life of the asset or the purpose for which the finance is to be used. Loans can be obtained for short-term, medium-term or long-term finance. Compared to an overdraft facility, which can be used as and when needed, a loan is more permanent. Repayment of the loan is negotiated at the time the loan is taken out and is generally at fixed intervals. They are often secured in the same way as overdrafts and if the repayment conditions are not met then the lender will take action to recover the outstanding amount.

Bank loans are often granted for a specified purpose and limitations may be imposed regarding the use of the loan and the raising of other finance while the loan is outstanding. Unlike an overdraft, the cost of this form of finance is known in advance as interest accrues from the time the business borrows the money irrespective of the fact that it may not use it straight away. In common with other forms of finance discussed so far, the rate of interest charged and the availability of this source of finance is dependent upon the size of the business and the lender's assessment of the risk involved. Thus, in general, the larger and more diversified a business, the easier will be its access to this form of finance.

KEY CONCEPT 9.5
Loans

Loans are generally for a fixed purpose and a fixed period of time. They have set repayment dates and costs include interest and set-up fees. They are normally secured on assets.

Hire purchase

An alternative way of financing the acquisition of an asset is through the use of hire purchase. Under a hire purchase agreement a finance company buys the asset and hires it to the business. Thus a business can acquire the asset and use it, even though it has not yet paid for it in full. During the period of the hire purchase agreement the finance company owns the asset. The hirer has the right to use the asset and carries all the risks associated with using that asset. Thus, for example, if a car is purchased on hire purchase, the hirer would be responsible for all the repairs and costs associated with the use of that car in the same way as if they had bought the car directly. At the end of the period of the hire purchase agreement the ownership of the asset is transferred to the hirer. A normal hire purchase agreement consists of a deposit and a set number of payments over a number of years.

This type of finance can only be used when a specific asset is purchased, i.e. the finance is for a specified asset purchase and therefore the amount borrowed is limited by the price of the asset. Hire purchase finance therefore cannot be directly used for financing working capital requirements or any other purpose. The hire purchase company actually pays the supplier of the asset directly and the asset belongs to the hire purchase company. If repayments are not made in accordance with the hire purchase agreement the hire purchase company has the right to repossess its property. The money borrowed is repaid by monthly instalments which include both a repayment of the capital borrowed and a charge for interest. The rate of interest charged will be dependent upon the market rate of interest, but is likely to be higher than the interest on a bank loan.

Hire purchase is available to all businesses and individuals, subject, of course, to the hire purchase company being satisfied with the creditworthiness of the person or business.

KEY CONCEPT 9.6
Hire purchase

Hire purchase is for a fixed period of time. Costs are in the form of interest charges. Ownership of the asset remains with the provider of the finance until all instalments are paid.

Leasing

A lease is an agreement between a lessor, the person who owns the asset, and a lessee, the person who uses the asset. It conveys the right to use that asset for a stated period of time in exchange for payment but does not normally transfer ownership at the end of the lease period. The period can vary from a very short period to ten or more years. In common with hire purchase, this form of finance is tied to a specific asset. Thus its use as a source of finance is limited to the purchase of capital items. Leasing companies will often provide leases tailored to the needs of an industry. For example, in the hospitality industry it is possible to obtain lease finance for the internal telephone system or even the complete furnishing of a hotel.

In general the cost of leasing is similar to that of hire purchase. The major difference between the two sorts of finance is that, in general, leases tend to be for a longer period of time and are frequently used as a source of finance for specialized assets. In essence there are two distinct types of leases – operating leases and finance leases. An operating lease is the same in reality as renting the equipment and usually applies to items such as photocopiers.

KEY CONCEPT 9.7
Leasing

Leases are for a fixed period of time; the costs are in the form of interest charges. Security is related to the asset in question.

The underlying economic substance of a finance lease, on the other hand, is equivalent to borrowing money from a finance company and then using that money to buy an asset. These differences are reflected in the definitions given in Key Concept 9.8.

KEY CONCEPT 9.8
Types of lease

An operating lease
A lease where the underlying substance of the transaction is a rental arrangement.

A finance lease
A lease where the underlying substance of the transaction is a financing arrangement.

The reason for emphasizing the difference between the two types of lease is that they are accorded different treatment in the accounts. In broad terms this means that in the case of an operating lease the payments are charged to the profit and loss account in the same way as rent. For a finance lease the treatment is the same as we have already illustrated in earlier chapters, where a loan preceded the purchase of one or more assets. In this case the profit and loss account is only charged with the interest, as would be the case with a loan. An example of some of the disclosure in respect of leases is provided in Case Study 9.1.

CASE STUDY 9.1
British petroleum

Commentary
The extracts from the notes to the accounts and the accounting policies statement of British Petroleum plc illustrate the disclosure in respect of finance leases. You will see that the accounting policy also covers operating leases where the rentals are charged against the profit of the year in which they are incurred.

Extract from the notes to the accounts of British Petroleum

		1992	*1991*
Obligations under finance leases		£m	£m
Minimum future lease payments payable within:	1 year	81	120
	2 to 5 years	487	608
	Thereafter	3 591	3 501
		4 159	4 229
Less finance charges		2 836	3 037
Net obligations		1 323	1 192

Extract from the accounting policies statement of British Petroleum

Leases

Assets held under leases which result in group companies receiving substantially all risks and rewards of ownership (finance leases) are capitalised as tangible fixed assets at the estimated present value of underlying lease payments. The corresponding finance lease obligation is included with borrowings. Rentals under operating leases are charged against income as incurred.

A number of variants on leases and hire purchase are available. These include contract hire, lease purchase, and sale and lease back. The details of these are, however, beyond the scope of this introduction.

Long-term finance

The number of alternative sources of long-term finance available is, to some extent, dependent upon the type of organization involved. We shall start our discussion with debt finance, such as long-term loans, which are more generally available, and then move on to discuss equity finance. The latter discussion will be sub-divided in terms of organization types, i.e. sole proprietorships, partnerships and limited companies, as these affect the type of equity finance available. In respect of limited companies, we shall limit our discussion to private limited companies.

Debt finance

This is the term given to any source of long-term finance that is not equity finance. Often, debt finance is seen exclusively as long-term interest-bearing finance. This is, in fact, a misconception, as all the finance we have discussed so far has been debt finance. We shall look at two broad categories of long-term debt finance, i.e. long-term loans, which are available to all organizations, and debentures and loan stock, which tend to be used by incorporated businesses.

Long-term loans

As we have said, loans can be used for short-term, medium-term or long-term finance. Interest rates are likely to be different for different loan periods as these will need to be adjusted to take into account the higher risk associated with lending money for a longer period of time. Long-term loans are often for a specific purpose, e.g. the purchase of property, and the time period is affected by the life of the asset, the repayments required and the willingness of the lender to lend money. For many small businesses these loans often take the form of a commercial mortgage on property.

Apart from loans related to property, the period of these loans is less in the UK than in Germany and Japan, where longer loan periods are more common. This may reflect a reluctance on the part of banks and other financial institutions to lend money for long periods of time. This was starting to change in the late 1980s and early 1990s, when building societies were beginning to take advantage of the deregulation of financial services to enter this market. Unfortunately, but perhaps understandably, a number of building societies got their fingers badly burned. This was probably due to a number of factors, including a lack of expertise, the start of the recession and the fact that interest rates were still rising. This meant that a number of businesses which had been operating on tight margins went out of business with consequential effects on the demand for, and price of, commercial property. The result of all this is that there are still limitations on the availability of long-term loans, especially for the purchase of assets other than property. As is the case with all the other types of finance we have discussed, the availability of this source of finance is also heavily dependent upon the lender's assessment of the credit-worthiness of the prospective borrower.

In the case of large companies, international groups and in particular multinationals, there is also the opportunity to raise funds from the European market and other markets around the world, as is evident from Case Study 9.2.

CASE STUDY 9.2
Forte

Extract from the notes to the accounts of Forte

18 Bank and other borrowings

	Company		Group	
	1990	*1988*	*1990*	*1988*
	£m	£m	£m	£m
Debenture and other loans – secured				
6.25% to 7.25% First Mortgage Debenture Stocks 1990/91	5	6	5	6
10.5% Mortgage Debenture Stock 1991/96	13	13	13	13
Other mortgage and secured loans (average interest rate 6.9%)	—	—	9	10
Debenture and other loans – unsecured				
10.25% Sterling Eurobond 1992	85	85	85	85
11.125% Sterling Eurobond 1990	50	50	50	50
8.25% US Dollar Eurobond 1991 (US$75 m)	45	42	45	42
8.625% French Franc Eurobond 1991 (FrFr400 m)	42	37	42	37
*Sterling Commercial Paper (average interest rate 15.0%)	99	153	99	153
*Eurodollar Commercial Paper (US$280 m) (average interest rate 8.3%)	170	150	170	150
*US Dollar Domestic Commercial Paper (US$182 m) (average interest rate 8.4%)	110	—	110	—
Other unsecured loans (average interest rate 9.5%)	11	17	21	26
Total debenture and other loans	630	553	649	572
Bank loans – secured				
Fixed Rate (average interest rate 9.6%)	—	—	13	13
*Veriable Rate (average interest rate 18.0%)	—	—	3	—
Bank loans – unsecured				
*14.9% Sterling loans 1990	6	60	6	60

	Company		Group	
	1990	*1988*	*1990*	*1988*
	£m	£m	£m	£m
*8.7% US Dollar loan 1990 (US$45 m)	—	—	27	—
*8.6% US Dollar loan 1990 (US$25 m)	—	—	15	—
*8.6% US Dollar loans 1989 (US$156 m)	—	88	—	88
*10.4% French Franc loans 1990 (FrFr600 m)	63	54	63	54
*8.3% Deutsche Mark loans 1990 (Dm34 m)	12	—	12	—
11.9% Irish Punt loan 1991 (I£20.8 m)	20	17	20	17
*8.6% Dutch Florin loan 1990 (Dfl46 m)	14	13	14	13
*13.3% Italian Lire loan 1990 (Lire33 b)	16	13	16	13
*12.8% Italian Lire loan 1990 (Lire30 b)	—	—	14	—
12.0% Spanish Peseta loans 2003/7 (Ptas2.65 b)	—	—	15	—
Other unsecured bank loans (average interest rate 9.1%)	—	7	47	37
Total bank loans	131	252	265	295
Total loans	761	805	914	867
Bills of exchange	41	—	41	—
Bank overdrafts	25	—	53	29
Total bank and other borrowings	827	805	1008	896
	£m	£m	£m	£m
Due within one year	215	158	341	220
Due after one year	612	647	667	676
	827	805	1008	896

Secured loans are secured by mortgages on certain hotel and other Group properties.
* Rates of interest vary in accordance with market rates. The rates quoted are those prevailing at the end of the period.

Commentary

As can be seen from the extract above, an international hotel group, in common with other international companies, has access to a number of different financial markets to raise finance. The study of the forms of finance available in the international market-place is a field of study in its own right and is outside the scope of this book.

Debentures and loan stock

These terms refer to particular types of long-term loans to limited companies. They basically mean the same thing and are essentially long-term loan finance. The main difference between these and long-term loans is that interest tends to be at a fixed rate and repayment tends to be at a fixed point in time, rather than over the period of the loan as would be the case for a commercial mortgage or other long-term loan. Debentures and loan stock are issued by the company raising the finance and can usually be traded on what are known as secondary markets. The price at which they can be sold and bought on the secondary market will not be the same as the price at which they were issued. This variation is related to changes in interest rates over time. In virtually all debenture deeds there is a right to repayment or appointment of a receiver if interest is not paid when due. The cost of this type of finance is similar to that for long-term loans and is affected by the market rate of interest, the security available, and the risk involved. For this reason, they are more commonly seen in the accounts of larger companies.

KEY CONCEPT 9.9
Debt finance – long-term

Long-term debt finance is generally for a fixed period of time and interest rates can be higher than for short or medium-term finance.

Equity finance

The other major source of long-term finance is equity finance, and here we need to look at organizational types, as this can have a major effect on both the type and the amount of equity finance available.

Sole proprietorships

In the case of a sole proprietorship, as we have seen, the only sources of equity finance are those supplied by the owner, and the retained profits. In many small businesses, the amount of funds that the owner has available to put into the business is often limited. This means that the only source of equity finance is retained profits. In a fast-growing business it is unlikely that there will be sufficient retained profits to finance expansion. As such, sole proprietorships, in common with many small businesses, become very reliant on debt finance and, as we shall see, this exposes them to more risk as a downturn in the market, or an increase in interest rates, could have a dramatic impact on their ability to service the debt. Unlike debt finance, equity finance has no limitations in terms of the use to which it is put.

Partnerships

Partnerships, as the name implies, are organizations that are owned, and often managed, by a number of individuals. They are most common among professionals, thus we see doctors, dentists, lawyers, architects and, of course, accountants working in partnerships. In essence, the sources of equity finance for partnerships are the same as for sole proprietorships, i.e. money contributed by the owners and retained profits. There are, of course, more people involved, so more equity can be raised through contributions by the owners. Partnerships are governed by the legislation contained in the 1890 Partnership Act and by case law. In general the main difference between partnerships and sole proprietorships is that, whereas the sole proprietor is the only person responsible for the debts, in a partnership the partners are *jointly and severally* liable. This means that if a partner cannot pay their share of the debts, the other partners must pay. The other important difference is related to the division of profits, which must be divided amongst the partners in accordance with the partnership agreement.

We shall be looking at the subject of partnerships in more detail in Chapter 10 where the accounting problems of partnerships will be discussed. For our purposes here, we can view partnerships as having the same sources of equity finance as sole proprietorships. The only difference is that they are likely to have access to a greater supply of funds. In addition there may be differences in relation to the availability of retained profits as some partners may leave more profits in the business than others. This will of course depend upon the individual partner's requirements for funds.

Limited companies

Limited companies have the advantage, from an investor's point of view, that the liability of the owners is limited to the amount they have invested in the company. As with partnerships and sole proprietorships, the major source of equity comes from the owners. However in the case of limited companies this is through the issue of ordinary shares.

Ordinary shares

In the case of companies, the equity is divided into ordinary shares, which represent contributed capital, and reserves, which represent profits made by the company. Each share normally has a nominal or par value, e.g. 10p or £1. This value has little significance in terms of the price at which the shares are bought and sold on the stock market. It is however, the figure at which the shares are shown in the accounts. In the case of an existing company any new shares issued after the company has been trading are likely to be issued at a price in excess of the nominal value. The difference between the nominal value and the price at which the share is issued is put to a special account known as the share premium account. This will be separately identified, as Case Study 9.3 illustrates.

CASE STUDY 9.3
Merrydown

Commentary

The extract from the balance sheet of Merrydown plc shows the capital and reserves broken down between the called-up share capital, the share premium account and the other reserves. The user is also referred to a note to the accounts where more details in respect of these sub-divisions is given.

Extract from the annual report of Merrydown

	Note	*1992*	*1991*
Capital and Reserves		£	£
Called-up share capital	17	1 819 229	1 613 863
Share premium account	18	881 570	1 065 281
Revaluation reserve	18	2 051 830	2 057 941
Profit and loss account	18	5 699 030	4 960 351
Shareholders' funds		£10 451 659	£9 697 436

As with any other form of organization, the other main source of equity capital is retained profits. Unlike a sole proprietorship or partnership, a company distributes its profits by way of dividends. The directors decide on the amount of dividend to be paid and the timing of the dividends, and until a dividend is declared by the directors, the shareholders have no *prima facie* right to a dividend. Dividends can be paid during the year and/or at the end of the year. If they are paid during the year they are referred to as interim dividends and the dividend at the end of the year is referred to as the final dividend. Dividends are treated differently from drawings which, as we have seen, are normally deducted from the owner's equity. These differences will be looked at in more detail in Chapter 10. A company has the advantage over a sole proprietorship or a partnership in that it can issue shares to whoever it wishes in whatever proportions it wishes. The shareholders do not have to take part in the management of the company, and in most large companies, the vast majority of shareholders play virtually no part in the management of the company. They merely invest their money and take the risk that they will get better returns, in the form of their share of the profits, than they would by investing in fixed interest investments. Ultimately, all the profits belong to the shareholders, so if they do not get their share of the profits in the form of dividends, i.e. the profits are retained in the company, their share of the profits and the future profits is reflected in the price at which they could sell their shares.

Preference shares

Apart from ordinary shares, a company can also issue preference shares. Unlike ordinary shares a preference share normally has a fixed dividend and even if more profits are made, the preference dividend remains the same. In addition they normally carry a right to preference in the order of payment in the event of the company going into liquidation. They are therefore less risky than ordinary shares and appeal to a different sort of investor. Whether these shares should be classified as equity or debt would depend on the particular type of preference shares in question and the rights attaching to them. Preference shares may be redeemable or non-redeemable. They may carry a right to dividends on a cumulative basis, i.e. if the directors do not pay any dividends in a year the preference shareholders will have a right to be paid that year's dividend and any others that have not been paid before the ordinary shareholders can be paid any dividend. Some preference shares are participating preference shares, whereby they get a share of profits if the profit is over a certain figure.

KEY CONCEPT 9.10
Equity finance

This is long-term permanent finance and comes from two main sources, i.e. contributed capital and retained profits.

Financing structures and financial risk

The mix of debt finance and equity finance is known as gearing, and it affects the financial risk of an enterprise. Basically the more reliant a business is on debt finance, i.e. the more highly geared, the greater the risk. The risk we are referring to here is that if interest rates go up or the profit margin comes down, the enterprise would not be able to pay the interest or repayments due on its debt finance. There are, of course, advantages of being highly geared as well as disadvantages, as Example 9.1 illustrates.

Example 9.1

Chansit has equity capital consisting of 20 000 ordinary shares of £1 each. It has retained profits of £10 000 and has £40 000 in loans on which interest at 3% above bank base rate, which currently stands at 12%, is due.

Solidco has equity capital consisting of 40 000 ordinary shares of £1 each. It has retained profits of £10 000 and has £20 000 in loans on which interest at 3% above bank base rate i.e. 15% is due.

Situation 1

Both companies make sales of £100 000 and their net profit before interest is 10% on sales.

The profit and loss accounts for the two companies would be as shown below.

	Chansit	*Solidco*
Sales	100 000	100 000
Costs	90 000	90 000
Net profit	10 000	10 000
Interest	6 000	3 000
Available for equity shares	4 000	7 000
Profit per share	0.20	0.17

The profit per share, which is normally referred to as earnings per share, is arrived at by dividing the profit by the number of shares in issue. Thus for Chansit the profit of £4000 is divided by 20 000 shares to arrive at the profit per share of 20p. The ordinary shareholders of Chansit are getting a better return than the shareholders of Solidco – 20p per share, as compared to 17p per share in Solidco. This is despite the fact that both companies have the same sales, costs and net profit. The differences arise as a result of the financing structure, its effect on the interest charges and the remaining profit after interest.

Situation 2 – Increased costs

In this situation, instead of making a net profit before interest of 10% of sales, the companies find that they can only make 8%.

In this case the profit and loss accounts of the two companies would be as follows.

	Chansit	*Solidco*
Sales	100 000	100 000
Costs	92 000	92 000
Net profit	8 000	8 000
Interest	6 000	3 000
Available for equity shares	2 000	5 000
Profit per share	0.10	0.13

In this case the profit margin of both businesses has fallen by the same amount. As a result, the profit available for the equity shares has dropped in both cases. However, the effect on the profit per share is more dramatic in the case of Chansit than it is in the case of Solidco, due once again to the effects of the financing structure. Thus, although in Situation 1 it looked as if Chansit had the better financing structure, we find from a shareholder's point of view that it is more vulnerable to a reduction in the profit margin than Solidco.

Situation 3 – Increased interest rates

In this situation the facts are the same as in Situation 2 above, i.e. the net profit before interest is 8% on the sales. However, in addition, bank base rate moves to 13% and therefore the interest on the loans moves up to 16%.

In this case the profit and loss accounts of the two companies would be as follows.

	Chansit	*Solidco*
Sales	100 000	100 000
Costs	92 000	92 000
Net profit	8 000	8 000
Interest	6 400	3 200
Available for equity shares	1 600	4 800
Profit per share	0.08	0.12

Once again both businesses are affected by the change in circumstances. However, the effect of the rise in interest rates is greater, in terms of the return to the shareholders, in Chansit than it is in Solidco.

These examples illustrate the effects of high gearing, which are to increase the returns to shareholders but at the same time make them more vulnerable to decreases in the profit margin. In addition, their returns are also affected more by increases in interest rates than those of a low-geared company.

It is worth mentioning that the lower the share of the business that is financed by equity, the more difficult it is to raise debt finance. Banks in the UK like to see a ratio of one to one, i.e. they will lend money, all other things being equal, so that the debt finance is equal to the equity share. There is often a clause to that effect included in the loan agreement. If the clause limits the amount of borrowing to the equity total, then decisions on how much profit to retain, whether to revalue land and buildings etc., can have a dramatic effect on a company's ability to raise finance.

Summary

In this chapter we have considered the main types of short-term, medium-term, and long-term finance that are available to all organizations. We have also looked at equity finance in the form of contributed capital and retained profits. The effects of different organizational forms on the sources of equity finance have been discussed and the effects of the mix of debt to equity finance on the returns to equity shareholders have been discussed and illustrated. It is important to remember that one vital point raised in this chapter was that the type of finance used should relate to the purpose for which that finance will be used.

Further reading

Arnold, J., Hope, T. and Southworth, A.J. (1985) *Financial Accounting,* Chapter 11, Prentice Hall.

Berry, A. (1993) *Financial Accounting: An Introduction,* Chapter 11, Chapman and Hall.

Pizzey, A. (1990) *Accounting and Finance: A Firm Foundation,* 3rd edn, Chapter 21, Cassell.

Review questions

1 Why is it important to match the type of finance with the purpose of raising that finance?
2 What are the forms of short-term finance discussed in the chapter?
3 What are the main differences between equity finance and debt finance?
4 What are the differences between drawings and dividends?
5 What does the term 'highly geared' refer to?
6 What are the advantages and disadvantages of being highly geared?
7 Which types of short-term finance require a business to provide some form of security?
8 What form of security is required for each of the forms of short-term finance discussed in the chapter?

Problems for discussion and analysis

1 A friend has been to see the bank manager about borrowing some money to finance the acquisition of a new van and a new machine. The bank manager has said that, in view of the current financial structure of the company, the bank would not be prepared to provide funds unsecured. The latest balance sheet of the company is given below.

Balance sheet

	Cost	Depreciation	
Fixed assets	£	£	£
Equipment	60 000	15 000	45 000
Vehicles	36 000	12 000	24 000
	96 000	27 000	69 000
Current assets			
Stock		3 600	
Cash		1 500	
		5 100	
Creditors: falling due within one year			
Trade creditors		7 500	
Taxation		10 800	
Bank overdraft		12 900	
		31 200	
Net current liabilities			(26 100)
Creditors: falling due after one year			25 000
			17 900
Financed by			
Ordinary shares			15 000
Retained profits			2 900
			17 900

(a) Advise your friend what alternative sources of finance are available and which would be appropriate for the purpose of buying a van and buying a new machine.

(b) Explain why, in your opinion, the bank manager was not prepared to lend unsecured.

2 Ben was planning to open a fish and chip shop. He has produced the following projections for the first year, based on his experience of the area and some careful research.

	£
Sales	36 000
Cost of ten-year lease	30 000
Refurbishment	3 000

Equipment	20 000
Stock of fish, etc.	1 000
Rent	2 000
Electricity	900
Wages	8 000
Personal drawings	5 000

Ben estimates that the costs of fish etc. required to make the sales target of £36 000 will be £12 000. He says that the equipment will last for five years and has no residual value. He has £40 000 in savings but is reluctant to invest the whole of that. He has been offered a loan of £20 000, to help buy the lease, at an interest rate of 10% per annum for the first year, with no repayments required during that year. After the first year the rate will be 4% above base rate. Base rate currently stands at 12%. Alternatively he can borrow money using a bank overdraft at a rate of 17% per annum.

(a) Calculate what Ben's profit would be if he put in all his own money and borrowed anything else he needs. Hint: The receipts and payments have to be looked at in terms of their regularity and their timing.
(b) Calculate what Ben's profit would be in the first year, assuming he takes the loan.
(c) Calculate what Ben's profit would be in the second year, assuming he does not take the loan and sales and costs are the same as the first year.
(d) Calculate what Ben's profit would be in the second year, assuming he takes the loan.
(e) Ben has asked you to advise him on the choice between the two alternatives. How would you advise him, and what reasons would you give?

10 Final accounts, partnerships and companies

Having established a base of knowledge about a simple form of organization, this chapter looks at alternative organizational forms and the impacts of each of these on the financial accounts produced. In addition it examines some of the underlying advantages and disadvantages of different organizational structures and also provides a bridge to other methods of illustrating double-entry systems.

The first section of this chapter has been included to assist readers who wish to continue with their studies using other textbooks. These are likely to use a more traditional approach for explaining accounting and the mechanics of accounting. It will also be helpful to readers who have had some exposure to that traditional approach as an aid to understanding how the exposition in this book and that in other texts relate to one another. In the next part of the chapter we shall move on to look at the trial balance and the final adjustments required before final accounts are extracted from the worksheet. In the remainder of the chapter we consider alternative formats of final accounts and how these relate to different forms of organization. This will involve some consideration of the advantages and disadvantages of the different organizational forms available. It will also require an examination of the ways in which the presentation of accounting information may differ. Before these new areas are discussed, however, we shall examine the traditional approach to accounting found in other textbooks and compare it with the worksheet approach.

The traditional approach

In this approach, instead of using columns to portray the individual accounts in an organization's accounting system, these accounts are represented by T accounts. In many basic book-keeping courses these

T accounts form a major part of the course and students are required to spend a lot of time practising entries to these accounts. Quite often this is done on the basis of rote learning. It is further complicated by the terminology used: 'debits' and 'credits'.

For people studying accounting for the first time the worksheet approach has been shown to be superior. Moreover, it is more in line with the increasing use of electronic spreadsheets. However, experience has shown that those who have already had some exposure to accounting often experience initial problems in converting from one representation of an accounting system to another. In this chapter we are going to work through a simple example to illustrate that the difference between the two methods is superficial and does not in any way change the principles involved.

Example 10.1

Brian started a business and during the first year the following transactions took place.

1 Opened a business bank account and paid in £10 000 of his own money.
2 Bought a van for £5000 and paid for it in cash.
3 Bought goods for £35 000 on credit and had paid £33 000 at the end of the year.
4 Sold goods for £45 000 all for cash.
5 Had goods in stock at the end of the year which cost £4000.
6 Paid expenses on the van of £1000.
7 Paid rent on his premises of £1500.

Let us first see what the worksheet would look like for Brian's business and we shall then see how the same transactions would be represented under the traditional method.

Brian's worksheet version 1

	Assets		=	Equity + Liabilities		
	Cash	*Van*	*Stock*	*Equity*	*Profit and loss*	*Creditors*
Item 1	10 000			10 000		
Item 2	−5 000	5 000				
Item 3			35 000			35 000
	−33 000					−33 000
Item 4	45 000				45 000	
Item 5			−31 000		−31 000	
Item 6	−1 000				−1 000	
Item 7	−1 500				−1 500	
Balance	14 500	5 000	4 000	10 000	11 500	2 000

You should make sure that you understand the entries on the worksheet above before moving on. If you do have problems refer back to the appropriate chapters. Now we record the same transactions using the traditional approach of T accounts.

Cash

Item 1	10 000	Item 2	5 000
Item 4	45 000	Item 3	33 000
		Item 6	1 000
		Item 7	1 500
		Bal c/d	14 500
	55 000		55 000
Bal b/d	14 500		

Stock

Item 3	35 000	Item 5	31 000
		Bal c/d	4 000
	35 000		35 000
Bal b/d	4 000		

Owners' equity

		Item 1	10 000

Van

Item 2	5 000		

Creditors

Item 3	33 000	Item 3	35 000
Bal c/d	2 000		
	35 000		35 000
		Bal b/d	2 000

Profit and loss

Item 5	31 000	Item 4	45 000
Item 6	1 000		
Item 7	1 500		
Bal c/d	11 500		
	45 000		45 000
		Bal b/d	11 500

Note: c/d, carried down; b/d, brought down.

A careful examination of the two systems will show that they have recorded the same transactions. All that has changed is the way in which the recording has been represented. This will be made clearer if we explain some of the items and the ways in which they have been treated.

For example, with the worksheet approach, to deal with item 1 where Brian puts some money into the business, we opened up a column entitled Cash and one entitled Equity on the other side of the worksheet. We then entered the amount involved, £10 000, in each of these columns. By contrast, under the traditional approach we opened two T accounts. One of these was for cash and the other for equity. We then entered the amount involved, £10 000, in these two accounts. All that is happening is that in contrast with the use of T accounts to represent accounts the worksheet uses columns.

Using T accounts, it is perhaps less clear which side of the account the entry should go on. In the case of assets the entry is put on the *debit* side, i.e. the *left-hand side*, and in the case of liabilities it is put on the *credit* side, i.e. the *right-hand side*.

> Under the traditional approach *assets* are shown as *debit balances* and *liabilities* are shown as *credit balances.*
>
> **KEY CONCEPT 9.1**
> ***Debits and credits***

We now consider the way in which item 2, the purchase of the fixed asset, is dealt with. We find that using the worksheet approach a new column is opened for the asset and the cash column is reduced by the amount paid for the new asset, i.e. £5000. The traditional approach also starts in the same way by opening a new account for the new asset, and puts the cost of £5000 on the left-hand side because it is an asset. So far, the methods are essentially similar. The other half of the transaction is perhaps slightly more difficult to follow as we have to *reduce* the cash balance. This is done by putting the £5000 on the right-hand side of the cash account. This is called crediting an account – in this case we are crediting a cash account.

Even at this stage it is perhaps becoming obvious that the worksheet approach is easier to follow as it relies less on jargon and rote learning than the more traditional approach. Another advantage of the worksheet approach is that we know at the end of the exercise that we have balanced our accounts and if they do not balance the error can be found by working back through the worksheet as described in Chapter 5. In the case of the more traditional approach we are as yet unsure that our accounts balance and so we would now extract what is commonly known as a trial balance. If having extracted this trial balance we found that it did not balance we would have to check through most if not all of the entries in our accounts to find the error. Hopefully that will not be the case with the trial balance for Brian's business which would be as follows:

Trial balance of Brian's business

	Debit	*Credit*
Cash	14 500	
Equity		10 000
Creditors		2 000
Van	5 000	
Stock	4 000	
Profit and Loss		11 500
	23 500	23 500

We can now see that the accounts do balance. You may have noticed that the columns are headed Debit and Credit and that all the accounts from the left-hand side of our worksheet, the asset accounts, are in the debit column and all the accounts from the right-hand side of the worksheet, those that relate to what the business owes, are in the credit column. In this case we have not made an error in our double entry as the trial balance balances and so we can move to the next stage. This is where final adjustments are made for accruals, depreciation etc. These adjustments are often referred to in accounting literature as end of period or end of year adjustments.

End of period adjustments

As we have said end of period adjustments refer to adjustments such as those required to provide for depreciation, bad debts, accruals and prepayments etc. These have all been covered in Chapters 6–8 and you should be familiar with the way in which they are dealt with via the worksheet. However, for the purposes of comparison we shall initially show how they are dealt with through the worksheet and then look at how they are dealt with through the traditional approach.

Example 10.1 continued

At the end of the year Brian decides that the van will have no scrap value and should be depreciated at £1000 a year for five years, and he also tells you that the rent is payable quarterly in advance so that only £1200 relates to this year.

Entering these adjustments on the worksheet would result in the worksheet shown below. You will notice that we have had to open two new accounts or columns to deal with the changes and then arrive at a new balance.

Brian's worksheet version 2

	Cash	*Van*	*Stock*	*Prepaid*	*Equity*	*Profit and loss*	*Creditors*	*Depreciation*
Item 1	10 000				10 000			
Item 2	−5 000	5 000						
Item 3			35 000				35 000	
	−33 000						−33 000	
Item 4	45 000					45 000		
Item 5			−31 000			−31 000		
Item 6	−1 000					−1 000		
Item 7	−1 500					−1 500		
Balance	14 500	5 000	4 000		10 000	11 500	2 000	
Adjustment						−1 000		1 000
Adjustment				300		300		
Balance	14 500	5 000	4 000	300	10 000	10 800	2 000	1 000

In the traditional approach we would also have to create the new accounts and then extract another trial balance. However, there is a shortcut which is often shown in textbooks and this involves making adjustments on what is effectively a type of worksheet. The difference between that worksheet and the one we use is that the rows become columns and vice versa. This worksheet is shown below and, as you can see, it merely extends our earlier trial balance to a new trial balance. This type of worksheet is often referred to as the extended trial balance.

The main difference between the two approaches in this respect is that when using the worksheet approach the final adjustments are automatically part of the double-entry system. Under the traditional approach they can be and often are outside the double-entry system. This can of course lead to errors and omissions which may be more difficult to trace. Let us look at the extended trial balance of Brian's business.

Brian's extended trial balance

	Debit	*Credit*	*Debit*	*Credit*	*Debit*	*Credit*
Cash	14 500				14 500	
Equity		10 000				10 000
Creditors		2 000				2 000
Van	5 000				5 000	
Stock	4 000				4 000	
Profit and loss		11 500	1 000	300		10 800
Depreciation				1 000		1 000
Prepaids			300		300	
	23 500	23 500	1 300	1 300	23 800	23 800

As can be seen the extended trial balance has also resulted in the need to open two new accounts and to make some adjustments to our existing profit and loss account. If these adjustments were done through double entry in the T accounts they would be shown as follows:

Prepaids

Adjustment	300		

Depreciation

		Adjustment	1 000

Profit and loss

Item 5	31 000	Item 4	45 000
Item 6	1 000		
Item 7	1 500		
Bal c/d	11 500		
	45 000		45 000
Adjustment	1 000	Bal b/d	11 500
		Adjustment	300

Discussion

We have seen that the differences between the two approaches are not differences of principle. Rather, they are alternative ways of depicting the same entries in the books of account of a firm. In the authors' opinion the advantages of the worksheet-based approach outweigh the advantages of the alternative approach and make it easier for those coming to the subject for the first time to assimilate the main principles involved in a double-entry book-keeping system. We shall now consider the way in which final accounts are produced and the rules and regulations governing their format.

Final accounts

Before we look at the regulations and the effects of different organizational forms we should remind ourselves of the way in which the final accounts, i.e. the balance sheet and the profit and loss accounts, are derived from the worksheet. This may be more readily understood if we consider the example of Brian's business. We shall extract the final accounts from the worksheet above.

Profit and loss account of Brian's business for the year ending 30 June 1999

Sales		£45 000
Cost of goods sold		31 000
Gross profit		14 000
Rent	1 200	
Van expenses	1 000	
Van depreciation	1 000	3 200
Net profit		£10 800

You will notice that the formal profit and loss account merely summarizes what is contained in that column of the worksheet. You may also have noticed that it is called the profit and loss account for the period ended on a certain date. This emphasizes that the profit and loss account is a period statement; we can contrast it with the heading of the balance sheet below. This as you can see, is at a particular point in time – a snapshot at a point in time.

Balance sheet of Brian's business as at 30 June 1999

	£	£
Fixed assets		
Van at cost	5 000	
Depreciation	1 000	4 000
Current assets		
Stock	4 000	
Prepaids	300	
Cash	14 500	
	18 800	
Current liabilities		
Creditors	2 000	
	2 000	
Net current assets		16 800
		20 800
Financed by		
Owner's equity		10 000
Profit and loss		10 800
		20 800

You will have noticed that the balance sheet merely takes the final line of the worksheet and classifies it under appropriate headings to enable the reader to interpret the information more readily. We shall be dealing with the subject of interpretation in more detail in Chapter 12. Prior to that, however, we need to consider the effect of different forms of organizational structure on the presentation of final accounts.

Forms of organization

As we said in Chapter 1 there are many forms of organization possible, from a sole proprietorship, through partnerships, companies and groups of companies to multinational conglomerates. In addition there are other less common forms such as co-operatives, friendly societies and provident societies. Each of these organizational forms requires slightly different accounts (see *Law in a Business Context*). This may be because the needs of the users are slightly different or because of other factors such as the requirements of legislation or other regulations, e.g. those imposed by the Stock Exchange. Rather than attempting to deal with all the different forms of organizations we shall concentrate our discussion on the simpler forms of organization: the sole proprietorship, the partnership and the limited company.

There are distinct differences in the presentation of final accounts which are related to the structure, size, patterns of ownership and goals of an organization. These influences operate at the organizational level of the 'Business in Context' model which was explained at the start of this book. Other influences which operate at the environmental level are legal requirements such as the reporting requirements of the Companies Acts and the Partnership Act and case law. These will be discussed in some detail here. Other influences at this level, such as the Stock Exchange requirements, are beyond the scope of an introductory text. We shall commence our discussion at the smallest and most common form of business organization: the sole proprietorship.

The sole proprietorship

This is a one-owner business, and is very simple to set up. All that is really required is a business bank account. Because it is so simple and because it has little recognition in law there are no formal guidelines for the format of the accounts. However, the fact that the business and the owner are not seen as separate legal entities could be a problem if the business gets into difficulties, as the owner is liable for all the debts of the business and may have to sell personal possessions such as the family home to meet them. In addition, as we discussed in Chapter 9, this form of organization relies heavily on the owner for finance and this can lead to problems if and when the business expands as owners tend to have fairly limited funds at their disposal.

Partnerships

A partnership exists where two or more people enter into an agreement to run a business together. This can have a number of advantages: the additional person may bring new finance to the business or new skills or contacts etc. In essence partnerships are fairly simple organizations and are similar to a sole proprietorship in that there are no rules governing the format of accounts, and so these can be tailored to meet the needs of the users of those accounts. However, as you can imagine there is more potential for conflict when there is more than one owner, and because of this there is considerable case law on partnerships as an organizational form.

For our purposes, all we need to do is to look at some of the more common issues arising in accounting for partnerships. We shall start, however, by considering the most basic situation where two people enter into an equal partnership, each putting in the same amount to the business and sharing profits equally. For accounting purposes all we need to do is to open a separate owner's equity account for *each* owner. These are generally referred to as 'partner's capital' accounts. We also need to open another account for each owner, or partner, to record other more short-term transactions. These are commonly referred to as 'partner's current accounts'. They record such things as the partners' entitlement to profit, their drawings etc. It is important in law that the capital transactions and other transactions are separated as different legal treatments may be applied to each of these amounts if the partnership were to be dissolved or cease to exist. For our purposes we can work on the basis that the capital account relates only to deposits and withdrawals of capital from the business and all other items are recorded via the current accounts. Let us use a simple example to illustrate how straightforward partnership accounting should be.

Example 10.2 Jane and John (Part 1)

Jane and John go into business together, sharing profits equally. Jane put in £1000 to the business whilst John put in £9000. They buy some fixed assets for £6000, some stock for £2000 and put the rest into a business bank account.

Before going on to the transactions of the period let us first examine how we would record the information to date on our worksheet.

Worksheet of Jane and John partnership version 1

	Assets			=	Equity + Liabilities	
	Cash	*Fixed assets*	*Stock*		*Jane's equity*	*John's equity*
Item 1	10 000				1 000	9 000
Item 2	−6 000	6 000				
Item 3	−2 000		2 000			

As you can see, all that we have had to do is to open a separate account for each partner which we have called Jane's equity and John's equity. More correctly these should be referred to as capital rather than equity.

Example 10.2 Jane and John (Part 2)

During the first year they sold goods for cash amounting to £30 000 and bought additional stock for £13 000; other expenses amounted to £4000 and they had goods in stock at the end of the year amounting to £3000. The fixed assets are to be depreciated over five years, using straight line depreciation, with no residual value.

Recording the above on the worksheet we find that at the end of the year there is a profit of £12 800 to be divided between the two partners. You will see that on the worksheet reproduced below we have opened partners' current accounts and have put their shares of the profits in their current accounts.

Worksheet for Jane and John in partnership

	Cash	*Fixed assets*	*Stock*	*Jane's equity*	*John's equity*	*Profit and loss*	*Jane's current*	*John's current*
Cash in	10 000			1 000	9 000			
Fixed assets	−6 000	6 000						
Stock	−2 000		2 000					
Sales	30 000					30 000		
Stock	−13 000		13 000					
Expenses	−4 000					−4 000		
Depreciation		−1 200				−1 200		
Cost of sales			−12 000			−12 000		
	15 000	4 800	3 000	1 000	9 000	12 800		
Balance						−12 800	6 400	6 400
Distribution	15 000	4 800	3 000	1 000	9 000	0	6 400	6 400

You should also have noticed that because the profit has been distributed to the partners via their current accounts the final balance on the profit and loss column is nil.

As you can see, the principles involved are very simple. It is really only a question of separating the various transactions. What often makes it more complex is the nature of the partnership agreement itself. For example it may require that interest is paid on the balances on the partners' accounts, or just on the balances on the capital accounts. It might require that certain partners get paid salaries or a bonus, and each of these may happen before or after profits are split. Finally a partnership agreement may require that profits are split according to some formula other than equal shares. Each of these situations can be easily handled if the partnership agreement is well drafted. All one does is follow the instructions contained in it.

Before we look at an example to illustrate how this is done let us examine some of the reasons why these requirements are included in partnership agreements.

Interest on capital

Interest on capital is usually included in a situation where the partners contribute uneven amounts. For instance, since Jane has put in £1000 to John's £9000 they may decide to compensate him for the fact that he has more money at risk by giving interest on the capital before dividing the profit. If this was the case and they decided that interest at 10% would be charged, the new worksheet would appear as shown below.

Worksheet for Jane and John in partnership after charging interest at 10%

	Cash	*Fixed assets*	*Stock*	*Jane's equity*	*John's equity*	*Profit and loss*	*Jane's current*	*John's current*
Cash in	10 000			1 000	9 000			
Fixed assets	−6 000	6 000						
Stock	−2 000		2 000					
Sales	30 000					30 000		
Stock	−13 000		13 000					
Expenses	−4 000					−4 000		
Depreciation		−1 200				−1 200		
Cost of sales			−12 000			−12 000		
Balance	15 000	4 800	3 000	1 000	9 000	12 800		
Interest						−1 000	100	900
Distribution						−11 800	5 900	5 900
	15 000	4 800	3 000	1 000	9 000	0	6 000	6 800

You can see by comparing this with the previous worksheet that the only effect is on the amount in each partner's current account (interest and distribution of profits).

Payment of salaries or bonus

A payment of salary or bonus is often done to reward particular partners for getting new business or for putting in more work in the business than the other partners. If for example Jane worked in the business every day of the week whereas John was rarely involved in the day-to-day running of the business they may decide that Jane should receive a salary of £5000 before interest was paid and before the profit was divided up. The resultant worksheet would be as shown below. Once again it is important to notice that the amount of the profit has not changed but the partners' shares of the profit have been altered to reflect their various inputs to the business. As before the final balance on the profit and loss account after the distributions is nil.

Worksheet for Jane and John in partnership after charging salary and interest at 10%

	Cash	*Fixed assets*	*Stock*	*Jane's equity*	*John's equity*	*Profit and loss*	*Jane's current*	*John's current*
Cash in	10 000			1 000	9 000			
Fixed assets	−6 000	6 000						
Stock	−2 000		2 000					

	Cash	*Fixed assets*	*Stock*	*Jane's equity*	*John's equity*	*Profit and loss*	*Jane's current*	*John's current*
Sales	30 000					30 000		
Stock	−13 000		13 000					
Expenses	−4 000					−4 000		
Depreciation		−1 200				−1 200		
Cost of sales			−12 000			−12 000		
Balance	15 000	4 800	3 000	1 000	9 000	12 800		
Salary						−5 000	5 000	
Interest						−1 000	100	900
Distribution						−6 800	3 400	3 400
	15 000	4 800	3 000	1 000	9 000	0	8 500	4 300

Uneven shares of profit

Because partners bring different skills, expertise and connections to a business venture it is not uncommon for partners to decide to share profits in some other ratio than equally. If, for example, Jane and John decided that, because John had a number of contracts which were the backbone of the business, he should take 60% of the profit and Jane would have the other 40%, the worksheet would be as follows:

Worksheet for Jane and John in partnership after charging salary and interest at 10% Profits split 40:60

	Cash	*Fixed assets*	*Stock*	*Jane's equity*	*John's equity*	*Profit and loss*	*Jane's current*	*John's current*
Cash in	10 000			1 000	9 000			
Fixed asset	−6 000	6 000						
Stock	−2 000		2 000					
Sales	30 000					30 000		
Stock	−13 000		13 000					
Expenses	−4 000					−4 000		
Depreciation		−1 200				−1 200		
Cost of sales			−12 000			−12 000		
Balance	15 000	4 800	3 000	1 000	9 000	12 800		
Salary						−5 000	5 000	
Interest						−1 000	100	900
Distribution						−6 800	2 720	4 080
	15 000	4 800	3 000	1 000	9 000	0	7 820	4 980

As before, the only alteration is to the distribution of the profit. The calculation of the profit itself is unaffected; this change in profit sharing arrangements, like the previous ones, only affects the balance on the partners' current accounts. It is worth noting whilst we are on the subject of current accounts that these accounts are used not only to record distributions of profits etc. at the end of the year but also to record withdrawals from the business. These take place throughout the year.

Partnership final accounts

Before leaving the subject of accounting for partnerships we should compare the format of the partnership final accounts with those of a sole proprietorship. The important aspects of partnership accounts which are reflected in the final accounts are (a) that each partner's equity should be separately identified and (b) that a split should be made between capital and other amounts due to the partners. The majority of the non-capital transactions will be reflected in the balances on the current accounts, although other kinds do occur, e.g. a partner may make a loan to the partnership. This would be dealt with separately, in the same way as any other loan, rather than being included in the partner's current account.

Profit and loss account of Jane and John's partnership for the year ended on xx. xxx. 199X

Sales		£30 000
Cost of goods sold		12 000
Gross profit		18 000
Expenses	4 000	
Depreciation	1 200	5 200
Net profit		12 800
Distributions		
Salary – Jane		5 000
		7 800
Interest – Jane	100	
– John	900	1 000
		6 800
Profit share – Jane	2 720	
– John	4 080	6 800
		Nil

If you compare the format of this profit and loss account with the one for Brian's sole proprietorship which we completed earlier you will see that the only difference is that the partnership profit and loss account has a 'distribution statement' added at the end. Although this is often shown as part of the profit and loss account there are no hard and fast rules. The way in which the accounts are presented is largely up to the partners involved. The balance sheet of the partnership would appear as follows.

Balance sheet of Jane and John's partnership as at xx. xxx. 199X

	£	£
Fixed assets		
Fixed asset	6 000	
Depreciation	1 200	4 800

	£	£
Current assets		
Stock	3 000	
Cash	15 000	
	18 000	
Current liabilities		
Creditors	Nil	
	Nil	
Net current assets		18 000
		22 800
Financed by		
Partners capital accounts		
Jane	1 000	
John	9 000	10 000
Partners current accounts		
Jane	7 820	
John	4 980	12 800
		22 800

We can see that the major difference in the balance sheet is in the section relating to how the business is financed. The owners' equity is divided between the owners and subdivided according to its permanency. The more permanent investment is in the capital accounts and the less permanent is in partners' current accounts.

As we have seen, the fact that a business is set up as a partnership provides us with more problems than if it were a sole proprietorship. But it can also potentially provide the business with greater access to skills and finance. However, the owners are still liable for all the debts of the business should it go bankrupt. It is mainly for this reason that many small businesses are set up as limited companies, and it is this popular form of business organization which we shall now consider.

Limited companies

Unlike the partnership and the sole proprietorship, a limited company is recognized as a separate legal entity quite distinct from its owners. The debts incurred in the normal course of business are those of the company. In the case of a default in payment it is the company which has to be sued rather than the owner. The fact that the owners may also be the managers and the only employees is irrelevant as in the eyes of the law all these roles are different.

Broadly companies are set up in a particular form to meet the requirements of the business concerned. For certain non-commercial organizations requiring the legal status of a company, it is normal for the company to be set up as a company limited by guarantee. This is an unusual form of incorporation. The members promise to contribute a guaranteed amount should the company go under, the amount of such a guarantee normally being limited to £1 per member.

For commercial organizations, the more common form of company is one in which shares are issued to the owners. In this case their liability is limited to the nominal value of the shares. The owners are referred to as shareholders or members. These companies can be either private companies or public companies, and in the latter category they can be listed or unlisted. 'Listed' is a term referring to the fact that the company's shares are traded on a recognized stock exchange. We need not dwell on the detailed differences between the various types of company as this is outside the scope of this book. However, we can broadly say that private companies are generally easier to form but their shares cannot be freely traded on a Stock Exchange, whereas public companies (Plcs) have shares which are freely transferable. They must also have a share capital in excess of £50 000. Public companies are subject to more restrictions and regulation than private companies and may well be subject to other forms of regulation: they must comply with accounting standards and Stock Exchange requirements which would not apply to private companies.

We shall limit our discussion to private companies and discuss the advantages of this type of organization over those already dealt with. The main advantage has already been mentioned: the limitation on the liability of the owners of the business in the event that the business goes bankrupt. Other advantages come from the ability to arrange distribution of profits and indeed of control of the company by means of the share ownership of the various parties concerned. For example, in the case of Jane and John, although they put unequal amounts into the business, under partnership law they both would have an equal say in any decision made, and so would any new partner they took on in the future. If they set up their organization as a company however, they could arrange the voting rights, and therefore control, as they wished. Each share issued normally carries the right to one vote, but non-voting shares can also be issued.

There are disadvantages to the limited company as an organizational form, however. This is because they are subject to various regulatory legislation. For example, they are required to produce accounts annually and to have these audited by a recognized firm of auditors. This can be expensive. A copy of the audited accounts must be lodged at Companies House where it is available for inspection by the public. The form of these accounts is also subject to the requirements of the Companies Acts which require that a company's accounts should consist of:

- the company's balance sheet;
- the company's profit and loss account;
- the directors' report;
- the auditors' report.

In addition to these general requirements there are detailed requirements covering the format and content of the actual accounts.

Clearly to go through these requirements in great detail is outside the scope of an introductory text. Instead we have included below a set of accounts for a private company. The following text highlights areas of difference between the accounts of the limited company and those of the other forms of organization considered. We consider first the profit and loss account.

Profit and loss account of Broll Ltd
for the year to xx. xxx. 199X

	Notes		*This year*	*Last year*
		£	£	£
Sales	1		60 000	45 000
Cost of sales			40 000	30 000
Gross profit			20 000	15 000
Distribution costs	2	3 000		(2 500)
Administration costs	2	11 000	14 000	(9 000)
Profit before taxation			6 000	3 500
Taxation	3		2 600	1 400
Profit after taxation			3 400	2 100
Dividends – interim	4	1 000		—
– final	4	1 600	2 600	1 100
Transfer to reserves			800	1 000

The first difference is in the title of the profit and loss account: the fact that Broll is a limited company must be stated. In addition the profit and loss contains comparative figures for the previous year, as well as references to a number of notes. These notes normally contain greater detail than can be shown on the face of the accounts and as such are an integral part of the analysis of the accounts of a company. This will be discussed in more detail in Chapter 12. We can see that down to gross profit the format is familiar. However, we then find that 'expenses' are classified into broad categories, i.e. distribution and administration costs. These categories are laid down in the legislation and need not concern us other than to note that by so doing a lot of detail is lost.

It is from the point at which the net profit is shown that the real differences arise. The most striking of these is that taxation is included in the profit and loss account. This is because the company is recognized as a separate entity for legal and tax purposes and its profits are liable to corporation tax. In contrast the sole proprietorship and the partnership are not separate legal or taxable entities, and the profit is only taxable as the income of the owners rather than in its own right. Moving on, we find that some of this is distributed by way of 'dividend' and some is transferred to 'reserves'. This part of the profit and loss account can be seen as analogous with the distribution statement in the partnership accounts which we have just considered. The dividends themselves are in fact a form of distribution to the owners (the shareholders) and are 'pro rata' to the number of shares held. There may be an interim and final dividend in one year but not in the other. This is not unusual: the declaration of any dividend depends upon the needs of the business and the availability of both profits and liquid funds to pay them. An interim dividend is in fact essentially a payment made part way through the year and is also dependent on both profitability and the availability of liquid funds. The final line of the profit and loss is the sum transferred to reserves: this is the residual balance being transferred to the profit and loss reserves, and is a profit in this case.

Let us now look at the balance sheet of a limited company and the differences that arise therein.

Balance sheet of Broll Ltd as at xx. xxx. 199X

	Notes		*This year*	*Last year*
		£	£	£
Fixed assets				
Intangible assets	5		10 000	11 000
Tangible assets	6		50 000	56 000
			60 000	67 000
Current assets				
Stocks	7	10 000		7 000
Debtors		10 000		4 000
Cash at bank and in hand		3 500		2 000
		23 500		13 000
Current liabilities				
Creditors		4 000		3 000
Taxation	3	2 600		1 400
Dividends	4	1 600		1 100
		8 200		5 500
Net current assets			15 300	7 500
			75 300	74 500
Capital and reserves				
Share capital	8		70 000	70 000
Retained profits	9		5 300	4 500
			75 300	74 500

As you can see, the top half of the balance sheet is very similar to those we have encountered before apart from the inclusion of dividends and taxation and the fact that a lot of the detail is left to the notes to the accounts. For example, note 6 would contain details of fixed assets bought and sold during the year, as well as the depreciation to date and that charged during the year.

The lower half of the balance sheet is somewhat different as the owners' equity is referred to as share capital and this may consist of different types of share capital. Each type may carry different voting rights etc. This would only be apparent if we looked at the detail contained in the notes. Similarly there may be a number of different types of reserves such as 'revaluation reserves' – a reserve for revalued assets such as land and buildings. However, in this case the only reserve is the retained profits, which is similar to the account for that purpose in the case of a sole proprietorship.

Many examples of published accounts are available but going back to one that we have used earlier provides another illustration (Case Study 10.1).

CASE STUDY 10.1
Merrydown

Profit and loss account
For the year ended 31st March, 1992

	Note	*1992* £	*1991* £
Turnover	1	17 308 782	16 758 701
Cost of sales (including excise duty)		8 715 094	8 858 952
Gross profit		8 593 688	7 899 749
Other operating expenses	2	6 242 618	5 370 317
Profit before interest payable		2 351 070	2 529 432
Interest charges	3	424 970	293 449
Trading profit on ordinary activities before taxation	1	1 926 100	2 235 983
Taxation	4	678 179	738 795
Profit on ordinary activities after taxation		1 247 921	1 497 188
Dividends	5	509 242	451 881
Retained profit for year	18	£738 679	£1 045 307
Earnings per ordinary share	7	17.15p	20.61p

		1992 £	*1991* £
Statement of retained profits for the year ended 31st March, 1992			
Retained profits at 1st April, 1991		4 960 351	3 915 044
Retained profit for year		738 679	1 045 307
Retained profits at 31st March, 1992	18	£5 699 030	£4 960 351

Balance sheets
As at 31st March, 1992

	Note	1992	1991
		£	£
Tangible fixed assets	10	8 239 294	7 348 731
Investment in subsidiaries	11	—	—
		8 239 294	7 348 731
Current assets			
Stock	9	6 078 309	5 307 898
Debtors	12	4 414 865	4 045 167
Cash at bank and in hand		21 617	112 897
		10 514 791	9 465 962
Current liabilities			
Creditors: amounts falling due within one year	13	7 576 136	6 390 220
Net current assets		2 938 655	3 075 742
Total assets less Current liabilities		11 177 949	10 424 473
Provisions for liabilities and charges	14	625 986	612 037
Accruals and deferred income	15	100 304	115 000
		726 290	727 037
Net assets		£10 451 659	£9 697 436

		1992	1991
		£	£
Capital and reserves			
Called-up share capital	17	1 819 229	1 613 863
Share premium account	18	881 570	1 065 281
Revaluation reserve	18	2 051 830	2 057 941
Profit and loss account	18	5 699 030	4 960 351
Shareholders' funds		£10 451 659	£9 697 436

Summary

In this chapter we have introduced you to the idea that different organizational forms require accounts in different forms and to the reasons for them. For example, in the case of a partnership there is a need to differentiate between the amounts belonging to each partner and to distinguish between those amounts that are more permanent in nature and those that are temporary. It should be clear that these requirements are in the main logical and that the differences that do exist are relatively minor in accounting terms. This is as it should be:

the most appropriate form of organization should be governed by sound business considerations rather than by accounting requirements or burdens imposed by legislation.

Review questions

1. Explain in your own words the meaning of the terms trial balance and extended trial balance.
2. Explain the meaning of the term 'final adjustments'.
3. Explain the difference between a sole proprietorship and a partnership.
4. Explain the reasons why partnership agreements often contain clauses relating to interest, bonuses, salaries and division of profits.
5. Why is it advantageous to set a business up as a limited company?
6. What are the differences between a sole proprietorship and a limited liability company?
7. Describe how the choice of organizational form determines the format of the final accounts.

Problems for discussion

The information below forms the basis for the questions which follow.

Susan sets up a business on her own as a sole proprietorship and has the following balance sheet at the end of year 1.

Balance sheet of Susan's business at the end of year 1

Fixed assets	*Cost*	*Depreciation*	*Net book value*
Equipment	12 000	2 400	9 600
Vehicle	6 000	1 500	4 500
	18 000	3 900	14 100
Current assets			
Stock		7 000	
Debtors		6 500	
		13 500	
Current liabilities			
Creditors		6 000	
Bank overdraft		4 500	
		10 500	
Net current assets			3 000
			17 100
Financed by			
Owner's equity			10 000
Profit for year		12 000	
Less: Drawings		4 900	7 100
			17 100

At the end of the first year Susan realized that although the business was profitable she could hardly take out enough money to live on because she was heavily reliant on her bank and creditors already. She also found that a lot of her time which could have been used to produce more goods was being taken up selling goods, collecting debts and generally doing administrative work.

She therefore decided at the start of the second year to take in a partner who would put an additional £5000 into the business and would be able to do some of the selling and other tasks after Susan had trained him. The agreement was a verbal agreement only on the first day of the new year and the two of them agreed to share profits equally.

In the second year the summarized transactions of the business were as follows:

sales, all on credit, £70 000; monies received from debtors, £62 000; purchases, all on credit, £40 000; monies paid to creditors, £38 000; monies introduced by new partner, Bob, £5000; other expenses incurred and paid, £7000; drawings by Susan £7000 and by Bob £5000; goods in stock at the end of the year, £9000.

1 The current partnership agreement between Susan and Bob has the advantage of being simple. If you were advising Susan would you suggest any alternatives to the present agreement and, if so, why?
2 What, if any, additional accounts need to be opened in the second year to cope with the fact that the business is now a partnership and for what reason are they needed?
3 Explain how you propose to deal with the following:

   the balance of £7100, i.e. the profit after drawings;
   the drawings from the business by Susan and Bob in year 2;
   the money introduced by Bob in year 2.

4 Produce the final accounts of the partnership for year 2 in a form suitable for a partnership.
5 Discuss what changes would need to be made if Susan and Bob decided to form a company to take over the business to protect both partners' interests as they stand under the current partnership agreement.

Cash flow statements

11

In this chapter we explore the importance of cash flows to an organization and introduce the cash flow statement as an additional mechanism that can be used to judge the financial health of an organization.

In this chapter we shall consider cash flow statements, the information they provide and their uses. At present, cash flow statements are additional or supplementary statements, although some have argued that a system based on cash accounting should be used as an alternative to the accrual accounting system, with which you are now familiar. Such arguments are beyond the scope of this chapter and the interested reader is referred to the further reading at the end of this chapter. We shall start with a discussion of the need for cash flow information and then move on to look at the contents of the cash flow statement. Finally we shall demonstrate how such statements are constructed and how the information is interpreted.

The need for cash flow information

In Chapter 1 we identified the users of accounts based on the discussion provided in the *Corporate Report* (1975). Apart from identifying the potential users of accounting information, that report also identified the type of information they would need. Amongst other types of information, it clearly identified the need for information on the liquidity of the enterprise. This need was also identified later that year in the report of the Committee on Inflation Accounting, commonly referred to as the Sandilands report. The initial action taken by the accounting profession was to require virtually all companies to provide a statement of source and application of funds. However, from 1992 the statement of source and application of funds has been replaced by a cash flow statement. This is claimed to be an improvement on the previous statement, which had a number of critics and had not gained widespread acceptance.

One of its major problems was that it was not well understood, which meant that it was not used as much as might have been expected. For example, research by Berry *et al.* (1987), showed that only 67% of bankers rated it as very important, compared with 91% rating the balance sheet and profit and loss account as very important. In terms of the bankers' detailed analysis of the information in the source and application of funds statement, this was used by less than 50% of the respondents. This was surprising, as the banking and accounting literature and indeed Egginton's earlier work (1975) would lead one to believe that bankers would be very interested in any statement relating to liquidity. However, comments from the bankers indicated that they redrafted the source and application of funds statement into a format which they could understand and which they felt was more appropriate to their needs.

In this chapter therefore we shall limit our discussion to the cash flow statement. Prior to that, however, it is worth considering what information such a statement provides, and why that information is important. We have already said that users need information about the liquidity of a business, but we need to know what this means in order to understand why they need it. At its most basic this information is about where money comes from and how it is used. To be useful, such information needs to differentiate between regular cash flows which are likely to be repeated, e.g. those arising in a retail business from buying and selling goods, paying wages etc., and other cash flows, e.g. new capital being introduced to the business or new fixed assets being purchased or sold. By separating out these two categories of cash flows the user should be better equipped to arrive at a judgement about what may happen in the future.

So we now know what type of cash flow information should be provided, but the questions that arise are: why do we need an additional statement? And why, at a general level, is cash flow information important? Taking the latter question first, it is important to appreciate that in order for a business to be successful it needs two things. The first of these is that it is profitable in the long run. The profit and loss account helps the user to arrive at a judgement in relation to the profitability of a business. The second requirement is that it is able to pay its debts as they fall due. As we explained in Chapter 9, if suppliers and lenders are not paid they will take action to call in a receiver and have the business wound up. The problem is that the profit and loss account and balance sheet provide very limited information on this aspect of the financial performance of a business.

Such information can be very revealing. For example, in the case of Polly Peck, which went into receivership in 1991, despite a trading profit of £139m. Polly Peck had a net cash outflow from operations of £129m. In other words, although it was making a profit it was paying out more than it was getting in. This example underlines the fact that in order to survive, a company needs to be both profitable and solvent. In the case of Polly Peck the company was profitable but was not solvent, even in the short term.

What does a cash flow statement show?

Having established the need for a statement of cash flows we need to look in more detail at what the statement shows. In broad terms, as we have pointed out, it tells us where we got money from, and how it was used. The money coming in is referred to as cash inflows, whilst money going out is referred to as cash outflows. The difference between the cash inflows and the cash outflows is known as the net cash flow, which can be either a net cash inflow or a net cash outflow, depending on the magnitude of the two components. Typical cash inflows would be moneys generated from trading, commonly referred to as cash flows from operations, moneys from new share issues or other forms of long-term finance, and any moneys received from the sale of fixed assets. Typical outflows would be moneys used to buy new fixed assets, to pay tax and dividends and to repay debenture holders or other providers of long-term capital. As we shall see, the cash flow statement separates these cash flows into various categories. The format we shall follow is that recommended in the accounting standard known as Financial Reporting Standard No. 1 (FRS 1) issued in 1991. We shall use the example of a cash flow statement shown as Example 11.1 as the vehicle for explaining what a cash flow statement contains. We shall then look at an example of how such a statement is constructed.

Example 11.1

Sample cash flow statement

Net cash inflow from operating activities		5000
Returns on investments and servicing of finance		
Interest paid	(200)	
Dividends paid	(2500)	
Net cash flow from returns on investment and servicing activities		(2700)
Taxation		
Corporation tax paid	(3000)	
Net cash outflow from taxation		(3000)
Investing activities		
Payment to acquire fixed assets	(900)	
Receipts from sales of fixed assets	50	
Net cash outflow from investing activity		(850)
Net cash inflow before financing		(1550)

Financing		
Issue of ordinary share capital	300	
Repayment of loan	(150)	
Net cash inflow from financing		150
Decrease in cash or cash equivalents		(1400)

As you can see, the cash flow statement shows cash flows under five separate headings. The first of these relates to cash flow from operating activities, broadly trading activities. This figure is arrived at by adjusting the profit figure by items that do not involve cash flows, e.g. depreciation, and by movements in creditors, debtors, stock, etc. It tells us what the cash flow from the normal activities of the business is. Clearly, in most cases this should be a positive cash flow, i.e. a cash inflow. The note below provides an illustration of how this figure is reconciled to the other figures in the balance sheet and the profit and loss account.

Reconciliation of operating profit to net cash flow from operating activities

Operating profit	4140
Depreciation charges	880
Loss on sale of fixed assets	12
Increase in stocks	(194)
Increase in debtors	(72)
Increase in creditors	234
	5000

You will note that an increase in stocks is shown in brackets, indicating that money has been used to pay for that increase in stocks. Similarly some money has been used to provide more credit to customers. This is shown as a cash outflow in respect of debtors. We can also see that some of these cash outflows have been financed by taking more time to pay our suppliers resulting in an increase in creditors.

The second heading in the cash flow statement relates to money earned from investments. This may be in the form of interest on surplus money invested or dividends from investments in other businesses. Also included under this heading are moneys paid to those people who provide finance. This may be in the form of dividends or interest. Each type is shown separately, allowing the user to identify from the rest of the information in the accounts whether these are discretionary, as is the case with dividends on ordinary shares, or compulsory, as is likely to be the case with interest. This separation is important, as although a business can delay the declaration and payment of dividends, it will need to cover its non-discretionary outgoings by its cash flow from operations if it is to survive in the short term.

The third heading relates to cash flows in respect of taxation, specifically money paid out and recovered in respect of corporation tax. We pointed out in Chapter 10 that, unlike unincorporated businesses such as sole proprietorships and partnerships, companies are liable to corporation tax on their profits. The calculation of the tax liability and the timing of the payment of this tax is subject to complex regulations, which you do not need to understand. It is important, however, to recognize that tax is normally payable in the year following the year in which the profit is made, so this is a recurrent cash flow, rather than a one-off. The amount of tax payable and therefore the amount of the cash flow will, however, differ from year to year.

The next heading is concerned with investing activities. This would include amounts received from the sale of fixed assets and cash outflows in respect of purchase of fixed assets. Clearly such cash flows are different from those we have discussed so far. They tend to be non-recurrent, as an individual fixed asset can only be sold or replaced once.

The final heading is the cash flows relating to the financing of the business. This would include amounts received from share issues, new loans or debentures – in other words, from long-term financing. It would also show amounts paid out in respect of loans or debentures that have been repaid during the year and in respect of any shares redeemed.

The final figure shown on the cash flow statement is the increase or decrease in cash or cash equivalents. This can be reconciled fairly easily with the information in the balance sheet. However, in order to do that we need to know what is included under this heading. The definition of cash equivalents included in FRS 1 is given in Key Concept 11.1.

KEY CONCEPT 11.1
Cash equivalents

Short-term, highly liquid investments which are readily convertible into known amounts of cash without notice and which were within three months of maturity when acquired, less advances from banks repayable within three months from the date of the advance.

Before moving on to work through an example of how these statements are constructed, it is worth reflecting on what the cash flow statement used in Example 11.1 tells us about the business in question. The first item to note is that, unlike Polly Peck, the business has a positive cash inflow from operations. However, if we look at the cash outflows that are recurrent, we find that those in respect of dividends and tax exceed the net cash inflow from operations. This may or may not be a cause for concern, depending upon two factors. The first is whether the tax due for next year is as much as that paid this year. The second factor is whether the dividends are likely to be the same next year. We can find out the answers to these questions from the balance sheet and the profit and loss account, as the tax and dividends will be included there.

The cash flow statement also highlights the fact that the business is investing in fixed assets and by looking at the information contained elsewhere in the accounts you could arrive at a judgement as to whether this is additional capacity or replacement of existing capacity. It is also worth noting that the business is raising new long-term capital – this may indicate future expansion. Finally, the fact that there is a decrease in cash and cash equivalents needs further investigation. This can be done either via the notes to the cash flow statement or directly from the movements on the balance sheet from one year to the next.

Having examined the end product in some detail, we shall now work through a simple example and use that as a vehicle for explaining the ideas involved. We shall start with a new business and see how the cash flow statement is prepared from the basic transaction information.

Example 11.2

On 1 April 19X1, Downsend Ltd started business, buying and selling electrical goods. They arranged an overdraft facility of £10 000 if they needed it. The transactions for the first 12 months are summarized below.

April

The owners bought 10 000 ordinary shares of £1 nominal value.

They purchased electrical goods for £8000 on one month's credit.

They purchased shop fittings for £10 000 and paid cash.

They sold goods for £4000 of which £3000 was cash and the rest was credit sales.

They paid the year's rent, in advance, of £6000 in cash.

May–March

The cash sales were £30 000 and credit sales were £25 000.

Cash amounting to £8000 was received from debtors.

They purchased another £40 000 of goods on credit and paid their creditors £34 000.

Paid wages to the assistant of £6500.

At the end of March 1992, the goods in stock had a cost price of £16 000. They decided to depreciate the fittings, which were unlikely to have any scrap value, over five years using the straight line method.

Their accountant calculated that they would owe corporation tax of £3000 and the directors decided to declare a dividend of £5000 for the year, none of which was paid in the year.

Stage 1

The first stage is to record the transactions on a worksheet. This would appear as shown below.

Worksheet of Downsend Ltd
for the year ended 31 March 1992

Description	*Bank*	*Fittings*	*Stock*	*Debtors*	*Shares*	*Profit & loss*	*Creditors*	*Tax*	*Dividend*
Capital	10 000				10 000				
Goods			8 000				8 000		
Fittings	−10 000	10 000							

Description	Bank	Fittings	Stock	Debtors	Shares	Profit & loss	Creditors	Tax	Dividend
Sales	3 000			1 000		4 000			
Rent	−6 000					−6 000			
Sales	30 000			25 000		55 000			
Debtors	8 000			−8 000					
Purchases			40 000				40 000		
Creditors	−34 000						−34 000		
Wages	−6 500					−6 500			
Cost of sales			−32 000			−32 000			
Depreciation		−2 000				−2 000			
Balance	−5 500	8 000	16 000	18 000	10 000	12 500	14 000		
Tax						−3 000		3 000	
Dividends						−5 000			5 000
Fainl balance	−5 500	8 000	16 000	18 000	10 000	4 500	14 000	3 000	5 000

From the worksheet we can now produce the cash flow statement. The first figure we need to arrive at is the net cash inflow from operating activities. We shall initially concentrate on using the information from the worksheet. However, in order to facilitate your understanding we shall also look later in this chapter at how the cash flow statement can be produced from the final accounts for Downsend Ltd.

Stage 2

Using the information contained in the worksheet, we first need to calculate the net cash flow from operating activities. We shall do this using the information contained in the profit and loss column and the cash column. We shall start by identifying those items in the profit and loss column that are associated with cash coming in to the business (the cash inflows) and cash being paid out of the business (cash outflows).

In terms of the cash inflows, we can see from the cash column that the money received in respect of sales amounted to £41 000, i.e. cash sales of £33 000 plus £8000 received from the debtors in respect of credit sales. In terms of the cash outflows relating to operations, we find that £34 000 was paid to creditors in respect of stock purchased during the year. In addition, Downsend paid £6000 for rent and £6500 for wages. If you look at all the other figures in the profit and loss column you will see that they do not affect the bank column and there is therefore no cash inflow or outflow. From this we can calculate our 'Net cash inflow from operating activities', as follows.

	£	£
Cash from cash sales and debtors		41 000
Less:		
Cash paid for purchases	34 000	
Rent	6 000	
Wages	6 500	46 500
Net cash outflow from operating activities		(5 500)

We now need to look for the other cash flows. These are easily identified on the worksheet by looking at the bank column. There is a cash inflow of £10 000 when the shares were issued, and a cash outflow in respect of the purchase of the fittings amounting to £10 000. As regards the tax liability and the dividend, neither of these amounts have been paid out during the year, so they do not affect the cash flow statement for this year. Thus we have all the information required to prepare our cash flow statement, and this would appear as follows.

Cash flow statement of Downsend Ltd

Net cash outflow from operating activities		(5 500)
Returns on investments and servicing of finance		
Dividends paid	—	
Net cash flow from returns on investment and servicing activities		—
Taxation		
Corporation tax paid	—	
Net cash outflow from taxation		—
Investing activities		
Payment to acquire tangible fixed assets	(10 000)	
Net cash outflow from investing activity		(10 000)
Net cash inflow before financing		(15 500)
Financing		
Issue of ordinary share capital	10 000	
Net cash inflow from financing		10 000
Decrease in cash or cash equivalents		(5 500)

Preparing a cash flow statement from final accounts

At the start of Example 11.2 we said that there were two ways of arriving at a cash flow statement. The easiest is working from a worksheet or the prime records, which is what we have done. The alternative is to work from the information in the final accounts, which although applying the same principles uses some different techniques. We shall now look at this technique in respect of Downsend Ltd. For this purpose we need to produce the final accounts of Downsend Ltd. These are reproduced below. You should note that as it is the first year, there is no opening balance sheet. However, in order to illustrate the technique we have included a comparative balance sheet with nil balances. The profit and loss account and balance sheet of Downsend Ltd are reproduced below.

Profit and loss account of Downsend Ltd
for the year ended 31 March 19X2

Sales	59 000
Cost of sales	32 000
Gross profit	27 000

Administration expenses	12 500	
Distribution expenses	2 000	14 500
Operating profit		12 500
Taxation		3 000
Profit after tax		9 500
Dividends		5 000
Retained profit		4 500

Notes
Depreciation on the fittings amounting to £2000 is included in the Distribution expenses.

Balance sheet of Downsend Ltd
as at 31 March 1992

	Cost	*Depreciation*	*19X2*	*19X1*
Fixed assets				
Shop fittings	10 000	2 000	8 000	0
	10 000	2 000	8 000	0
Current assets				
Stock		16 000		0
Debtors		18 000		0
		34 000		0
Creditors: Falling due within one year				
Creditors		14 000		0
Tax		3 000		0
Dividend		5 000		0
Bank overdraft		5 500		0
		27 500		0
Net current assets			6 500	0
			14 500	0
Financed by				
Ordinary shares			10 000	0
Retained profit			4 500	0
			14 500	0

The first figure we need to identify is the cash flow from operations. This we can do by extracting the figures from the profit and loss account and balance sheet. From the profit and loss we need the operating profit and all those items not involving cash flows – in this case, depreciation. These non-cash-flow items need to be added back to the profit to get to a figure representing the cash flows. We than need to identify any amounts included in the figures used in arriving at the profit for which a cash flow has not yet taken place. These are sales on credit where the cash has not yet been received i.e. the increase in debtors, and increases in stocks. Similarly we need to identify any purchases for which no payment has been made, the increase in creditors. This can be done from the balance sheet. A useful technique is to add an extra column to the balance sheets to show these changes, as shown below.

Balance sheet changes of Downsend Ltd

	Cost	Depreciation	19X2	19X1	Changes
Fixed assets					
Shop fittings	10 000	2 000	8 000	0	8 000
	10 000	2 000	8 000	0	8 000
Current assets					
Stock		16 000		0	16 000
Debtors		18 000		0	18 000
		34 000		0	34 000
Creditors: Falling due within one year					
Creditors		14 000		0	14 000
Tax		3 000		0	3 000
Dividend		5 000		0	5 000
Bank overdraft		5 500		0	5 500
		27 500		0	27 500
Net current assets			6 500	0	6 500
			14 500	0	14 500
Financed by					
Ordinary shares			10 000	0	10 000
Retained profit			4 500	0	4 500
			14 500	0	14 500

We can now arrive at the figure for the net cash flow from operating activities, as shown below.

Operating profit	12 500
Depreciation – fittings	2 000
Increase in stock	(16 000)
Increase in debtors	(18 000)
Increase in creditors	14 000
Net cash outflow from operating activities	(5 500)

If we now look at the balance sheet changes column this will provide us with the basis to complete the rest of the statement. We can see that we have invested in fixed assets as there is an increase in fixed assets of £8000 shown in our changes column. However, we know from the 19X2 balance sheet that this figure is arrived at after taking off depreciation. We also know from Chapter 8 that depreciation does not involve any cash flows so we need to add this back to find what we spent of the fixed assets as follows.

Net change in fixed assets	8 000
Add: Depreciation charge for the year	2 000
Actual change in fixed assets	10 000

In reality, with fixed assets there are likely to have been many movements. However, the purchases for the year can normally be found in the note to the accounts relating to fixed assets. Working down the balance sheet changes column we have already dealt with the changes in stock, debtors and creditors in arriving at the cash flow from operations. This takes us to the tax and the dividends, which are still owing in this case so have not involved any cash flow. Once again in reality there is usually an opening balance and a closing balance which when combined with information from the profit and loss account will enable us to identify the cash flows. For example, if we calculated that what we owed in tax for the year was £30, we would show this as the tax charge in the profit and loss account. If at the start of the year we owed £10 in tax and we owed £25 at the end of the year, we could then calculate what had been paid during the year as follows.

	£
Tax owing at the start of the year	10
Tax charge for the year	30
	40
Tax owing at the end of the year	25
Therefore the tax paid is	15

A similar calculation could be done in respect of dividends. These calculations can be fairly complex in reality; however, you need only be concerned with the principle in order to facilitate your understanding.

Returning to the changes column on our balance sheet, we find that there has been a change in share capital, which in this case represents moneys paid in to the business. We need to bring this in to our cash flow statement under the appropriate heading. The only other change is to retained profit and we have already dealt with profits in arriving at our cash flow from operations so this has already been dealt with. We are now able to draw up the cash flow statement, which would of course be the same as the one already completed.

Before leaving the discussion of Downsend Ltd it is worth returning to the cash flow statement and commenting on what information it gives us. We can see that although the business is profitable, it has a net cash outflow during the year. This is caused by the fact that all the money introduced by the owners at the start of the year was used in buying shop fittings, leaving no money for the purchase of stock or for financing the credit sales. From our reconciliation of the operating profit with the cash flow from operations, we can see that part of this has been financed by the creditors. We can also see from the bottom of the cash flow statement that the rest has been financed from a decrease in cash and cash equivalents – in this case a bank overdraft. Thus the business is heavily reliant on its creditors and the bank for its continued existence. However, as an overdraft limit of £10 000 was set up when the business was started, there may not be a problem.

Summary

In this chapter we have introduced the cash flow statement and looked at the ways in which it can be produced. More importantly, we have tried to give an indication of what information can be obtained from

CASE STUDY 11.1
Merrydown

Group cash flow statement
For the year ended 31st March, 1992

	Note	1992 £	1992 £	1991 £	1991 £
Operating activities					
Cash received from customers		19 236 634		17 606 611	
Cash payments to suppliers		(12 000 773)		(11 464 361)	
Cash paid to and on behalf of employees		(2 988 810)		(2 736 954)	
Other cash payments		(2 883 101)		(2 824 156)	
Net cash inflow from continuing operating activities	a		1 363 950		581 140
Returns on investments and servicing of finance					
Interest paid		(424 970)		(293 449)	
Dividends paid		(459 954)		(408 845)	
Net cash outflow from returns on investments and servicing finance			(884 924)		(702 294)
Taxation					
UK corporation tax paid			(764 816)		(679 037)
Investing activities					
Purchase of tangible fixed assets		(1 309 311)		(1 295 825)	
Sale of plant and machinery		9 184		6 731	
Net cash outflow from investing activities			(1 300 127)		(1 289 094)
Net cash outflow before financing			£(1 585 917)		£(2 089 285)
Financing					
Issue of ordinary share capital	d	(21 655)		—	
Govermment grant		(1 602)		(210 000)	
Net cash inflow from financing			(23 257)		(210 000)
Decrease in cash and cash equivalents	c		(1 562 660)		(1 879 285)
			£(1 585 917)		£(2 089 285)

Notes to the cash flow statement
For the year ended 31st March, 1992

a. Reconciliation of operating profit to net cash inflow prom operating activities

	1992	1991
	£	£
Operating profit	2 351 070	2 529 432
Depreciation charges	403 453	329 270
Amortisation of government grant	(16 298)	(95 000)
Decrease/(increase) in stocks	(770 411)	(1 345 407)
Decrease/(increase) in debtors	(369 698)	(1 137 972)
Increase/(decrease) in creditors	(234 166)	300 817
Net cash inflow from continuing operating activities	£1 363 950	£581 140

b. Analysis of changes in cash and cash equivalents during the year

	1992	1991
	£	£
Balance at 1st April, 1991	(3 091 766)	(1 212 481)
Net cash outflow	(1 562 660)	(1 879 285)
Balance at 31st March, 1992	£(4 654 426)	£(3 091 766)

c. Analysis of the balances of cash and cash equivalents as shown in the balance sheet

	1992	1991	Change in year
	£	£	£
Cash at bank and in hand	21 617	112 897	(91 280)
Bank overdrafts	(4 676 043)	(3 204 663)	(1 471 380)
	£(4 654 426)	£(3 091 766)	£(1 562 660)

d. Analysis of changes in financing during the year

	Share capital (including premium)
	£
Balance at 1st April, 1991	2 679 144
Cash inflow from financing	21 655
Balance at 31st March, 1992	£2 700 799

such a statement and why that information is important. Perhaps the major message that the reader should take from this chapter is that a business cannot survive merely by being profitable. It also needs to stay solvent, and this aspect of the business also has to be properly managed. We shall be discussing how cash flows can be managed later in this book. Before leaving cash flow statements, it is worth looking at an example from a set of published accounts, one of which is shown as Case Study 11.1.

References

Accounting Standards Steering Committee (1975) *The Corporate Report*, ASC.
Inflation Accounting: Report of the Inflation Accounting Steering Committee (1975), Cmnd. 6225, HMSO.
Financial Reporting Standard No. 1, FRS 1 (1991) *Cash Flow Statements*, Accounting Standards Board.
Berry, A., Citron, D. and Jarvis, R. (1987) *The Information Needs of Bankers dealing with Large and Small Companies*, Certified Accountants Research Report 7, Certified Accountants Publications.
Egginton, D. 'The changes that Britain's bankers would like to see', *Accountants Magazine*, 27 July 1975, pp. 14–15.

Further reading

A. Berry, *Financial Accounting – An introduction*, Chapter 13 (Chapman and Hall, 1993).
T.A. Lee, *Cash flow accounting* (Van Nostrand Reinhold, 1984).

Review questions

1 What is the main aim of a cash flow statement?
2 What are the claimed advantages of the cash flow statement?
3 How does 'net cash flow from operating activities' differ from operating profit?
4 How does an increase in the depreciation charge affect the operating profit and the 'net cash flow from operating activities'?
5 What is meant by 'cash and cash equivalents'?

Problems for discussion and analysis

1 Discuss the impact of each of the items below on the balance sheet, profit and loss account and cash flow statement, giving reasons for your answer where appropriate.

(a) During the year the company sold a fixed asset with a net book value of £5000 for £3000.
(b) The company also revalued its land from its original cost of £130 000 to £200 000.
(c) The building which had cost £90 000 and on which depreciation of £30 000 had been provided was revalued to £100 000.
(d) The company had also made an issue of 100 000 8% £1 preference shares at a price of £1.20 per share.
(e) The company had paid back a long-term loan to the bank of £80 000.

2 The information on the transactions of Newspurt Ltd in its first year of trading are given below.

May 19X2
Issued 50 000 £1 ordinary shares for £50 000.
Purchased a machine for £30 000 and paid immediately.
Bought a delivery van for £10 000 and paid immediately.
Paid tax and insurance on the van of £400.
Paid a quarter's rent in advance of £2000.
Purchased raw materials costing £10 000 on one month's credit.

June 19X2–April 19X3
Made sales of £90 000 all on credit.
Purchased raw materials costing £40 000, all on credit.
Paid four quarters' rent in advance, amounting to £8000.
Paid creditors £38 000.
Received £70 000 from debtors.
Paid wages of £25 000.

At the end of the year Newspurt Ltd had raw materials in stock which cost £3000. The directors decided to depreciate the van over five years and the machine over four years using straight line depreciation and assuming no residual value. The accountant had calculated that no corporation tax liability would arise and the directors had decided not to pay any dividends.

(a) Produce a worksheet for Newspurt Ltd.
(b) Produce a cash flow statement for Newspurt Ltd.
(c) Identify any additional information about Newspurt Ltd that the user can get from the cash flow statement that would not have been apparent in the profit and loss account and balance sheet.

12 Financial statement analysis

The concepts, uses and limitations of financial analysis are explored in this chapter, in which we return to the different users and their needs to provide a framework in which an informed analysis can take place. Some of the basic techniques of analysis are explained and explored through the use of a single case study. Finally, the chapter looks at the limitations of financial analysis, including the impacts of price changes and different accounting choices.

In the previous chapters we have considered the way in which accounting information is produced and what the components of financial statements mean. In this chapter we shall consider the statements themselves and more specifically the ways in which they can be analysed. This chapter is not intended to be comprehensive in its approach to the subject of financial analysis but to offer some guidelines to the subject and to provide the reader with some basic tools of analysis. We shall consider the needs of the person for whom the analysis is being undertaken or, in other words, the 'user group'. Using this approach it is possible to establish the form of analysis most appropriate to these needs. The 'user groups' are discussed at the start of the book.

Investor group

The investor group was discussed previously as a homogeneous group with similar needs, but there are in fact different types of investor. For sole traders and partnerships the investor is the owner or partner. The equivalent of this type of investor in a company is the ordinary shareholder. These investors will be referred to from now on as equity investors. We need to establish what this group has in common, and what distinguishes the equity investor in a large company from the equivalent in a sole proprietorship. In general, equity investors take on all the risks associated with ownership and are entitled to any rewards after other prior claims have been met. For a sole trader the equity investor, i.e. the owner, is also likely to be heavily involved in the management and day-to-day running of the business. Where there is this direct involvement his needs will be the same as for managers (discussed below). In the case of larger organizations, such as large private companies and all public companies, there is likely to be a separation of ownership and management. For large businesses the final accounts meet the information needs of the shareholders, who are in the main properly characterized by the term 'absentee owners'. In general, the smaller the organization and the greater the direct involvement of the owners in the day-to-day running of the business, the more detail will be required. However, the information required to meet the needs of equity investors is broadly the same irrespective of the type of ownership involved. We therefore suggest that the basic needs of this group of users can be met with information about:

- profitability, especially future profitability;
- management efficiency (for example, are assets being utilized efficiently?);
- return on their investment
  - within the firm;
  - compared with alternatives;
- risk being taken
  - financial risk;
  - business risk;
- returns to owners
  - dividends;
  - drawings etc.

Preference shareholders

For investments in companies it is also possible to purchase a share known as a preference share. These shares are generally seen as less risky than ordinary shares and therefore do not normally earn as great a reward. Although it is difficult to generalize on the differences between these shares and ordinary shares (this varies from share to share), normally preference shareholders will be entitled to a *fixed* rate of dividend and to repayment before ordinary shareholders in the event of the business being 'wound up'. Because of the nature of the shares, these users are likely to be interested in:

- profitability, mainly future profitability;
- the net realizable value of the assets;
- the extent by which their dividends are covered by profit.

If we compare the needs of these two groups of investors we can see that this group is more likely to be interested in the extent to which income is safe, rather than in the growth of the business. This is because in most cases it is only ordinary shareholders who will benefit from such growth. The preference shareholders' return is in the form of a dividend at a fixed rate irrespective of the profits made.

In many ways this type of investment is similar to long-term loans (we shall deal with these in more detail later.) The similarity is at a fairly superficial level in that the return is at a fixed rate. There are important differences beyond this superficial similarity, however. In the case of a loan the interest has to be paid whether or not profits are made, whereas preference dividends, like dividends on ordinary shares, are not due to be paid until they are declared by the directors of the company. This is one of the reasons why the interest on loans is treated as an expense in arriving at the profit before taxation, whereas the preference dividend is shown as an appropriation of profit after tax. The differences in the way in which they are dealt with in the accounts also reflects the different treatments in tax legislation. The interest on the loan is allowed for tax purposes. It is an expense in arriving at the taxable profit. Another reason for the difference in treatment is that loans are repayable at some specified point in time whereas, unless specifically stated (as in the case of redeemable preference shares, preference shares are *permanent capital*. In this way they are more similar to ordinary shares: the capital is only repaid if the business ceases to exist. We can now move on to look at other providers of capital who are also users of accounting information.

Lenders

Lenders, as we saw in Chapter 9, can be conveniently subdivided into three subgroups: short-term creditors, medium-term lenders and long-term lenders.

Short-term creditors are normally trade creditors, i.e. those who supply the business with goods on credit. Their areas of interest would be:

- liquidity/solvency, short term;
- net realizable value of the assets;
- profitability and future growth;
- risk (financial and business).

Medium-term lenders may well be bankers and other financial institutions. Their areas of interest would be:

- profitability (future profits provide cash for repayment of loans);
- security and the nature of the security;
- financial stability.

Long-term lenders will have the same needs as medium-term lenders, except if they are 'secured' lenders. A secured lender is someone who has a legal charge on the assets of the business and can claim those assets if the business does not repay or service the lending in accordance with the lending agreement. In the case of secured lenders their areas of interest are likely to be:

- risk, especially financial risk;
- security – net realizable value of specific assets;
- interest cover – how well their interest is covered by the profits being made.

As can be seen these different types of lender have broadly the same needs for information. It is the emphasis that changes depending on whether one is looking from a short- or a long-term perspective.

Employees

Employees are interested in judging job security and in assessing their wages especially their relative fairness. Their areas of interest are likely to be:

- profitability – average profits per employee for the purposes of productivity bargaining;
- liquidity – future trends in profits.

There has been considerable debate over the extent to which these needs are met by conventional accounts and whether an alternative statement such as a statement of value added would meet these needs better.

Auditors

Auditors are not normally seen as a user of accounting information. However, in order to carry out an audit efficiently an analysis of accounts is frequently carried out. For the purposes of planning and carrying out their audit, the auditors are likely to be interested in:

- trends in sales, profit, costs, etc.;
- variations from norms;
- accounting policies.

Management

It is very difficult to describe the needs of managers as they will vary greatly from situation to situation. They will be interested in all the information above, however, as they are likely to be judged on their performance by outside investors or lenders. In addition, they will require detailed information on the performance of the business as a whole and on the parts of the business to enable them to manage the business on a day-to-day basis. This information could include such items as profitability by major product, costs per product, changes in sales or component mix etc.

The list of users dealt with above is not intended to be comprehensive. We have tried to give the reader a flavour of the differing needs of the various groups discussed and to indicate that some of these will not be provided by the annual accounts. At this stage we need to establish what, if any, needs are common and what other factors need to be considered.

Some common needs which can be readily identified are profitability, liquidity and risk. The problem is how these are measured and how to judge good or bad performance. Before going on to discuss these issues in detail, let us first examine the common needs in more detail and look at the context in which the financial analysis is to be carried out.

Common needs

The most obvious need that virtually all these groups have in common is the need for information about the profitability of the business. This can be divided into two components, one relating to past profitability and the other to future profitability. Another factor that is common to a number of groups is the requirement for information about financial risk and about 'liquidity' or 'solvency', as it is often called. Other themes that emerge concern the return on the investment in the business. This has associated measures such as the riskiness of the return (dividend cover or interest cover). There are also a number of needs that are more specific to particular user groups. A good example of these is the security measures used by lenders. We shall examine how the common needs can be analysed in some detail after we have established the context in which the analysis should take place.

Context for financial statement analysis

Before doing any analysis it is important to remember that it must be seen in a wider context than merely a mechanical exercise using various techniques. Some of the factors that are directly relevant to any analysis of business performance are as follows.

KEY CONCEPT 12.1
Financial analysis

Good financial analysis requires that the *person* for whom the analysis is being done is clearly identified together with the *purpose* of the analysis. It is unlikely to be usefui if it does not take into account as many relevant factors as possible.

The size of the business

The fact that a business is the size of ICI makes it less vulnerable to the decisions of others outside the organization. For example a banker might lend money to a small business at a rate of 3% or 4% above base rate, whereas for ICI or BP the rate would be much lower. Similarly the banker is likely to ask for security from the small business whereas with ICI the name itself is enough security.

The riskiness of the business

Apart from size the nature of the business needs to be taken into account: a gold prospecting business will have a different level of risk and return than a building society. Other factors which affect the risk, known as business risk, are the reliance on a small number of products, the degree of technological innovation and, of course, vulnerability to competition.

The economic, social and political environment

Examples of the way in which the economic, social and political environment affects industry can be found in virtually any daily paper. For example, if the pound goes down relative to the dollar this will affect imports and exports and some firms will gain or suffer accordingly. Changes in interest rates often have sharp effects on firms that are financed by a large amount of borrowing (loans or overdrafts). The effects of the social environment tend to be more subtle. A study of recent history shows a movement towards acceptance of profit as the prime motivation for business, whereas in some countries this is balanced with regard for the environment or for ensuring full employment. These social changes frequently coincide with political changes, although the environmental issue is a good example of a social effect which is likely to transcend political changes. This was very apparent in the debate in 1989 on the privatization of the water industry.

The industry trends, effects of changes in technology

In order to make any judgements about performance and more especially about the future it is vital to understand the way the industry is going. For example, in the late 1970s and early 1980s most of the major British toy manufacturers went bankrupt. This was in part due to changes in the nature of the industry and the product. The industry was being affected by cheap imports, the impact of large buyers, and the high rates of inflation and interest. The product required in the market place was also changing towards electronic toys rather than the traditional die cast model cars such as Dinky toys.

Effect of price changes

We have just mentioned high rates of inflation. The effect of price changes may be more specific. For example, the price of property in recent years has been rising faster than the general change in prices. Over the last 20 or more years there have been a number of proposals for taking account of price changes in corporate reports, none of which has gained general acceptance. However, the fact that the perfect solution has not been found does not mean that the problem can be ignored as even low rates of inflation of 5% can mean that what appears to be a gentle growth of sales is in fact a decline. It should be pointed out that although we normally think of price changes in terms of price rises, there are many examples where the effects of new technology, competition and economies of scale have led to reductions in price. The most obvious examples are in the electronics industries and the computer industry. For example, a calculator cost approximately £15 for the most basic model at the start of the 1970s; an equivalent today would be less than £5.

Projections and predictions of the future

While we can all take a guess at the future, clearly there is a case for taking into account the opinion of those more closely involved with the business and those who have expertise in the industry and in analysing likely economic trends. Financial analysis must, after all, relate not only to what has happened but also to what is going to happen.

Having looked at some of the factors which need to be taken into account it should be clear that, although a set of accounts may contain some of the information, a lot of other information will have to be obtained from other sources. These other sources of information can be conveniently subdivided into sources external to the business and those internal to the business. Some examples of these other sources are discussed below.

Sources external to the business

- **Government statistics**, such as the monthly *Digest of Statistics*, Department of Trade and Industry statistics and HMSO publications.
- **Trade journals** These may be specific to the trade or more general professional or business journals such as *Management Today* or *Marketing Weekly*.
- **Financial press** A lot of information can be gleaned from the financial pages of quality newspapers, from the *Financial Times* and from specialist publications such as the *Investors' Chronicle*.
- **Databases** There are now a number of on-line databases, such as Datastream, which can be accessed for information. These contain information about other companies, industry statistics, and economic indicators.
- **Specialist agencies** may provide an industry-wide analysis, general financial reports, credit-scoring services and many other services.

The first three of these sources are likely to be fairly readily accessible in good libraries. The others are more specialist and access may be more limited and much more expensive.

Sources internal to the business

Chairman's statement or review of the year's activities

In the case of public companies a chairman's statement is included with the annual accounts. It contains summarized information for the year, as well as some predictions for the future. The information contained should not be taken at face value as it is likely to reflect one point of view which itself may be biased. The statement often highlights only the positive side. As a senior lending banker commented, 'It is as important to ascertain what is left out as it is to ascertain what has been included'.

Directors' report

This is a statutory requirement for all companies and the information contained in it is laid down in the Companies Acts. The statutes, however, lay down a *minimum* and that is therefore normally *all* the information that is given.

The balance sheet

This will give information about the position at a point in time. The information is therefore really only valid at that point in time and given that the median time for publication by large companies is over three months after the balance sheet date and for small companies it is thought to be at least ten months, the information may have very little bearing on the current position. This question of how timely the information is has a major bearing on what can be achieved from an analysis of the accounting information contained in the published accounts.

The profit and loss account

As with the balance sheet the information contained is probably fairly old by the time it is published. Another problem is that the information tends to be summarized information which may mean that the performance of the weaker parts of a business are not necessarily readily apparent as they are offset by the performance of the stronger parts.

The accounting policies statement

As we have seen, there are a number of different ways of dealing with such items as stocks. Is FIFO or average cost being used? For depreciation, is reducing balance or straight line being used? Many other items are subject to similar preconditions, and so it is vital to understand the basis which has been adopted. This should be stated in the statement of accounting policies. Unfortunately, all too often, these statements are of such generality that they are fairly meaningless. It is not uncommon to find a statement on depreciation which says that 'depreciation is charged on the straight line method over the useful life of the assets'. The problem with such a statement is that different assets have different lives and different residual values. In fact it is quite likely that different businesses will come to different estimates of both of these for the same asset. This leads to problems of comparability between different companies as the basis adopted will affect the profits, balance sheet values etc. Within the same business the problems are to some extent alleviated by the requirement to follow the basic accounting concept of *consistency*:

KEY CONCEPT 12.2
Consistency

This important concept says that:

once an accounting policy is adopted it should not be changed from year to year. This is applied fairly rigorously to limited companies as their financial reports are covered by legislation and are subject to an audit report. For unincorporated businesses such as sole proprietorships and partnerships it is likely to be less rigorously applied.

Notes to the accounts

These are vital to any financial analysis as they contain the detailed information. Without that information the level of analysis possible is likely to be very superficial, especially in complex business organizations. However, users often find that the level of detail contained and the complexity and technical language used are not helpful to their understanding of the treatment of various items in the accounts.

Cash flow statement

This is a statement contained in the accounts of medium and large size limited companies. The purpose of the statement is to provide some information about the origin of the cash coming into the business and how that cash was spent. It broadly distinguishes between the cash flows arising out of the normal operations of the business and other cash flows. The latter group are then further sub-divided into those relating to returns on investments and servicing of debt, those to do with taxation, those arising from the purchase or sale of fixed assets and those from changes in the long-term financing of the business. Finally the statement reconciles the above with the movements in cash and cash equivalents.

Auditors' report

Every company is subject to an annual audit of its accounts. Included in the accounts is a report from the auditors stating whether, in the opinion of the auditors, the accounts show a 'true and fair' view. As far as financial analysis is concerned this report is best treated as an exception report: unless it is qualified in some way no account needs to be taken of it. It is worth mentioning that for most bankers it does add credibility to the figures. It does not, however, mean that the accounts are correct in all their details: quite often the report contains a number of disclaimers in respect of certain figures.

The common needs explained

We have identified common needs such as profitability, liquidity, financial risk etc. but before we can carry out any analysis we need to know what is meant by these terms. We shall therefore discuss what each term means and identify what we are trying to highlight with our analysis. For this purpose we shall use the example of Broll Ltd. You are already familiar with this example which we introduced in Chapter 10. It is reproduced below.

Example 12.1

Profit and loss account of Broll Ltd
for the year to xx. xxx. 199X

	Notes		*This year*	*Last year*
		£	£	£
Sales	1		60 000	45 000
Cost of sales			40 000	30 000
Gross profit			20 000	15 000
Distribution costs	2	3 000		(2 500)
Administration costs	2	11 000	14 000	(9 000)
Profit before taxation			6 000	3 500
Taxation	3		2 600	1 400
Profit after taxation			3 400	2 100
Dividends – interim	4	1 000		—
– final	4	1 600	2 600	1 100
Transfer to reserves			800	1 000

Profitability

Looking at the first of our needs relating to profitability it is intuitively obvious that the starting point for this information should be the profit and loss account. Before looking at the information contained in the profit and loss we need to establish what information is needed.

We need some sort of relative comparison. Is the business more profitable than in was last year? Is it more profitable than a similar business, or even a dissimilar business? Each of these questions requires us to measure the profit *relative* to something else. The last question cannot be answered by simply looking at one set of accounts. We need to compare a number of different businesses and to do this we have to make sure that the accounts are comparable. Are they depreciating the assets over the same time period? Remember that the shorter the time period the greater the charge, and therefore the smaller the final profit figure. It is for these comparisons that the accounting policies statement is required. Let us look at comparisons over time within our own business. If we look at Broll Ltd we find that the business made more profits this year, when it earned £6000 profit before taxation, than last year when the figure was only £3500. The question that now arises is whether it is more profitable because it is selling more, i.e. £60 000 this year compared with £45 000 last year, or whether it is more efficient, or whether it is a combination of the two.

We can go some way to answering this by simply working out what the increase in sales was and what the increase in profit was. In this case the sales increased by 33%, i.e.

$$\pounds 60\,000 - \pounds 45\,000 = \frac{\pounds 15\,000}{\pounds 45\,000} \times 100 = 33\%$$

The profit, however, increased by over 70%, i.e.

$$\pounds 6000 - \pounds 3500 = \frac{\pounds 2500}{\pounds 3500} \times 100 = 71\%$$

Thus we have discovered that not only is Broll making more profit by selling more but it is also making a greater profit on each sale. However, we do not know whether this seemingly favourable change is because this year was a good year or last year was a bad year nor do we know whether we have had to invest a lot of money in order to increase the profitability. The former question can only really be satisfactorily answered by comparisons over a longer period of time than two years and by then comparing Broll Ltd with a similar business in the same industry. The second question can perhaps be answered in the case of a small company by looking at what return the profit represents relative to the amount invested. This then begs the question what is the amount invested, as often in the case of small businesses the major investment made by the owner is the time spent in the business. In the case of a public company, on the other hand, there is normally very little relationship between the amount shown in the accounts and the amount you would have to pay to buy the company.

Whilst not ignoring those problems, for the present we can look at the balance sheet, reproduced below, as a rough guide in the absence of anything better. We can see that in this case the investment in the form of capital and reserves has hardly changed – £74 500 last year and £75 300 this year. Therefore we can be reasonably certain that there is a real increase in efficiency from last year.

Example 12.1 Continued

Balance sheet of Broll Ltd as at xx. xxx. 199X

	Notes	This year		Last year
		£	£	£
Fixed assets				
Intangible assets	5		10 000	11 000
Tangible assets	6		50 000	56 000
			60 000	67 000

	Notes	This year £	£	Last year £
Current assets				
Stocks	7	10 000		7 000
Debtors		10 000		4 000
Cash at bank and in hand		3 500		2 000
		23 500		13 000
Current liabilities				
Creditors	3	4 000		3 000
Taxation	4	2 600		1 400
Dividends		1 600		1 100
		8 200		5 500
Net current assets			15 300	7 500
			75 300	74 500
Capital and reserves				
Share capital	8		70 000	70 000
Retained profits	9		5 300	4 500
			75 300	74 500

Before leaving the question of profitability we need to discuss the future profitability of the business, as this was identified as a common need for many users. The fact that a company has been profitable is comforting but if you want to make a decision about whether to buy into a business or sell up you need information about the future, not the past. This information is not contained in the profit and loss account, although it could be argued that information on the past is the best guide to the future. In practical terms the only way you can form an opinion about the future is by using a combination of information including past profits, knowledge of the industry, predictions about the economy and many other factors.

Profitability – summary

- Profitability requires comparisons:
  - over time;
  - with other businesses.
- Profitability relates to:
  - the past for evaluation;
  - the future for prediction.

Liquidity and financial risk

We shall deal with these two together as they are both related to the financing of the business. The area of financial risk or solvency is of vital importance as there are many cases where a business has gone bankrupt because of cash flow problems even though it was profitable. There are also cases where two companies in the same line of business produce dramatically different results purely because of the way they are financed. For example, if you make a return of 15% on every pound invested and can borrow money at 10% it is worth borrowing money because the excess return goes to the owners. However, there is some risk involved in such a course of action as you will lose if the interest rate rises to, say, 17% and you are still only making 15%. A way of measuring the financial risk is to look at the balance sheet of a business and identify the amount of debt finance, i.e. loans, debentures, bank overdrafts and other borrowing, and to compare this with the amount of equity finance, i.e. owners' capital plus reserves.

In the UK, in general, debt finance does not normally exceed the equity finance although the extent to which this generalization holds true is to some extent dependent on the size of the business. This is largely as a result of the banks' policies of lending on a pound-for-pound basis, i.e. for each pound of your money that you put in the business the bank will lend a pound. Whilst this is not a hard and fast rule it is effectively used as the benchmark by bank managers in the clearing banks in the UK. It is interesting that different countries seem to adopt different benchmarks. For example, banks in Germany and Japan tend to lend well above the one-for-one norm.

In the case of Broll Ltd there is no long-term borrowing, nor is there even a bank overdraft. This may be a good thing as the company is only making £6000 on the capital invested of over £75 000. This is less than 10% and, at the time of writing, below the rate at which money could be borrowed.

Looking now at liquidity: what is generally understood by this is, can you meet your commitments as they fall due? In general the major area for concern is the short term, which is often taken to be a year. This is convenient as it fits in with the definition used for current assets and current liabilities, and so we have a suitable measure simply by looking at the balance sheet. For example, Broll has current assets of £23 500 and current liabilities of only £8200. This means that it should get enough money in during the next year to pay what it is currently due to pay out in that year.

One of the problems that arises with this apparently simple measure is that current can mean due tomorrow or in 12 months or even more. In the case of some current assets, for example stock, it first has to be sold and then the money has to be collected. Another, problem is the question of what is the correct liquidity level for the business. If for example there is a lot of cash in the bank, that is hardly an efficient use of resources. In the case of Broll the amount of £3500 in the bank may be far in excess of its true needs. There is also the question of whether £10 000 tied up in debtors is excessive on sales of £60 000, especially if we compare this to last year where the debtors were £4000 on sales of £45 000.

Other problems with interpreting the information may arise if we try to compare different businesses. For example an aircraft manufacturer will have different needs from a food wholesaler. Even within the same industrial sector the needs will differ. For example, a whisky distiller will have different needs from a brewery, as the former has a product that has to be matured over years whereas the latter has a product that is produced in a few months and has a fairly limited shelf life.

Financial risk – summary

- Financial risk involves long-term and short-term solvency.
- Requirements and norms differ widely from industry to industry.

The importance of considering the type of industry is aptly illustrated by the balance sheets contained in Case Study 12.1.

Once again the general conclusion to be drawn is that on its own the analysis of the financial statements is only a small part of the story and that analysis needs to be put into a wider context of knowledge of the industry and the environment. The maxim that a little knowledge is a dangerous thing applies equally to business analysis as it does elsewhere. With that firmly in mind we can now move on to look at some of the techniques that can be used to analyse the financial information.

Techniques of analysis

Many techniques are used in financial analysis from simple techniques such as studying the financial statements (in a manner similar to the exercise we have just done) and forming a rough opinion of what is happening to sophisticated statistical techniques. It should be pointed out that this rough analysis based on 'eyeballing' the accounts is vital as it forms the base on which the more sophisticated techniques can be built. If, for example, we fail to notice that a business has made a loss for the past few years the application of the most sophisticated techniques will not help as we have failed to grasp an essential point.

We shall limit ourselves to an examination of some of the simpler techniques. The choice of technique is once again a function of what you are trying to do and the purpose of your analysis. For example managers and auditors may be interested in establishing any variations from past norms and explaining these and, where necessary, taking appropriate action. However, for a shareholder in a large company such an analysis, even if it were possible, would be inappropriate as no action could be taken and the level of detail is too specific.

Comparison of financial statements over time

With limited data a simple comparison of the rate and direction of change over time can be very useful. This can be done both in terms of absolute amount and in percentage terms. Both are normally required in order to reach any meaningful conclusions. For example, a 50% change on £1000 is less significant than a 50% change on £50 000. However, if you only have £1000 to start with a change of £500 may well be significant. Thus it is not only the absolute figure but also the amount relative to other figures that is important.

CASE STUDY 12.1
ASDA plc and J. Sainsbury plc

ASDA Group Plc annual report 1992

Balance sheets

	Note	Group		Company	
At 2 May 1992		*1992*	*1991*	*1992*	*1991*
		£m	*£m*	*£m*	*£m*
Fixed assets					
Tangible assets	10	2003.6	2136.0	0.2	0.3
Investments	11	104.5	103.5	830.5	244.0
		2108.1	2239.5	830.7	244.3
Current assets					
Stocks	14	307.3	379.1	8.1	16.4
Debtors	15	117.8	156.5	1230.9	1597.2
Investments	16	0.4	2.5	—	—
Cash at bank and in hand		38.4	82.8	—	1.5
		463.9	620.9	1239.0	1615.1
Creditors: amounts falling due within one year					
Borrowings	17	(282.7)	(460.7)	(262.2)	(446.8)
Other creditors	19	(553.9)	(622.1)	(432.3)	(316.3)
		(836.6)	(1082.8)	(694.5)	(763.1)
Net current (liabilities)/assets		(372.7)	(461.9)	544.5	852.0
Total assets less current liabilities		1735.4	1777.6	1375.2	1096.3
Creditors: amounts falling due after more than one year					
Borrowings	17	(433.9)	(569.9)	(221.7)	(353.7)
Other creditors	19	(0.7)	(0.8)	—	—
Provisions for liabilities and charges	20	(193.5)	(69.8)	2.3	5.8
		1107.3	1137.1	1155.8	748.4
Capital and reserves					
Called up share capital	23	557.4	293.4	557.4	293.4
Share premium account	24	122.7	29.3	122.7	29.3
Revaluation reserve	24	86.6	82.8	161.5	34.8
Profit and loss account	24	340.6	731.4	314.2	390.9
Minority interests		—	0.2	—	—
		1107.3	1137.1	1155.8	748.4

Commentary

You will note that in the case of ASDA the current liabilities are far in excess of the current assets. This is because of the industry within which they operate. It is also the case for Sainsbury's as is illustrated by the balance sheet included in their annual report and accounts for 1993 reproduced below.

J. Sainsbury Plc annual report 1993

Balance sheets
13th March 1993

	Note	Group		Company	
		1993	*1992*	*1993*	*1992*
		£m	*£m*	*£m*	*£m*
Fixed assets					
Tangible Assets	1	4448.5	3809.2	3662.0	3123.5
Investments	2	29.4	27.6	624.9	574.7
		4477.9	3836.8	4286.9	3698.2
Current assets					
Investments	5	78.5	189.6	78.5	139.2
Stocks	6	448.2	386.5	261.0	229.1
Debtors	7	95.3	80.8	56.1	63.0
ACT Recoverable		37.6	37.3	37.6	37.3
Cash at Bank and in Hand		144.4	173.9	90.7	87.6
		804.0	868.1	523.9	556.2
Creditors: due within one year	8	(1524.6)	(1468.2)	(1319.5)	(1274.5)
Net current liabilities		(720.6)	(600.1)	(795.6)	(718.3)
		3757.3	3236.7	3491.3	2979.9
Total assets less current liabilities					
Creditors: due after one year					
Convertible	8	(200.0)	(200.0)	—	—
Other	8	(513.2)	(377.9)	(674.0)	(478.9)
Deferred Tax	10	2.0	(1.7)	9.4	5.5
Minority Interest		(17.4)	(16.2)	—	—
		3028.7	2640.9	2826.7	2506.5
Capital and reserves					
Called up Share Capital	11	443.7	439.4	443.7	439.4
Share Premium Account	12	895.4	837.5	895.4	837.5
Revaluation Reserve	13	26.8	26.8	28.1	28.1
Profit and Loss Account	14	1662.8	1337.2	1459.5	1201.5
		3028.7	2640.9	2826.7	2506.5

Commentary

In both these examples you will note that there are two balance sheets, one for the Company and one for the Group. A group is where there are a number of companies which are owned by another company referred to as the parent company or holding company. Most of the companies quoted on the Stock Exchange are in fact groups of companies taking advantage of the protection offered by setting up individual companies with limited liability, so that if one part has a problem it does not automatically bankrupt the rest of the operation.

The period of time chosen is also worth considering. Too short a time period will not be very meaningful. This was the case with Broll where we could only say that the profit had increased but had no idea about whether that was part of a trend or whether it was because last year was a particularly bad year. Similarly, one has to be careful not to take too long a period as the nature of the business or the environment may have altered drastically. Finally, it must be borne in mind that there may be other changes which have affected the figures; for example, the business may have decided to depreciate its vehicles over three years instead of four. Having taken account of these warnings let us now look at how we could do the comparisons.

Trend analysis

Trend analysis is normally used for time periods in excess of two to three years in order to make the results easier to understand and interpret. It involves choosing a base year and then plotting the trend in sales or profits or whatever from there on.

KEY CONCEPT 12.3
Trend analysis

In trend analysis the choice of an appropriate base year is vital. If the base year chosen is not typical the resultant analysis will at best be extremely difficult and at worst actually misleading.

Example 12.2 ABC Ltd

ABC Ltd profit and loss summary

	1987	*1988*	*1989*	*1990*	*1991*
	£000	£000	£000	£000	£000
Sales	12 371	13 209	16 843	14 441	13 226
Cost of sales	9 605	9 981	12 807	9 858	10 812
Gross profit	2 766	3 228	4 036	4 583	2 414
Distribution expenses	619	660	842	1 011	926
Administration expenses	1 070	1 123	1 432	1 300	1 190
Operating profit	1 077	1 445	1 762	2 272	298
Interest charges	215	252	460	768	676
Pre-tax profit	862	1 193	1 302	1 504	−378
Taxation	464	529	875	579	98
Profit after tax	398	664	427	925	−476
Dividends	164	185	336	337	112
Retained profit	234	479	91	588	−588

If we take the cost of sales figure it is clear from a casual examination of the figures that it rises in 1987 and 1988 to a peak in 1989 after which it falls in 1990. If we plotted that on a graph it would look like Figure

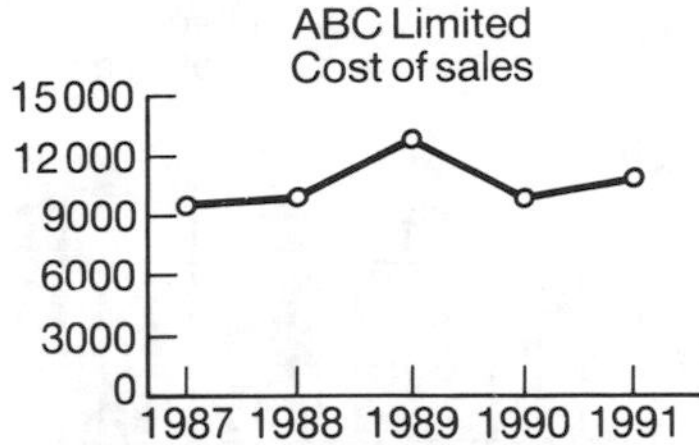

Figure 12.1

12.1. As you can see the information contained is fairly limited; it merely reflects what we have already found. To make any sensible comment we need to see how these costs are behaving in relation to something else. This could be in relation to another item in the profit and loss account such as sales or in relation to the costs in a comparable company. To do the latter comparison, however, we first have to find some common means of expression as the companies being compared are unlikely to be exactly the same size. One way of doing this is to use index numbers to express the figures we are looking at and the way in which they change from year to year.

Index number trends

As with other forms of trend analysis this technique is normally used for time periods in excess of two to three years. It is intended to make the results easier to understand and interpret. It does this by choosing a base year, setting that base year to 100 and expressing all other years in terms of that base year.

If for example we used 1987 as the base year and set that at 100 we would be able to calculate the sales trend as follows:

$$\frac{\text{1988 sales}}{\text{1987 sales}} \times 100 = \frac{13\,209}{12\,371} \times 100 = 107$$

For 1989 the calculation would be

$$\frac{\text{1989 sales}}{\text{1987 sales}} \times 100 = \frac{16\,843}{12\,371} \times 100 = 136$$

Using the same formula we can find the index for each of the other years and we can then look at the trend. In this case the figures are:

1987, 100; 1988, 107; 1989, 136; 1990, 117; 1991, 107

We could do the same for the cost of sales and the profit figures and then these could be analysed. In the case of sales we can see that the sales peaked in 1989 and then declined to the same level as in 1988. This can be seen more easily in Figure 12.2 which shows the sales in the left-hand blocks and the cost of sales in the right-hand blocks for each year.

Figure 12.2 is thus much more informative as it relates sales to cost of sales; in addition the use of index numbers allows us to compare this

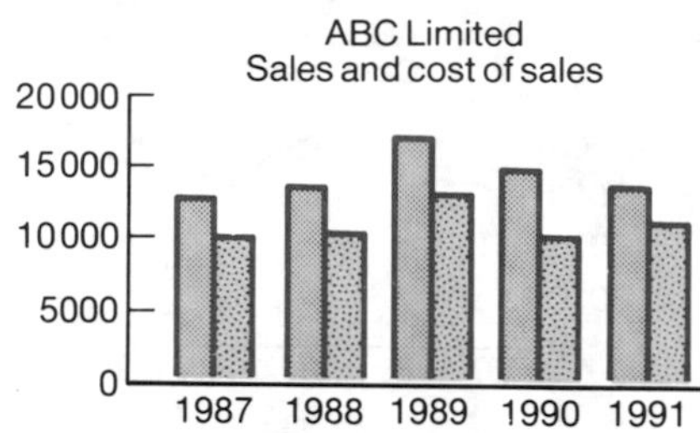

Figure 12.2

company with another irrespective of size. The graph in this case shows that both sales and cost of sales peak in 1989. After that, however, we see that although sales fall in both 1990 and 1991 the cost of sales rises again in 1991.

Percentage changes

Another technique often used in trend analysis is to identify the percentage change from year to year and then examine the trends in this. For example, if we look at the sales we find that the change from 1987 to 1988 was 7%, whilst that from 1988 to 1989 was 27%. These figures are calculated using the following formula:

$$\frac{\text{This year's sales}}{\text{Last year's sales}} \times 100 = \frac{13\,209}{12\,371} \times 100 = 107 \text{ or } 7\% \text{ up}$$

Once again it should be pointed out that these trends are of most use if they are compared with other trends, either in the business itself or in the industry. You should also bear in mind that these percentage increases are often illusory as they merely reflect the increase that would be expected as a result of the rate of inflation in the particular period and the particular country concerned.

Common size statements

A technique which can be used to turn the large numbers we often encounter in accounts into more digestible information is 'common size' statements. This technique, as the name implies, deals with the problem of comparisons of differently sized companies. It involves expressing the items in the balance sheet, for example, as precentages of the balance sheet total. Once again this is best illustrated by looking at ABC Ltd, the balance sheets of which are reproduced below. We can derive certain information and questions from just looking at the balance sheets, but it is not easy to identify exactly what is happening. For example, why has the Land and buildings gone up in 1989 by a greater amount than the other fixed assets? Where did the intangibles come from, and what are they? These questions can often be answered, in part at least, by using the detailed information contained in the notes to the accounts.

Example 12.2 ABC Ltd Continued

ABC Ltd summary balance sheets

	1987	1988	1989	1990	1991
Fixed assets	*£000*	*£000*	*£000*	*£000*	*£000*
Land and buildings	639	660	682	1 070	1 103
Plant and equipment	875	849	959	863	767
Other fixed assets	450	554	486	663	683
	1 964	2 063	2 127	2 596	2 553
Intangibles			470	451	460
Current assets					
Stocks	3 645	3 952	3 903	3 289	3 255
Debtors	2 259	2 389	3 012	2 776	2 508
Cash	400	464	183	15	41
	6 304	6 805	7 098	6 080	5 804
Creditors: Amounts falling due in one year					
Creditors	3 701	3 706	4 842	3 311	4 277
Taxation	110	415	196	44	48
Dividends	121	137	224	225	1
Bank overdraft	0	3	86	427	663
	3 932	4 261	5 348	4 007	4 989
Net current assets	2 372	2 544	1 750	2 073	815
Creditors: Amounts due after one year					
Loans	297	148	0	427	92
Provisions for liabilities and charges					
Deferred tax	922	843	620	369	0
	3 117	3 616	3 727	4 324	3 736
Financed by					
Share capital	1 447	1 459	1 471	1 476	1 476
Share premium	137	145	153	157	157
Reserves	1 533	2 012	2 103	2 691	2 103
	3 117	3 616	3 727	4 324	3 736

The problem when looking at standard balance sheets is that the figures often disguise what is really happening. If, however, we convert the statements to some common measure the underlying trends become clearer. We could take for example the share capital for 1987 and express it as a percentage of the balance sheet total. We find that it is 46% in that year compared with 40% in 1988. To calculate this we simply divided the share capital figure by the balance sheet total and then multiplied the result by 100. Thus for 1989 we would have

$$\frac{\text{share capital}}{\text{total}} \times 100 = \frac{1471}{3727} \times 100 = 40\%$$

Following this procedure for all items in the balance sheets produces common size statements as follows.

ABC Ltd common size balance sheets

	1987	*1988*	*1989*	*1990*	*1991*
Fixed assets	%	%	%	%	%
Land and buildings	21	18	18	25	30
Plant and equipment	28	23	26	20	21
Other fixed assets	14	15	13	15	18
Tangible fixed assets	63	56	57	60	69
Intangibles			13	10	12
Current assets					
Stocks	117	109	104	76	87
Debtors	72	66	81	64	67
Cash	13	13	5	1	1
	202	188	190	141	155
Creditors: amounts falling due in one year					
Creditors	(117)	(102)	(130)	(76)	(115)
Taxation	(4)	(11)	(5)	(1)	(1)
Dividends	(4)	(4)	(6)	(5)	(0)
Bank overdraft	0	(0)	(2)	(10)	(18)
	(125)	(117)	(143)	(92)	(134)
Net current assets	77	71	47	49	21
Creditors: Amounts due after one year					
Loans	(10)	(4)	0	(10)	(2)
Provisions for liabilities and charges					
Deferred tax	(30)	(23)	(17)	(9)	0
	100	100	100	100	100
Financed by					
Share capital	46	40	40	34	40
Share premium	4	4	4	4	4
Reserves	50	56	56	62	56
	100	100	100	100	100

One of the things that we can see from an analysis of these statements is that the net current assets have shown a very marked decline over the period from 77% of the balance sheet total in 1987 to only 21% in 1991. We can also see that 1990 was in many ways an atypical year, e.g. the stock levels, debtor level and creditor level were out of line with other years. By 1991 the bank overdraft had risen to its highest level ever and stocks, debtors and creditors had gone back to the levels of 1989. It should be noted that with this technique the choice of the base year is just as important as it was with trend analysis.

The technique of common size statements can be applied just as easily to the profit and loss account as to the balance sheet. In the case of the profit and loss account it is normal to express all items as a percentage of sales as illustrated below.

ABC Ltd common size profit and loss account

	1987	*1988*	*1989*	*1990*	*1991*
	%	%	%	%	%
Sales	100	100	100	100	100
Cost of sales	78	76	76	68	82
Gross profit	22	24	24	32	18
Distribution expenses	5	5	5	7	7
Administration expenses	8	8	9	9	9
Operating profit	9	11	10	16	2
Interest charges	2	2	3	5	6
Pre-tax profit	7	9	7	10	−4
Taxation	4	4	5	4	1
Profit after tax	3	5	2	7	−5
Dividends	1	1	2	2	1
Retained profit	2	4	0	5	−6

Apart from the obvious rounding errors which occur when working in whole numbers the statement above is fairly self-explanatory. An item that is worth highlighting is that the cost of sales in 1991 has squeezed the operating profit down to only 2% return on sales in a year when the interest charges are seen to be 6% of sales. This illustrates the risk of high gearing which we referred to earlier in Chapter 9 and in this chapter.

Common size statements and the other techniques that we have examined so far have largely ignored the relationship between the two components of the financial statements of a business. The effect of this is that we have not been able to extract everything we could from the information available. Other techniques of analysis are available which look at the relationship between items in the balance sheet and items in the profit and loss account. The most common of these techniques is known as ratio analysis and this is explored more fully below.

Ratio analysis

Although ratio analysis is seen in virtually every accounting textbook most students, whilst having little difficulty in calculating ratios, find extreme difficulty in understanding what they mean once they have been calculated. Because of this we shall not deal extensively with all the possible ratios that can be calculated but instead we shall try to concentrate on the relationships that we are trying to express through the ratios we calculate. This approach will increase your understanding of the reasons for calculating these ratios and will therefore enable you to interpret the results from a sound basis of understanding. We shall first discuss some ratios which express relationships between items in balance sheets, and then we shall discuss those ratios based upon items in the profit and loss account. Finally we shall examine ratios which combine information from the two statements.

KEY CONCEPT 12.4
Ratio

A ratio R is quantity A divided by quantity B:

$$R = A/B$$

In essence a ratio is merely a shorthand notation for the relationship between two or more things. It is the relationship that it is expressing that must be understood. Without that understanding the ratio, no matter how precisely calculated or sophisticated, is meaningless.

Before doing that, we need to understand exactly what a ratio is. This is defined in Key Concept 12.4.

Apart from understanding the relationship underpinning the ratio we also need to examine ratios in a wider context. For example, if we want to work out how many police we need to police a football match we could work on the basis of one policeman to a number of spectators. If we found that we needed 200 police for a crowd of 40 000 spectators the ratio would be one to 200 or 1:200.

Obviously this ratio is meaningless on its own as it does not tell us whether we are using the *right* number of police. To decide this we would need to establish whether there were still problems of violence or, if not, whether we could achieve the same result with fewer police. The former problem would require additional information whilst the latter could perhaps be judged, in part at least, by looking at what other football clubs do and what ratio of police to spectators they use. This simple example serves to illustrate the fact that the ratio on its own cannot tell us very much. It needs to be looked at in the context of other information and experience.

Ratios based on the balance sheet

As we have already said, the important point to bear in mind is what the ratio is attempting to illustrate. For example, we could look at the balance sheet of ABC and calculate the ratio of plant and equipment to other fixed assets but this would be of little use unless we knew what the relationship meant and what we expected. The calculation of ratios is not an end in itelf. There are some relationships, however, that do mean something. For example, earlier in this chapter we discussed the need to find out about liquidity and financial risk. We said that financial risk was related to the amount of debt finance compared with equity finance. If we wanted to express this as a ratio, using ABC Limited for example, we could take the loans in 1987 and compare them with the equity in that year. The figures for loans for that year were £297 000 and the equity figure was £3 117 000. The ratio could be calculated by dividing the equity figure by the loans figure as follows:

$$\frac{£3\,117\,000}{£297\,000} = 10.5 \times \text{ or } 10.5:1$$

This tells us that for every £1 of loan finance there is £10.5 of equity finance or that there is 10.5 times more equity than debt. If we compare this with 1990 we find that the ratio in that year is

$$\frac{£4\,324\,000}{£427\,000} = 10.1 \times \text{ or } 10.1:1$$

If we had calculated this ratio for all years we would find that it goes up and down, which is something we could have established by looking at the common size statements. We still do not know whether this is good or bad or why it is going up and down. To answer those questions we need to look at the environment, industry norms, and what else is happening in the particular business we are analysing.

To illustrate the latter point we can look in more detail at the balance sheets for the two years in question. We find that, apparently, the ratio we have just calculated suggests that the business is almost as reliant on debt in 1990 as it was in 1987. In fact this is not the case as the short-term debt, in the form of the bank overdraft, has gone from a position in 1987 of having £400 000 in cash and at the bank to having only £15 000 in cash and having an overdraft at the bank of £427 000. Thus the ratio we calculated only tells us part of the story as ABC is now relying on short-term as well as long-term borrowing.

One way to overcome this problem is to calculate more than one ratio to establish the relationship between debt and equity. For example we could also calculate the ratio of total debt to equity or the ratio of the total debt less cash balances to equity. All these ratios attempt to give some indication of the financial risk involved.

Other balance sheet ratios that are commonly used relate to the relationship between current assets and current liabilities and to the relationship between current monetary assets, such as debtors and cash, and current liabilities. These relationships are used to express what is happening in relation to what is often referred to as 'short-term liquidity'. They are calculated by dividing, for example, the current assets figure by the current liabilities figure. Once again, on its own the result of this calculation does not necessarily tell us very much. We need to look at trends and take into account the nature of the business. For example, we would expect a high street greengrocer to be in a different situation with regard to the optimum level of stock held than, say, a car manufacturer. This is because the greengrocer's stock, being perishable goods, has a limited shelf life. Apart from the nature of the business we also need to take into account the industry norms and the size of the business.

Turning now to the trends in ABC's liquidity ratios we can see whether they give us any idea of what is happening.

$$\text{Current ratio: } \frac{\text{current assets}}{\text{current liabilities}}$$

$$1987 = \frac{£6\,304\,000}{£3\,932\,000} = 1.6 \times \text{ or } 1.6:1$$

The ratio for the other years are as follows:

1988, 1.6:1; 1989, 1.3:1; 1990, 1.5:1; 1991, 1.2:1

These show that the ratio is declining, but what does this mean? To answer that we need to think about the relationship being expressed, i.e. the relationship between those assets that will be turned into cash in the short term and the amounts we potentially have to pay out in the short term. If the ratio is going down it means that we have less cover and therefore there is more risk. If using this measure we find that the risk is increasing we may then wish to use a more sensitive measure. One such measure simply excludes the stock from the current assets and compares the remaining current assets with the current liabilities. The reasoning behind the exclusion of stock is that it will first have to be sold and then the debtors will have to pay before we can use the cash to pay our creditors.

This ratio, i.e. the ratio of current assets, excluding stock, to current liabilities is often referred to as *the acid test* or *quick ratio* and is defined as follows:

$$\text{Acid test or quick ratio} = \frac{\text{current assets} - \text{stock}}{\text{current liabilities}}$$

Calculating this ratio for 1987 we obtain

$$\frac{£6\,304\,000 - £3\,645\,000}{£3\,932\,000} = 0.67 \times \text{ or } 0.67:1$$

The fact that the ratio is less than one to one tells us that we could not pay our current debts if we were called upon to do so. Or, to put it another way, the ratio tells us that we have 67p to pay each £1 of current liabilities. The question is: does this matter? ABC has after all stayed in business well after 1987. In fact the business on which ABC is based carried on for a further five years.

The interpretation of the information obtained from calculating this ratio, as with all the other ratios, can only make sense if it is judged by comparison with a set of industry norms. Even this is not as straightforward as it sounds, as there are often different norms within an industry depending on the size and relative power of the firms in that sector. There is also the point that any norm based on a number of firms will be the average rather than the best and so care has to be exercised when looking at these norms and applying them to a particular firm. This all seems to imply that comparisons with norms may not be meaningful in any case. This is certainly true if it is done without adequate attention to what it is that the results are being compared with.

The question of the usefulness or otherwise of an industry norm does not apply in the case of ABC Ltd as we do not have that information. What we do have is the information base to calculate a trend and the trend in the quick ratio for ABC is shown below:

1988, 0.67:1; 1989, 0.6:1; 1990, 0.7:1; 1991, 0.5:1

Once again the trend shows an overall decline with 1990 being the odd year out. As before we can conclude that the risk is increasing but can say very little about whether this is in line with what is happening generally because we are looking at the company in isolation. In reality we would know from our knowledge of what was happening in the economy generally whether credit was getting tight or easing off and this knowledge would help us in our interpretation of the trend shown above.

Another invaluable aid to arriving at a judgement of an organizations liquidity position is the cash flow statement, which we discussed in Chapter 11. Unlike the balance sheet ratios which relate to one point in time, and are therefore capable of some manipulation, the cash flow statement relates to a period of time and is therefore less susceptible to manipulation. By using a combination of an analysis of the balance sheet ratios and an analysis of the cash flow position over a period of time you should be able to arrive at a reasonable judgement of the liquidity position of any organization.

You may like to look at the cash flow statement of ABC Ltd for 1991 which is reproduced below and identify what additional information it provides.

Cash flow statement of ABC Ltd for 1991

Net cash inflow from operating activities		1 776
Returns on investments and servicing of finance		
Interest paid	(676)	
Dividends paid	(336)	
Net cash flow from returns on investment and servicing activities		(1 012)
Taxation		
Corporation tax paid (including ACT)	(94)	
Net cash outflow from taxation		(94)
Investing activities		
Payment for redundancies	(11)	
Payment to acquire tangible fixed assets	525	
Payment to acquire intangible assets	(9)	
Net cash outflow from investing activity		(90)
Net cash outflow before financing		125

Financing		
Debenture loan repayment	(335)	
Net cash outflow from financing		(335)
Decrease in cash or cash equivalents		(210)

The cash flow statement tells us that there is a net cash outflow of £210 000. It also shows us that the cash inflow from operating activities of £1 321 000 is used mainly to pay interest and tax. A closer look at the cash inflow from operations is provided in the reconciliation of this with the profit figure.

Reconciliation of operating profit to net cash flow from operating activity

Operating profit	298
Depreciation charges	210
Increase in stocks	34
Decrease in debtors	268
Increase in creditors	966
	1776

This reconciliation reveals that most of the cash inflow from operations comes from the increases in creditors. This, of course, reveals an increasing reliance on short-term financing which is further evidenced by the increase in the overdraft level.

Having looked at some of the balance sheet ratios for measuring financial risk let us now turn our attention to the profit and loss account.

Ratios based on profit and loss

Most ratios that relate solely to the profit and loss account are really expressions of costs as a percentage of sales, e.g. the gross profit or net profit expressed as a percentage of sales. These relationships are also made apparent with common size statements, which we have already examined. Therefore we shall not discuss them further here. Instead we shall consider some of the relationships between the profit and loss account and the balance sheet.

Profit and loss and balance sheet relationships

For example, if we have an increase in sales we would expect our debtors to increase; we would probably have to buy more goods to sell and so our creditors may rise and in all probability our level of stocks would also have to rise to cope with the increased demand. In the case of ABC the sales have risen as have the debtors. At this stage we are not sure whether the increase in debtors is solely due to the increase in sales or whether it is in part caused by the debtors taking longer to pay up. The use of a ratio that compares sales and debtors would provide answers to questions such as this.

When calculating ratios that relate balance sheet items to profit and loss account items we have to bear in mind that if prices are changing the relationship can be distorted. This is because the balance sheet represents prices at one point in time, whereas the profit and loss account represents the results of operations for a period. This can be shown diagrammatically as follows:

T_0	Profit and loss account	T_1
←		→
Opening balance sheet		Closing balance sheet

Thus the opening stock figure or debtors figure would be expressed in start-of-the-year prices, the profit and loss figures in average prices and the closing figures in end-of-year prices. Added to this problem of a changing price level is the fact that the volume will also change. For example, as sales increase we need to hold more units of stock to provide the same service. Thus we have two problems i.e. changes in prices and in volumes. One way to compensate for this is to use the average of the opening and closing balance sheet figures and compare that average figure for stocks, debtors etc. with the figure from the profit and loss account which is already expressed in average prices. Thus to calculate the relationship between sales for 1991 and the debtors we would take the debtors at 1990 and at 1991 and take the average of the two figures. This would give us a better approximation of the true level of debtors required to sustain that volume of sales.

The relationship thus calculated can be expressed either as the turnover of the balance sheet figure, e.g. debtors turnover or as the number of days debtors take to repay. We shall use the latter for the purposes of illustration, as experience shows that this is more readily understood.

To calculate this ratio the formula we require is

$$\text{debtor collection} = \frac{\text{average debtors}}{\text{sales}} \times 365$$

Thus for 1991 for ABC the debtor collection period is

$$\frac{\frac{1}{2}(2776 + 2508)}{13\,226} \times 365 = 73 \text{ days}$$

Once again we cannot comment on whether this is good or bad without some reference point and some more information. For example, if the sales mix had changed and ABC had moved into overseas markets this may mean that it takes longer to collect money.

A number of other ratios of this type can be calculated, e.g. the number of days stock's are held or the period taken to pay creditors using cost of sales and purchases respectively. However, as this is an introductory text we shall not deal with these other ratios in depth; instead we encourage you to identify the relationships which will aid your understanding and derive your own ratios. If, having done that, you are interested in looking at some of the more commonly used ratios you should make reference to one of the texts suggested at the end of this chapter.

Before leaving the subject of financial analysis and in particular ratio analysis, it is worthwhile reminding ourselves of some of the points made in this chapter about putting the analysis into context and also reiterating the limitations of this sort of analysis.

Summary of major issues

There is no point in using sophisticated techniques for analysis without an understanding of the following.

- The wider context, i.e. the environmental context: What is meant here is the economic social and political pressures, the type of industry and where the industry as a whole is going.
- The organizational level: We need to appreciate the type of organization we are dealing with. Is it a charity? Does it have an American parent company? How are these factors affecting the information that is being presented and the way in which that information is presented, and how should they affect our analysis?
- The strategic context: What sort of organization are we dealing with? What business is it in? How big is the organization? These are all relevant questions that have to be answered if the analysis is to be carried out properly.
- Who the analysis is for: As we have seen, different users have different needs in terms of analysis and, even when their needs appear to overlap, the emphasis is frequently different from group to group.
- Any analysis will only be as good as the base data: In this case we are dealing with analysis based on historic cost accounts, which assume that prices do not change, when in practice this is not the case. Even if we overcome that problem, there is the question of how up to date or out of date the information is. There are also issues of comparability because different accounting policies are adopted and because the size of the organization affects norms. And what do norms actually mean?

Finally we need to be clear what the point of the analysis is. Are we providing the base for a decision about the future actions of a user of accounting information and, if so, what alternatives in terms of decisions is that user facing? Having identified in our case that ABC seems to have some problems we now need to identify what, if any, action can be taken to solve some of those problems. In general, the role of the outside user is probably limited to that of problem identification as in most cases there is little that the outside user can do in terms of problem solving. This is a task that should be carried out by the management of the company.

In order for management to be able to carry out this task, as we have already suggested, they will need more detailed information and often they will also require different forms of information. For example, the fact that the costs are rising does not help as they need to know which costs are actually rising. They also need to know whether the problem is due to the fact that at a lower level of sales they are losing the economies of scale. Then they need to know the level of sales and costs they would expect in 1992 and thereafter so that they can take appropriate actions to improve the performance of their business. In the next chapters we shall consider these additional needs of managers and how they are met through the analysis of past information, whether it be in the form we have already seen or in a different form. We shall also consider what other information is needed for planning, decision making and control, where this is obtained, and how it is used.

Before moving on to that discussion it is worth briefly summarizing some of the key features and limitations of financial statement analysis.

Key features

- Financial analysis has to be looked at in the wider context of the industry, the environment etc.
- Financial analysis has to be targeted to meet the needs of the user of the analysis.
- Financial analysis is only as good as the base information that is being analysed.
- Financial analysis involves both inter-temporal and inter-firm comparisons and this imposes limitations.

These key features point to some limitations that have to be borne in mind when discussing financial analysis. These can be usefully summarized under three headings as follows.

Key limitations

Information problems

- The base information is often out of date, i.e. timeliness of information leads to problems of interpretation.
- Historic cost information may not be the most appropriate information for the decision for which the analysis is being undertaken.
- Information in published accounts is generally summarized information and detailed information may be needed.
- Analysis of accounting information only identifies symptoms, not causes, and thus is of limited use.

Comparison problems – inter-temporal

- Effects of price changes make comparisons difficult unless adjustments are made.

- Changes in technology affect the price of assets, the likely return and the future markets.
- A changing environment affects the results and this is reflected in the accounting information.
- Potential effects of changes in accounting policies on the reported results.
- Problems associated with establishing a normal base year to compare other years with.

Comparison problems – inter-firm

- Selection of industry norms and the usefulness of norms based on averages.
- Different firms have different financial and business risk profiles and this affects the analysis.
- Different firms use different accounting policies.
- Impacts of the size of the business and its comparators on risk, structure and returns.
- Different environments affect results, e.g. different countries, homebased versus multinational firms.

Thus there are a number of issues that you need to bear in mind when carrying out your analysis and interpreting and reporting the results. They should not, however, be used as a reason not to attempt the analysis.

Further reading

A full discussion of techniques of financial analysis can be found in *Financial Statement Analysis – a New Approach* by B. Lev (Prentice-Hall, 1974).

Review questions

1 Identify the main user groups and their common needs in terms of financial analysis.
2 How do the needs of long-term lenders differ from those of equity investors?
3 What factors do we need to take into account in order to put our analysis in context?
4 What sources of information outside the business are available to you and how would you use this information in your analysis?
5 What information would you derive from reading the Chairman's Statement?
6 What other parts of the annual report would you use in your analysis?
7 Explain briefly what the difference is between financial risk and business or commercial risk.

8 How would you measure financial risk in the short and long term?
9 What are the limitations to our analysis which are inherent in the accounting data we are using?

Problems for discussion and analysis

Belper

Given below are the summarized accounts of Belper Ltd for the past five years. These form the basis for the questions which follow.

Summarized balance sheets of Belper Ltd

	19X1	*19X2*	*19X3*	*19X4*	*19X5*
Fixed assets	*£000s*	*£000s*	*£000s*	*£000s*	*£000s*
Freehold land and buildings	14 058	14 571	20 559	20 598	29 721
Leasehold land and buildings	2 349	2 490	5 184	5 193	12 564
Plant and machinery	8 082	11 541	26 781	30 000	47 172
Total gross fixed assets	24 489	28 602	52 524	55 791	89 457
Depreciation freehold					597
Depreciation leasehold	117	147	345	774	858
Depreciation plant etc.	4 197	5 325	8 259	11 277	18 747
Total depreciation	4 314	5 472	8 604	12 051	20 202
	20 175	23 130	43 920	43 740	69 255
Intangible fixed assets					
Goodwill	789	807	849	936	936
Investments	486	795	393	303	393
Patents and trademarks	3 972	3 618	6 063	8 730	9 345
Current assets					
Stock	20 031	23 034	53 091	74 823	99 606
Debtors	17 589	24 693	60 270	48 987	66 768
Bank and cash	4 698	6 801	7 839	3 273	9 747
	42 318	54 528	121 200	127 083	176 121
Creditors: due within one year					
Creditors	16 197	24 588	55 659	41 130	72 831
Taxation	459	768	4 302	2 712	3 444
Dividends	801	1 812	3 339	3 738	3 672
Bank loans and overdraft	10 581	4 026	18 180	29 316	37 638
	28 038	31 194	81 480	76 896	117 585
Net current assets	14 280	23 334	39 720	50 187	58 536
Creditors: due after one year					
Loans	14 793	15 477	35 241	28 695	61 110
	24 909	36 207	55 704	75 201	77 355

Financed by					
Ordinary share capital	2 229	2 829	3 396	6 792	7 077
Share premium account	2 931	7 530	14 598	11 247	12 387
Retained profits	19 749	25 848	30 975	43 692	41 734
Revaluation reserves			6 735	6 734	16 157
	24 909	36 207	55 704	68 465	77 355

Notes

(i) During 19X5 some of the freehold properties were revalued.
(ii) Loans amounting to £22 million were repaid during 19X5.
(iii) No fixed assets were disposed of during the year.

Summarized profit and loss accounts of Belper

	19X1 *£000s*	*19X2* *£000s*	*19X3* *£000s*	*19X4* *£000s*	*19X5* *£000s*
Sales	93 930	116 232	259 470	278 340	372 753
Cost of sales	81 750	102 543	230 349	239 820	346 205
Trading profit	12 180	13 689	29 121	38 520	26 548
Depreciation	1 023	1 380	3 678	4 065	8 151
Interest	2 727	2 652	7 707	10 167	14 082
Net profit before tax	8 430	9 657	17 736	24 288	4 315
Taxation	2 517	1 746	9 270	7 833	2 601
Net profit after tax	5 913	7 911	8 466	16 455	1 714
Dividends	801	1 812	3 339	3 738	3 672
Retained profits	5 112	6 099	5 127	12 717	−1 958
Retained at start of year	14 637	19 749	25 848	30 975	43 692
Retained at end of year	19 749	25 848	30 975	43 692	41 734

1 From a review of the information above identify the areas which you would concentrate on in your analysis of the position of Belper Ltd.
2 Produce common size profit and loss accounts for the five years and analyse these statements with particular reference to the profitability of Belper.
3 Calculate the trends in the sales and cost of sales and comment on the information disclosed by your analysis.
4 Using whatever form of analysis you consider appropriate comment on the financial risk profile of Belper Ltd for the five years under review.
5 Based on your analysis write a brief report for the bank advising them on whether to continue to provide finance for Belper Ltd.
6 Apart from the information arising from your analysis what other information would you advise the bank to consider when making their decision?
7 Discuss how your analysis would have been altered if you were carrying out the analysis on behalf of a prospective shareholder.

Metaltin

The information below relates to Metaltin Ltd.

**Profit and loss account of Metaltin Ltd.
for the year ended 30 April 19X2**

	Notes	*19X2*	*19X1*
Sales		4 814	5 614
Cost of sales	1	4 298	5 039
Operating profit		515	575
Interest charges		156	53
Profit before tax		359	522
Taxation	2	193	292
Retained profit		166	230

Balance sheet of Metaltin Ltd as at 30 April 19X2

	Notes	*19X2*	*19X1*
Fixed assets			
Land and buildings	3	360	227
Fittings	3	285	320
Motor vehicles	3	221	162
		866	709
Current assets			
Stocks	4	1 763	1 194
Debtors		1 259	1 004
Cash		5	61
		3 027	2 259
Creditors: Falling due within one year			
Creditors		1 370	1 147
Taxation	2	215	332
Bank overdraft		676	255
		2 261	1 734
Net current assets		766	525
Creditors: Falling due after one year			
Loans	5	200	130
		1 432	1 104
Financed by			
Share capital	6	545	483
Retained profit	6	787	621
Revaluation reserve	6	100	0
Total equity		1 432	1 104

Extracts from the notes to the accounts

1 Included in the cost of sales are the following charges.

	£
Depreciation	123
Auditors' remuneration	55
Directors' remuneration	240
Hire of plant	30
Profit on sale of fittings	20

3 Fixed assets

	Land	*Buildings*	*Fittings*	*Motor vehicles*
Balance at 1 May 19X1	120	140	600	440
Additions			100	140
Revaluations	60	40		
Disposals	180	180	700	580
			90	
Balance at 30 April 19X2	180	180	610	580
Depreciation				
Balance at 1 May 19X1		33	280	278
Charge for year		(33)	75	81
Disposals		0	355	359
			30	
Balance at 30 April 19X2		0	325	359
Net book value 19X2	180	180	285	221
Net book value 19X1	120	107	320	162

5 A long-term loan amounting to £70 was repaid during the year. This was replaced with a new loan of £140 repayable in ten years.

6 Share capital and reserves

	Share capital	*Retained profit*	*Other reserves*
Balance at 1 May 19X1	483	621	
Share issue	62		
Movements in year		166	100
Balance at 30 April 19X2	545	787	100

Cash flow statement of Metaltin Ltd
for the year ended 30 April 19X2

Net cash inflow from operating activities		17
Returns on investments and servicing of finance		
Interest paid	(156)	
Net cash outflow from returns on investment and servicing activities		(156)

Taxation		
Corporation tax paid	(310)	
Net cash outflow from taxation		(310)
Investing activities		
Payment to acquire tangible fixed assets	(240)	
Receipts from sales of fixed assets	80	
Net cash outflow from investing activity		(160)
Net cash outflow before financing		(609)
Financing		
Issue of ordinary share capital	62	
Issue of new loan	140	
Repayment of loan	(70)	
Net cash inflow from financing		132
Decrease in cash or cash equivalents		(477)

Notes to the cash flow statement

1 Reconciliation of operating profit to net cash flow from operating activities:

Operating profit	515
Depreciation charges	123
Profit on sale of fixed asset	(20)
Increase in stocks	(569)
Increase in debtors	(255)
Increase in creditors	223
	17

2 Analysis of changes in cash and cash equivalents during the year:

Bank balance at 1 May 19X1	(194)
Net cash outflow for the year	(477)
Bank balance at 30 April 19X2	(671)

3 Analysis of changes in cash and cash equivalents:

	1992	*1991*	*Change*
Cash in hand	5	61	(56)
Bank overdraft	(676)	(255)	(421)
	(671)	(194)	(477)

4 Analysis of changes in financing during the year:

	Share capital	*Loans*
Balance at 1 May 19X1	483	130
Cash inflow from financing	62	70
Balance at 30 April 19X2	545	200

Workings

Taxation	£
Balance at 1 May 19X1	332
Charge for the year	193
Less:	525
Balance at 30 April 19X2	215
Paid in the year	310

1 Produce a common size balance sheet and profit and loss account for Metaltin Ltd and comment on each of these statements.
2 Calculate the percentage changes in the balance sheet and the profit and loss account from 19X1 to 19X2 and comment on what this analysis reveals.
3 Using all the information and techniques available to you comment on the performance of Metaltin Ltd as reflected in the accounts and the cash flow statement.

13 Internal users and internal information

Having been concerned in previous chapters with external reporting and the needs of external users, we now return to internal users and their needs. Their needs are discussed under the headings of decision making, planning and control. The impacts of organizational size and structure on these needs is then examined to provide a context for the remainder of the book.

In Chapter 12 we discussed external users of information, their information needs and the ways in which they used the accounting information available. This information was derived from the financial reports via the annual accounts of the enterprises being analysed. The underlying information for these financial reports comes from the organizations' accounting system. This accounting system may be very simple or extremely sophisticated depending on the size of the business and the information needs of the users of the accounting information. One of these users is management and we stated that management would not only need more detailed information than that normally contained in the financial accounts but that it would need more up to date information and indeed some different types of information. This does not mean that the information which management may need is not useful to other users that are external to the enterprise; it may in fact be very useful to them if they had it. The reason it is not used by many of the external user groups we discussed in Chapter 12 is that in some cases they do not have the power to demand access, as for example in the case of the larger public companies such as GEC Plc. In other cases, the enterprises are too small and their internal accounting system too unsophisticated to produce any information other than that required for the annual accounts, as would be the case with, for example, your local fish and chip shop.

We shall now examine the needs of management in terms of the information they may require in order to make decisions between alternative opportunities, to plan the enterprise activities and to ensure that the plans are carried out. It is this information which is primarily prepared for internal users which may be available to external users if they have sufficient power to demand and obtain access.

Management's information needs

As a starting point we shall examine the situation of an existing business where management has already decided on the course of action to follow. In this situation management will be interested in the outcomes of those past decisions. They can obtain certain information from the annual accounts, but often this will be insufficient for this purpose because, for one thing the annual accounts often contain summarized and simplified information. This is almost certainly true in anything other than the smallest of enterprises. This summarized information may alert management to the fact that profit is lower than anticipated, but it is unlikely to be sufficiently detailed to identify the cause of this variation. This means that for management purposes there is almost invariably a need for more detailed information about the results of their past decisions and actions than that which is contained in the annual accounts.

As the name implies, annual accounts are only drawn up once a year, and this is another reason why they are unlikely to be sufficient to meet the needs of managers, who need more regular and up to date information. The fact that annual accounts are only produced at the year end means that even if they are able to establish why the results have varied from those anticipated it may well be too late to take appropriate action. For example, if an enterprise has a January year end for accounting purposes, its accounts will normally not be available until some time after the end of January. Thus any corrective action is correspondingly delayed. Although management would have access to the year's results much earlier than they are published there may still be considerable delays. These delays will not be as great as for the published accounting information where the time span between the year end and the actual production of the annual accounts varies from about three to four months for quoted companies to periods in excess of ten months for smaller enterprises.

KEY CONCEPT 13.1
Management Information needs

Management generally need more detailed information
They need up to date information
They need more frequent information
They need information suited to the decisions they are required to take

We have established some needs of management that are not satisfied by the production of annual accounts. The reason that management is likely to require information more frequently is so that they can monitor the results of their actions and decisions and fine tune the business as and when required. This is not to imply that none of the needs of managers are met by the financial information system on which the annual accounts are based. For example, although the annual accounts only show one figure for debtors, the accounting records will contain much more information about the individual debts making up that debtors figure. This will include information about when the sales took place and the customer's past payment record. This detailed information allows management to collect the money more quickly and to chase the slow payers. By doing this management will be able to ensure that the business does not face more problems because of poor cash flow than are absolutely necessary.

There are, of course, other examples of information contained within the accounting system that, if presented and used in different ways from that required for drawing up annual accounts, meet management needs better. For example, as we indicated in Chapter 6, the basic information required for both marginal and absorption costing is available from the accounting system. You will also recall that in that chapter we discussed the impact of the accounting standard SSAP 9 on the choice between absorption and marginal costing for reporting purposes. Chapter 16 contains a fuller explanation of these alternative systems and the problems associated with their use in practice. This provides the basis of understanding required for an appreciation of the discussion of the relative merits and limitations of these alternatives when looked at from the point of view of management. From that discussion you will see that depending on the decision faced by management they may need information presented in different ways. For example, to make a decision about whether to continue making a particular product or not they will require forward-looking information in the form of forecasts. They may, for example, wish to know the point at which the revenue is going to be equal to the cost, i.e. the breakeven point, and how likely it is that such a point will be reached. Whilst the latter question of the likelihood of sales reaching the level to provide a breakeven position is a question for the sales and marketing department, the question of what the cost of the product is at different levels of output is one that accountants will be called upon to answer.

A full discussion of the way in which costs behave and how to establish the breakeven position is contained in Chapter 15. An understanding of these principles is vital if appropriate decisions are to be made by management, whatever industry is being considered. For example, Sir Freddy Laker of Laker Airways argued that in the airline industry you needed to know a breakeven position that would cover costs, a breakeven position that would cover costs plus the interest charges incurred in buying planes and a third position at which you were profitable. In that case the breakeven positions could be expressed in terms of seat occupancy. Unfortunately, as it turned out, this was not the only information necessary to run a successful airline and Laker Airways subsequently went bankrupt.

Having said that management needs other information possibly in different forms, it is important to understand that the base information used to produce the annual accounts is also used as the source for many different reports that are provided to meet the specific needs of management. It should be borne in mind that, as with the other users referred to in Chapter 12, for management purposes financial information is only one of a number of types of information needed in order to make decisions about the future direction and actions of the business. It is not our intention to deal with these other types of information as they are outside the scope of this text but they could include marketing information, employment legislation etc. We shall continue our discussion of management's information needs within the relatively narrow confines of financial information.

The discussion to date has suggested that management needs more frequent and more detailed information, and that information may be required in a different format from that contained in the annual accounts. We suggested that this information was used to monitor progress and take appropriate actions to fine tune the business. Implicit in this process of monitoring is that the results are judged against some expectations. These expectations may be rough plans carried in the head of the owner of a small business or detailed plans and budgets in the case of a larger enterprise. The process of planning and control and the ways in which the information is derived and used is discussed in more detail in Chapter 14 where we look at the process of setting objectives and the problems of goal congruence in more detail. The budgeting process is also discussed in greater detail in Chapter 19 which contains a detailed analysis of the ways in which budgets can be used within an organization as a discipline to help planning, as a control mechanism and as a motivator of people.

As we have said, most if not all of this information may also be useful to users other than managers. However, some of the information is commerically sensitive and achievement of the goal of an enterprise may be dependent on its plans being kept secret from its competitors. Thus not all external users will be able to demand access to the information and the question of whether they have access will depend not only on who they are but also upon their importance to the enterprise. We shall now consider what these external users' needs may be, who they are, and the factors, such as relative power, competition and confidentiality, that determine their access or lack of access to internal information. The arguments of commercial sensitivity do not apply to some of the nationalized industries such as the Post Office. An example of the type of information that the Post Office produces is reproduced in Case Study 13.1.

CASE STUDY 13.1
The Post Office

The Post Office
Business Brief 8

Business Performance
The overall performance of the postal business in recent years can be judged from:

- profit on turnover against target
- ability to finance investment from profits and meet external financing limit targets (see Business Brief 7)
- delivery performance against targets (quality of service)
- productivity improvements
- real unit cost trends

Quality of service is the one area which has fallen short of target. However, an intensive campaign to improve performance followed by a radical agreement on efficiency measures (Spring 1985) between the Post Office and its major union has resulted in an improving trend in service reliability since the start of the 1985–6 financial year.

Productivity improvements
In the late 1970s quality of service problems were accompanied by declining productivity – partly caused by falling mail volume against high fixed collection and delivery costs. The problem was acute in inner London, where business volume fell by 30% between 1968 and 1978 and productivity by 20%–25%.

Inner London letter post was referred in 1979 to the Monopolies and Mergers Commission, which reported a year later with 43 recommendations, all but three of which were adopted. Following the report, productivity in inner London had improved by 27% by the end of the 1984–5 financial year.

The Monopolies and Mergers Commission examined the letter post as a whole in 1984. The Post Office accepted all but two of the 78 recommendations in this second report (September 1984) on financial control, quality of service, efficiency, personnel and mechanization (see Post Office Report and Accounts 1984–5, page 26). More than half will be implemented by March 1986.

Nationally, productivity in 1984–5 rose by 3%, making an improvement of 16% since 1979–80. A key factor has been productivity schemes agreed with the Union of Communication Workers – originally on a voluntary basis but with full participation as one of the terms in the major agreement with the UCW referred to above.

Commentary
The Post Office highlight six measures of business performance of which three relate to financial information and three to service delivery. Of those that relate to financial information, one which is of specific interest here is the measurement of actual profitability as measured by the financial accounting system against the profitability targets which would have been set as part of the planning function, which is supported by what is commonly referred to as the management accounting system.

External users' information needs

One external user group who can demand access to internal accounting information is the taxation authorities. The nature of the information they require will vary but will normally be either more detailed breakdowns of particular expense headings or details of the timing of purchases and sale of fixed assets. The reason for this is that the taxation system is based upon a different set of rules for arriving at the taxable profit from those used to arrive at the accounting profit. The taxation authorities, which include both the Inland Revenue and the Customs and Excise who deal with value-added tax (VAT), have a statutory right of access to information.

Another external user who often is in a sufficiently powerful position to demand and obtain further information is the enterprise's bankers. The information they demand will of course depend on the circumstances. For example, if the enterprise is doing well the information demanded will be quite different from what would be required if the enterprise had problems. We shall discuss at a general level some of the additional information they may require and why this is required before going on to examine what determines whether or not this information is available to these external users.

In general, the information demanded by an enterprise's bankers can be divided into two categories: that required for routine monitoring and that required to arrive at judgements about the future needs of the enterprise. The former category would include regular management accounts such as monthly profit statements, an analysis of debts in terms of how old they are (this is known as an 'aged debtors analysis') and other up to date information such as the amount owed by the enterprise, i.e. the monthly creditors balance. All this information is required to monitor the health of their customer's business on a more regular basis than would be possible if they had to rely on the information provided by annual accounts which, as we have already said, are likely to be a few months out of date when they are produced.

Bankers also required other information to make judgements about the future needs and prospects of the enterprise in order to ascertain whether to lend money, when it is likely to be repaid and the risk involved. The information on future prospects is normally required in the form of projected cash flow statements and profit and loss accounts, but would also include information about other loans that the enterprise may have and their due dates for repayment. The financial information is of course only part of the information that the banker may require; this could also include future orders, plans, analysis of competitors etc.

As we have already indicated, there are circumstances where, like other external users such as shareholders and competitors, the banker cannot get access to this additional information. We shall examine those circumstances in our discussion of the impact of organizational size and structure on the information produced for management purposes, which is, of course, one factor which determines what these external users have access to.

Impacts of organizational size

We have discussed the needs of management in terms of information to make decisions about the future, to plan future actions and to control the business on a day-to-day basis. It should be clear that the more complex and sophisticated the business is, the more likely it is that it will require additional information. For example, the local garage owner may be able to carry in his head all the information needed to enable the business to be run effectively on a day-to-day basis. This is because the business is sufficiently small and the proprietor, who is of course in this situation also the manager, is directly involved in the running of the business and is on the spot to take whatever action is necessary.

On the other hand, in a large and complex business there is a need for a more formalized system for a number of reasons. Firstly the amount of information required in, for example, a multi-product firm is such that it is unlikely that the management would be able to carry, in their heads, all the detail necessary to run the business effectively. (A fuller discussion of the problems faced by multi-product firms and the techniques available to solve those particular problems is contained in Chapter 18 where we look at the effects of resource constraints and at make or buy decisions.) Secondly, with larger businesses it is probably the case that the larger the business the more the senior managers will be removed from the day-to-day operations. This will not only change their information needs to requiring information of a more strategic type but will also impose a requirement for additional information to control the activities and actions of those below them.

Thus the size of the organization will influence the information needs of its managers and the way in which these needs are met, i.e. the need for more formal systems as the size of the business increases. We have also suggested that the nature of the business has an effect on the information needs – thus a multi-product business will require more sophisticated information systems than a single-product business. Consider for example the different information required to run a restaurant where the only product is food compared with that required to run a hotel. In the latter case not only do you need information about the food operation, but information is also required on bed occupancy rates, the bar profit etc.

However, in discussing the information needs of managers it has to be borne in mind that information is not cost free. In general the more sophisticated the information system the more it costs to set up and run. Thus the need for better and more up to date information always has to be balanced against the costs and benefits of obtaining that information. However, as we point out in Chapter 14, although there is considerable literature on cost–benefit analysis the practical implementation of such an approach is fraught with difficulties. We should also remember that more up to date information is not in itself better *per se* as it also needs to be relevant to the use to which it is to be put. A fuller discussion of what constitutes relevant information in relation to costs and benefits and how these relate to short-term decisions is contained in Chapter 17. This issue of obtaining relevant information at a reasonable cost is part of the explanation of why in the case of many small businesses there is little in the way of formal management information. In many of these cases the information if it exists at all is held in the owner–manager's head in a form that is not readily accessible to others. In these situations bankers are often able to exercise considerable influence as a major provider of finance; however, in the end, no matter how much pressure is exerted they cannot access information that does not exist. They therefore have to rely on the annual accounts and such other information as is available.

We have shown that the information available is influenced not only by the needs of managers but also by the size and complexity of the organization's products. We have also suggested that the nature of the product or products can influence the information systems. There are of course many other factors which will have an influence on what is required and what is produced. Consider, for example, the differing needs of high technology industries and the impacts of flexible manufacturing systems and of management techniques such as Just-in-time. These, like the particular industry, will lead to specific needs. A full discussion of these is outside the scope of this book although in subsequent chapters we have tried to look at different industries in both the manufacturing and service sectors. Rather than pursuing the effects of differing industries further we shall now consider a more general influence upon the information needs of managers, i.e. the structure of the organization.

Impacts of organizational structure

It is clear from looking at a few well-known examples that different organizations have different structures and this means that their information needs may also differ. If we consider retailing, it is obvious that a business such as Marks & Spencer that operates both within the UK and overseas is going to need information relating to a Paris branch that may be different from that for a London branch if for no other reason than the effect of different currencies. Thus in general an organization that has a multinational operation will have different information requirements than one whose operations are solely in the domestic market.

Similarly, many department stores such as Debenhams are organized round departments as profit centres and the departments' profits are identified separately. This implies that both the cost records and the takings from sales have to be identified and recorded by department. It may well be the case in such organizations that management is rewarded on the basis of schemes such as profit sharing, or by comparing profits achieved against predetermined targets. In such circumstances the information system would have to be designed to meet the structural requirements of the organization. These and similar matters are touched on in the discussion of department and divisional accounting in Chapter 17 and the impact and uses of budgets in Chapter 19.

We could of course find many more examples of different organizational structures apart from those referred to above as the organizational structure will depend on and to some extent be determined by the product, the market in which a business operates and the competitive environment, as well as more mundane factors such as geography and location of its component parts or outlets. To do so would be extremely time consuming and outside the requirement of this text. However, in general terms the more decentralized an organization is, the more complex the information system will be.

Summary

In this chapter we have looked at the information needs of internal users. We have shown that the broad term management covers a wide range of people in the organization who may each have differing information needs. These will vary from the detailed information needs of the manager of a department within a store to the more strategic needs of the general manager of the whole department store. This analysis can of course be applied to other organizations where there are multiple layers of management ranging from those involved in the day-to-day running up to the board of directors. We have also indicated that the size and complexity of the organization as well as its structure will affect the information requirements of those within the organization and the relative availability of this information to those external users who may have the power to access such information. However, the common thread that runs throughout is that management needs detailed up to date information for the purposes of planning, decision making and control of organizations. It is to a more detailed examination of these areas that we turn in the following chapters.

Review questions

1. What are the main reasons why management would require additional information to the annual accounts?
2. One of the major improvements that bankers wish to see in respect of financial information is an improvement in the timeliness of information. Explain what this means and why it is important to bankers. How might this differ for managers?
3. What is likely to be the major impact of organizational size on the information needs of managers?
4. What useful management information is available from the accounting system from which the annual accounts are produced?
5. What additional information would bankers wish to have and what purpose would they use this for?

Problems for discussion and analysis

1 Would the way in which managers use the information you have identified in your answer to question 5 above differ from the way it is used by bankers and if so how would it differ?

2 In each of the situations outlined below identify what you believe your information needs would be.

Situation 1
You are the manager of a local branch of a national retail organization. All buying is done centrally and prices are fixed. You are in charge of the day-to-day management and hiring and firing of staff. Your annual remuneration is fixed.

Situation 2
The situation is the same as above except that in addition to your annual salary you receive a bonus of £1 for each £100 profit made above that expected.

Situation 3
As in situation 2 above except that you are able to decide on the selling price yourself.

Situation 4
You have been so successful as a branch manager that the company has promoted you to the position of regional manager in charge of 20 shops all of whose managers work under the conditions outlined in situation 3 above.

3 You work for an organization primarily involved in health care which runs a number of nursing homes for the elderly and has a head office staff consisting of yourself and two owner directors. Each of the nursing homes has a matron in charge who looks after the day-to-day running of the nursing home, but the advertising of the service etc. is carried out by one of the directors whilst the other director looks after the billing of the patients and collection of monies due. The overall profitability of your organization has fallen drastically in the last year and you have been asked to investigate the situation.

Identify what information you would need and what level of detail would be required in order for you to start your investigation.

Planning and control

14

This chapter examines the planning and control process, which is divided into four stages: the setting of objectives, making strategic decisions, making operating decisions and monitoring and corrective action. Those factors that will affect the design and application of the planning and control process are also considered.

To be able to make decisions wisely, individuals and organizations need to have some vision about the future. A decision made without any thought to the future may well result in undesirable consequences; this is particularly so in the business context. For example, one of the main reasons identified for the failure of small businesses is the lack of planning of cash requirements. These businesses often fail despite the fact that they trade profitably. Apart from the need to make plans there is also a need to monitor actual performance to ensure that the plans are being attained. This monitoring activity is an essential part of the control exercised by organizations to help secure their survival and efficiency.

In this chapter we examine the planning and control process using a framework which not only explains the process itself but also provides an essential foundation for the analysis and discussions in subsequent chapters.

It is important to recognize that the planning and control process cannot be examined in isolation. There are a number of factors that will influence its design and application. In this chapter we also discuss some of the more significant factors, such as technology, that may influence the design of accounting information systems in the context of the planning and control process, and it is appropriate here to consider some of the main limitations inherent in the application of the process.

The planning and control process

KEY CONCEPT 14.1
Planning and control

Planning involves the determination of objectives and expressing how they are to be attained. The control process is the means of ensuring that the plans will be achieved.

A number of stages have been identified in the planning and control process:

Stage 1 Setting of objectives
Stage 2 Making strategic decisions
Stage 3 Making operating decisions
Stage 4 Monitoring and possible corrective action

We will begin by considering the four stages in the planning and control process before turning to the technical aspects of this process and factors that may influence the design of the accounting system within the process.

Objectives

From both a practical and a theoretical perspective, the determination and setting of objectives is probably the most complex stage of the planning and control process in a business organization. However, in the absence of any explicit objectives there is no basis for management to evaluate whether the business is succeeding, nor any criterion for choosing between alternative business opportunities.

Organizations themselves do not have objectives *per se*; the objectives of the organization will reflect those of the people involved with that organization. These individuals will each have their personal goals and it is likely that some may conflict with other participants. A sales manager's objective may be the maximization of sales, in volume terms, without any strong consideration to profitability. This may conflict with the objectives of the financial management of the firm whose primary concern could be to maximize profits through the introduction of higher prices with lower volumes of sales. This conflict in objectives is commonly referred to as a lack of goal congruence.

The problem of goal congruence is more acute in large business organizations because of the number of participants and their varying vested interests. In the case of a company, it is likely that employees would find an increase in remuneration desirable and possibly one of their personal goals. However, this may conflict with the interest of

KEY CONCEPT 14.2
Goal congruence

Goal congruence is the alignment of organizational goals with the personal and group goals of the individuals within an organization.

shareholders if it reduces the amount available to them for payment of dividends.

From a wider social perspective, there is a growing awareness of the need to recognize the interests of parties external to the organization itself when it sets its objectives. In particular, customers, government and the local community will all have an interest in the survival and the activities of the organization. For example, in recent years there has been a growing public concern about environmental issues. Through public pressure a number of firms have had to change policies regarding their production activities. A good illustration of this is the change in policy of petrol companies to produce unleaded petrol.

If a business organization's objectives are to be effective there must be congruence of goals. Horngren (1991) suggests that: 'Goal congruence exists, for example, when managers working in their own best interests also act in harmony with the goals of the organization as a whole.' When an organization sets its objectives the interests of all the participants will need to be recognized and common goals identified.

A number of academics maintain that it is not important to consider the goals of each individual, since their major interests will tend to converge to form group objectives. For example, it is likely that more pay will be a common goal for all employees. However, for an organization, there still remains the problem of identifying and setting objectives that satisfy all interested groups.

Lowe and Chua (1983) suggest that by looking at the common ground shared by the participants it is possible to establish organizational goals. They start by designating the possibilities open to organizations as 'activity spaces', which are defined by the interests of the varying groups involved with the organization. For example, the activity space for shareholders of a company might be to reduce labour costs, whereas that of employees (and possibly of governments) would be to maintain jobs and wage levels. Figure 14.1 shows the activity space for each interested group.

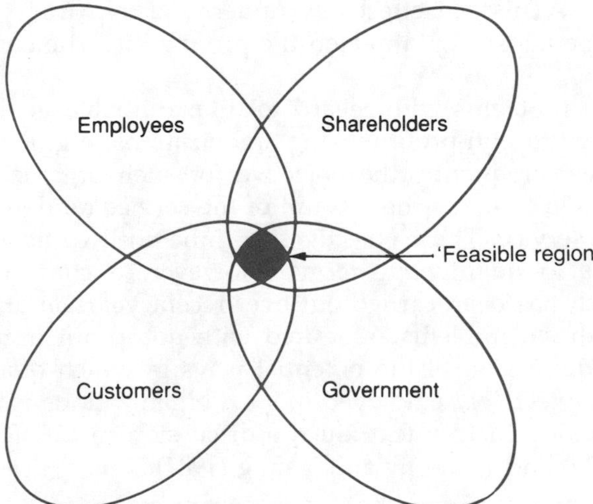

Figure 14.1

Where the boundaries of the activity space for each group overlap in Figure 14.1 are regions where the acceptable activity is common to more than one group. The area where the activity spaces for all groups overlap is described as the 'feasible region'. Lowe and Chua argue that it is the task of management of an organization to confine its activities within this 'feasible region'.

The most obvious activity in the 'feasible region' for a business organization in a capitalist economy is the making of profit. Where markets are, by and large, unregulated and competitive, profit making is an essential element in ensuring a firm's survival. Profits are by nature quantifiable and targets can readily be set in terms of formulating objectives. The quantifiable nature of profits also means that they are measurable. This attribute is very attractive to managers as deviations from the set objectives during an accounting period can easily be identified. This feature is particularly important in the control process, which will be discussed later in the chapter. It is common, in practice, to find the profit objective stated, more precisely, in terms of maximization of profits.

Qualitative objectives, in contrast with those of a quantitative nature, suffer from the problems associated with measurement. For example, the quality of a product (in meeting its purpose and customer requirements) is far more difficult to define in measurable terms, and difficulties also arise when comparing the objective set with actual performance in the control process. Although product or service quality is often cited as a prime objective of a business, in reality it is often disregarded or assessed inappropriately through movements in sales revenue.

Because of the difficulty often faced in setting unquantifiable goals, such as a quality definition or social responsibilities, most firms tend to compromise on the easier option of profit setting as the major (or sole) criterion for expressing their objectives. Although this gives a simple version of the firm's objectives, it has the disadvantage of conferring a blinkered view of the interactions which take place with various other interests. This can effectively undermine the firm's performance and even, paradoxically, threaten the profit which the company has put in esteem.

These problems with regard to unquantifiable goals are particularly pertinent to non-profit-making organizations, e.g. local authorities and charities. Frequently the objective for such organizations will be expressed in terms of the amount of the service rendered and the quality of that service. These objectives are inherently difficult or impossible to express in quantitative terms. However, a considerable amount of research has been carried out over recent years in an attempt to overcome these problems associated with non-profit organizations. A detailed discussion of the potential ways in which qualitative objectives can be effectively employed in such organizations is outside the scope of this introductory text. Such a discussion can be found in Henley *et al*. (1989) and Anthony and Young (1984).

Strategic decisions are those that determine the long-term policies of the firm and that are necessary if the firm is to meet its objectives.

KEY CONCEPT 14.3
Strategic decisions

Making strategic decisions

Strategic decisions in a business organization will invariably relate to policy changes in respect of the products or services that are currently being offered and the markets where they are sold.

The nature of the environment in which businesses operate is uncertain and outside the control of management. Some typical examples of the uncertain variables that can confront an organization are changes in taste, high inflation, recession and competitiveness. If organizations remain static and do not consider alternative policies in such an environment, it is likely that their objectives will not be met, which could threaten their survival in the long term. Often, strategic decisions have been made to maintain long-term profitability by diversifying, which has also made businesses less dependent on their traditional markets. For example, Ladbrokes, who primarily concentrated in the betting shop market, have invested in hotels and the leisure industry.

Drury (1993) suggests that to make effective strategic decisions management should be pro-active in 'identifying potential opportunities and threats in its current environment and take specific steps immediately so that the organization will not be taken by surprise by any developments which may occur in the future'. He argues that firms should be constantly searching for alternative courses, and developing:

- new products for sale in existing and new markets;
- new markets for existing products.

It is also maintained that because of the importance of strategic decisions they will tend to be taken at the higher levels of management of organizations. These decisions are of a long-term nature, and this is one of the features that differentiates them from operating decisions.

Operating decisions are decisions that focus on the efficient use of the resources available to the firm in the short term.

KEY CONCEPT 14.4
Operating decisions

Making operating decisions

The majority of operating decisions in an organization will be concerned with pricing and output, e.g. price setting and the determination of production volumes and stock levels.

To be effective the decisions must be made with reference to the objectives and strategic policies of the organization. However, as these decisions are taken in the current economic environment, often there will be constraints on the levels of sales and production. These constraints may prevent an organization, in the short term, meeting its objectives. For example, an organization may be confronted with shortages of skilled labour which will effectively constrain output levels in the short term. If the maximization of profits is an objective of the organization in this situation, the constraint will also effectively result in limiting the extent to which the objective can be met in the short term. In the long term usually these constraints can be relieved. In the case of shortages in labour skills, training can be given. In circumstances where resource constraints exist, although the long-term objectives cannot be satisfied, it is still important to allocate scarce resources efficiently. Management accounting techniques have been developed to allocate scarce resources efficiently in these circumstances and they will be considered in detail in a later chapter.

The long-term plans of an organization, as previously mentioned, will be formulated through the making of strategic decisions with reference to the overall objectives of the organization. In cases where, in the short term, the targets embodied within the long-term plans cannot be met, there may be a need to amend or revise these plans in the light of the current economic situation. The process of re-examining long-term plans, in such circumstances, is an important feature of managing organizations effectively in a dynamic economic environment.

Operating decisions will be translated into a short-term plan which is referred to as a budget. Budgets are simply plans of action expressed in money terms. The process of aggregating operating decisions into a plan compels management to look ahead and co-ordinate their activities. For example, from this aggregation process the required level of stocks for production activities over the planning period can be identified. Without forward plans that co-ordinate production activities the business may drift along meeting undesirable situations, such as not having enough stocks to meet production requirements, that should have been anticipated and avoided. The budget also acts as a basis for judging performance, through the comparison between actual and budgeted figures. This comparison can help to highlight strengths and weaknesses within the organization. It is important that budgets should be communicated to personnel in an organization so that they are aware of the planned (budgeted) targets. This will enable them to act in accordance with the plan.

The degree of sophistication and detail given to these budgets will depend inevitably on the size of the organization and the needs of internal users within the organization. Often the budgets will cover a period of one year and be broken down in monthly intervals. Primarily the reason for periodic monthly budgets is for control reasons, to enable a comparison of budget and actual activity at regular intervals so that timely monitoring of the plan is facilitated.

The process of preparing budgets and the types of budgets that are commonly employed will be examined in detail in Chapter 19.

Monitoring and corrective action

Essentially monitoring and corrective action are the major parts of the control activities of any organization. The first element in this stage is the monitoring of actual performance against budget. Inevitably, from this comparison, differences (commonly referred to as 'variances') will be identified – it is unlikely that the actual performance will be exactly the same as the budget. The reason for this is that the operating decisions embodied in the budget will normally be determined well in advance of actual performance and the process of forecasting cost and revenues in a dynamic economic environment is surrounded by uncertainty.

KEY CONCEPT 14.5
Monitoring and corrective action

Monitoring is the process of comparing actual performance with a predetermined target (plan). It provides the basis from which corrective action can be planned and taken.

To monitor performance effectively, personnel in an organization who incur expenditure and generate revenues will be identified and made responsible for these costs and revenues. The underlying approach adopted here is known as 'responsibility accounting'. The approach recognizes various decision centres throughout an organization and traces cost and revenues to individual managers who are primarily responsible for making decisions and controlling the cost and revenues of the centre. The manager's knowledge of the centre places him/her in a relatively advantageous position, within an organization, to ensure that budget targets are achieved. These responsibility centres will normally take the form of departments or divisions within an organization.

In effective responsibility accounting systems managers will, to some extent, also participate in the preparation of their own budgets. There is evidence from research suggesting that in certain circumstances participation by responsible managers in the setting of budgets enhances the probability that an effective planning and control system is employed within an organization.

There is a need for a reporting system, in an organization, to communicate relevant information to support a system of responsibility accounting effectively. The reports will show the actual performance, the budget, and the deviations (variances) from budget. The mode in which budgeted and actual costs and revenues are collected and then reported, e.g. by product, labour or material input costs, will be determined by management. The major factors influencing management in deciding the extent and sophistication of the reporting system will be the costs of installing such a system compared with the benefits generated from the system. A more detailed discussion of the cost and benefits of information systems will be covered later.

When variances have been identified it is necessary to determine the reason for them in order that corrective action may be taken. If deviations from budget, assuming the budget reflects realistic targets, are not corrected it could be harmful to the organization in the long run. For example, material usage in a production process may exceed the budget in a particular control period, which could result in losses and consequently threaten the profitability of the organization if action is not taken.

Whilst the methods for identification of variances and their causes are outside the scope of this text, it is appropriate that you have some insight into the general nature of the causes of variances.

Traditionally texts have tended to concentrate on variances that have been caused through operating problems, e.g. the prices of raw materials are greater than anticipated in the budget, perhaps because of inefficient buying practices by buyers. A few academics, in particular Demski (1967) and Bromwich (1980), have argued that there could be other causes of variance that have tended to be overlooked in the control process. Basically they identify three causes of variances:

1 Operating variances are related to human or mechanical factors that result in the budget targets not being achieved.
2 Random variances are caused by divergences between actual and planned costs that arise at random; i.e. they occur by chance and there is no means of controlling these variances. For example, in some chemical processing the output can vary per unit of input because such variations are inherent in the process; in particular evaporation often occurs in these types of process.
3 Planning variances will occur if plans are not realistic at the time of actual performance, even if operations have been efficiently carried out. Put simply, the plans may be out of date. For example, during the planning stage material costs may have been set with due care, but because of rapid inflation these planned costs are out of date in the control period and therefore do not represent realistic budget targets to compare actual and planned activities.

You should now read Case Study 14.1 on variances.

CASE STUDY 14.1
Mark Plc Variances

Mark Plc employs a budgeting system to control costs. The original budget for 19X1 included material A, which was estimated to cost £5 per kilogram. It was anticipated that 1000 kg would be used during the year. Therefore the budget in total cost terms was £5000. During the year, however, although 1000 kg was used, the cost was £6000.

Traditionally, the analysis of the variance between actual and budget would be presented as follows:

	Actual	*Budget*	*Variance*
	£	£	£
Material A 1000 kg	6000	5000	(1000)

The brackets around the variance of £1000 indicate that it is 'unfavourable', i.e. actual costs exceed budget (plan).

This analysis, however, does not give any indication as to the cause of the variance. For example, it could be because of inefficient buying practices by the purchaser of the materials or because prices have increased through inflation during the year. The former cause implies that the variance is due to operating problems and actions may be taken in the future to ensure that more efficient buying practices are used. In contrast, if the variance is caused through inflation since the price was set in the original budget, it implies that the variance is because the plan is out of date. In this case it is unlikely that the firm can take any action to prevent such variances occurring again.

Let us now assume that the firm has information at the end of the year 19X1 indicating that a realistic planned price taking account of inflation during the year would be £5.50 per kilogram. The variances could then be analysed as follows:

	Actual £	*Budget* £	*Variance* £
Variance caused through inefficient operations	6000	5500	(500)

	Original budget £	*Updated budget* £	*Variance* £
Variance caused by the plan being out of date	5000	5500	(500)

In this analysis the causes of the variance are clearly identified, i.e. £500 relates to operating problems and £500 is because the original budget was out of date. The information presented in this way is more informative and useful for management purposes.

Although the analysis of operating, random and planning variances is on the whole theoretically sound, there are a number of practical problems which may explain its limited use in practice. For example, in Case Study 14.1 the up to date budget of £5500 was established at the end of the year. In other words this budget was established in hindsight after the purchase of the material. To establish a realistic budget reflecting the recent past operating conditions these budgets, by their nature, must be determined after the event. Whilst such budgets are useful for variance analysis purposes, they do not give any targets for management to work to during the actual production period. This is a major deficiency in the use of these types of budgets. There are a number of other major criticisms. The most critical commentator being Lloyd Amey (1973).

In the context of this book, as has already been mentioned, it is not necessary for us to delve too deeply into the details of the causes of variances nor to examine the criticisms in detail. It is important, however, to recognize, from the work of Demski and Bromwich in this area, the limitations of traditional variance analysis, which can restrict the effectiveness of the planning and control process in its practical application.

Another effective limitation to this stage of the process is the cost of investigating the cause of variances. The activity of investigation can be costly. It may be considered not worth the time and money to carry out such an investigation for the benefits derived. Therefore, a variance may not be seen as sufficiently significant.

The control system

The accountant's control system, the monitoring and corrective action stage of the process, is often compared with those of an engineer, using the analogy of a central heating system. Figure 14.2 is a relatively simplistic diagram of a central heating system. In this system the desired temperature is set and the comparator compares this with the actual room temperature. If there is any deviation from the set temperature action is automatically taken by the system to fuel the boiler to enable it to compensate for any temperature variance. This system thus involves the process of monitoring actual output against a desired output, and when a variance is identified corrective action will automatically be taken.

Earlier, when we were examining the planning and control process, very similar stages were identified and described. However, there are a number of interesting differences between the two systems, some of which will give us a greater insight into the limitations of the planning and control process.

An important difference is that the central heating model is a physical system where there are *automatic* responses to outputs. That is, corrective action is taken to obtain the desired temperature automatically, and without any reference to operatives. In contrast, the control model,

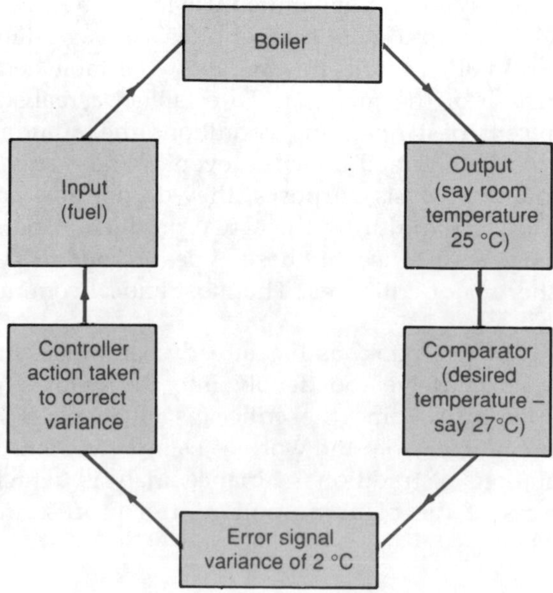

Figure 14.2

within the planning and control process, is normally dependent upon humans. In this system the response to deviations from the budget is not taken automatically. Time lags will be experienced in all accounting reporting systems and people will have to be motivated to respond to variances and take corrective action if it is perceived to be necessary.

The extent of these time lags in reporting will depend upon the sophistication of the accounting information system. In the case of some large companies the monitoring of performance will be on a weekly basis and, with computerization helping to speed up the reporting process, the capability of taking corrective action is relatively quick. However, in the majority of organizations control reports will normally be generated on a monthly basis. The main restriction to implementing more timely systems will be the installation and running cost, which once again relates to the cost and benefits of information systems, i.e. an information system should only be installed if the benefits generated from the system exceed the cost of installing the system. The variances that are reported in an accounting information system can, of course, only be used to guide future operations. An organization cannot remedy past mistakes.

It is now well recognized that the effectiveness of accounting information systems is very much dependent upon the attitudes of individuals associated with the organization. For a detailed explanation of accounting and its relationship with human behaviour, reference should be made to Hopwood (1976). Although a considerable amount of attention is now correctly given to the influence of individuals on accounting information systems, there is still considerable scope for further research as well as the appreciation in practice that human behaviour can distort the effectiveness of accounting systems.

In the context of the control systems, the process of setting targets will be influenced and affected by the behaviour of individuals. For example, a sales manager may respond negatively if he is set a target that, in his opinion, he is unable to achieve. Another example is the required action to correct further undesirable variances: this action will very much depend upon the reaction and motivation of the responsible manager and his subordinates. If a manager perceives that targets are unrealistic it is unlikely that he/she will be motivated to take corrective action to ensure that they are met in the future. The accountant's control system is therefore limited in its application by the motivation of individuals in setting budgets and taking action on variances that have been identified.

The cost and benefits of accounting information systems

An accounting information system is a commodity in much the same way as household goods such as detergents, soap and food. That is, there is a cost, often considerable, in installing and running the system. The benefits from employing the system should exceed the cost or otherwise it would be questionable whether the system should be installed.

The optimal system for any organization will be the system that generates the greatest amount of benefits net of costs. Horngren (1987) contrasts this approach with choosing a system because it is more accurate or a truer approximation of economic reality. The cost–benefit approach does not use accuracy as a criterion but focuses on the net benefits derived from alternative systems, giving preference to the system that generates the greater net benefits.

The practical implementation of the cost–benefit approach, however, is rather complex. Whilst it may be feasible to determine the cost of alternative systems, the benefits, e.g. the quality of information, are invariably difficult to measure as they tend to be qualitative. Although this is a problem, and cost–benefit approach is relevant in the choice of systems and is particularly relevant to the systems within the planning and control process described earlier.

Organizational and environmental context

A number of writers and researchers argue that the installation of effective planning and control processes in businesses requires consideration of individual and organization factors. Earlier we briefly examined individual behavioural considerations with reference to the setting of budgets and the motivation required to take corrective action to maintain control of costs and revenues within the organization. Now we briefly consider other organizational and environmental issues.

Businesses are affected by and dependent on their environment. Emmanuel, Otley and Merchant (1990) stress that a firm's 'ultimate survival is determined by the degree to which it adapts and accommodates itself to environmental contingencies (uncertain events)'. Therefore the design of planning control systems must be carefully tailored to match their environment and the organizational context in which the system will be employed. This approach is not new in practice; it has been implicitly recognized by accountants for a number of years.

Traditionally writers of texts have suggested that there is one best way in which in a particular task can be carried out regardless of the environment in which the organization operates, e.g. the nature of the market and the production process. Accounting information systems as illustrated in texts have invariably adopted this approach, and have not differentiated the various needs of accounting for different organizations. This approach very much follows the classical management and scientific management theories propounded by, for example, F.W. Taylor (1947). The *contingency theory* of organizations, in contrast, accepts that different types of organization will require differing types of accounting information to enable them to function effectively.

Emmanuel and Otley identify three major classes of contingent factors:

1 technology, e.g. the nature of the production process – labour-intensive *vis-à-vis* machine-intensive operations;

2 environmental, e.g. the degree of competition and the degree of predictability;
3 structural, e.g. the size and type of the organization.

These contingent factors will affect the accounting information systems, and in particular the effectiveness of the planning and control process. For example, in the context of planning, businesses that are in a relatively risky market will tend to invest more in planning in an attempt to predict outcomes and analyse alternative opportunities to lessen their risk. The design of planning and control systems should take account of these wider issues if a firm is to survive and cope in its environment.

Users of planning information and the impact of organizational size

Very little reference has been made to small businesses *vis-à-vis* large businesses, so far, in the context of installing and employing planning and control systems. Clearly, there are constraints for small businesses in their use and choice of such systems. One of the major constraints relating to the cost and benefits of installing these systems was described earlier. Nevertheless, there is increasing evidence to suggest that there is a greater chance of survival if small firms do use budgets to plan their future and employ control mechanisms to ensure that these plans are met. The reason often cited for the high failure rate in the UK of this size of firm is the lack of planning and control of cash resources. Therefore, much of what has been said so far regarding the need for planning and control it would appear is relevant to this size of enterprise.

Summary

For organizations to operate efficiently in a dynamic and uncertain environment there is a need for them to plan and control their businesses. Four important stages of the planning and control process were identified and examined in this chapter.

The setting of objectives is clearly critical to the process. The other stages in the process are very dependent upon clear objectives being set and communicated to personnel within an organization. In the uncertain environment that confronts business organizations it is important that they constantly make and review strategic decisions to maintain their position in the market place and to exploit the opportunities for growth. In the short term organizations must manage their resources efficiently in their day-to-day operating decisions which are embodied within short-term plans known as budgets. If an organization is to ensure that it is meeting its objectives in the long and short term it is necessary to monitor results and take corrective action when relevant. This was examined in the last stage of the process.

A number of problems were also identified relating to these four stages in the planning and control process. Potentially these problems can limit the effectiveness of the process. However, there is growing evidence that the more successful organizations invest heavily in planning and control information systems.

References

Amey, Lloyd (1973) Hindsight vs expectations in performance measurement, in *Readings in Management Decisions* (ed. L. Amey), Longman.

Anthony, R.N. and Young, D.W. (1984) *Management Control in Nonprofit Organizations*, Richard Irwin.

Bromwich, M. (1980) 'Standard costing for planning and control', in *Topics in Management Accounting* (eds J. Arnold, B. Carsberg and R. Scapens), Philip Allen.

Demski, J.S. (1982) 'Analysing the effectiveness of traditional standard cost variance model', in *Information for Decision-Making*, 3rd edn (ed. A. Rappaport), Prentice-Hall.

Drury, J.C. (1993) *Management and Cost Accounting*, Chapman and Hall.

Emmanuel, C.R., Otley, D.T. and Merchant, K. (1990) *Accounting for Management Control*, Chapman and Hall.

Henley, D., Holtham, C., Likierman, A. and Perrin, J. (1989) *Public Sector Accounting and Financial Control*, 3rd edn, VNR.

Hopwood, A. (1976) *Accounting and Human Behaviour*, Prentice-Hall.

Horngren, C. and Foster, G. (1991) *Cost Accounting – a Managerial Emphasis*, 7th edn, Prentice-Hall.

Lowe, E.A. and Chua, W.F. (1983) 'Organizational effectiveness and management control', in *New Perspectives in Management Control* (eds E.A. Lowe and J.L.F. Machlin), Macmillan.

Taylor, F.W. (1947) *Scientific Management*, Harper and Row.

Further reading

For a more detailed analysis and discussion regarding the influence of the environment and its relations to business organizations and organizational objectives reference should be made to Chapters 2 and 3 of David Needle's book in this series 'Business in Context' (Chapman & Hall, 1989).

Public Sector Accounting and Financial Control by Henley *et al.* (VNR, 1989) gives a comprehensive analysis of accounting for non-profit organizations in the context of the public sector. This book contains chapters examing local government, nationalized industries and the National Health Service. Of particular interest in relation to this chapter is the discussion concerning the objectives of these non-profit organizations. Another text, *Management Control in Nonprofit Organizations* by Anthony and Young (3rd edn, Irwin, 1984), provides a useful insight into the role of planning and control in non-profit organizations.

A useful and interesting analysis of organizational control systems in an accounting context can be found in the first part of *Accounting for Management Control* by Emmanuel, Otley and Merchant (2nd edn, Chapman & Hall, 1990).

Review questions

1 There are a number of stages in the planning and control process. Identify these and give a brief description of each stage.
2 In recent years external users of accounting information have required from firms their internal management accounting information. Explain why such information is useful to these users.
3 Define responsibility accounting with reference to the planning and control process.

Problems for discussion and analysis

1 Discuss the main differences between the control models of accountants and engineers. Detail any limitations to the planning and control process that can be identified through this comparison.
2 Give illustrations of how the behaviour of individuals can affect the planning and control process.
3 For plans to be effective management should consider the wider environmental factors that relate to the firm. Discuss.
4 Describe why it is important to set objectives in the firm and comment on the problems of setting objectives.

15 Cost behaviour and cost–volume–profit analysis

To be able to predict future costs for planning and decision making it is necessary to understand how costs behave in relation to activity levels. The chapter begins by examining the nature of cost behaviour, classifying costs into fixed and variable. This classification is then employed within the context of cost–volume–profit analysis.

For managers to be able to choose between alternative business opportunities, they need information regarding future costs and revenues and the way in which these may vary at different levels of activity. In order to use this information effectively, in the business environment, they also need to understand how costs are determined and the way in which costs and revenues behave.

In this chapter we begin by examining cost behaviour and the ways in which costs are predicted, and then we consider the application of this information to decision making using the technique of cost–volume–profit (CVP) analysis. This technique examines the interrelationships between cost, volume and profits at differing activity levels to aid managers in their decision making. We also critically appraise the traditional methods and models that are used and the underlying assumptions.

Cost behaviour

To understand how costs behave it is first necessary to understand the nature of costs. Some costs are essentially fixed in nature, e.g. the standing charge for the domestic telephone service. Others vary with usage or activity, e.g. the cost of each telephone call made. These costs are known as variable costs. Unfortunately, not all costs fall neatly within these categories and therefore it may be necessary to make some simplifying assumptions about how costs behave for the purpose of decision making.

Before examining fixed and variable costs and how they behave it is worthwhile to start with the examination of cost functions.

> **KEY CONCEPT 15.1**
> ***Variable costs***
>
> Variable costs are the same per unit of activity and therefore total variable costs will increase and decrease in direct proportion to the increase and decrease in the activity level. The activity level may be measured in terms of either production/service output or sales output. The choice will depend upon what is being measured.

> **KEY CONCEPT 15.2**
> ***Fixed costs***
>
> A cost is fixed if it does not change in response to changes in the level of activity.

Linear cost functions

A basic notion of science is the idea that one thing will depend on another according to some mathematical relation. It is likely that in your study of economics you have come across the application of this concept. For example, when considering the relationship between the total spending (c) of a nation on all consumption goods in one year and the total income (y) of all persons in the nation in one year economists use the expression:

$$c = f(y)$$

This expression states that consumption is a function of the level of income. That is, the level of consumption in one year will be dependent upon the level of income.

Similarly, this basic notion is also applied in accounting in order to understand the functional relationships between cost and activity levels.

There are two important variables involved in the construction of cost functions. (We shall use the example of the cost of travelling to illustrate the nature of these variables and their interrelationship.)

- The dependent variable y is the cost to be predicted – the total cost for an activity, e.g. the cost of petrol for a journey.
- The independent variable x is the level of activity, e.g. the number of miles to be travelled on the journey.

The dependent variable is expressed as a function of the independent variable:

$$y = f(x)$$

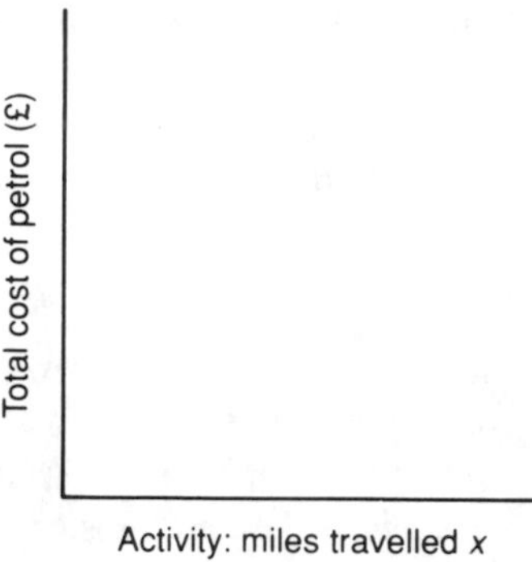

Figure 15.1

In our example, similar to the functional relationship of consumption and income described above, this relationship can be expressed as follows:

> The total cost of petrol for a journey is a function of (or dependent upon) the number of miles travelled.

In this relationship we have assumed that there is only one independent variable, i.e. the number of miles travelled. However, in this example, and in general, there is more than one independent variable. In the case of the cost of petrol for a journey the consumption of petrol and thus cost will also be dependent upon, for example, the speed that the vehicle travels at.

The relationship between the dependent and independent variables is illustrated in Figure 15.1, where the vertical axis is the dependent variable, measuring total cost of petrol, and the horizontal axis is the independent variable, measuring the activity, i.e. the miles travelled. The cost for the number of miles travelled can be plotted on the graph to produce a cost function. The function may be linear or non-linear. Traditionally accountants assume cost functions to be linear, which is not necessarily a realistic assumption as often costs behave in a non-linear fashion.

KEY CONCEPT 15.3
Linear cost functions

Mathematically we can express the linear cost function as follows:

$$Y = a + bx$$

where Y is the total cost to be predicted; a is a constant, i.e. the element of cost that remains unchanged whatever the activity level (in accounting terminology this is known as the 'fixed cost', e.g. the road tax payable on a car); b is the cost that will be the same for each unit of activity, and thus as the activity varies so will the cost (this cost is known as the variable cost, e.g. the cost of petrol); x, as before, is the level of activity, measured in units of output.

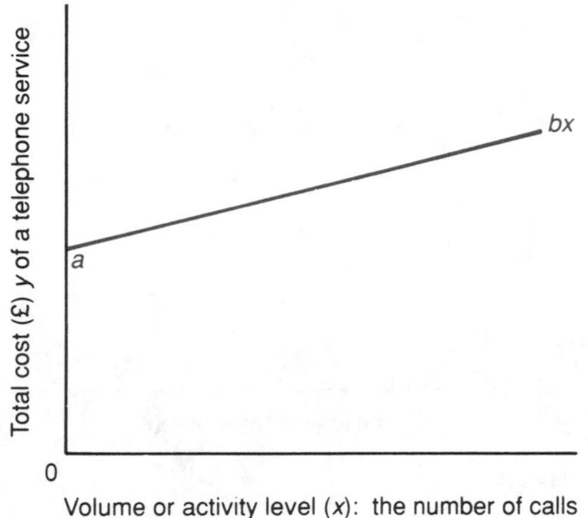

Figure 15.2 Total cost function

Figure 15.2 illustrates a linear cost function of a telephone bill, which was referred to earlier. Point *a* represents the fixed costs, which remain the same for any level of activity – in our example the standing charge. The line *bx* illustrates the variable cost *b* (the cost per call), rising in proportion to increases in activity *x* (the number of calls made).

We can determine the total cost of the use of the telephone using the above expression if we know the cost of the standing charge, the cost per call and the number of calls to be made:

$$\text{standing charge } a = £14$$
$$\text{cost per call } b = 4\text{p } (£0.04)$$

The number *x* of calls to be made is 1500. Thus if *Y* is the total cost of the bill,

$$Y = £14 + £0.04 \times 1500 = £74$$

If the number of calls increases to 1800, the total cost of the bill will be:

$$Y = £14 + £0.04 \times 1800 = £86$$

To help you to understand this expression and its usefulness you should examine a recent telephone bill for your household and calculate the total cost of the bill if the number of calls made increased by say 50%. This exercise may also result in your spending less time on the telephone!

The choice of the independent variable

Often, as previously mentioned, there will be more than one independent variable that will affect the total cost of an activity. The speed that the vehicle travels, as well as the miles travelled, was cited as a variable that can affect the amount of petrol consumed and thus the total cost of petrol for a journey. However, invariably it is too complex to take account of all independent variables that affect total costs. Because of

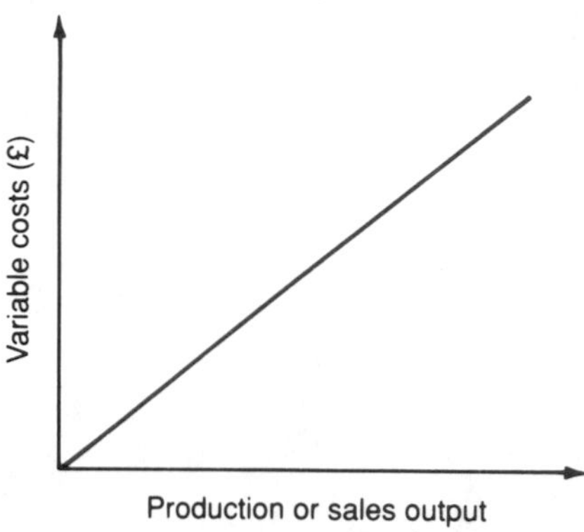

Figure 15.3 Variable cost function

this, the independent variable that is chosen, when there is more than one, should be the most influential variable in relation to the movement of costs. In the case of the cost of petrol for a journey it is likely, in general, that the most influential variable will be the miles travelled rather than, for example, speed.

In some cases the selection of the most influential variable will be obvious. However, in other cases it may not be so obvious. In such cases past costs should be examined at different activity levels to establish which of the independent variables are most influential. In the example of the cost of a journey, the consumption of petrol could be measured for a journey of, say, 5 miles at differing speeds. A decision, based on the evidence of this journey and judgement, will then have to be made as to whether the miles travelled or the speed is the most influential variable in the cost of petrol for the journey.

The cost of raw material is a good example of a cost that varies with the level of production output. For example, if one unit of output requires 2 kilograms of material A and the cost per kilogram of the material is £1.50, then the material cost for 50 units of output will be (2 kilograms × £1.50 per kilogram) = £3.00 per unit × 50 units = £150.

Sales commission is an example of a cost that would normally vary with sales output. For example, if a salesperson receives 10% commission on every unit that is sold and the selling price per unit is £20, the commission that will be received will be £2 per unit. If the salesperson sold 3000 units during the year the total commission received would be 2 × 3000 units = £6000.

Labour paid on a hourly basis is conventionally classified as a cost that varies with production output. In reality, however, this category of labour will invariably be paid a fixed wage which bears no direct relationship to output levels. There may be some incentive bonus included in the pay structure that will be linked with output, but primarily the main proportion of the remuneration will be fixed for a fixed working week. Nevertheless for decision-making purposes it is assumed that this category of labour is variable because, physically (ignoring the basis of remuneration), production levels will normally be a function of the labour input.

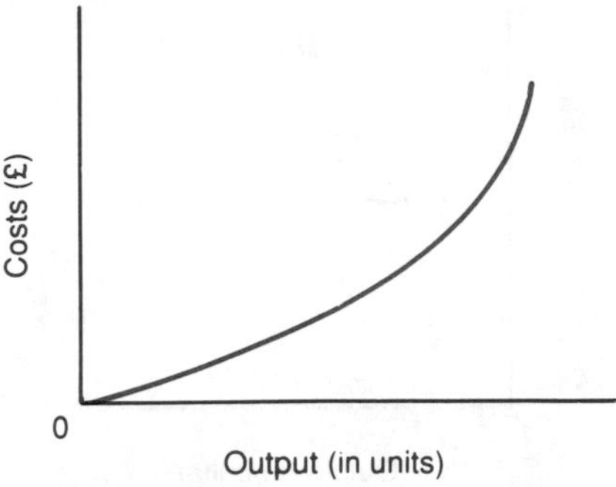

Figure 15.4 Curvilinear cost function

Figure 15.3 illustrates the movement of variable costs over activity levels. In this illustration you will see that at the intercept, in which the cost function meets the vertical axis, costs and activity are zero. This is because variable costs relate directly to activity levels; thus if activity is zero the variable costs will be zero and as activity increases the variable cost function (i.e. the total variable costs) will increase. This can be compared with Figure 15.2 where the fixed costs were also included in the illustration.

In reality it is unlikely that costs that are traditionally classified as variable will behave strictly in a linear fashion. The variable cost function therefore tends to be curvilinear. The following examples illustrate some of the reasons why variable costs are not strictly linear.

- In the case of raw materials purchased at certain stages of activity, manufacturers are likely to benefit from bulk discounts.
- Prices of resources tend to increase as a scarcity arises due to demand.
- Diminishing returns: for example, attempts to sell more units may well entail transporting the extra units over longer distances to reach more distant markets and therefore distribution costs may increase at a faster rate than activity. Assuming that selling prices are constant these greater distribution costs will result in diminishing profit margins.

Figure 15.4 shows a variable cost function with diminishing returns.

Fixed costs

Examples of costs that will normally be classified as fixed are rent, rates, salaries of administrators, and the standing charge for a telephone service referred to earlier. Fixed costs of this type will normally also be classified as *overhead costs*, which are described in Chapter 16. Figure 15.5 illustrates the traditional graphical representation of the way in which fixed costs behave over activity levels.

However, the concept that fixed costs are constant over all levels of activity is not realistic. In reality a fixed cost will only be fixed over a

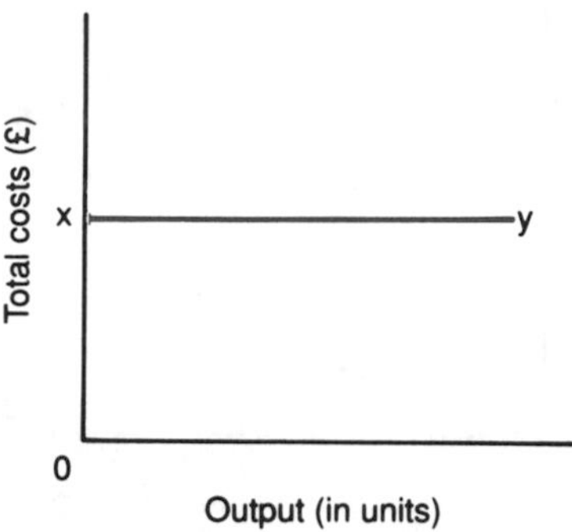

Figure 15.5 Fixed cost function

limited range of output. For example, in the case of a telephone, the standing charge is fixed if only one phone is rented; if an extension is required the standing charge increases. Similarly, a factory has a limited capacity; if production were to exceed that capacity another factory would be required, and thus the costs would increase. Therefore these types of cost tend to behave in a stepped fashion. Figure 15.6 illustrates a stepped cost function in the case of renting a factory. The rent is £2000 for one factory which has a capacity in output terms of 1000 units. Another factory will be required for output levels exceeding 1000 units, and the total rent will increase to £4000 (assuming that the rental and the capacity are the same). This cost will remain at £4000 up to 2000 units, when another factory will be required and costs will increase in the same fashion and so on.

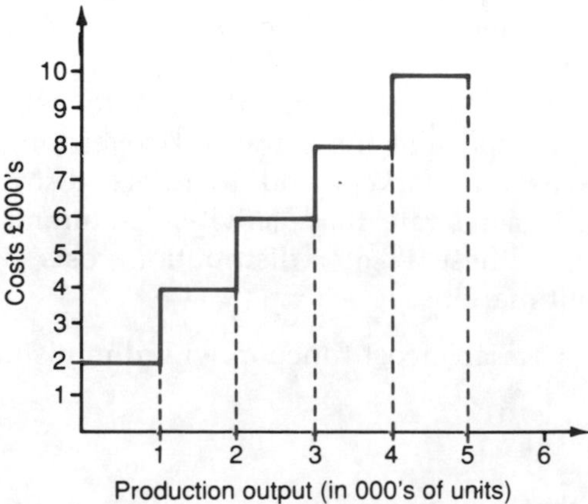

Figure 15.6 Stepped cost function

The relevant range of activity

In predicting future cost behaviour, assuming that the intention is to operate in the relevant range of activity, we can be reasonably confident about the pattern of cost behaviour. This confidence is important

The relevant range of activity relates to the levels of activity that the firm has experienced in past periods. It is assumed that in this range the relationship between the independent and dependent variables will be similar to that previously experienced.

KEY CONCEPT 15.4
The relevant range of activity

to managers as the information regarding the way in which costs behave will be the basis for future decision making. If the costs do not behave as predicted this could lead to decisions being taken that may jeopardize the organization's future.

Outside the relevant range we cannot be confident that the relationship between the variables will hold. Figure 15.7 shows a cost function in the relevant range of activity and other cost functions outside this range, which are not of a similar pattern. Therefore, if an organization is intending to operate at an activity level not experienced before, it must be extremely cautious in the prediction of future costs, relying more on forecasting methods than on predicting costs on the basis of past behaviour. The examination of forecasting methods is outside the scope of this text; you can find references to the methods in most advanced management accounting texts.

Conventionally, for convenience, graphical representations of the relations between cost and volumes do show cost functions that are the same for all levels of activity, i.e. the same pattern of costs is shown inside and outside the relevant range of activity. This is the case in all the graphical representations showing cost functions illustrated before Figure 15.7 in this chapter.

Cost behaviour – assumptions and limitations

As we have already mentioned, accountants conventionally employ cost functions that are linear for use in making operating decisions. This practice is based on a number of assumptions and we have

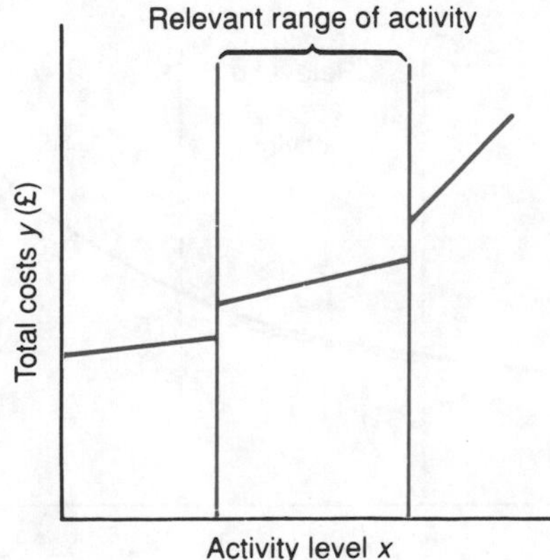

Figure 15.7 Relevant range of activity

discussed most of them. For clarity, however, they are summarized below.

- All costs can be divided into either fixed or variable costs.
- Fixed costs remain constant over different activity levels.
- Variable costs vary with activity but are constant per unit of output.
- Efficiency and productivity remain constant over all activity levels.
- Cost behaviour can be explained sufficiently by one independent variable.

From our earlier analysis it will be recognized that these assumptions are a little simplistic and tend to be approximations of reality. Therefore the question arises: are the cost functions used by accountants justified? The answer to this question is often difficult to establish with much confidence. Primarily this is a cost–benefit question (this approach was generally considered in Chapter 14): are the net benefits greater when accountants' linear cost functions are used compared with the more sophisticated cost functions such as curvilinear functions? The non-linear functions will invariably be more costly to establish because of their sophistication. Although the cost and benefits of an information system, as previously mentioned, are difficult to establish, it is theoretically a sound concept, and therefore should be borne in mind when deciding in practice what models to employ. It is also the case that the relatively recent developments in information technology have tended to reduce the cost of developing and using these more sophisticated models.

Arnold and Hope (1990) argue that the use of a linear cost function 'is not unreasonable as statistical studies have presented evidence which suggests that within specified output limits [the relevant range of activity], organizations do have cost functions which are approximately linear'. Figure 15.8 shows how a curvilinear cost function approximates to a linear function within the relevant range of activity.

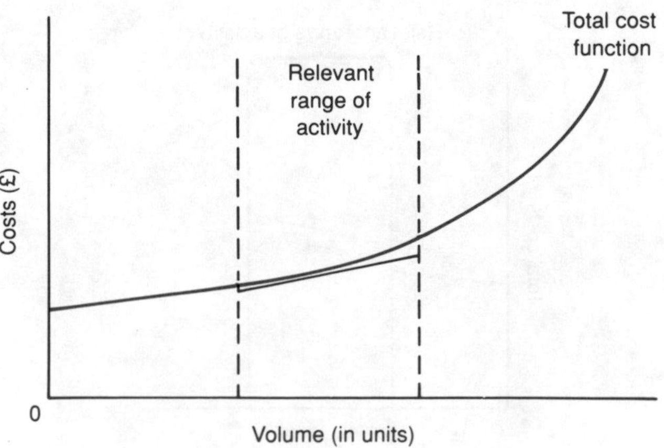

Figure 15.8

Cost estimation relates to methods that are used to measure past (historical) costs at varying activity levels. These costs will then be employed as the basis to predict future costs that will be used in decision making.

KEY CONCEPT 15.5
Cost estimation

Cost estimation

There are many methods of cost estimation. Detailed knowledge of each of these methods is not necessary at this stage of your studies. However, it is important that you appreciate the basic principles and limitations of cost estimation. For a detailed examination of the methods see Horngren and Foster (1991).

The methods of cost estimation that can be used range from those that are simple to others that are mathematically complex. The essential factor is to choose the estimation technique that generates the greatest benefits net of the costs of deriving the information. This to a great extent will depend on the size of the organization. The smaller the organization the less likely it is that a sophisticated method will be employed, as the costs will be relatively high compared with the benefits that will be generated from the use of such a method.

Cost estimates will be based on historical cost accounting data, i.e. on the costs of past production, service and sales activity. One of the simplest methods is the account classification method, which involves simply observing how costs behave in a previous period from past accounting data and classifying these costs as fixed or variable. The method relies on much subjective judgement and thus is limited in its ability to predict the future behaviour of costs accurately.

A more sophisticated method of cost estimation is regression analysis. The linear regression model involves making a number of observations from past cost behaviour and statistically analysing the data to produce a line of best fit. Figure 15.9 shows graphically a number of points that have been determined from past cost behaviour at varying levels of activity, and a line of best fit is established using the mathematical technique of regression analysis. A clear pattern of behaviour, i.e. where the points are closely clustered together over the ranges of activity, indicates a high correlation between cost and output (activity), whilst a widely dispersed arrangement of points indicates a low correlation. For further explanation see a text on quantitative methods, such as *Quantitative Techniques in a Business Context* by Slater and Ascroft (1990). In the example illustrated in Figure 15.9 there is a fairly clear pattern of behaviour and thus we can conclude that there is a relatively high correlation between cost and output.

There are more sophisticated statistical techniques using regression analysis for estimating costs. These include multiple regression, which takes account of more than one independent variable, and curvilinear regression.

The use of past data to determine future costs and the way in which

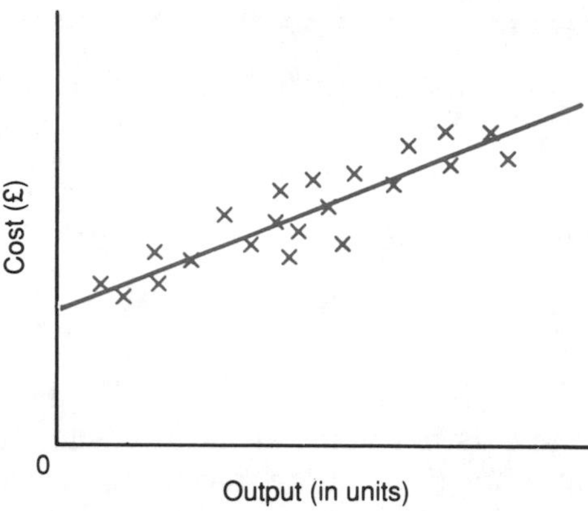

Figure 15.9 Line of best fit

they behave does have its problems. The following briefly summarizes some of these.

- Relevant range of activity: As previously mentioned, little confidence can be placed in cost estimates beyond the range of activity from which the data have been derived. It is therefore dangerous to extrapolate cost trends well beyond the levels of output previously experienced.
- The number of observations: It is important in statistical analysis to derive *many* observations of output and cost levels in order to be able to make accurate predictions about future behaviour. The greater the number of observations the higher the accuracy of the estimate and therefore the better the prediction.
- Changes in prices: Past costs may not reflect current price levels and they will bias the estimates downwards. There is thus a need to adjust these prices to current levels.
- Changes in technology: Only observations made under current production procedures should be included in the analysis. Costs of work practices using, for example, machinery that is no longer used is irrelevant to future decisions.
- Incorporating past inefficiencies: If operations were performed in an inefficient manner in the past and cost estimates are derived from this past period, they will incorporate inefficiencies.

With the development of more sophisticated techniques there is increasing use of industrial engineering methods in measuring future costs. Using time and motion studies, input and output analysis and production control productivity surveys it is possible to specify relatively accurately the relationship between labour time, machine time, materials and physical output. These techniques look to the future physical levels of resources and then convert them into money values instead of using past data as the basis of estimating future costs.

Cost–volume–profit analysis

Organizations are constantly faced with decisions relating to the products and services they sell such as the following.

- Should we change the selling price, and if so what would be the effect on profit?
- How many units must be sold to break even?
- How many units must be sold to make a specified target profit?
- Should more money be spent on advertising?

KEY CONCEPT 15.6
Cost–volume–profit (CVP) analysis

CVP analysis is a tool used by organizations to help them make decisions by examining the interrelationships between cost, volume and profits.

The cost data used in CVP analysis will be derived from the prediction of future costs discussed earlier in this chapter.

Sales revenue

It is normally assumed in CVP analysis that sales revenue, like costs, behaves in a linear fashion over varying output levels. That is, the sales price per unit sold will be the same for all levels of output. Figure 15.10 illustrates a sales revenue function; the vertical axis represents the total sales revenue and the horizontal axis is the sales output levels. It can be seen that the sales revenue function increases in direct proportion to sales output. This is because the selling price is the same for every unit sold.

The assumption that the selling price will remain constant for all levels of sales is rather unrealistic. For example, often you will find quantity discounts being offered with consumable goods at supermarkets; i.e. if you buy one tablet of soap the price is 30p, whereas if you buy two tablets the price is 50p (i.e. 25p each). This limitation to the application of CVP analysis will be considered in more detail later.

CVP analysis: the equation

CVP analysis is based on the following relationship that can be expressed as an equation:

$$\text{profit} = \text{sales} - (\text{fixed cost} + \text{variable cost})$$

This expression can be rearranged as follows:

$$Sx = \text{VC}x + \text{FC} + P$$

Where S is the selling price per unit, x is the number of units to be sold, VC is the variable cost per unit, FC is the fixed cost and P is the expected profit. The nature of this equation is very similar to the cost functions considered earlier. You will notice that only one independent

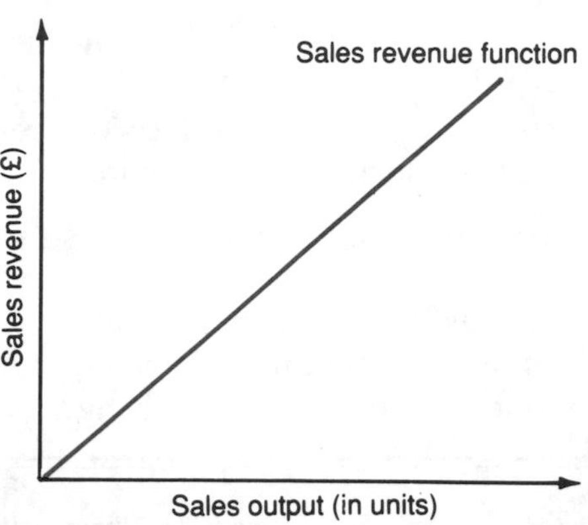

Figure 15.10 Sales revenue function

variable is being accounted for: the activity, measured in units. Also the fixed and variable costs are expressed in a similar way and when added together are equal to total cost. The only additional variables are sales price, which was discussed above, and profit, profit being the difference between sales revenue and total costs.

To illustrate the application of CVP analysis in decision making we consider the example of Boycott Industries.

Example 15.1: Boycott Industries

Boycott Industries produce only one product. The following revenues and costs have been estimated for the forthcoming month:

Selling price	£70 per unit
Variable costs	£40 per unit
Fixed cost	£2400

The management of the firm wish to know the following.

1 How many units need to be sold to break even (i.e. to make neither a profit nor a loss)?
2 How many units must be sold to make a profit of £600?
3 Would it be a worthwhile policy to introduce advertising at a cost of £1200 and to increase sales output from 300 to 350 units?
4 What should the selling price be to make a profit of £4320 on sales of 120 units?

Solution

1 The number of units to breakeven is obtained from the equation

$$Sx = \mathrm{VC}x + \mathrm{FC} + P$$

To break even $Sx = \mathrm{VC}x + \mathrm{FC}$; we drop P (profit) from the original equation because at the breakeven point profits will be zero. Using the data given we have the following equation:

$$70x = 40x + 2400$$

Therefore $x = 80$ units.

Proof

	£	£
Sales (£70 × 80 units)		5600
Less costs:		
Variable cost (£40 × 80 units)	3200	
Fixed costs	2400	5600
Profit		0

2 For the number of units that have to be sold to make a profit of £600,

$$Sx = VCx + FC + P$$

Using the data given we have the following equation:

$$70x = 40x + 2400 + 600$$

Therefore $x = 100$ units.

3 Advertising cost £1200; sales output increases from 300 to 350 units. Rearranging the equation in 1 above:

$$P = Sx - (VCx + FC)$$

The profit for 300 units is therefore

$$\text{Profit} = 70 \times 300 - [40(300) + 2400]$$
$$= £6600$$

Advertising costs will increase fixed costs by £1200 and the profit for 350 units will be

$$\text{Profit} = 70 \times 350 - [40(350) + 3600]$$

Therefore the profit is £6900. Presumably the firm will go ahead and advertise the product as it generates greater profits.

4 For the selling price to make a profit of £4320 on sales of 120 units we again use

$$Sx = VCx + FC + P$$
$$S(120) = 40(120) + 2400 + 4320$$

Therefore $S = £96$.

The breakeven chart

A useful method of illustrating the relationships between cost, volume and profits is through the medium of what is commonly referred to as a breakeven chart. The relationship between these variables is plotted on a graph. The cost functions and the sales revenue function, which in previous illustrations have been shown separately, are now included together in the breakeven chart.

Figure 15.11 shows the breakeven chart for Boycott Industries, using the data given earlier. You will notice that in the construction of this particular chart the variable costs are plotted above the fixed costs,

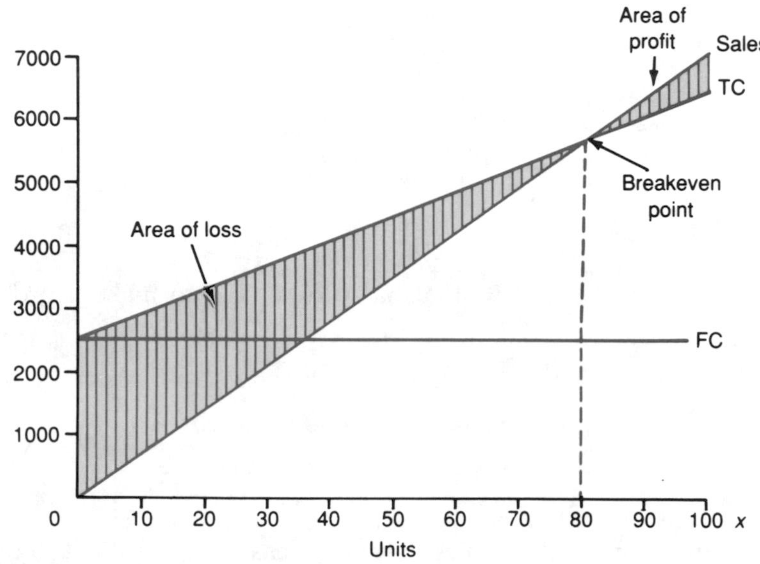

Figure 15.11 Breakeven chart

resulting in a total cost function that rises from the intercept at £2400 and increases at the rate of £40 per unit. There is another way of constructing the total cost function in breakeven charts which will be illustrated later. The main advantage of the chart to management is that from the chart the breakeven point and the areas of loss and profit can clearly and quickly be identified. This enables management to establish the effect of varying output levels that they may wish to consider. For example, the profit at an output level of 90 units can easily be read from the chart without the need to solve an equation.

The contribution margin method

The contribution margin is equal to the sales price per unit less the variable cost per unit. It is also common to find the contribution margin described as the contribution per unit. Using the data from Boycott Industries the contribution margin is as follows.

	£
Sales price per unit	70
Less: variable cost per unit	40
Contribution margin	30

Figure 15.12 is another version of the breakeven chart, once again using the data relating to Boycott Industries.

The total cost function is constructed by first plotting the variable costs and then the fixed costs. By constructing the total cost function in this way we can identify the contribution margin, i.e. the difference between the sales and variable cost functions, as shown on the chart.

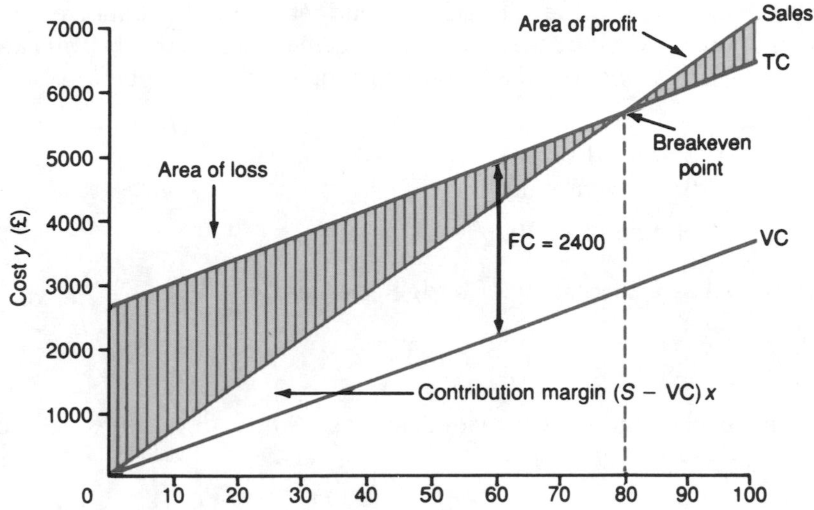

Figure 15.12 Breakeven chart illustrating the contribution margin

The interesting point to notice is that each unit sold will make a contribution of £30. The contribution initially reduces the loss incurred by fixed costs by £30 per unit. When fixed costs have been covered by the contribution generated by sales at the output level of 80 units (i.e. at the breakeven point) every unit sold thereafter contributes £30 to profits. For example, at the origin (i.e. no sales) a loss is made of £2400 which is the sum of the fixed costs. When one unit is sold it contributes £30, thereby reducing the loss to £2370 (2400 − 30). As sales output increases the loss will be reduced by £30 per unit to the breakeven point where the fixed costs are now totally covered. After the breakeven point each unit sold increases profit by £30 per unit; thus if 81 units are sold a profit of £30 would be made.

The contribution margin is an important concept and is used widely in accounting to aid managers in making decisions. We shall be examining the concept in more detail in Chapters 17 and 18.

Using the contribution margin approach we can answer the problems posed earlier, e.g. the breakeven point for Boycott Industries:

$$Sx = \mathrm{VC}x + \mathrm{FC} + P$$

Rearranging this expression in terms of the contribution margin, where $Sx - \mathrm{VC}x =$ contribution margin C, we have $Cx = \mathrm{FC} + P$, and for the breakeven point $Cx = \mathrm{FC}$ and it follows that $x = \mathrm{FC}/C$. Using the data from Boycott Industries: $x = 2400/30 = 80$ units.

Margin of safety

The margin of safety is the amount by which actual output, normally measured in terms of sales, may fall short of the budget without incurring a loss. It may be expressed as a percentage of budgeted sales. It is therefore, a crude method of measuring risk that the business might make a loss if it fails to achieve budget. Using the data from the example of Boycott Industries, if the budgeted sales were 100 units and the breakeven point 80 units, the margin of safety would be:

	Units
Budgeted sales	100
Breakeven point	80
Margin of safety	20

Expressed as a percentage of budgeted sales:

$$\frac{20}{80} \times 100 = 25\%$$

A further illustration is provided in Case Study 15.1: Amex Sounds Ltd.

CASE STUDY 15.1
Amex sounds ltd

Amex Sounds Ltd are a company which specialize in the sale of domestic electronic sound equipment. The company purchases goods from manufacturers and sells them to the retail trade. A high proportion of the goods they sell are manufactured abroad and imported. Since starting up five years ago they have been very successful, in terms of sales and profit growth. The Managing Director has recently been offered an exclusive contract to sell a cassette recorder that is manufactured in South Korea. Although this recorder has been sold successfully in the USA it has yet to be sold in the European market.

The company are currently assessing whether or not to enter into the contract. The following gives information relating to the estimated costs and revenues of the contract.

- A market survey has been completed with the help of a marketing consultant. At a price of £40 per recorder the estimated sales in the first year would be 9500 recorders. This is considered to be the most realistic price and volume level in the forthcoming year taking account of competition.
- The price paid for each recorder will be £19.50. This includes the cost of packaging and shipment. The contract specifies that this price will be fixed for one year from the contract date.
- Variable costs, other than the cost of the recorder, are estimated to be £3.00 per recorder sold.
- The company are currently trading from a rented warehouse in Islington. However, there is very little space for further expansion. After due consideration of location and costs it is decided that if the contract is accepted a warehouse in Peterborough will be rented and used exclusively for the sale of these recorders. Peterborough has been chosen primarily because of the relatively lower cost of renting premises and the better employment situation. The rent of this warehouse will be £46 000 per year and it is estimated that salaries will be £65 000 per year.
- Other fixed costs are anticipated to be £15 000.

The following summarizes the cost that will be incurred in selling the recorder.

	Costs per unit
	£
Variable costs	
Purchase price of recorders	19.50
Other variable costs	3.00
	22.50
Fixed costs (per year)	
Rent of warehouse	46 000
Salaries	65 000
Other fixed costs	15 000
	126 000

In the decision whether or not to accept this contract CVP analysis will be a useful aid. We shall therefore begin by determining the profit at the estimated output level of 9500 and the breakeven point employing the equation method and the notation used earlier:

$$Sx = \text{VC}x + \text{FC} + P$$

We can rearrange the equation in terms of profits and contribution per unit where $S - \text{VC}$ is the contribution per unit:

$$P = x(S - \text{VC}) - \text{FC}$$
$$P = 9500(40 - 22.50) - 126\,000 = £40\,250$$

The contribution per unit is therefore £17.50. (40 – 22.50)

To determine the breakeven point in terms of units sold we rearrange the equation using the contribution per unit approach.

The breakeven point is given by: contribution (x) = FC

$$17.50x = 126\,000$$

Therefore the breakeven point is 7200 units.

The difference between the breakeven point and the estimated sales in terms of units is 9500 – 7200 = 2300 units; this would give the company a margin of safety in percentage terms of (2300/9500 × 100) 24% approximately.

Clearly the information derived from our analysis will be useful in the assessment of this contract. In particular the determination of the breakeven point gives the management of the company a basis to evaluate an element of the risk associated with the contract. Knowledge that there is a margin of safety of 2300 units will be useful in this assessment.

We now extend our analysis to consider an advertising scenario. It will be assumed that costs and revenues above remain constant with the exception of any effect on costs and revenues associated with advertising.

The company consults an advertising firm regarding the sales of the recorder. Two separate strategies are proposed: expenditure on advertising of

- £16 000 will increase the sales volume in the year to 10 300 units, or
- expenditure of £30 000 will increase the sales volume in the year to 11 500 units.

These two strategies will be considered separately and compared with the original analysis above taking into account the profit and breakeven levels.

Advertising costs £16 000, sales volume 10 300 units

The advertising costs would be classified as fixed costs; therefore fixed costs will now be £126 000 + £16 000 = £142 000. Using the equation method we can determine the profit:

$$P = x(S - VC) - FC$$
$$P = 10\,300 \times 17.50 - 142\,000$$

Therefore the profit is £38 250. The breakeven point is given by: contribution x = FC

$$17.50x = 142\,000$$

Therefore the breakeven point is 8114 units (to the nearest whole number).

This proposal, we can safely say, will not be attractive to the company as profits are £40 250 − £38 250 = £2000 lower than the original proposal and the risk is greater as the breakeven point will be higher by 8114 − 7200 = 914 units.

Advertising costs £30 000, sales volume 11 500 units

Fixed costs will now increase to £126 000 + £30 000 = 156 000.

$$P = x(S - VC) - FC$$
$$P = 11\,500 \times 17.50 - 156\,000$$

Therefore profit will be £45 250. The breakeven point is given by: contribution (x) = FC

$$17.50x = £156\,000$$

Therefore the breakeven point is 8914 units (to the nearest whole number).

In this case the decision whether to use advertising is somewhat more complex. Firstly, the profit will increase by (£45 250 − £40 250) £5000, which presumbly will be attractive to the company. However, the risk measured in terms in breakeven analysis is greater as the breakeven point has risen from 7200 to 8914 units.

The analysis of these advertising strategies, in terms of profit and breakeven points, is clearly useful in determining whether the company should use advertising. However, it is important to appreciate that this information will only be a part of the total information necessary to evaluate proposals. For example, it will also be necessary to consider the effect on cash flows. It is likely that the company will require additional investment to support an advertising campaign and this should be taken into account.

CVP analysis: Linear functions – the assumptions and limitations

The cost–volume–profit model that has been examined and illustrated in this chapter has been assumed to be linear. The assumptions and limitations of a linear cost function were described earlier in the section relating to cost behaviour, and these are relevant to the CVP model.

The sales function, as was previously discussed, is also assumed to be linear and thus it is assumed that the sales price will remain constant over all levels of activity. Empirical evidence suggests that this is unlikely for the majority of goods and services. A more realistic sales function would be represented by a curvilinear pattern. However, although the assumption of a linear function seems to be too simplistic, there is evidence that within the relevant range of activity the sales function, like cost, does approximate to a linear pattern.

The choice of employing a linear or a non-linear function to represent sales in the analysis will once again depend on the costs and benefits of the information.

In the examples of the application of CVP analysis we have assumed a one-product firm (Boycott Industries). In reality the majority of firms produce more than one type of product. This assumption has been made because there are particular problems associated with the application of CVP analysis in multi-product firms.

There may be interdependences between the production and demand of two or more of the firms' products. For example, the demand for one product, e.g. the sales of butter, may be affected by the demand for another product, e.g. margarine. In these cases it will be necessary to examine the CVP relationships together. This will not cause a problem if the sales mix (the proportion of sales volumes of the interdependent products) and the profit margins are the same. If the mix changes, the overall volume targets may be achieved but the effects on profits will depend on whether the product of higher or lower margin predominates in the mix.

Fixed costs represent another problem in the application of CVP analysis in multi-product firms. If the fixed cost can be identified with particular products there is no cause for concern. But if fixed costs are of a general nature, e.g. head office expenses, these costs will have to be apportioned and/or allocated on some fairly arbitrary basis. This could be misleading and lead to inaccurate decisions.

If one or more of the resources available to a firm is scarce, there will be a constraint on the potential total sales output. The problem is how the resources should be allocated among the products. This will depend on how effectively each product uses the resource. We shall be examining this problem in more detail in Chapter 18.

Summary

In this chapter we examined the nature of fixed and variable costs and the way in which these costs behave over activity levels. We explained the way in which these costs are measured for use in predicting future costs. In practice, important decisions will be made by organizations based on the understanding of cost behaviour and the ability to predict future costs accurately. However, it was stressed that often rather simplistic assumptions were made in deriving this information. Whilst the adoption of these assumptions limits the accuracy of the information, invariably we can derive reasonable approximations of the real world by using methods that may not be considered wholly realistic. CVP analysis was examined. This is an extremely useful technique in the decision-making process of organizations, although it is also limited by the rather simplistic assumptions underlying the determination of future costs and revenues over varying activity levels.

References

Arnold, J. and Hope, T. (1990) *Accounting for Management Decisions*, 2nd edn, Prentice-Hall.
Hongren, C. and Foster, G. (1991) *Cost Accounting – A Managerial Emphasis*, 7th edn, Prentice-Hall.
Slater, R. and Ascroft, P. (1990) *Quantitative Techniques in a Business Context*, Chapman and Hall.

Further reading

For a more detailed analysis of methods of cost estimation reference can be made to Horngren and Foster (1991).

Another book in this series, *Economics in a Business Context* (1989), examines curvilinear cost functions from an economics perspective in Chapter 4.

The CVP model that we have examined ignores risk and uncertainty, which will inevitably be relevant in practice. This aspect is considered in *Managerial Accounting: Method and Meaning* by R.M.S. Wilson and W.F. Chua (Chapman & Hall, 1992), 2nd edn, Chapter 4.

Review questions

1 It is often assumed that there is only one independent variable in cost behaviour. Explain the nature of independent variables and why this assumption is made.
2 Explain what is meant by the relevant range of activity and its significance in CVP analysis.
3 Variable and fixed costs are traditionally assumed to be linear. Explain why this assumption is unrealistic.
4 What are the problems associated with CVP analysis in a multi-product firm?

Problems for discussion and analysis

1 In the table below fill in the blank spaces:

Sales	*Variable costs*	*Fixed costs*	*Total costs*	*Profit*	*Contribution*
£	£	£	£	£	£
1 000	700		1 000		
1 500		300		500	
	500		800	1 200	
2 000		300		200	

2 Clean-it Plc makes washing machines and with its existing plant capacity the maximun production possible is 1000 units per year.

Fixed costs are estimated at £18 000 per annum and the selling price of each machine is £120. Sales for the next year are expected to drop to 800 units.

The cost of each washing machine is calculated as follows:

Direct material cost £20
Direct labour cost 10 hours at £4 per hour

(a) Calculate (i) the breakeven point, (ii) the maximum profit and (iii) the profit at an estimated sales level of 800 units.
(b) Costs alter by the following proportions:

Direct materials increase by 20%
Fixed costs come down by £6000
Direct labour costs increase by £1 per hour

What will be (i) the new breakeven point and (ii) the new profit at the estimated sales level of 800 units?

3 Cords Plc manufactures a style of corduroy trousers that it sold last year at £18 a pair. The cost specifications for these trousers were as follows:

		£
Variable costs per pair of trousers		
Materials		6.50
Labour		3.50
Fixed overheads per month	£26 400	

Cords Plc made a profit of £11 040 each month.

(a) How many pairs of trousers did Cords Plc sell each month?
(b) Cords Plc is now planning next year's operations. The Sales Director is proposing to boost sales by reducing the selling price to £17 and spending an additional £3000 per month on advertising. She estimates that these actions will enable the company to sell 5800 pairs of trousers each month.

Evaluate the Sales Director's proposals taking into account their expected impact on profits and on the breakeven point. State any assumptions you need to make.
(c) If the Managing Director of Cords Plc were to require that next year's profit show a 15% increase over last year's performance, how many pairs of trousers would have to be sold each month (i) assuming that the Sales Director's policies were adopted and (ii) assuming that they were not.

16 Accounting for overheads and products costs

This chapter focuses on how overhead costs are dealt with in determining the cost of products. Two costing methods are examined: absorption costing and marginal costing.

The profit and loss account summarizes all the costs and revenues of an organization over a defined period of time. Whilst this information is extremely useful in determining the overall profitability of the organization, there is also a need to determine the costs and the profitability of individual products.

We shall examine a number of the reasons why management requires product costing information.

- **To control costs** Product costs will be compared with planned costs. If the actual costs deviate from the plan management may need to take corrective action so that predetermined management targets are met in the future.
- **To aid planning** Product costs are a useful base for estimating future product costs in the planning process. But when using past costs for this purpose, management must be careful to take account of any potential changes in the level of costs in the future, due to inflation.
- **For valuing stocks** Product costs need to be determined so that the value of products that are complete (finished goods) and products that are partially complete (work in progress) can be established at the end of each accounting period for inclusion in the balance sheet and profit and loss account.
- **To aid the setting of selling prices** The cost of products may influence the setting of prices. From a marketing viewpoint it can be argued that the price will be determined through market forces, i.e. from consideration of what the market can bear. However, in a number of situations, particularly where there is little or no competition, prices will often be set with reference to the cost.

- **To ascertain the relative profitability of products** In times of scarce resources when a firm is constrained as to its level of output it is likely that management will favour selling only its most profitable products. In these circumstances knowledge of product costs is essential.

When firms only manufacture one product the process of product costing is relatively straightforward. This is because all the costs of the business are directly attributable to the single product that is produced by the firm. The complexity of product costing occurs when an organization produces more than one product. In these types of organizations, known as multi-product firms, management is confronted with two main problems. Firstly, it is necessary to set up a system to account for those costs that can be directly attributed to individual products. These costs are known as direct costs. For example, the amounts of raw materials used to produce individual products can normally be identified and a system is required to account for this direct cost. The second problem, which is more complicated, is to account for costs that are not directly attributed to any one product. There are two terms in accounting terminology that are used to describe these types of costs – indirect or overhead costs. An example of an indirect cost is the cost of renting a factory in a multi-product firm where it is impossible to attribute the cost to individual products directly.

KEY CONCEPT 16.1
Direct and indirect costs

A direct cost is one that is traceable, and thus attributable, to a product. Indirect costs (also known as overhead costs) are those that cannot be easily and conveniently identified with a particular product.

In this chapter we focus on two main approaches used in the determination of product costs in multi-product firms; namely marginal costing and full costing. Under the marginal costing approach it is only direct costs that are included in the cost of the product. Costs that are not directly identifiable with products (indirect costs) are excluded from the cost of individual products. In contrast, the full costing approach includes not only direct costs but also indirect costs. It is argued, by those who favour the full costing approach, that to facilitate the fair and equitable computation of product costs, overheads must be included.

Before examining these two approaches it should be stressed that the need to identify the costs and revenues is not restricted to manufactured products but extends to services provided and to organizations that are purely service oriented. An insurance broker, for instance, will need to identify costs of selling different types of policy, for example car insurance and life assurance, to determine the profitability of the varying policies that are sold. This information may influence what policies are sold and the mix of policies. For the purposes of our analysis we shall tend to focus on manufacturing organizations.

We begin our analysis by examining the full costing approach for determining the cost of products.

Full costing

Definitions of full costing

In a manufacturing organization the costs incurred in producing and selling a product consist of production costs and other business expenses such as administration, selling and distribution expenses. The costs to be included in the full costing approach may include all these costs or just some, e.g. the production costs. The definition of full costing adopted will depend upon the purpose for which the full costing of products is being used and the preferences of management. For management purposes, accounting information, as has already been emphasized, is not regulated by any external forces, such as the law or accounting standards set by the professional accountancy bodies. Management may adopt definitions and use accounting data at their discretion to meet their organization's requirements.

For the purposes of our analysis we shall adopt the definition of full costing that only includes production costs. This is the definition of full costing that is conventionally used for the purpose of valuing finished stocks and work in progress, which was discussed in Chapter 6. In the context of stock valuations, it is argued that it is only appropriate to include those costs that are incurred prior to sale of the stock. Normally, these costs will consist of only those related to production.

Figure 16.1 shows the flow of costs associated with a manufacturing organization when the full costing approach is adopted, where 'full cost' represents only those costs associated with production whether they are direct or indirect costs. Here materials and labour are classified as both direct and indirect costs. For example, in the case of manufacturing labour the arrows are directed to both work in progress (i.e. directly into the production process, thereby indicating that they are a direct cost) and indirect production costs (i.e. indicating they can be indirect cost). The classification of these costs into direct and indirect, not surprisingly, will depend upon whether the cost can be identified directly with products or not.

KEY CONCEPT 16.2
Full costing

The full cost of a product consists of the direct and indirect costs of production.

On some occasions it may be more convenient to classify a cost as indirect although it would be possible to identify the cost directly with

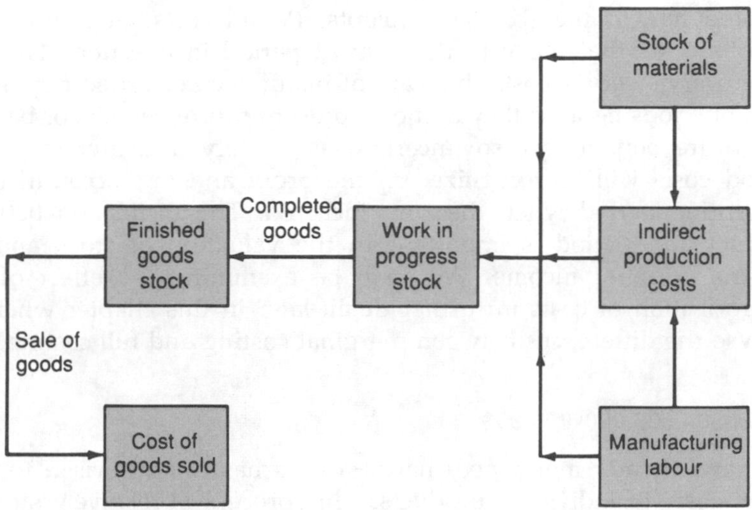

Figure 16.1

a product. Consider, for example, the labour costs of a supervisor who is responsible for a group of employees working on a number of different products. An elaborate system would have to be set up to record the time supervising each employee and then to relate this time (and thus costs) to particular products. In this case it may be considered more cost effective and convenient simply to classify supervision costs as indirect.

An example of indirect material cost is the cost of machine lubricant. Indirect costs, other than materials and labour, can typically be in the form of costs related to heating, lighting, training and the depreciation of machinery and premises (if owned). All indirect production costs will be 'absorbed' into the products being produced, so that at any point in time the value of work in progress and finished goods will consist of materials, labour and indirect costs. The cost of goods sold will be matched with the revenue from the sales of these goods in the profit and loss account. When full costing is applied, as in our definition, the cost of goods sold will consist of both direct and indirect production costs, as indicated in Figure 16.1.

Product and period costs

Before examining the procedures that are used to absorb indirect costs into product costs it is appropriate to consider another classification of costs, namely period costs. Any costs not categorized as product costs will normally be classified as period costs.

Product costs, as we have already mentioned, will only be recognized in the profit and loss account when the product is sold. Prior to the sale, the cost of products will be shown as an asset (either as work in progress or finished goods) in the balance sheet, thereby indicating that these items have some future benefit to the business. The principle adopted here is the accruals concepts. Period costs, in contrast, are seen as costs that relate to the current period in question. They are therefore viewed as costs that cannot justifiably be carried forward to future periods because they do not represent future benefits or because the future benefits are so uncertain as to defy measurement. Thus period costs will be recognized in the profit and loss account in the accounting period when they are incurred. The distinction between product and period is important in the valuation of stock and the determination of income. We shall be examining the effect of this categorization of costs in further detail later in this chapter when we analyse the differences between marginal costing and full costing.

The absorption of overheads

We have already mentioned that a system has to be devised to trace direct costs to individual products. This process is relatively straightforward because direct costs can be identified precisely with a particular product. For example, when materials are obtained from stock, the cost of these materials will be recorded against product and accounted for as a cost to the product. The complexity arises when we are to share out indirect costs to products. The objective is to share out costs equitably. The method adopted should therefore take into account the amount of indirect services used to support the manufacture of products. The term used for the process of sharing out indirect costs to products is 'absorption of overheads'.

Production overhead costs will be incurred by cost centres that support the production activity. The cost centres can be divided into two categories – production and service cost centres. Production cost centres are departments where the manufacturing activity physically takes place; e.g. an assembly department. Service cost centres are primarily engaged in servicing the production function, but are not directly involved in the production activity. A 'goods in' department, whose function it is to ensure that goods and materials received from suppliers are of the standard and quantity ordered, is a typical example of a service cost centre in a manufacturing organization. The overhead costs of both the production and service cost centres must be absorbed into the product to establish the full cost of products.

At this stage it is appropriate to summarize the stages in the absorption of overheads. Figure 16.2 shows the three stages in this process.

The following is a further explanation of the stages detailed in Figure 16.2.

Stage 1

The first stage in the absorption of overhead costs is to identify and collect overhead costs associated with both the production and service cost centres. Some of these costs can be relatively easily 'allocated' to particular cost centres. The word allocated, in the context of product costing, means that the cost can be directly traced to a cost centre. For

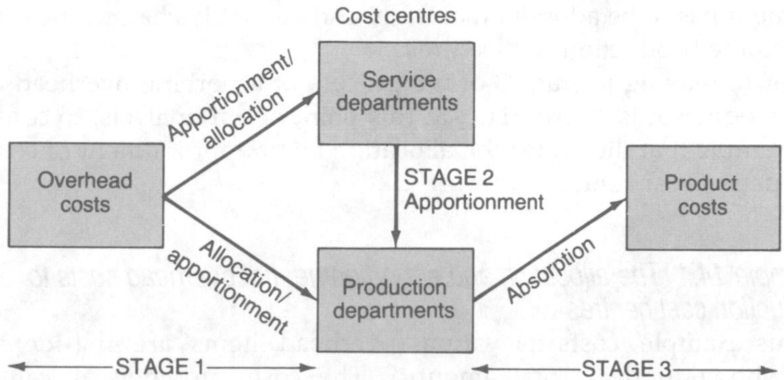

Figure 16.2

example, in a drawing office, classified as a service cost centre because it provides a service to a number of production cost centres, the salaries of draughtsmen can be identified with the centre by recording the salary payment from the payroll against the cost centre. In contrast, the cost of heating and lighting consumed by the drawing office may not be so easy to establish. The cost of heating and lighting may, for example, be billed for the whole building, in which the drawing office is only one of many occupant cost centres. In such cases, because the cost is difficult, if not impossible, to identify accurately with any one cost centre a method of 'apportioning' these costs on a fair and equitable basis must be adopted. The term apportioning describes the sharing out of overhead costs that cannot be directly traced to a cost centre. A reasonable method of apportioning heat and lighting costs that relates to the benefits (i.e. heating and lighting) enjoyed by the drawing office may be on the basis of the area that the office occupies. For example, if the total cost of heating and lighting is £15 000 and the area used by the drawing office, measured in square metres, is say 6000 out of a total area of the building of say 30 000 metres, the cost apportioned to the drawing office would be £15 000 × 6000/30 000 = £3000.

Stage 2

When all the overhead costs, allocated and apportioned, have been established for each service cost centre it is then necessary to charge these costs to the production cost centres. Once again some method of apportionment will have to be used. The reason for this is that the service cost centres will normally be servicing more than one production cost centre and the costs of the service are unlikely to be easily identified with any one production cost centre. Using the example of the drawing office again, it is likely that the service supplied by this office will spread over a number of production cost centres and it may well be impractical to identify the accurate cost of this service with production departments. In these circumstances, a method of apportionment has to be adopted that fairly and equitably charges the service cost to the production cost centres.

Prior to moving to stage 3 of the process of absorbing overhead costs into products it is appropriate, at this point of our analysis, to consider an example that illustrates the allocation and apportionment of costs to production cost centres.

Example 14.1 The allocation and apportionment of overhead costs to production cost centres

In this example, costs for various overhead 'items' are first identified and shown under 'Total amount'. The costs are then allocated or apportioned to production and service cost centres. In the case of indirect labour and materials the costs are allocated to these cost centres as they can be directly identified to the centres. With reference to the table on page 305, of the total amount of indirect materials consumed (£20 000), £8000 has been directly identified with production cost centre A. In contrast, the costs related to power, rent and rates and insurance cannot be directly identified with the cost centres. Therefore these costs will be apportioned to the centres using some equitable basis reflecting the benefits the centres have enjoyed. In the case of the cost of power, for example, the number of machine hours consumed by the cost centres is considered an equitable basis for apportionment. If you refer to the information relating to the use of machine hours in the example you will notice that machinery was only used in the two production cost centres. Of the total of 110 000 machine hours 50 000 were consumed by production cost centre A and 60 000 hours by cost centre B. The cost of power for each of these production cost centres is then calculated with reference to the consumption by the two departments; the following shows the calculation.

Production cost centre	£
A 50 000 hours/110 000 hours × £22 000 =	10 000
B 60 000 hours/110 000 hours × £22 000 =	12 000
Total cost of power	22 000

Therefore the apportioned charge to production cost centre A is £10 000 and to B is £12 000.

Similar calculations using different assumptions are made to establish the apportioned charge to the cost centres for rent and rates and insurance.

Table showing the allocation and apportionment of costs

Item	*Basis*	*Total amount*	*Production cost centres* A £000	B £000	*Service cost centres* X £000	Y £000
Indirect materials	Allocated	20	8	4	5	3
Indirect labour	Allocated	30	14	6	4	6
Power	Machine hours	22	10	12	—	—
Rent and rates	Area	10	2	5	2	1
Insurance	Book value	8	3	2	3	—
Total overheads		90	37	29	14	10
Service X to Prod	Number of employees		5	9	(14)	
Service Y to Prod	D/L hours		8	2		(10)
Total overheads		90	50	40	—	—

Data used for apportioning overheads

Item	*Quantity*				
Machine hours	110 000 h	50 000 h	60 000 h	—	—
Area	30 000 sq ft	6 000	15 000	6 000	3 000
Book value fixed assets	£96 000	£36	£24	£36	—
No. of employees	7 000	2 500	4 500		
Direct labour hours	20 000 h	16 000	4 000	—	—

These costs relate to one year.

After allocating and apportioning the overheads to the production and service cost centres the next stage is to apportion the service centre costs to the production cost centres. The basis of apportionment chosen, in the case of the costs of service cost centre X, is the number of employees in each production cost centre. The number of direct labour hours worked by employees in the production cost centres is the basis of apportionment used for service centre Y. As previously mentioned the basis of apportionment should reflect the benefits enjoyed by the consuming production cost centres. For example, it may be that service cost centre X is the works canteen. If so, the number of employees in each production cost centre may be a reasonable basis for calculating the amount of use made of this facility by each of the two production cost centres. The calculation of the apportioned charge to the production cost centres is very similar to the calculation described above for apportioning power costs. Thus in the case of service cost centre X the calculation will be as follows:

Production cost centre

		£
A	2500/7000 × £14 000	5 000
B	4500/7000 × £14 000	9 000
Total cost of service cost centre X		14 000

It can be seen that the whole of the costs of service centre X are now apportioned to the two production cost centres. Similar calculations will be made to apportion the cost of service cost centre Y to the two production cost centres. Finally, the overhead costs are aggregated for each of the two production cost centres as can be seen in the final line in the example.

Stage 3

As has been mentioned previously the productioon cost centres are where the manufacturing activity actually takes place. Units of products will physically pass through these cost centres in the course of the manufacturing cycle. As the products pass through the centre a proportion of the overhead cost is charged to the product (or absorbed into product). The objective here, once again, is to charge out overheads to units of production on some equitable basis. Normally an absorption rate is used for this purpose. The absorption rate is determined by the following formula:

$$\frac{\text{Total overheads of a production cost centre}}{\text{Level of activity}}$$

We have already discussed how the numerator in this formula is determined in stage 2 above. The denominator, the activity level, will be chosen with reference to the types of products passing through the production cost centres and the main activities of these centres. If, for example, the particular products passing through the centre are homogeneous, i.e. similar in construction, the appropriate activity to be chosen is likely to be the number of units worked on in the production centre. In these circumstances the activity, units of production, should represent an equitable basis for absorbing the overheads as the benefits enjoyed by each unit from the expenditure of overheads should be equal or very similar. For example, if it was estimated that 10 000 units were to be worked on in the year by production cost centre A, in Example 16.1 above, and assuming the products were homogeneous, the absorption rate would be £50 000/10 000 units = £5 per unit. This rate would then be applied to each unit of production worked on in the cost centre and would represent a reasonable share of the overhead cost appropriate to each product.

In contrast, if the products are not homogeneous it is then necessary to choose an activity measure that corresponds more closely with the overhead expenditure of each production cost centre. If, for example, overhead expenditure of a production cost centre is mainly incurred in supporting the direct labour function, the measure chosen should be based on this activity. In these circumstances the number of direct labour hours would probably be a suitable measure.

In practice the most common activity measures used to absorb overheads into product costs are chosen from the following list:

- direct labour hours
- direct labour cost
- machine hours
- cost of materials

The following shows the calculation of the absorption rate with reference to the data given in Example 16.1 for production cost centre A assuming that machine hours is the appropriate activity measure:

$$\frac{\text{Total overheads of cost centre A}}{\text{Level of activity}} = \frac{£50\,000}{50\,000 \text{ machine hours}}$$

Therefore the absorption rate is £1 per machine hour. This rate will be applied to units of product passing through cost centre A. For example, if one of the products passing through cost centre A uses up 40 machine hours in the manufacturing process, the charge to the product will be

$$40 \text{ hours} \times £1 \text{ per machine hour} = £40$$

Predetermined overhead absorption rates

In practice, overhead absorption rates are normally determined once a year in advance of the actual cost being incurred. Thus the two elements of the above formula will be estimates. That is, the total overheads of each production cost centre and the level of activity chosen will be based on estimates rather than actual costs.

There are a number of reasons why estimates are used rather than actual costs. Two of the main reasons are as follows. Firstly, some overhead costs are only known some months after they have been incurred. For example, electricity costs are normally billed to consumers every quarter in retrospect. Therefore, an organization would have to wait three months before they could determine this overhead cost, and only then could they charge the cost to products that may have already been manufactured and sold. Clearly, such a delay in determining costs would have a detrimental affect on the timeliness of management information. Secondly, a number of overhead costs are seasonal, for example, heating costs. Seasonal variations can distort the costing of products. For example, if a product is manufactured in the summer, the cost of heating absorbed into the product cost is likely to be zero. In contrast, if the product was manufactured in the winter the cost would include a charge for heating. Thus the cost of a product could then depend upon when it was produced. It can be argued that such circumstances would distort the costing of products and would also require a firm to set up complex costing systems to reflect these seasonal variations.

The use of estimates in determining the overhead absorption rate does create problems. The actual overheads incurred in a period may not be equal to the overheads that have been absorbed into product costs because the absorption rate is based on estimates. Therefore the amount of overheads absorbed over a period will only be the same as the cost actually incurred if the actual overhead cost of the production cost centre is equal to the estimates cost (the numerator in the formula) and the actual level of activity is equal to the estimated activity level (the denominator in the formula). Normally, any difference between the total overheads absorbed and the actual overheads incurred during a period will be directly charged to the profit and loss account for that period. These differences in costs will not be allocated or apportioned to products, but will be classified as a period cost. The reason for that this is that it is generally seen as impractical and too costly to identify these differences with individual products, but large differences may need to be investigated.

Example 16.2 below illustrates the process of absorbing overheads into units of production where the actual overhead cost is different from the original estimates on which the absorption rate was based.

Example 16.2

The following are estimates relating to the manufacture of a number of similar products for the forthcoming year 19X1:

Estimated units to be produced during the year	100 000
Estimated overhead cost during the year	£150 000

Therefore the overhead absorption rate will be

$$\frac{\pounds 150\,000}{100\,000 \text{ units}} = \pounds 1.50 \text{ per unit}$$

The actual units produced in 19X1 were 110 000 units; thus the charge to products passing through the cost centre will be 110 000 units × £1.50 (the absorption rate) = £165 000.

However, the overheads actually incurred during 19X1 were £176 000. Thus the difference between actual overhead costs and what was absorbed during the year is £176 000 − £165 000 = £11 000. This £11 000 will be charged to the profit and loss account as an 'under-recovery of overhead' during the year, and thus will be classified as a period cost because it is not identified with any of the units of production produced during the year.

In this example, the cost and the activity level were underestimated during the year. Differences between estimates and actual costs and activity levels will often occur, in practice, because it is very difficult to estimate precisely what the actual costs and activity levels will be in advance of the event.

CASE STUDY 16.1
PHJ Machines

PHJ Machines Ltd has organized its production cost centres by the types of machines it uses to manufacture its products. There are four production cost centres which are known by the machine type – machine type 1, 2, 3 and 4. The company desires to establish an overhead absorption rate for each of these cost centres based on a machine hour rate. The company also wishes to determine the cost per unit of one of its products XDC.

The management of the company have made the following estimates for the forthcoming year 19X3.

	£	£
Indirect materials		
Machine type 1	300	
Machine type 2	600	
Machine type 3	700	
Machine type 4	400	2 000
Maintenance costs		
Machine type 1	700	
Machine type 2	800	
Machine type 3	1 200	
Machine type 4	900	3 600
Other overhead expenses		
Power		1 400
Rent and rates		3 200
Heat and lighting		800
Insurance of buildings		800
Insurance of machinery		1 000
Depreciation of machinery		10 000
Supervision		4 800
Total overheads		27 600

Other relevant information (based on estimates):

Machine type	*Effective horse power*	*Area occupied (square metres)*	*Book value of machinery* £	*Working hours*
1	10	400	5 000	2 000
2	15	300	7 500	1 000
3	45	800	22 500	3 000
4	30	500	15 000	2 000
	100	2 000	50 000	8 000

To determine the machine hour rate we must first allocate costs that can be directly identified with the four cost centres, i.e. the indirect materials and the maintenance costs. We then need to apportion those overheads that cannot be directly identified with a cost centre, i.e. those described in our example as 'other overhead expenses'. This has to be carried out by sharing out these overheads to the cost centres based on some equitable method that reflects the use made of these resources. The following sets out the apportioning of costs to the four cost centres. The basis of apportionment is indicated in parentheses against the cost item.

Types of machines	1	2	3	4
	£	£	£	£
Costs allocated				
Indirect materials	300	600	700	400
Maintenance costs	700	800	1 200	900
Costs apportioned				
Power (effective horse power)	140	210	630	420
Rent and rates (area)	640	480	1 280	800
Light and heating (area)	160	120	320	200
Insurance – building (area)	160	120	320	200
Insurance – machines (book value of machine)	100	150	450	300
Depreciation of machines (book value of machine)	1 000	1 500	4 500	3 000
Supervision (working hours)	1 200	600	1 800	1 200
Total overheads	4 400	4 580	11 200	7 420

The calculation of the apportioned costs to the cost centres in this example is similar to that shown in Example 16.1. To illustrate this computation further the calculation of the apportioned costs of rent and rates to cost centres is shown below.

Cost centre machine type		£
1	400 sq. metres/2000 sq. metres × £3200 =	640
2	300 sq. metres/2000 sq. metres × £3200 =	480
3	800 sq. metres/2000 sq. metres × £3200 =	1 280
4	500 sq. metres/2000 sq. metres × £3200 =	800
	Total cost of rent and rates apportioned	3 200

The basis of apportionment for each type of overhead cost, we can assume, has been chosen because it represents a reasonable method for sharing out the cost and reflects the benefits enjoyed by the cost centre from the resource. For example, the supervision cost has been apportioned on the basis of working hours and it is likely that this basis would reasonably reflect the benefits enjoyed from this resource by each cost centre.

Now that the total overheads have been collected for each of the four cost centres we can divide these costs by the estimated working hours of each machine to obtain the absorption rate.

Machine type		*Machine hour rate*
		£
1	£4400/2000 h =	2.20
2	£4580/1000 h =	4.58
3	£11 200/3000 h =	3.73
4	£7420/2000 h =	3.71

(to the nearest penny)

An alternative system that could be adopted by the company would be to absorb the total overhead cost by the total estimated machine hours. In this case it would not be necessary to allocate and apportion costs over individual cost centres because the same rate would be applied to all cost centres. The overhead absorption rate would therefore be

total costs/total working hours = £27 600/8000 h
= £3.45 per machine hour

This rate would then be charged to all items of production passing through all cost centres. Although this method is appealing, in that far less time is spent in calculating the overhead absorption rate, it does not take account of the resources consumed by the individual cost centres in the production process. It is therefore likely that such a system would excessively distort the costing of individual products.

Turning now to the product costs of XDC, the following information is also given: 2000 units were produced in the year. The direct costs incurred were

	£
Direct material	870
Direct Labour	940

The machine hours actually worked in the year producing 2000 units of XDC were as follows.

	Hours
Machine type 1	400
Machine type 2	400
Machine type 4	200

To determine the cost per unit we first need to determine the total cost associated with the manufacture of the product. The direct costs are given above. The overhead costs to be absorbed into the product will be based on the overhead absorption rate, the machine hour rate and the actual hours worked in these cost centres on the product. The total cost of product XDC is as follows.

		£
Direct material		870
Direct labour		940
Machine type 1,	400 h × £2.20	880
Machine type 2,	400 h × £4.58	1 832
Machine type 3,	200 h × £3.71	742
Total cost		5 264

It is now necessary to divide the total cost by the number of units produced to determine the cost per unit.

£5264/2000 units = £2.63 per unit (to the nearest penny)

Case Study 16.1 illustrates a number of the procedures and principles regarding the absorption of overheads that have been discussed above:

Different types of production processes

In the examination of full costing above, we have discussed the general principles of costing systems that take into account direct and indirect costs. In practice there are a number of different types of costing systems that are contingent on the type of technology used in the production process and the type of product being produced. Traditionally, the systems are classified into two categories: job costing and process costing.

At this stage of your studies it is not necessary to examine these two systems in detail. However, it is appropriate to give you some insight into the systems. Job costing systems will be used when the costs of each unit of production, or a batch of units, can be identified at any time in the manufacturing cycle. The examples we have looked at earlier closely mirror the job costing system. In contrast, in a system of process costing, individual products cannot be identified until the manufacturing process is complete. A number of similar products will be manufactured at the same time within the process. Costs are accumulated on a process or departmental basis and are then divided by the number of units produced to obtain an average unit cost. In such cases product costs will represent the average unit costs of production.

Marginal costing

In this chapter so far no specific reference has been made to fixed and variable costs. Variable costs, as previously defined, vary proportionally with production. The term marginal cost refers to the change in total costs resulting from the production of one more (or less) unit of production. Invariably the marginal cost will be synonymous with the variable cost of a product and in the context of product costing we shall assume that these two terms have the same meaning.

The classification of costs that we have tended to concentrate on in this chapter is direct and indirect costs. We have defined a direct cost as one that is traceable, and thus attributable, to a given cost objective, in our case a product. In the context of a multi-product firm the only direct costs that can be identified with a product will be those costs that change when production increases or decreases, i.e. marginal costs. Indirect costs will therefore normally only consist of fixed costs, i.e. costs that do not change as production increases or decreases.

KEY CONCEPT 16.3
Marginal costing

Only direct production costs are included as product costs in marginal costing.

Earlier, when we defined product costs, in the case of full costing we said that both direct and indirect costs of production should be included in the cost. It follows that product costs, in this case, will include both fixed and variable costs of production. The process of absorbing overheads, and in particular the apportionment of costs, although based on clearly identified criteria, is relatively arbitrary. Often a number of bases for apportioning overhead costs are available each having the quality that they are equitable. However, the use of these different bases will invariably result in differing amounts of costs being apportioned to products. In Case Study 16.1 above, heating and lighting costs were apportioned on the basis of area occupied. It could have been argued that working hours would have been just as equitable as a base for apportioning these costs. The result, in terms of the amount of costs that are apportioned to the four cost centres, however, would be very different. The cost of a product will therefore often depend on the choice of the basis used to apportion costs. It is part of the job of a management accountant to examine the basis of apportioning costs.

In the following chapters relating to decision making it will be argued that fixed costs should normally be ignored in the decision-making process, i.e. they are irrelevant to the decision. This is another argument in support of marginal costing *vis-à-vis* full costing.

It is not difficult to appreciate the argument that the use of the full costing method can distort costing and the value placed upon products. Those who support this argument advocate that the only costs that should be classified as product costs are those that are direct, which we are assuming in this analysis are only marginal costs. All other production costs, i.e. fixed overheads, are classified as period costs.

Whilst the argument for marginal costing of products is attractive and convenient, it implies that fixed costs are not incurred in the production process. This is clearly not true. Expenditure on fixed costs is just as essential in the manufacture of products as marginal costs are. In recent years the case for inclusion of fixed costs in product costs has gained further momentum as the proportion of fixed costs incurred in the manufacture of products has grown as a result of automation. The majority of the costs associated with automation, such as the cost of machinery, are of course fixed costs. Another argument in support of full costing is that if fixed costs are ignored the cost of products will be seen to be undervalued. For example, if the costs of a unit of production consist of £2 of marginal costs and £10 of fixed costs, the value given to this product for stock valuation purposes under the marginal costing regime will be just £2. The cost of resources employed in the production of this unit, and thus its true value, is clearly more than £2! It is therefore not surprising that in practice firms tend to favour full costing for stock valuation purposes.

The arguments for and against these methods of costing all have their virtues and it is not easy to resolve which method is preferable. To some extent the method preferred is dependent on its application. For example, in the case of future decision making the arguments in favour of marginal costing as the preferred method are well documented, as we shall see in Chapters 17 and 18. However, the preference is not quite so clear when other applications are considered. We can therefore only conclude that the preferred method will depend on individual subjective judgements regarding the strengths and weaknesses of the two methods.

Perhaps the most controversial debate regarding the use of full and marginal costing relates to stock valuation and its effect on income measurement. It is therefore appropriate to examine these two methods of product costing in more detail.

Income measurement and stock valuations

In Case Study 16.2, for clarity, we consider a firm that produces only one product. In such a situation all the costs would by definition be identifiable with the one product and therefore would be classified as direct costs whether or not they are fixed or variable. However, in practice the distinction between these two classifications will still be valid in this situation. The reason for this, as was previously mentioned in the discussion on overhead absorption rates, is that many of the indirect costs will only be known some months after they have been incurred. For management purposes it is often preferable to absorb these costs using estimates rather than wait until the actual cost can be determined. In Case Studies 16.2 and 16.3 we treat fixed factory overheads in a similar way to their treatment in a multi-product firm.

CASE STUDY 16.2
Foot Lighting Company

The Foot Lighting Company Ltd manufactures and sells one design of desk lamp. The following are the costs of production for 19X1:

Marginal costs (direct cost) £3.00 per unit
Fixed factory overhead absorption rate £2.00 per unit

The fixed factory overhead rate is based on estimates of overhead costs of £40 000 and an activity level of 20 000 units. Actual fixed overheads incurred in 19X1 were £40 000. The sales price is £8.00 per unit.

Sales and production data for 19X1 in units is as follows.

	Units
Opening stock of finished goods	1 000
Production	20 000
Sales	20 000
Closing stock of finished goods	1 000

During 19X1 selling expenses were £1600 and administration expenses not associated with production were £1000.

We shall begin by producing an income statement for 19X1 using the absorption costing approach and assume that any over- or under-absorption of overheads is charged or credited to the income statement as a period cost.

Income statement for 19X1 (using absorption costing)

	£	£
Sales (£8 × 20 000)		160 000
Less cost of goods sold		
Opening stock of finished goods (£5 × 1000)	5 000	
Plus production (£5 × 20 000)	100 000	
Cost of goods available for sale	105 000	
Less closing stock of finished goods (£5 × 1000)	5 000	100 000
Gross profit		60 000
Period costs:		
Administration	1 000	
Selling	1 600	
Over- or under-absorption of overheads	—	2 600
Net profit		57 400

The following is a brief commentary on the above statement.

The production and the opening and closing stock of finished goods in this statement, using the absorption costing approach, are costed at the full cost of the product, i.e. the direct costs of £3 and the overheads absorbed at £2 per unit. You will also note that there are no movements in the opening and closing stocks during the year. This is because the units produced are equal to those sold.

The period costs are represented by selling and administration expenses; thus they are not included in the product cost.

There is no over- or under-absorption of overheads. This is because the total overheads absorbed (£2 per unit multiplied by the number of units produced (20 000), i.e. £40 000) are the same as the actual overheads incurred during the year.

Income statement for 19X1 (using marginal costing)

	£	£
Sales		160 000
Less cost of goods sold		
Opening stock of finished goods (1000 × £3)	3 000	
Production (20 000 × £3)	60 000	
Cost of goods available for sale	63 000	
Less closing stock of goods sold (1000 × £3)	3 000	60 000
Contribution		100 000
Less period costs		
Fixed factory overheads	40 000	
Administration	1 000	
Selling	1 600	42 600
Net profit		57 400

That is, the net profit is the same in both cases.

From the above statement it can be seen that the main differences between absorption and marginal costing are as follows.

- The product costs: the production costs and the values of opening and closing stocks of finished goods consist only of the direct costs of £3 per unit.

- Fixed factory overheads are classified as period costs under the marginal costing approach and are not included as product costs.
- The summation of sales revenue less cost of goods sold represents the contribution; contribution was earlier defined as sales less marginal costs (see Chapter 15).
- Both methods of costing in this Case Study produce the same profit figure.

CASE STUDY 16.3
The Foot Lighting Company

We shall assume that the costs and sales price are the same as in Case Study 16.2 for the following years 19X2 and 19X3.

The sales and production data, in terms of units, for 19X2 and 19X3 are as follows.

	19X2	*19X3*
	Units	*Units*
Opening stock of finished goods	1000	6000
Production	22000	16000
Sales	17000	21000
Closing stock of finished goods	6000	1000

We shall also assume that the overhead absorption rate, actual overheads incurred, administration and selling expenses are the same as in Case Study 16.2.

We begin our analysis by considering the absorption costing method.

Income statement (using absorption costing)

19X2	£	£
Sales (17000 × £8)		136000
Less cost of goods sold		
Opening stock of finished goods (1000 × £5)	5000	
Production (22000 × £5)	110000	
Cost of goods available for sale	115000	
Less closing stock of finished goods (6000 × £5)	30000	85000
Gross profit		51000
Less period costs		
Over- absorption of overheads – see note below	(4000)	
Administration costs	1000	
Selling costs	1600	(1400)
Net profit		52400

Over-absorption of overhead

	£
Overheads absorbed during the year 22000 units × £2 =	44000
Actual overheads incurred during the year	40000
Over-absorption of overheads	4000

The £4000 represents the amount that we have overcharged to products during the period. That is, we have charged £44000 through applying the absorption rate, which is based on estimates, whilst the actual overhead costs were £40 000. The difference will therefore be credited to the income statement.

19X3	£	£
Sales (21 000 × £8)		168 000
Less cost of goods sold		
Opening stock of finished goods (6000 × £5)	30 000	
Production (16 000 × £5)	80 000	
Cost of goods available for sale	110 000	
Less closing stock of finished goods (1000 × £5)	5 000	105 000
Gross profit		63 000
Less period costs		
Under-absorption of overheads – see note below	8 000	
Administration	1 000	
Selling	1 600	10 600
Net profit		52 400

Under-absorption of overheads

	£
Overheads absorbed during the year 16 000 × £2	32 000
Actual overheads incurred during the year	40 000
Under-absorption of overheads	8 000

In this case we have absorbed less than we estimated by £8000 and this amount will therefore be charged to the income statement as a period cost.

Income statement (using marginal costing)

19X2	£	£
Sales		136 000
Less cost of goods sold		
Opening stock of finished goods (1000 × £3)	3 000	
Production (22 000 × £3)	66 000	
Cost of goods available for sale	69 000	
Less closing stock of finished goods (6000 × £3)	18 000	51 000
Contribution		85 000

19X2	£	£
Less product costs		
Fixed factory overheads	40 000	
Administration	1 000	
Selling	1 600	42 600
Net profit		42 400

19X3	£	£
Sales		168 000
Less cost of goods sold		
Opening stock of finished goods (6000 × £3)	18 000	
Production (16 000 × £3)	48 000	
Cost of goods available for sale	66 000	
Less closing stock of finished goods (1000 × £3)	3 000	63 000
Contribution		104 000
Less period costs		
Fixed factory overheads	40 000	
Administration costs	1 000	
Selling	1 600	42 600
Net profit		61 400

The following summarizes the differences between the net profits of the methods used above.

	19X2	*19X3*
	£	£
Marginal costing	42 400	61 400
Absorption costing	52 400	52 400
Net profit difference	(10 000)	9 000

The difference in net profit over these two years is a direct result of the methods used. In the case of absorption costing fixed costs are classified as product costs and are therefore included in the valuation of stocks. When there is an increase in stocks during a period (i.e. in year 19X2) the fixed costs associated with these stocks will be included in the stock value rather than being included (recognized) as a cost in the 'cost of goods sold' computation. In contrast, when there has been a decrease in stock during a period (i.e. in year 19X3), which means a proportion of the goods sold (5000 units in our example) has been obtained from the opening stocks rather than production, the fixed costs related to these stocks are released as expenses and matched against sales. In the case of the marginal costing approach all fixed costs during a period, because they are classified as period costs, will be charged in the income statement in the period in which they are incurred.

The following summarizes the movement in stocks over the two year period.

Movement in finished stocks	*19X2*	*19X3*
	Units	*Units*
Opening	1000	6000
Closing	6000	1000
Difference	5000	(5000)

In 19X2 there has been an increase in stocks of 5000 units. Under the absorption costing approach the fixed cost element of these stocks (5000 units × £2 absorption rate = £10 000) will not be included as a cost in the period. But in the case of a marginal costing approach these fixed costs (£10 000) will be charged, as period cost, to the income statement in 19X2, i.e. when they were incurred. The net profit in the case of absorption costing is £10 000 more than the profit under the marginal costing approach.

The reverse situation arises in 19X3. In this year the fixed costs associated with the decrease in stocks, under absorption costing, are released as costs and matched against the sales during the period. Thus 5000 units × £2 absorption rate = £10 000 is now recognized as a cost in the cost of goods sold. These fixed costs are excluded in the case of marginal costing because they were not incurred during the year as they relate to the previous year. Therefore the net profit calculated under absorption costing will be £9000 less than the profit under the marginal costing method.

We will now consider another Case Study (16.3) where there is a movement in stocks over the two year period. Here the units produced are greater (19X2) or less (19X3) than those sold.

From the Case Studies we can summarize the differences between the methods as follows.

- When sales equal production (i.e. when there is no movement in stock) marginal and absorption costing will yield the same profit. The amount of fixed costs charged to the income statement will be the same.
- When production exceeds sales (i.e. when stocks are increasing) absorption costing will show a higher profit than does marginal costing. Under absorption costing a portion of the fixed production costs is charged to stocks and thereby deferred to future periods.
- When sales exceed production, absorption costing shows a lower profit than does marginal costing. This is because the fixed costs included in the stocks are charged to the later period in which the stocks are sold.

In the long run the profit figures disclosed by the two methods must even out because sales cannot continuously exceed production, nor can production continuously exceed sales.

The differences in profits derived from the application of the two methods can be reconciled by the following arithmetical expression:

fixed overhead absorption rate × the movement in stocks during a period = difference in profits

Summary

The determination of product costs for management information purposes is clearly critical in the planning, control and decision-making process of organizations. However, the values given to products very much depend upon the form of costing method adopted. Two methods have been examined in this chapter – full costing and marginal costing. The main difference between the two methods is the way in which production overheads are accounted for.

Under the full costing method, production overheads are included as a product cost. In multi-product firms overheads will always be difficult if not impossible to trace directly to products. There is therefore a need to adopt some system that equitably shares out the overheads to products. In this chapter we examined absorption costing as a means of sharing out overhead costs to products. It is important to recognize the advantages and the problems associated with the adoption of this method, in particular the necessity of choosing a basis to apportion costs that by its very nature is discretionary but does have the advantage that it takes account of all the costs of production.

The marginal costing method, in contrast, treats overheads as a period cost, and it follows that the only expenses that are included in product costs are direct costs. Whilst this method overcomes the problems associated with absorbing overheads it does ignore a significant element of the production cost in the valuation of cost of sales and stocks.

An example of the application of these costing methods was illustrated at the end of the chapter, applying both of these costing methods to stock valuations. The example showed the differences in values and net profit obtained when these two methods were applied. It is important that you understand the reasons for these differences and appreciate the arguments for and against the application of the methods to product costing.

Further reading

A well-analysed example of absorption costing applied in a marketing context is given in *Managerial Accounting: Method and Meaning*. Chapter 3, by R.M.S. Wilson and W.A. Chua (Van Nostrand Reinhold, 1988).

Review questions

1 Explain why it is important to determine the cost of products.
2 Define direct and indirect costs.
3 Give examples of expenditure that would be classified, in a manufacturing organization, as direct costs and indirect costs.
4 What are period costs?
5 Explain why it is necessary to use estimates in determining an absorption rate.
6 Discuss the advantages and disadvantages of applying marginal costing for product costing.

Problems for discussion and analysis

1 Barclay Plc uses a predetermined overhead rate in applying overheads to product costs on a direct labour cost basis for cost centre X and on a machine hour basis for cost centre Y. The following details the estimated forecasts for 19X1:

	X	Y
Direct labour costs	£100 000	£35 000
Production overheads	£140 000	£150 000
Direct labour hours	16 000	5 000
Machine hours	1 000	20 000

(a) Calculate the predetermined overhead rate for cost centres X and Y.

(b) BNH is one of the products manufactured by Barclay. The manufacturing process involves the two cost centres X and Y. The following data relate to the resources that were used in the manufacture of the product during 19X1:

	X	Y
Direct materials	£20 000	£40 000
Direct labour	£32 000	£21 000
Direct labour hours	4 000	3 000
Machine hours	1 000	13 000

Determine the total production cost for product BNH using full costing.

(c) Assuming that product BNH consists of 20 000 units, what is the unit cost of BNH?

(d) At the end of the year 19X1 it was found that actual production overhead costs amounted to £160 000 in cost centre X and £138 000 in cost centre Y. The total direct labour cost in cost centre X was £144 200 and the machine hours used were 18 000 in cost centre Y during the year. Calculate the over- or under-absorbed overhead for each cost centre.

2 Drawrod Plc has three manufacturing cost centres: Punching, Stamping and Assembly. In addition the company has two service cost centres: Maintenance and Inspection.

The following details the estimated production overhead expenses for the year to the 31 December 19X2:

	£	£
Indirect materials		
Punching	12 000	
Stamping	14 000	
Assembly	10 000	
Maintenance	8 000	
Inspection	4 000	48 000
Indirect labour		
Punching	24 000	
Stamping	30 000	
Assembly	14 000	
Maintenance	36 000	
Inspection	10 000	114 000

Other overhead expenses		
Power	56 000	
Rent and rates	128 000	
Heat and light	32 000	
Insurance of buildings	32 000	
Insurance of machines	40 000	
Depreciation of machines	40 000	328 000
Total		490 000

The following are additional estimates relating to manufacturing for the year ended 31 December 19X2:

	Punching	*Stamping*	*Assembly*	*Maintenance*	*Inspection*	*Total*
Area occupied (sq. metres)	18 000	12 000	24 000	3 000	3 000	60 000
Working hours	52 500	45 000	30 000	15 000	7 500	150 000
Book value of machines	200 000	140 000	60 000	—	—	400 000
Machine hours	51 200	64 000	44 800	—	—	160 000
Number of employees	180	150	240	30	60	660

The costs of the service cost centre are to be apportioned as follows:

	Maintenance (%)	*Inspection* (%)
Punching	40	20
Stamping	30	30
Assembly	30	50
	100	100

The company's bases for the absorption of overheads are as follows.

Punching	Machine hours
Stamping	Machine hours
Assembly	Working hours

(a) Calculate the absorption rates for the Punching, Stamping and Assembly cost centres (calculations to the nearest penny).

(b) Specify and explain the factors to be considered in determining whether to use a single factory-wide overhead absorption rate for all factory overheads or a separate rate for each manufacturing cost centre, with reference to the system applied to Drawrod Plc.

3 The management of Absent Ltd has been studying the first three years' results of this newly formed company and are a little concerned with the figures produced. They tend to think of profits as being directly related to the volume of sales and find it confusing that for one year the reported sales are higher than those of the previous year but the reported net profit is lower.

The following figures are applicable to the years under consideration:

	19X1	*19X2*	*19X3*
Actual sales (units)	36 000	50 000	60 000
Actual production (units)	58 000	35 000	53 000

In each of the years the estimated production volume was 45 000 units and the estimated fixed overheads were £67 500.

The selling price was £4 per unit and variable costs were £1.50 per unit for all three years.

Actual costs equalled estimated costs in all years. Selling and administrative expense for each year were £10 000. The company had no opening stock. The management accountant was having considerable difficulties explaining to management that fluctuations in profits resulted from differences between volume of sales and the volume of production within an accounting period, together with the system of product valuation used.

(a) Prepare income statements for Absent Ltd using marginal costing and absorption costing for each of the three years to aid the management accountant's explanation.
(b) Reconcile the net profit reported under the costing methods.
(c) Which costing method would you recommend for management decision-making purposes and why?

17 Accounting for decision making: when there are no resource constraints

In terms of decision making, the relevant costs and benefits which relate to the decision are future costs and benefits. These future costs can be categorized into incremental costs and benefits, opportunity costs, avoidable costs and replacement costs. In this chapter we consider these categories of costs in relation to business problems where there are no resource constraints.

For planning, management will need to make decisions about future business opportunities to ensure that the organization's objectives are met. A large proportion of these decisions will relate to the short term and will be expressed in financial terms in the organization's budget (see Chapter 19). Management will also be required to make decisions of a more immediate nature which relate to opportunities that were not anticipated at the planning stage. To ignore profitable opportunities because they have not been specifically included in the budget would clearly be irresponsible in a dynamic business environment. These decisions can be categorized as follows.

- Decisions where there are no resource constraints: In these circumstances organizations will be free to make decisions, knowing that the decision will not affect other opportunities, e.g. the decision to introduce a new product, where the decision will not affect, in any way, the demand and production levels of other products. These decisions can also be simply described as 'accept or reject' decisions.
- Decisions where there are resource constraints: This situation occurs when an organization experiences a shortage of physical resources, e.g. a shortage of a particular material. In such cases an organization will be unable to accept all potential desirable opportunities. To

decide which of these opportunities to choose it will be necessary to implement a priority (ranking) system.

- Mutually exclusive decisions: These are decisions where the acceptance of one opportunity will mean that the others will be rejected, e.g. the decision to make or buy a component to be embodied within one of the firm's products – the decision to make will mean that the option to buy is rejected. Mutually exclusive decisions can include situations both with and without resource constraints.

In this chapter we shall be examining the methods used by accountants to provide information for management to make efficient short-term decisions, and the application of these methods to different types of decision when there are no resource constraints. Decisions where an organization *is* subject to resource constraints and the make or buy type of decision will be considered in the next chapter.

The reference to the short term will be interpreted to mean decisions that will affect the firm within a period of a year. This is the convention. It will be assumed that the values of cash inflows and outflows throughout the year will be of an equivalent value. This tends to be a little naive in that clearly all individuals and firms will prefer to receive, for example, cash today rather than in 11 months' time. For clarity, however, it is convenient in our analysis to make this assumption, as complexities arise when we begin to take account of the time value of money in the decision-making process which is considered later on in Chapter 20.

Relevant costs and benefits

Decision making

Decisions relate to the future and the function of decision making is to select courses of action for the future that satisfy the objectives of the firm. There is no opportunity to alter the past, although past experience may help us in future decisions. For example, the observation of past cost behaviour may help to determine future levels of cost.

Relevant costs and benefits can therefore be defined as those costs and benefits that will result from making a specific decision. A more precise definition will be established after we have examined the underlying principles of relevant costs and benefits and considered some examples of the application of these principles.

The relevant costs for decision making are different from those used in accurals accounting. This is not surprising as the principles of traditional costing (e.g. overhead absorption methods) evolved from the need to report historical events, rather than to determine future costs and benefits. A number of methods adopted by accountants to account for decisions about the future are derived from economic theory and therefore may be familar to you.

We now consider the principles underlying relevant costs for decision making and the application of these principles to specific types of decisions. The differences between the application of relevant costs and traditional costing will also be discussed in this analysis.

Future and past (sunk) costs

Costs of a historical nature, which are normally referred to as sunk costs, are incurred as a result of a past decision and are therefore irrelevant to future decisions and should be ignored.

KEY CONCEPT 17.1
Sunk costs

Sunk costs or past costs can easily be identified in that they will have been paid for or they are owed under legally binding contracts. The firm is committed to paying for them in the future.

CASE STUDY 17.1
Wellings plc

A firm has an obsolete machine that was purchased and paid for two years ago. The net book value of the machine, as shown in the accounts of the firm, prior to its becoming obsolete is £72 000. The alternatives now available to the firm are

- to make a number of alterations to the machine at an estimated cost of £20 000 and then to sell it for £40 000, or
- to sell it for scrap, the estimated selling price being £15 000.

The net book value of £72 000 represents the original cost of purchasing the machine less the accumulated depreciation (charge for depreciation over the two year period). The original cost is the result of a past decision. It was incurred two years ago and therefore it is a sunk cost. It is irrelevant to the future decision whether they alter the machine and sell it, or sell it for scrap. The depreciation is also based on the original cost of the machine and is thus irrelevant to this future decision. The only relevant costs and benefits in this example are those related to the future; we can analyse these as follows.

	Alter	*Scrap*
	£	£
Future benefits	40 000	15 000
Future costs	20 000	—
Future income	20 000	15 000

From the analysis of relevant costs and benefits it can be seen that the firm will be £5000 better off altering the machine and selling it rather than selling it for scrap.

Differential (incremental) costs

Another important principle in the determination of relevant costs and benefits is that only differential (incremental) costs and benefits are relevant to future decisions. The application of the principles underlying differential costing will be illustrated by considering in Case Study 17.2 the opportunity offered to a firm, which has spare capacity, to accept a special order. Through a comparison of the costs and benefits associated with the opportunities available to the firm we are able to identify differential costs and benefits. It is these costs and benefits that are relevant to decisions between competing opportunities.

KEY CONCEPT 17.2
Differential costs

Differential (incremental) costs are the differences in costs and benefits between alternative opportunities available to the organization. It follows that when a number of opportunities are being considered costs and benefits that are common to these alternative opportunities will be irrelevant to the decision.

CASE STUDY 17.2
Haslemere Plc

Haslemere Plc manufactures dressing gowns. The current capacity is 120 000 gowns per year. However, it is predicted that in the forthcoming year sales will only be 90 000 gowns. A mail order firm offers to buy 20 000 gowns at £7.50 each. The acceptance of this special order will not affect regular sales and will take a year to complete. The Managing Director is reluctant to accept the order because £7.50 is below the factory unit cost of £8 per gown.

The following gives the predicted total income and the predicted income per unit, in a traditional costing format, if the order were not to be accepted.

		Total		Per unit
	£	£	£	£
Sales: 90 000 gowns at £10 each		900 000		10.00
Less factory expenses				
Variable	540 000		6.00	
Supervision	90 000		1.00	
Other fixed costs	90 000	720 000	1.00	8.00
Gross profit		180 000		2.00
Selling expenses				
Variable	22 500		0.25	
Fixed	112 500	135 000	1.25	1.50
Profit		45 000		0.50

The Management Accountant with the Production and Sales Manager is requested to review the costs of taking on the special order. These are their conclusions.

1 The variable costs of production relate to labour and materials and these will be incurred at the same rates as for the production of their normal production units.
2 There will be a need for additional supervision. However, it is anticipated that four of the current supervisors can cover this requirement if each of them works

overtime of 5 h per week. Supervisors are paid £10 per hour and overtime is paid at a premium of £2 per hour. There are 48 working weeks to the year. Therefore the additional costs will be

$$5\text{ h} \times £12 \text{ per hour} \times 48 \text{ weeks} \times 4 \text{ supervisors} = £11\,520$$

3 Other fixed costs relate to costs such as factory rent and the depreciation of plant. It is anticipated that these will remain the same if the order is accepted.
4 There will be a need to hire an additional machine costing £10 000 if the contract is accepted.
5 The variable sales costs relate to salespersons' commission, and this cost will not be incurred on the special order.
6 The fixed sales expenses relate to the administering of sales. These costs will remain the same except that it is anticipated that a part-time clerk will be required to help with the additional workload if the special order is accepted. The salary will be £6000 per year.

Using the differential costing approach we can compare the total income for the year for Haslemere Plc if the order is accepted or rejected.

	Accept	*Reject*	*Differential cost and revenue*
	£	£	£
Sales	1 050 000	900 000	150 000
Factory expenses			
Variable costs	660 000	540 000	120 000
Supervision	101 520	90 000	11 520
Other fixed costs	90 000	90 000	—
Hire of plant	10 000	—	10 000
	861 520	720 000	141 520
Sales expenses			
Variable costs	22 500	22 500	—
Fixed costs	118 500	112 500	6 000
Total costs	1 002 520	855 000	147 520
Profit	47 480	45 000	2 480

From the differential analysis it can be seen that Haslemere will be £2480 better off if the special order is accepted. Also it can be observed that a number of the costs are irrelevant in the decision analysis. That is, they are the same whether or not the order is accepted; for example, 'other fixed costs' are £90 000 for both the accept and the reject decisions. Therefore the analysis of data could have been simplified by only considering the differential costs and revenues related to the special order. If the differential analysis of costs and revenues results in a profit, from a purely quantitative perspective, the order should be accepted.

Avoidable and unavoidable costs

An alternative way of determining whether a cost is relevant or irrelevant in decisions (such as the special order for the dressing gowns illustrated above), instead of using the differential analysis is by asking the question: will a cost be avoided if the company did not proceed with the special order? If the answer is positive the cost is relevant and should be included. For example, consider this question with regard to the cost of plant hire for the special order above: will the cost of plant hire be avoided if the company does not proceed with the order? The answer is yes, i.e. the cost is relevant to the decision as it will only be incurred if the order is accepted. Alternatively, a cost is described as unavoidable if the cost will be incurred whether or not the decision is to accept or reject, i.e. the cost is irrelevant to the decision.

KEY CONCEPT 17.3
Opportunity cost

The opportunity cost of a resource is normally defined as the maximum benefit which could be obtained from that resource if it were used for some alternative purpose. If a firm uses a resource for alternative A rather than B, it is the potential benefits that are forgone by not using the resource for alternative B that constitute the opportunity cost. Therefore the potential forgone benefits, the opportunity cost, are a relevant cost in the decision to accept alternative A.

Opportunity cost

The economists' concept of opportunity cost has been adopted by accountants for decision-making purposes. This concept relates to the cost of using resources for alternative opportunitites.

The following is an example of the concept of opportunity costs: Basil Sums, a qualified accountant, is a sole practioneer. He works 40 hours per week and charges clients £20 per hour. Basil is already overworked and will not work any extra hours each week. A circus offers Basil £1000 per week to become a lion tamer. In the decision to become a lion tamer Basil must consider the benefits he would forgo from his accounting practice, i.e. £20 × 40 hours = £800 per week; this is the opportunity cost of Basil's becoming a lion tamer. Assuming that Basil is only concerned with financial rewards he will accept the offer as he will be £1000 − £800 = £200 per week better off.

Replacement costs

In cases where a resource was originally purchased for some purpose other than an opportunity currently under consideration, the relevant cost of using that resource is its replacement cost. This cost has come about as a direct result of the decision to use the resource for a purpose not originally intended and the need to replace the resource. The following example will help you to understand the application of this principle.

Hick Bats Ltd has been approached by a customer who would like a special job done. The job would require the use of 500 kg of Material A. Material A is used by Hicks Bats for a variety of purposes. Currently the company holds 1000 kg in stock which was purchased one month ago for £6 per kilogram. Since then, the price per kilogram has increased to £8. If 500 kg were used on this special job it would need to be replaced to meet the production demand from other jobs.

The relevant cost of using material A on this special job is the replacement cost 500 kg × £8 = £4000. This is because the material will need to be replaced and as a result of its use the replacement will cost £4000. The cost of £4000 will have arisen as a direct result of accepting the special order and therefore is relevant to the decision. It should be noted that the original cost of £6 per kilogram is irrelevant to the decision as it relates to a past decision and has already been incurred (i.e. a sunk cost).

Case Study 17.3 illustrates the application of the principles of relevant costs described above compared with traditional costing methods.

CASE STUDY 17.3
Hutton Plc

Hutton Plc is considering whether to accept the offer of a contract to undertake some reconstruction work at a price of £73 000. The work would begin almost immediately and will take about a year to complete. The company's accountant has submitted the following statement.

	£	£
Contract price		73 000
Less costs		
Cost of work already incurred in drawing up detailed costings		4 700
Materials		
A	7 000	
B	8 000	15 000
Labour		
Direct	21 000	
Indirect	12 000	33 000
Machinery		
Depreciation on machines owned	4 000	
Hire of special equipment	5 000	9 000
General overheads		10 500
Total cost		72 200
Expected profit		800

The management of the company is rather apprehensive as to whether it is advisable to incur the inevitable risks involved for such a small profit margin. On making further enquiries the following information becomes available.

1 Material A was bought two years ago for £7000. It would cost £8000 at today's prices. If not used on this contract, it could be sold for £6500. There is no alternative use for this material.

2 Material B was ordered for another job but will be used on this job if the contract is accepted. The replacement for the other job will cost £9000.
3 The trade union has negotiated a minimum wage agreement, as a result of which direct wages of £21 000 will be incurred whether the contract is undertaken or not. If not employed on this contract, it is thought that these employees could be used to do much needed maintenance work, which would otherwise be done by an outside contractor at an estimated cost of £18 500.
4 The indirect labour is the wage of a foreman who will have to be taken on to supervise the contract. A suitable person is ready to take up the appointment at once.
5 The machine which is already owned is six years old. £4000 is the final instalment of depreciation required to write off the balance on the asset account. There is no alternative use for the machine, and its scrap value is negligible, because of the high cost of dismantling and removal.
6 The general overhead absorption rate is 50% of direct labour. Over-heads are expected to rise by £4000 if the contract is accepted.

With reference to the above information and the principles of relevant costs discussed earlier we can now consider the individual items of costs that should be accounted for in the decision whether to accept or reject the contract.

1 Material A: The £7000 originally paid for the material is a sunk cost and is thus irrelevant. We are told that the current replacement cost is £8000. However, the company can only obtain £6500 if it was sold, i.e. the net realizable value. This is the benefit the company forgoes (the opportunity cost) by using the material on this contract. Thus £6500 is the relevant cost.
2 Material B: The fact that this material has already been ordered means that the company is legally committed to pay the supplier of the material. Thus this cost of £8000 can also be considered as a sunk cost and is irrelevant to the decision. The only alternative is to use the material on the other job. If so the company would have to purchase some more material at a cost of £9000. This is the opportunity cost of using the material on this contract.
3 Direct labour: These employees will be paid whether the contract is accepted or not; therefore this cost is unavoidable and irrelevant. However, if they were not employed on this contract the company would save £18 500 in fees to the outside contractor for maintenance. The £18 500 is therefore a relevant cost as this is the opportunity cost of using them on the contract.
4 Indirect labour: The cost of £12 000 for employing the foreman is an incremental cost, i.e. it will only be incurred if the contract is accepted, and therefore is relevant to the contract.
5 Depreciation on the machine owned: The cost of depreciation relates to a past cost (i.e. sunk cost) and is thus irrelevant to the decision. A relevant benefit would be the machine's scrap value. However, as this is negligible it is ignored.
6 The hire of special equipment: The cost of £5000 will only be incurred if the contract is accepted and therefore the cost is an incremental cost and is relevant to the decision.
7 General overhead: The only cost that is relevant is the increase in cost of £4000 if the contract is accepted. That is, this cost is incremental and is thus relevant to the decision. All the other costs related to general overheads are unavoidable and therefore irrelevant.

8 Cost of work already incurred in drawing up costings (£4700, detailed at the beginning of the schedule): This cost is irrelevant to the contract as it is a sunk cost and therefore should be excluded.

We are now in a position to draw up an amended statement of costs for the contract.

Relevant costs and benefits

	£	£
Contract price		
		73 000
Less costs		
Materials:		
A	6 500	
B	9 000	15 500
Labour		
Direct	18 500	
Indirect	12 000	30 500
Hire of special equipment		5 000
Overheads		4 000
Total costs		55 000
Expected profits		18 000

In this particular case study, it is apparent that by considering only costs that are relevant the contract is more attractive to the company. In the original schedule of costs and revenues, which were based on traditional costing methods, the expected profit was only £800 compared with £18 000. It should be stressed that the higher profits yielded from the analysis of *relevant* costs and benefits compared with the traditional analysis will not always be the rule. The result depends on the particular circumstances of the firm making the decisions.

The principles underlying the relevance of costs and benefits to decisions, described and illustrated in Case Study 17.3, tend to focus on costs rather than revenues. However, the same principles apply to revenues. That is, only those revenues that will be generated as a result of the decision should be brought into the decision model and are therefore relevant to that decision. Relevant benefits by their very nature relate to the future. All benefits that have been received or are due to be received from a prior commitment are irrelevant to future decisions.

The meaning of relevance

Earlier in this chapter relevant costs and benefits were defined, in general terms, as those costs and benefits that will result from a specific

Relevant costs and benefits are those that relate to the future and are additional costs and revenues that will be incurred or result from a decision.

Costs that are relevant to a decision may also be

- the cost of replacing a resource that was originally purchased for some other purpose
- the opportunity cost of using a resource that could be used for some alternative purpose

KEY CONCEPT 17.4
Relevant costs and benefits

decision. We are now in the position to derive a more precise definition.

There are also costs and revenues that are incurred or generated by an organization that will not be relevant to a decision, i.e. will not be affected by a decision. It is important to be able to identify these costs and benefits so that we can eliminate them from our analysis.

Fixed and variables costs and the contribution approach to decision making

The concept of contribution was introduced in Chapter 15. The contribution is the difference between the sales revenue and the variable costs. We reintroduce the concept here in the context of relevant costs and decision making.

It is normally assumed that costs will behave in a linear fashion. That is, fixed costs are constant over all volumes and variable costs will vary in direct proportion to volume. Therefore in a number of situations in decision making fixed costs will be irrelevant to decisions as they will remain the same whether or not the decision is accepted or rejected, i.e. they are unavoidable. Thus when there are no scarce resources in the making of a decision and the sales revenue exceeds the relevant variable costs an accept decision will be made. This decision rule is applicable to a number of types of decisions.

A word of caution: there will be some situations when costs will not necessarily behave in a linear fashion, and so variations in unit variable costs or in fixed cost levels might occur. For example, the cost of new machinery specifically purchased for a future contract would be classified as a fixed cost, but it is relevant to the contract as it is avoidable. When fixed costs are directly attributable to opportunities they will be relevant to the accept/reject decision. However, unless you are given a clear indication to the contrary, you should always assume that costs do behave in a linear fashion. It should be noted that this assumption was also adopted in Chapter 15.

The contribution approach can be applied to a number of types of decisions that management must take in the course of running a business. The following examples illustrate the concept.

The range of products to be manufactured and sold

The management of an organization will be confronted with a number of opportunities each year and will have to decide which opportunities should be embodied within their plans. In Case Study 17.4 the products are independent of each other. We can derive a simple rule from this study: if a product makes a positive contribution it is worth considering for acceptance within the firm's production programme. The fixed costs have been apportioned to products. This is the convention under absorption costing which was described in Chapter 16. It is where overheads are absorbed into products using predetermined rates based on budgeted figures for overhead costs and activity levels. Normally these overhead costs will be unavoidable and thus not relevant, as in the example above. Overhead costs will only be relevant if they are incremental in nature.

CASE STUDY 17.4
Nelson's Oil and Fat Products plc

A firm has the opportunity to manufacture and sell three products A, B and C in the forthcoming year. The following is a draft summary of the profit or loss on the products.

	Total	*A*	*B*	*C*
	£	£	£	£
Sales revenues	200 000	30 000	20 000	150 000
Variable costs	136 000	21 400	13 200	101 400
Fixed costs	44 000	3 400	7 400	33 200
Total costs	180 000	24 800	20 600	134 600
Profit (loss)	20 000	5 200	(600)	15 400

The fixed costs of £44 000 represent overhead costs which have been apportioned to the products and will remain the same whether or not all or some of the products are sold during the year.

Because of the loss shown by product B the management propose to eliminate that product from its range.

The firm would be making a profit of £20 000 if all three products are manufactured and sold. However, if only A and B were sold, as the management suggest, the profit would be reduced.

	Total	*A*	*C*
	£	£	£
Sales	180 000	30 000	150 000
Variable costs	122 800	21 400	101 400
Contribution	57 200	8 600	48 600
Fixed costs	44 000		
Profit	13 200		

This reduction in profit is because product B makes a contribution of £6800 (£20 000 − 13 200) and the fixed costs remain the same at £44 000 whether or not A, B or C are manufactured and sold.

Closing an unprofitable department/division

In a dynamic business environment, organizations will inevitably need, at times, to appraise the economic viability of their departments and divisions. Although the decision whether or not to close or keep open a department/division is a very different decision from those involved in the determination of the range of products to be manufactured and sold (described above) the same underlying principles of relevance are adopted.

Invariably, in practice, there are a number of costs that are allocated to departments which are outside their control and relate to overheads that are incurred by the firm as a whole. A typical example is head office expenses, which relate to the administrative costs of running the business. These types of cost are irrelevant as they are unavoidable.

The rule to be applied in such decisions is that if a department makes a positive contribution, i.e. revenue exceeds variable costs, the department should remain open and vice versa. However, when there are fixed costs that are directly attributable to a department, and therefore are avoidable, the rule can be amended and expressed as follows. If the revenue generated by a department exceeds the costs directly attributable to that department, it should remain open and vice versa. An example of such a decision is given in Case Study 17.5.

Unfortunately in practice a number of organizations still persist in ignoring the principles of relevant costs and benefits in making future decisions. This can only distort decision making and result in organizations taking wrong courses of action. A good example of this was in 1984 at the beginning of the National Coal Strike. A team of academic accountants argued that the decision by the National Coal Board (NCB) to close a number of pits was incorrectly taken because costs not directly related to those pits (i.e. irrelevant costs) were included in the decision making process. The example that was cited was Cortonwood Colliery, whose closure started the dispute. The academics estimated that 23.1% of the pit's total costs, representing in monetary terms £11.70 per tonne of coal, were external to the operation of the pit and would not be saved by closing the pit. These costs related to central overheads and past (sunk) costs and were therefore irrelevant costs. For example, £2.37 per tonne that was included in the costs related to past surface damage, which clearly is a sunk cost. The academics concluded that if only relevant costs were included in the decision-making process Cortonwoord Colliery would in fact be contributing £5.5 per tonne rather than the loss of £6.2 per tonne that was estimated by the NCB. It is of interest to note that the NCB tried to prevent the disclosure of this analysis in the accounting press by means of a court injunction!

CASE STUDY 17.5
Recaldin Engineering plc

The following are the costs and revenues of three departments X, Y and Z, summarized in a traditional costing format.

	X	*Y*	*Z*	*Total*
	£000	*£000*	*£000*	*£000*
Revenue	80	40	60	180
Department costs	24	15	46	85
Apportioned costs	20	10	20	50
Total costs	44	25	66	135
Profit/(loss)	36	15	(6)	45

The apportioned costs of £50 000 in total are unavoidable and relate to Head Office overhead costs.

From the way in which the data are presented it could be argued that Department Z should be closed down as it makes a loss of £6000. Currently, the total profit of the three departments is £45 000. However, if Department Z were closed the profit would be reduced.

	Total	*X*	*Y*
	£000	*£000*	*£000*
Revenue	120	80	40
Department costs	39	24	15
Departmental profit	81	56	25
Apportioned costs	50		
Profit	31		

The reduction in profit to the firm as a whole of £14 000 is due to closing Department Z which in fact makes a departmental profit of £14 000 (£60 000–£46 000) which contributes to the Head Office overhead costs and the firm's overall profit. Thus Department Z should remain open.

Summary

In this chapter we have considered decisions that organizations are required to make regarding future opportunities where there are no constraints in respect of physical resources. In the context of all the types of decisions considered it is clear that the application of traditional costing methods will not result in organizations satisfying the assumed objective of maximizing future cash flows. It was illustrated that the maximization of cash flows will only be satisfied when the principles of relevant costs are applied to such decisions. The costs and benefits that are relevant were described and are summarized below:

- future costs and benefits;
- differential and incremental costs and benefits;
- avoidable costs;

- replacement costs;
- opportunity costs.

The main limitation to the analysis is that only quantitative information has been considered. In practice many of these decisions will be made on the basis of qualitative criteria. This will be discussed at the end of Chapter 18 after examining the methods used to make decisions where there are scarce resources.

Further reading

Inevitably decision making involves risk and uncertainty. We have in the main assumed a world of certainty. There are a number of techniques that can be adopted in an attempt to cope with this problem. Whilst risk and uncertainty are outside the scope of this text you may wish to consider some of the techniques that can be applied. A text that illustrates such techniques is *Managerial Accounting: Method and Meaning*, by R.M.S. Wilson and W.F. Chua (VNR, 1988). Those concepts in economics which are relevant are discussed in *Economics in a Business Context* by A. Neale and C. Haslam (VNR, 1989).

Review questions

1 Discuss the reasons why accrual accounting methods are not appropriate to future decision making.
2 In the context of decision making explain the meaning of:

- sunk costs;
- differential costs;
- avoidable and unavoidable costs;
- opportunity costs.

3 Depreciation is an important concept in the determination of profit. Discuss why it is classified as an irrelevant cost in decision making.
4 In the majority of cases fixed costs will be irrelevant in decision making, but on some occasions they may be relevant. Describe the circumstances when fixed costs are relevant to future decisions.

Problems for discussion and analysis

1 Calculators Plc manufacture and sell pocket calculators. The sales price of these calculators is £22. The company's current output is 40 000 units per month, which represents 90% of the company's productive capacity. Noxid, a chain store customer who specializes in selling consumable electronic goods, offers to buy 2000 calculators as a special order at £16 each. These calculators would be sold under the name of Noxid.

The total costs per month are £800 000 of which £192 000 are fixed costs.

(a) Advise Calculators Plc whether they should accept the special order.
(b) Would your advice change if Nixod wanted 5000 calculators?

2 Spinks Ltd produce three products, A, B and C. The following is an estimate of costs and revenues for the forthcoming year:

	A	*B*	C
	£	£	£
Sales	32 000	50 000	45 000
Total cost	36 000	38 000	34 000
Net profit (loss)	(4 000)	12 000	11 000

The total cost of each product comprises one-third fixed costs and two-thirds variable costs. Fixed costs will be constant whatever the volume of sales.

The Managing Director argues that as product A makes a loss the production of this product should be discontinued.
Comment on the Managing Director's argument.

3 Eatitnatural Ltd is a company which specializes in the manufacture and sale of health foods. The company has just completed market research on a new type of organic toothpaste called Abrasive. The budget estimate derived from the market research for one year's production and sales, which was presented to the Board by the Marketing Manager, is as follows.

Abrasive Toothpaste

	£	£
Cost of production (100 000 kg)		
Labour		
Direct wages	50 000	
Supervisory	30 000	80 000
Raw materials		
Ingredients X	17 000	
Ingredients Y	7 000	
Ingredients P	9 000	
Ingredients Z	1 000	34 000
Other variable costs		10 000
Fixed overheads (60% of direct labour)		30 000
Research and development		20 000
Total costs		184 000
Sales (100 000 kg at £1.60 per kg)		160 000
Loss		(24 000)

The Board of Directors are very disappointed with this budget in view of the research and development costs already incurred of

£20 000 and the need to make use of the spare capacity in the factory. Fred Sharpe, the Managing Director, suggests bringing in a consultant to examine the costs of the new product.

The following additional information is available.

(i) 60% of the direct labour requirement would be transferred from another department within the company. The monthly contribution of this department (£5000), subject to introduction of a special machine into the department at a hire cost of £4000 per year, would fall by only 20% of its current level as a result of the reduction in the labour force. The remainder of the direct labour requirement would have to be recruited. It is anticipated that their wages will be the same as those transferred from the other department. In addition, it is estimated that the cost of recruitment, e.g. advertising, will cost £3000.

(ii) Two supervisors would be required at a cost of £15 000 per year each. One would be recruited; the other, Reg Raven, would remain at work instead of retiring. The company will pay him a pension of £5000 per year on his retirement.

(iii) Stocks of ingredient X are currently available for a whole year's production of Abrasive, and are valued at their original cost. The price of this ingredient is subject to dramatic price variations, and the current market price is double the original cost. It could be resold at the market price less 10% selling expenses or retained for use later in another new product to be manufactured by the company, by which time it is expected that the market price will have fallen by about 25%.

(iv) Ingredient Y's price has been very stable and is used for other products currently manufactured and sold by the company. There are no stocks available for the production of Abrasive.

(v) Ingredient P is another commodity with a fairly static price. Half of the annual requirement is in stock and the other half will have to be purchased during the year at an estimated cost of £4500. The materials in stock could be resold for £4000 less 10% selling expenses, or could be used to produce another product after some further processing. This processing, which would take 2000 h in the Mixing Department where labour is paid £12 per hour, would save the company additional purchasing costs of £5000. The Mixing Department has sufficient idle capacity to do this amount of work only.

(vi) Ingredient Z was bought well in advance and is in stock. It has no alternative use. Fred Sharpe is beginning to regret the decision to buy this ingredient in advance as it will deteriorate in store and may become dangerous before the end of the budget period. It cannot be sold and will cost the company £500 to dispose of it if it is not used to produce Abrasive.

(vii) The other variable costs can all be avoided if the contract is not accepted.

(viii) Fixed overheads of the company are expected to increase by

£2000 per year as a result of manufacturing and selling Abrasive.

As the consultant employed by the company, you are requested to re-examine this statement, taking account of the additional information, and to recommend any necessary action. Clearly state any assumptions that you make.

Accounting for decision making: resource constraints and decisions which are mutually exclusive

18

This chapter examines decision making within a business environment when resource constraints exists. Finally, qualitative factors, that can play a significant part in decision making, are considered.

In Chapter 17 we examined the principles of relevant costs and the application of these principles in making accounting decisions. These decisions related to situations where there were no resource contraints and their acceptance or rejection did not affect the demand or production levels of any other products. In practice, however, a decision taken by an organization will often necessitate giving up other opportunities, either because of the lack of resources or because the decision is mutually exclusive (i.e. where the acceptance of one opportunity will mean that others will be rejected). In this chapter we shall be examining decisions where there are resource constraints and the make or buy decision. The make or buy decision is probably the most common type of mutually exclusive decision that confronts organizations.

In the case of decisions where there are resource constraints, we shall be restricting our analysis to the problem when there is only one scarce resource. Decision making when there are two or more scarce resources is outside the scope of this introductory text. However, the same principles apply to this type of decision in the determination of an optimal solution. The main difference is that when there are two or more scarce resources more complex mathematical skills are required in the computation of the solution.

In Chapter 17, in our analysis of short-term decisions, we assumed that only quantitative factors (e.g. cost and revenues) are relevant in the decision-making process. Initially, in the consideration of decision making in this chapter we shall continue with this assumption. Often in reality, however, qualitative factors will also be influential in the decision-making process. It is appropriate therefore to conclude our examination of short-term decision making by considering the nature of qualitative factors and some examples that will often be influential in the decision-making process in practice.

Decision making with constraints

For the situation where there are no constraints and fixed costs are unavoidable (i.e. irrelevant), as described in Chapter 17, we derived a *decision rule*:

> All opportunities should be accepted if they make a positive contribution to fixed costs and profits.

KEY CONCEPT 18.1
Decision making with constraints-objective

When there are resource constraints the objective that should be applied is to establish the optimum output within the constraints to maximize contribution and thus profits.

If the availability of one or more resources is restricted, however, an organization will be unable to accept every opportunity that yields a positive contribution. It is therefore necessary to derive a decision-making rule that takes account of these resource constraints to enable organizations to maximize profits.

Before considering this process to determine the optimum output it is appropriate to examine the nature of constraints that an organization may be subjected to in the context of its operations.

Traditionally, in accounting texts, the constraints that are usually considered relate to shortages of manufacturing resources, such as particular types of materials, labour skills and the size of manufacturing plant. However, organizations in the service sector could similarly be restricted in their earning capacity as a result of such constraints. For example, it could be the case that an accounting practice is restricted as to the number of clients it can accept for audit work because of the shortage of qualified accounting staff available to the practice. The principles to be applied, when there are constraints, will be same for both manufacturing and service sectors.

The constraints described relate to the short term and can invariably be eliminated in the long term. For example, a firm has the opportunity to manufacture and sell two products, X and Y, both of which yield a positive contribution per unit. But due to a shortage of skilled machine operators the firm cannot satisfy the demand for these products. Clearly, this constraint is only a short-term phenomenon as the firm could train machine operators now to ensure that there will not be a shortage in the long term. However, in the short term this will be an effective constraint on production and ultimately income.

The contribution approach with one scarce resource

In determining the optimum output, as detailed in Key Concept 18.2, it should be noted that the analysis only takes account of quantitative factors. However, it is often the case that qualitative factors will also be influential in the decision process. For example, unprofitable products may be included in the range offered to customers to maintain customer loyalty to all products sold by the firm. This should always be borne in mind when making such decisions.

Example 18.1 illustrates the stages of the process described above.

KEY CONCEPT 18.2
The optimum output with one constraint

To determine the optimum output with one constraint we must first determine the contribution of all opportunities and eliminate those that yield a negative contribution. Secondly, we must establish the contribution per unit of the constraint for all those opportunities that yield a positive contribution. For example, say product A yields a positive contribution of £16 per unit and takes 4 labour hours to produce; assuming that labour is the only effective production constraint, then the contribution per labour hour in producing product A is £16/4 h = £4 per labour hour. This provides the crucial information about the efficiency of the use of the constrained resource in terms of contribution and thus profitability. The next stage is to rank these opportunities, preferring those that yield the highest contribution per constraint. If, for example, product B generates a positive contribution per labour hour of £3, product A will be ranked higher, in the absence of other factors, as it yields a contribution of £1 more per labour hour. The optimum plan can then be derived within the total resources available. In the example above this will be total labour hours available to the firm in a defined period.

Example 18.1

The Directors of Fame Plc are in the process of drawing up the production plan for the forthcoming year. There are five products that are under consideration: A, B, C, D and E. The following statement of the contribution per unit of these opportunities has been prepared by the company's accountant.

	A	*B*	*C*	*D*	*E*
	£	£	£	£	£
Selling price	10	24	48	13	22
Variable costs					
Materials	7	3	2	3	2
Labour	4	7	10	2	5
Total variable costs	11	10	12	5	7
Contribution per unit	(1)	14	36	8	15
Estimated demand in units	800	700	800	600	400
Labour hours per unit	4	7	10	2	5

All labour is paid at the rate of £1 per hour. The total of fixed costs for the year is estimated to be £14 990 and will not vary with the range of products actually produced and sold.

The labour position has become very difficult and it is anticipated that only 7000 h will be available next year.

We begin our analysis to determine the optimum production plan, within the labour constraint confronted by Fame Plc, by accepting all opportunities that yield a positive contribution and rejecting those that yield a negative contribution. All the opportunities with the exception of product A yield a positive contribution. Product A, which has a negative contribution, will therefore, at this stage, be eliminated from the company's possible future range of products.

Before we continue it is wise to check whether the labour constraint of 7000 h is an effective constraint on the company's activities. We can do this by calculating the total labour hours required to meet the demand of the four products identified that yield positive contributions. We will begin with product B and follow alphabetical order:

Product	*Demand in units*	*Per unit*	*Labour hours total*	*Cumulative*
B	700	7	4 900	4 900
C	800	10	8 000	12 900

It can be seen from the cumulative labour hours column that if we satisfied the demand of only products B and C the company would exceed the labour hours it has available (i.e. 7000 h). Thus we can conclude that labour hours are an effective constraint on the company's level of production and that the company will be unable to accept all the opportunities available to it.

We can now calculate, for the four remaining opportunities, the contribution per labour hour by dividing the labour hours per unit into the contribution per unit and ranking the opportunities in order of the highest contribution per labour hour:

	B	*C*	*D*	*E*
Contribution per labour hour	£14/7 h = £2	£36/10 h = £3.6	£8/2 h = £4	£15/5 h = £3
Ranking	4	2	1	3

From the table above it is apparent that product D is ranked first as it yields the highest contribution per labour hour (£4), followed by product C with a contribution of £3.60 per hour and then products E and B. This priority ranking can now be applied to determine the products that will be included in the optimum plan and to establish the total contribution that is generated from this plan:

Product	*Demand units*	*Labour hours per unit*	*Labour hours total*	*Contribution (£) per unit*	*Contribution (£) total*
(1) D	600	2	1 200	8	4 800
(2) C	580	10	5 800	36	20 880
			7 000		25 660

It can be seen that the company is able to satisfy the total demand for product D, which was ranked first, within the labour constraint, leaving 7000 − 1200 = 5800 h available for the production of other products. Product C is the next product preferred within the ranking order and the total demand for C is estimated to be 800 units. However, to satisfy the demand for C will use up 800 units × 10 h per unit = 8000 h and we only have 5800 hours available. Therefore the company will be restricted to producing 5800 h/10 h = 580 units of product C because of the shortage of labour. Products B and E are excluded from the plan as there are no more labour hours available.

This is the optimal plan because it takes account of two important variables, contribution and the scarce resource – labour hours. If the production plan had been based on a priority ranking scheme that only took account of the contribution, ignoring the constraint, the ranking order in terms of the highest contribution per unit would be as follows.

Ranking	*Product*
1	C
2	E
3	B
4	D

The total contribution that would be yielded from this ranking order would have been as follows.

Product	*Demand*	*Labour hours*		*Contribution (£)*	
	units	*per unit*	*total*	*per unit*	*total*
C	700	10	7 000	36	25 200

It can be seen that only product C, which was ranked first using the ranking order based on the highest contribution per unit, will be produced and sold by the company. This is because the maximum demand for product C is 800 units and because of the restriction on labour hours available only 700 units can be produced (i.e. 10 h × 700 units = 7000 h). The important point to recognize, however, is that the contribution of £25 200 generated from this ranking order is less than the contribution (£25 680) from using the order of ranking based on contribution per labour hour described earlier. The comparison of profitability using these two approaches clearly shows that if an organization is to maximize its profits and when there are resource constraints, these constraints *must* be included within the decision process.

The contribution per unit of scarce resource and the internal opportunity cost

The use of the contribution per unit of scarce resource in establishing an organization's optimum production plan leads us to some interesting insights into the measurement of the opportunity cost of scarce resources. In Chapter 17 we defined the opportunity cost of a resource as 'the maximum benefit which could be obtained from that resource if it was used for some alternative purpose'. Invariably, the opportunity cost of a resource that is scarce will be greater than its purchase price. This is because there will be competing opportunities for the resource within the organization. A number of examples were shown in the last chapter where the relevant cost of using a resource (the opportunity cost) exceeded the purchase price of the resource.

The concept of opportunity cost can also be applied in the selection of products to be included in an organization's optimum production plan. We shall continue with the example of Fame Plc to illustrate the application and to help us to understand further the concept of opportunity costs in this type of decision.

In the case of Fame Plc labour hours were scarce, and there were competing alternative opportunities for this resource within the company. In particular, there were only enough labour hours to satisfy the demand for product D and partially to satisfy the demand for C, producing 580 units out of a total demand of 800. The contribution per labour hour of product C was £3.60 and only opportunities that yield a higher contribution per labour hour would therefore be preferred. In the case of products B and E, the contribution per labour hour was less; thus C was preferred. Indeed, if any new opportunities became available to Fame they would only be included in the optimium production plan if they generated a contribution per labour hour greater than £3.60.

Product C can therefore be described as the *marginal product* within the production plan and the contribution per labour hour of £3.60 as the *the marginal return* on one hour of labour. That is, if Fame had one more labour hour available the return on this hour would be £3.60, or conversely, if one hour fewer was available the company would lose £3.60, in terms of contribution. In terms of the production of product C, an extra labour hour will produce one-tenth of one C, as it takes 10 hours to produce one unit. Thus we assume here that product C is divisible, i.e. that we can make and sell one-tenth of a unit more or less of C. The following shows the increase in contribution from one more hour used in producing one-tenth of C.

	£
Selling price (£48/10)	4.80
Less costs	
Materials (£2/10)	0.20
Labour (£10/10)	1.00
Total variable costs	1.20
Increase in contribution	3.60

This computation would be the same if one less hour were to be available, but would result in a loss in contribution of £3.60.

At this stage it is appropriate to summarize the three main points that have been derived from our analysis so far and to examine their implications.

1. *If one more labour hour becomes available it will contribute £3.60 per hour*

In the case of Fame, the contribution of £3.60 per hour will be generated from an additional 2200 h, if these hours were available. 2200 hours represents the number of hours that would be used in making another 220 units (220 × 10 h per unit) of product C, the unsatisfied demand of C (Total demand 800 units minus 580 units that are planned to be produced within the original labour constraint). If more than 2200 hours became available, assuming there were no new opportunities, labour would then be used to produce product E, which would generate £3 per hour. The number of units of E produced would clearly depend upon how many hours became available. 2000 h would be required to satisfy the total demand for E. If any more hours were available these would be employed on the least preferred product B.

This information at the planning stage can be extremely useful to managers in considering scenarios. For example, management may be unsure as to the exact number of hours it may have available, and could ask the question: if 300 additional labour hours became available, in the coming year, what would be the increased contribution? This can be quickly calculated when the contribution per labour hour is known, by simply multiplying the contribution per labour hour by the number of hours; in this example £3.60 × 300 h = £1080.

2. *If one less hour is available, Fame would lose £3.60 per hour in contribution*

The loss in contribution of £3.60 per hour would continue for every hour lost up to 5800 h. 5800 h (580 h × 10 h per unit) are the total hours required to satisfy the original constrained demand of 580 units of product C. This information, similarly, could be useful to management at the planning stage in considering scenarios. For example: what would be the loss in contribution if 600 labour hours were lost due to machine breakdowns during the year? Knowing the loss in contribution for every labour hour lost, the calculation is simple and quick, i.e. 600 h × £3.60 = £2160.

3. *If future opportunities became available they would have to contribute at least £3.60 per labour hour before they would be considered for inclusion in the future production plan*

It would not be necessary, in such cases, to recalculate the contribution from each product and then to rank each product etc. in coming to this conclusion. All that is necessary is to calculate the contribution per labour hour for any *additional* opportunities that become available. These should then be compared with the contribution per labour hour generated from the current opportunities included in the optimum plan. If these new opportunities yield a higher contribution per labour hour they will displace those currently in the plan. Once again this information will be extremely useful to management.

From the view point of planning the future profitability of an organization we can therefore conclude that the knowledge of contribution from the use of constrained resources is extremely useful to management in making decisions.

The contribution per labour hour is also known as the internal opportunity cost of labour. The term internal opportunity cost is more appropriate when it is used in examining the efficient use of resources within an organization. In the example of Fame, labour was paid £1 per hour, but there is the additional cost of labour (i.e. the internal opportunity cost of £3.60 per hour) that relates to its use within the organization because there are competing opportunities for the use of the scarce resource. The cost of labour per hour is therefore represented by two elements of costs:

1 the cash cost of employing the labour which can be described as the 'external opportunity cost';
2 the internal opportunity cost which reflects the cost of using the resource *within the organization itself* due to competing opportunities.

These costs can be summarized in a table as follows:

	£
Cash cost of employing labour (the external opportunity cost)	1.00
Internal opportunity cost for the use of labour in the organization	3.60
Total cost of labour	4.60

The determination of the internal opportunity cost is extremely useful as it indicates how much Fame would be willing to pay to obtain one more labour hour. For example, to release more labour hours to produce additional units of product C, the company may decide to offer overtime to their employees at a premium, but are unsure what premium to offer. The total opportunity cost of £4.60 per hour is the maximum the company should be willing to pay for an additional labour hour. The payment of a higher rate will result in a loss. On the basis of this information the company may decide to offer its employees £3 per hour (i.e. a premium of £2 per hour) for any overtime worked, which is £1.60 less than the maximum they can afford to pay. The contribution generated from one labour hour to produce one-tenth of product C will then be:

	£	£
Selling price (one-tenth of £48)		4.80
Less costs		
Materials (£2/10)		0.20
Labour		
External opportunity cost	1.00	
Premium for overtime	2.00	3.00
Total costs		3.20
Contribution		1.60

If the company anticipated that their employees would be willing to work 350 h of overtime during the period the additional total contribution will be £1.60 × 350 h = £560.

In this analysis we have used the example of a labour constraint. However, the principles applied in this example are relevant to any situation where a resource is scarce: we must determine the opportunities that use these resources most efficiently.

A make or buy decision involves the problem of an organization choosing between making a product or carrying out a service using its own resources, and paying another external organization to make or carry out a service for them.

KEY CONCEPT 18.3
Make or buy decisions

Make or buy decisions

An example of a make or buy decision is the decision whether an organization should design and develop their own new computer system or whether an external software house should be hired to do the work.

The 'make' option should give the management of the organization more direct control over the work. However, an external contractor will often have specialist skills and expertise for doing the work. As with the majority of decisions considered in this chapter, make or buy decisions should not be made on the basis of cost alone. Factors other than the costs and benefits of a decision, which are normally referred to as 'qualitative factors', will be considered in more depth at the end of this chapter.

We begin our analysis by first examining whether to make or buy when an organization has spare capacity. We shall then consider the situation when capacity is restricted because of shortages of resources.

Where there is spare capacity

We assume an organization is not working at full capacity and thus has enough resources available to make a product or component, if it so wishes,without affecting the production of other products.

Example 18.2 illustrates the principles that should be applied to make and buy decisions.

Example 18.2

Hughes Plc is a company that is confronted with the problem of whether to make or buy three components, A, B and C. The respective costs are as follows.

	A	B	C
Production units	1000	2000	4000
	£	£	£
Variable costs per unit			
Materials	4	5	2
Labour	10	12	5
Total variable cost	14	17	7

The fixed costs per annum that are directly attributable (avoidable costs) to the manufacture of the components and are apportioned (unavoidable costs) to components are as follows.

	£
Avoidable costs	
A	1 000
B	5 000
C	13 000
Apportioned fixed costs	30 000
	49 000

A subcontractor has offered to supply units of A, B and C for £12, £21 and £10 respectively.

The relevant costs to be taken into account in this decision are the differential costs associated with making or buying. In this example the differential costs are the differences in unit variable costs and the directly attributable fixed costs. The following is a summary of the relevant costs.

	A	B	C
	£	£	£
Variable cost per unit, making	14	17	7
Cost per unit, buying	12	21	10
Additional cost per unit of buying	(2)	4	3
Production units per annum	1 000	2 000	4 000
	£	£	£
Additional total variable cost of buying	(2 000)	8 000	12 000
Fixed costs saved by buying	1 000	5 000	13 000
Additional total cost of buying	(3 000)	3 000	(1 000)

The organization would therefore save £3000 per annum by subcontracting component A (this is because the variable cost per unit to make the component is greater than the purchase price), and £1000 per annum by subcontracting component C (this is due to the saving of £13 000 of fixed costs directly attributable to making the component). In the case of component B the organization will be £3000 better off making the component.

It should also be noted that the apportioned fixed costs are irrelevant because they are unavoidable to this decision.

In such decisions there will normally be another consideration that is relevant. If components A and C are to be purchased from a subcontractor it is likely that the organization will have spare capacity. It is also likely that this spare capacity has some value to the organization; for example, it may decide to let the space to an outside party which would generate additional income. This additional income should then be included as a relevant cost of making the components as the revenue will be forgone if the component is made. It is an opportunity cost.

As previously mentioned, in these types of decisions there will inevitably be other qualitative factors that should be taken into account. In this example, the organization may be apprehensive about the quality of the work of the subcontractor. This factor may lead the organization to favour making components A and C, although in cost terms this policy would be unprofitable.

Where there is no spare capacity

A firm may be confronted with the decision whether to make or buy a component when it is currently working at full capacity. To make the component, it will be necessary for the firm to stop or restrict its current production output. In such cases the cost of making must include not only the costs directly attributed to making but also the loss in contribution of the production that has been displaced by the decision to make. The loss in contribution is the internal opportunity cost, which was discussed earlier.

Example 18.3 illustrates the application of the concept of the internal opportunity cost in the make or buy decision when capacity is restricted.

Example 18.3

Lee Plc is in the process of deciding whether to make or buy a component that is to be embodied in one of the products it manufactures and sells. Labour is in short supply and the factory is currently working at full capacity. The following are the estimated costs per unit to make the component:

	£
Direct labour (5 h at £4 per hour)	20
Direct material	15
Fixed overheads	5
Total cost per unit	40

The fixed overhead costs are apportioned to the product and will be unavoidable whether or not the component is made. Thus this cost is irrelevant to the decision whether to make or buy. All the other costs are directly attributable to the cost of producing the component and are thus relevant. The relevant cost associated with making the component is therefore £35.

The alternative is to buy in the component from another firm. The cost of buying the component is £38 per unit.

If labour was not in short supply, the firm should make the component rather than buying it because the relevant costs of making (£35) are less than the purchase price of buying (£38).

However, in view of the shortage of labour we must consider the contribution forgone by the decision to make. To do so we must account for the contribution generated from the current production activity that is to be restricted in opting to make the component. The following data relate to the revenue and cost per unit associated with a product that is to be displaced by producing (making) the component:

	£	£
Selling price		26
Less costs		
Direct labour (3 h at £4 per hour)	12	
Direct material	8	20
Contribution per unit		6

The contribution per hour of labour generated from this product is £2 (i.e. contribution £6 divided by 3 h labour time). This is the internal opportunity cost of using the labour on the manufacture of this product. If labour is to be efficiently diverted to making the component instead of this product it must therefore yield a contribution of at least £2 per hour. We can also conclude that the effective cost of labour employed on making the component consists of two elements: the cash paid to employees for their labour of £4 per hour (i.e. the external opportunity cost) plus the internal opportunity cost of £2 per hour. These two elements of cost should therefore be included in the calculation to decide whether to make or buy the component. The following summarizes all the relevant costs in making the components.

	£	£
Direct labour		
Cash paid to employees (the external opportunity cost) £4 × 5 h	20	
Internal opportunity cost £2 × 3 h	6	26
Direct materials		15
Total relevant costs		41

The inclusion of the internal opportunity cost as a relevant cost to the decision to make has resulted in a cost for making the component of £41. This exceeds the buying price of £38; thus purely on financial grounds the decision should be to buy rather than make.

The principle that the internal opportunity cost should be included in the relevant costs of a make or buy decision applies to all situations where there is no spare capacity because resources are scarce.

Qualitative factors

In our analysis of decision making in this and the last chapter all the decisions made were based only on financial criteria. Often, however, qualitative factors will be of great influence in such decisions. Indeed, on some occasions an opportunity would be rejected on purely quantitative (financial) criteria but for other reasons, primarily of a qualitative nature, the opportunity is accepted.

Qualitative factors are factors which cannot be quantified in terms of costs and income. They may stem from either non-financial objectives or factors which could be quantified in money terms but have not been because there is insufficient information to make a reliable estimate.

The nature of these qualitative factors will vary with the circumstances under consideration. The following are some examples of qualitative factors that may influence decisions.

Customers

The inclusion or exclusion of a product from the range offered or the quality of the product and after-sales service will invariably affect demand for the product and customer loyalty. For example, the exclusion of one product from a range because it is uneconomic to produce and sell could affect the demand for other products. Products manufactured by firms are often interdependent and this interdependence can be calculated before a decision is made.

Employees

Decisions involving the closure of part of a firm or relocation or changes in work procedures will require acceptance by the employees. If the changes are mishandled bad labour relations could lead to inefficiencies and losses.

Competitors

In a competitive market, decisions by one firm to enhance their competitive advantage may result in retaliation by competitors. For example, the decision to reduce selling prices in order to raise demand will not be successful if all competitors take similar action.

A firm may decide to produce an unprofitable product or to offer a service at a loss because otherwise it would be leaving the market for competitors to enjoy. The firm considers that continued service to customers will eventually affect the demand for its other products.

Legal constraints

A opportunity may occasionally be rejected because of doubts about pending legislation. The decision to open a hotel, for example, may be influenced by pending legislation on safety requirements that would result in additional costs which are too complex to estimate.

Suppliers

A firm may rely heavily on a good relationship with a particular supplier for the prompt delivery of supplies. Some decisions may affect that supplier and the relationship must be considered in any decision.

Collectively, these constitute the environmental, organizational and structural constraints of the Business in Context model (see Needle, 1989).

Summary

In this chapter we have developed a number of the concepts introduced in Chapter 17. In particular the concept of opportunity cost was examined and the two elements of cost, the external and internal opportunity costs, were identified.

The concept of opportunity cost was shown to be a very powerful tool in determining the optimal production plan when an organization is experiencing a shortage of resources. In particular it ensures that scarce resources are used efficiently.

Lastly, in this chapter we examined the nature of the qualitative factors that may influence decisions. A number of examples were given which illustrate their importance in the decision-making process.

References

Needle, D. (1989) *Business in Context*, VNR.

Further reading

An excellent analysis of decision making when there is more than one constraint can be found in Chapters 9 and 10 of *Accounting for Management Decisions* by J. Arnold and T. Hope (Prentice-Hall International, 1983).

Review questions

1 Many organizations, at particular times, will be subject to shortages of resources. These shortages will effectively restrict their ability to meet the demand for their products or services. Describe four examples of these types of constraints, two from a manufacturing firm and two from a service firm.
2 Explain why a shortage of resources in an organization is a short-term phenomenon.
3 Discuss the importance and usefulness of the concept of internal opportunity cost in the making of decisions.

4 The opportunity cost of a resource, in some circumstances, may be higher than the resource's purchase price. Explain why this may be the case.

5 Qualitative factors are often influential in the decision-making process. Describe the nature of qualitative factors and give three examples that may influence a decision to make a component rather than buying it from another firm.

Problems for discussion and analysis

1 Coyle Plc at present manufactures all the components that go to make up its finished products. A salesman from a components supplier has just offered to provide the firm's requirements for two components, the BC100 at £7.75 each and the BC200 at £2.00 each. If the firm buys in components the capacity utilized for these components at present would be unused. The firm currently manufactures 50 000 units of each component and the current costs of production are as follows:

	BC100	*BC200*
	£	£
Materials	2.50	1.00
Labour	3.00	1.25
Fixed overheads	3.50	1.75
Total cost per unit	9.00	4.00

(a) On a quantitative basis should the firm continue to manufacture BC100 and BC200 or should it buy in both or either of the components?

(b) Discuss the qualitative factors which are likely to have an influence on this decision.

2 Pigeon Proprietory Ltd proposes a production plan for 19X1, aiming to maximize profits. The following details are available.

Product	A	B	C	D	E	F
	£	£	£	£	£	£
Selling price	20	28	8	36	16	40
Costs						
Direct materials	4	4	1.2	2.4	2.8	1.6
Direct labour	4	6	2.4	8.8	3.6	3.2
Fixed overheads	4	6	2.4	8.8	3.6	3.2
Total cost	12	16	6.0	20.0	10.0	8.0
Profit	8	12	2.0	16.0	6.0	32.0
Labour hours per unit	6.4	7	4	9	5	12
Machine hours per unit	3	2	1	3	1	8
Maximum demand	2500	1200	700	1100	900	2900

Fixed overhead, which is estimated to cost £10 000 irrespective of what is produced and sold, is applied at 100% of direct labour cost.

A maximum of 64 000 direct labour hours is expected to be available.

(a) Calculate the optimal profit-maximizing production plan and explain the reasons for your choice.
(b) Explain the following hypothetical internal opportunity costs:
- direct labour hours £2.40;
- machine hours £1.70.

3 You have recently been appointed as a consultant to the Murphy Manufacturing Company. The management of the company had prepared a report showing certain data concerning the two products, Mox and Tox. The following information has been extracted from this report.

	Mox	*Tox*
	£	£
Selling price	3.0	1.5
Costs		
Direct materials	0.8	0.5
Direct labour	1.0	0.2
Fixed overheads	1.4	0.5
Total cost	3.2	1.2
Profit/(loss)	(0.2)	0.3
Monthly sales in units	1000	2000

In view of the poor results shown by Mox the following changes have been proposed by the management.

(i) Abandon the production of Mox and buy in 1000 per month for £2800. The quality is identical and selling price will remain unchanged.
(ii) Use the spare capacity to make Cox. It is estimated that 1000 units could be sold at £1 each. Material costs are £0.4 per unit and labour costs £0.2.

All overheads are fixed and are not expected to change from the present cost of £2000 per month. No stocks are held.

(a) Comment on the suitability of the management's statement for assessing product profitability and indicate any ways in which you think it could be improved.
(b) Prepare a monthly profit and loss statement for the present and proposed new programmes. Do the proposed changes appear to be profitable? Explain the reasons for any misunderstandings which may have arisen as a result of the management's proposal.

4 Burco Ltd produces and sells two products: X and Y. During the last year 700 labour hours were worked and the operating results were as follows.

	X	*Y*	*Total*
Units sold	1000	1000	2000
	£	£	£
Sales	1000	2000	3000
Variable costs			
Labour	200	500	700
Materials	550	900	1450
Total variable costs	750	1400	2150
Contribution	250	600	850
Fixed costs			600
Net income			250

All variable costs are a linear function of output. The material used for X is quite different from that used for Y but both may be produced with the same labour force.

Five units of X can be made in one labour hour, whilst only two units of Y can be made in one labour hour. Labour hours are expected to be limited to 800 next year.

The following information about the market for X and Y for next year is available.

	X	Y
Maximum quantity that may be sold next year (units)	1100	1200
Minimum quantity that must be sold next year to retain market (units)	600	800

(a) Assuming plant capacity is fully used, what is the optimum mix of X and Y?

(b) Assuming that the price of material for Y decreases by 20%, what is the optimal mix of X and Y? Do not assume any change in the price of X or Y.

(c) Assuming that the cost of labour increases by 20%, prices can only be put up by 10% without affecting sales limits and the number of labour hours available is reduced to 600, what is the optimal mix of X and Y?

(d) What is the net income in each case for scenario (a), (b) and (c) above?

(e) Discuss the limitations of your analysis.

19 Budgets

The focus of this chapter is on short-term planning. Budgets are the medium by which these short plans are operationalized within a business environment. The budget process is examined with associated contingent factors such as the level and type of technology.

In the chapter on Planning and Control (Chapter 14) four stages of the planning and control process were identified. The third stage, which was described as 'Making operating decisions', focused on the use of resources and the individual decisions necessary to use these resources consistently within the overall objectives of an organization. In this stage it was also stated that the decisions would be translated into a short-term plan, normally referred to as a 'budget'. Budgets were defined as 'plans of action expressed in monetary terms'. In this chapter we shall be examining the purpose of budgets, the budgeting process, and the preparation of budgets.

It should be stressed that different types of organization will require different types of budgets to enable them to function effectively. The budget must match the organization's particular situation. In Chapter 14 we mentioned the application of contingency theory to all accounting information systems. The major contingency factors identified were technology, the environment and the structure of the organization. Similarly, these factors will affect the type of budget to be employed in an organization. To illustrate this point, we can briefly compare the information content and design of a retail organization's budget with that of a manufacturing organization. In a retail organization the budget will deal mainly with the level of consumer sales and the purchases of goods necessary to satisfy these sales. In contrast, the budget of a manufacturing organization will tend to focus on the sales of products that will be manufactured and the production activity necessary to meet these sales. However, there will be some similarities between the two types of budget and a common basis for preparing the budget of different types of organization. We shall concentrate, in this chapter, on large manufacturing organizations, which traditionally have relatively sophisticated budgets.

The purpose of budgets

Below are listed a number of the traditional purposes of budgets. Although we said earlier that budgets, and thus the purpose of budgets, will depend on the type of organization, those given below are appropriate to most organizations.

To compel planning

The introduction of budgets within an organization forces management to look ahead and set short-term targets. By looking to the future, management are then in a good position to anticipate potential problems. For example, the identification of shortages of cash at particular times in the budget period will give management the opportunity to ensure that provisions are made to supplement this shortage, e.g. to negotiate an overdraft facility with their bank.

Co-ordination of the different functions within an organization

The preparation of budgets will tend to increase the co-ordination between different departments and units within an organization as it is essential that the individual plans of managers are integrated. The managers are therefore forced to consider the relationships between various departments. For example, it is important that a purchasing department is aware of the material requirements for manufacture so that buying and stock levels are maintained to service the needs of the manufacturing activity during the budget period.

Communication

A budget will often be a useful means by which top management can formally communicate their objectives and strategies for the forthcoming budget period. This function will be reinforced, normally periodically, through a control mechanism, which will be referred to later, that reviews actual performance against the budget during the budget period.

To provide a basis for responsibility accounting

Individual managers are identified with their budget centres and are made responsible for achieving the stated budget targets. These targets may be in terms of expenditure, income and output that are considered to be within the manager's control. Responsibility accounting was previously outlined in Chapter 14. Within the context of budgets responsibility accounting represents an important feature of the delegation of responsibility within an organization.

To provide a basis for a control mechanism

The budget may be used as a basis for comparing actual performance with a plan and identifying any deviation from that plan. The identification of these deviations gives management the opportunity to take corrective action so that such deviations do not persist in the future. When budgets are used in the context of a control mechanism the term 'budgetary control' is normally used.

Authorization of expenditure

The budget may act as a formal authorization of future expenditure from top management to those individuals who are responsible for the expenditure. The fact that an item of expenditure, for example, is contained in the budget that has been approved by the top management of the organization implies that the item has been approved and no further approval will normally be required.

A means to motivate employees to improve performance

The budget may be used as a target to motivate employees to reach certain levels of attainment. For example, in a previous budget period a salesperson may achieve sales of products to the value of £30 000; management may in the next period set a target of, say, £40 000 believing, rightly or wrongly, that this new target will motivate the salesperson to reach higher levels of attainment than in the previous period.

It is also the case that budgets may mean different things to different people within an organization. For example, whilst a budget may be introduced by management in an organization with the aim of monitoring production costs, production managers may perceive the main purpose of the budget as a device to monitor their performance. Budgets can therefore lead to much misunderstanding, frustration and friction within an organization.

The budget process

The following analysis focuses on the main features of the budget process.

The products that will be manufactured and sold, in a budget period, will be determined via the operating decisions, as previously described in Chapters 17 and 18. These decisions are initially made in isolation from a number of functions within an organization that are there to support the manufacture and sales of the products that have been

> The term 'the budget process' refers to the sequence of operations necessary to produce a budget for a particular organization. The sequence of operations will depend upon the type of organization and its perceived requirements for planning and control.
>
> **KEY CONCEPT 19.1**
> ***The budget process***

chosen in the decision-making process. In the context of a manufacturing organization these supportive functions will normally relate to purchasing, production, marketing, administration and finance. Each of these functions will also require investment in resources, such as personnel necessary to perform the support function. It is at the beginning of the budget process that consideration is given to the operating decisions collectively and their interrelationships with these functions. At this stage the resource implications of the decisions are analysed to determine the extent to which they will draw upon the functions that were described above. From this analysis guidelines will be formulated for the preparation of the budgets. The guidelines represent a framework for the preparers of budgets, identifying the overall levels of activity and the organization's policies on performance criteria, e.g. productivity. The personnel involved at this stage will be the top management of the organization. These managers will include those that have overall responsibility for the sales and production activities and those that are responsible for ensuring that the activities are co-ordinated, e.g. an accountant who has responsibility for the co-ordination of the accounting information input, often referred to as the budget accountant. Thus the vitally important management task of co-ordination of the various interrelated aspects of decision making begins in the budgeting process.

In a manufacturing organization, for example, the main task of co-ordination will inevitably be concerned with the overall policy on the level of sales and production activities. The co-ordination of these activities will involve ensuring that the level of production output is sufficient to meet the sales demand for products and any stock of finished goods that is also required by management. For example, if the sales demand for a product is 150 units and the desired closing finished goods stock level is 30 units, assuming there are no opening stocks of finished goods available, 180 units will have to be manufactured to meet the sales and stock requirements in the budget period. The functions such as marketing and finance necessary to support these levels of output will also be considered at this stage. So will the formulation of management policies on the levels of performance for the budget period.

When the output levels and associated policies have been determined by top management they must then be communicated to the preparers of the budgets. As previously mentioned the preparers will be given guidelines and it will be the responsibility of these preparers to formulate the budgets within these guidelines. Budgets will be prepared for individual responsibility centres which have been defined by the organization's hierarchy. These centres will be managed by personnel who are responsible for particular functions within the organization, e.g. generating sales, producing products and those supporting the sales and production functions.

There is some debate on the extent to which managers who are responsible for spending and income-generating departments should be involved in the preparation of their own budgets. It is normally the case, however, that managers of these responsibility centres will have some influence over the content of the budget. The extent of influence will vary from organization to organization and will depend on the management style of the organization. For example, the top management of some organizations may adopt a regime of imposing rules on subordinates without any discussion with them. The problem is that if managers are solely responsible for the preparation of the budget it is likely that the budget will reflect a bias in favour of the manager which may not be in the best interests of the organization as a whole. For example, it is likely that a manager who is responsible for the sales of a particular product range will set a budget that can easily be attained. The attainment of such targets will invariably be looked upon favourably by the manager's superiors. It is likely, however, that a manager of a responsibility centre will have a greater degree of knowledge and understanding of the operation of his own centre than any other personnel within the organization, and this knowledge is important in the formulation of budgets. Thus there is a strong case for at least some involvement by the manager of a responsibility centre in the preparation of the centre's budget.

Typically, in the budgeting process of an organization, individual budgets for each responsibility centre will be the subject of negotiations before approval and adoption by the organization. The parties in this negotiation stage will normally include the manager of the responsibility centre, the preparer of the budget (if not the manager) and the manager's superior. The accountant who is responsible for budgets within the organization will normally act as an intermediary in this negotiation process. Often in large organizations the negotiation process will be in a number of stages as the budget moves up the management hierarchy for approval. Figure 19.1 illustrates a typical hierarchy for the production management of an organization and the stages of negotiation of the production budget for three products that collectively represent a range of products.

In the figure the production budgets in terms of costs and output levels would be determined for products A, B and C. It has been assumed here that a product manager is responsible for the production of each of the products. As mentioned above, it likely that the product manager will prepare his/her own budget or at least be influential in its content. When the budgets have been prepared the first stage in negotiation will take place between the individual product managers and the production manager who has overall responsibility for the production of this range of products. After the individual budgets have

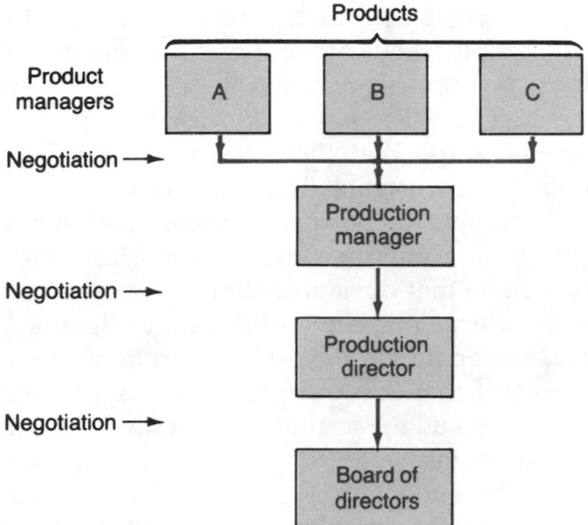

Figure 19.1

been agreed the combined budgets for the range are then negotiated with the production director who has responsibility for all production of the organization. The last stage of negotiation of the production budget will be at Board level where eventually the budget will be approved.

At each stage of the negotiation process, as described, bargains are struck between the managers responsible for the budget and their immediate superiors. The negotiations between managers in the hierarchy of an organization in effect therefore represent a bargaining process where the individual goals of managers are formulated for a forthcoming budget period.

At Board level the final fine tuning of the respective budgets will take place. This process involves ensuring that all the budgets are consistent with each other, e.g. that the required material stock levels are sufficient to meet the production requirement throughout the year. When all the individual budgets have been finalized and approved at this level they are summarized into what is commonly referred to as a master budget. The master budget will normally take the form of a budgeted balance sheet and profit and loss account for the budget period. The information within the master budget is in effect a summary of all the individual budgets referred to earlier. Thus the master budget represents the overall plan for an organization. It is useful as it clearly sets out the targets for the organization in an easily understandable form and can be compared with the actual balance sheet and profit and loss account.

After the final approval at Board level the budgets will be passed down the organization to the respective responsibility managers. It will be these managers who will be delegated to carry out the plans contained within each individual budget.

Plans in the form of budgets are extremely useful to an organization.

A number of the purposes identified earlier for budgets highlight their usefulness. For example, they compel organizations to look ahead and thereby anticipate any particular problems that may arise in the future. The nature of budgeting that has been described so far tends to be rather static, in the sense that the planning process is based upon certain assumptions and events that will occur in the forthcoming budget period. However, the business environment in reality tends to be dynamic, and thus events may not turn out as anticipated in the budget. It may well be that deviations from the budget are harmful to the organization; for example, the cost of producing a product may be greater than that anticipated in the budget and losses may be made. It is therefore important that these actual events in a budget period are monitored against the budget so that action may be taken to alleviate any undesirable situations.

Deviations from the budget in a period, however, may be due to events within the control or outside the control of the organization. For events that are within its control, the organization can take action, if they are undesirable, to ensure that such deviations will not occur in the future. In contrast, events outside the control of the organization, such as a downturn in the economy, may mean that it will be necessary for the organization to reconsider its plans. Typically, this will often result in organizations 'trimming' their operations to lower levels of activity or diversifying into other markets. The point here is that undesirable situations may be averted if an efficient system of control is imposed, and if the actual and budgeted performances are compared sufficiently frequently.

The budget time period

At this point of our analysis it is appropriate to consider the budget period. The budget period normally employed by organizations is one year. The reason for a period of a year appears to relate to the periodic reporting requirements for published accounts regulated by the law. Public companies, for example, are required by law, with few exceptions, to publish accounts annually. It should also be recognized that there is normally a link between the information content of budgets and the annual accounts. For example, an organization's budget will normally include the planned total sales for the period whilst the annual accounts will show the actual sales achieved in the same period. Mainly for control purposes the budget for the year will be broken down into quarterly, monthly and weekly periods. The extent to which the budget is broken down to these shorter periods will depend on the needs of the particular organization and the state of the economy. For example, if an organization operates in a very competitive market it is likely that management will desire to monitor performance on a fairly regular basis to ensure that the organization is maintaining its competitive position, as reflected in actual revenues, costs and output.

The master budget will normally consist of the budgeted profit and loss account and balance sheet, representing a summary of the individual functional budgets of the organization as a whole.

KEY CONCEPT 19.2
Master budget

Preparation of budgets

The master budget

The master budget is extremely useful to management as it clearly sets out the objectives and the targets for the forthcoming budget period and is in a form that is easy to comprehend. It also provides a basis for co-ordinating individual functional budgets. The importance of co-ordination was emphasized earlier in this chapter. In a medium to large manufacturing organization these functional budgets will normally consist of sales, production, administration, distribution and cash budgets.

For small organizations, frequently the profit and loss account, balance sheet and cash budget will be sufficient for the organization's management requirements. The information contained in these three budgeted statements can provide management with a reasonable base to analyse the forthcoming period. In particular, a number of ratios and indicators can be derived such as those relating to profitability, liquidity and financing. The use of these ratios and indicators was discussed in Chapter 12.

We shall begin, for clarity, by considering the preparation of a profit and loss account, balance sheet and cash budget for a small firm just starting up (Example 19.1).

Example 19.1

Sivraj Ltd was formed on 1 July 19X1 with a share capital of £40 000. £24 000 of this capital was immediately invested into fixed assets, leaving £16 000 cash.

The fixed assets, it is estimated, have a 10-year life, and will have no value at the end of 10 years. The company have decided to depreciate these assets using the straight line method of depreciation. Therefore the depreciation charge per year will be £24 000/10 years = £2400, or expressed in monthly terms £2400/12 months = £200.

Prior to starting, business plans have been formulated for the first six months of the first year of operations. These plans are set out below.

Sales for the six months are estimated to be £600 000. However, the company operates in a seasonal market and will also be allowing some of its customers to take credit. The company anticipates the following receipts of cash over the six month period from sales:

	Sales receipts
	£
July	40 000
August	50 000
September	50 000
October	70 000
November	120 000
December	170 000
	500 000

From this breakdown of the anticipated cash received over the six month period it is apparent that at the end of the period there will be money owing from customers (i.e. debtors) of £600 000 − £500 000 = £100 000.

The materials required to meet the demand for sales are estimated to be £240 000. To enable the company to maintain a stock (to ensure against any shortages) £260 000 worth of materials will be purchased in the period. However, because of the production cycle and the credit that the company will be obtaining from its suppliers the pattern and amount paid to suppliers will be as follows:

	Payment to suppliers for materials
	£
July	60 000
August	60 000
September	20 000
October	20 000
November	20 000
December	20 000
	200 000

At the end of the six-month period the company have purchased materials costing £260 000 but have only paid £200 000 for them; thus the company will owe (i.e. have creditors of) £60 000 at the end of December 19X1.

The estimated labour cost that will be incurred over the six months will be £180 000. In addition the firm anticipates that overheads (excluding depreciation) of £138 000 will also be incurred over this period. Overheads and wages will be paid evenly over the six-month period.

We shall also assume that any cash deficits are financed by a bank overdraft.

To ensure that sufficient cash resources are available the company wishes to calculate a cash budget (forecast) on a monthly basis as well as a budgeted profit and loss account for the period and a balance sheet at the end of the period.

We shall begin by constructing the three budgeted statements from the information given. This will be followed by a commentary con-

Table 19.1 Cash budget for 6 months Sivraj Ltd

	July £	*August* £	*September* £	*October* £	*November* £	*December* £
Cash inflows						
Share capital	40 000					
Sales receipts	40 000	50 000	50 000	70 000	120 000	170 000
Total cash inflows	80 000	50 000	50 000	70 000	120 000	170 000
Cash outflows						
Materials	60 000	60 000	20 000	20 000	20 000	20 000
Wages	30 000	30 000	30 000	30 000	30 000	30 000
Overheads	23 000	23 000	23 000	23 000	23 000	23 000
Fixed assets	24 000					
Total cash outflows	137 000	113 000	73 000	73 000	73 000	73 000
Net cash flow	(57 000)	(63 000)	(23 000)	(3 000)	47 000	97 000
Balance brought forward	—	(57 000)	(120 000)	(143 000)	(146 000)	(99 000)
Balance carried forward	(57 000)	(120 000)	(143 000)	(146 000)	(99 000)	(2 000)

cerning the usefulness of these statements to management. The cash budget will be considered first (Table 19.1).

It can be seen from the cash budget for Sivraj that the inflows and outflows of cash are recorded in the budget statement when the cash is actually received or paid. There are a few main points to remember when constructing a cash budget.

- The dates of receipt and payment of cash, not the date of sale or purchase, are relevant; thus allowance must be made for any credit period given or received. For example, in the case of Sivraj the relevant sales are when the cash is actually received and not when the sales are earned in the period.
- Provisions should be excluded as they do not affect cash flows; for example depreciation on fixed assets is excluded as the cash flow associated with fixed assets occurs when the asset is paid for. Thus the relevant cash outflow £24 000, which was paid out for the fixed asset when it was purchased. The depreciation charge is irrelevant and should be ignored.
- Any inflows of capital and outflows such as drawings, payment of tax and dividends must also be included. In the example of Sivraj the only relevant item of this nature is the capital which was injected into the business on start up.
- The format of the cash budget is very similar to the worksheets which were introduced in an earlier chapter. In the case of cash budgets the horizontal headings should relate to the discrete time period chosen for the budget. Thus, in this example, the requirement is monthly for six months to the end of December 19X1. The company could have chosen weeks, for example; in such a case

there would be a column for each week of the six month period. The time dimension will depend upon the requirements of the managers of the organization.

Table 19.2 Profit and loss account for the six months ending 31 December 19X1

		£
Sales		600 000
Cost of sales	£	
Materials	240 000	
Wages	180 000	420 000
Gross profit		180 000
Less	£	
Depreciation	1 200	
Overheads	138 000	139 200
Net profit		40 800

The profit and loss account, for convenience, has been constructed in a summary form rather than through the use of a worksheet (Table 19.2). Unlike the cash budget, the profit and loss account is constructed by applying the concept of accruals accounting (i.e. matching revenues with costs associated with the revenues) rather than cash flow accounting. Thus, in our example, the material cost is the cost of materials included in the sales rather than the cash paid for the materials. The depreciation charge for the six months is calculated by taking the monthly charge of £200 and multiplying by six.

The balance sheet, similarly to the profit and loss account, has been constructed without the use of a worksheet (Table 19.3). The following is a brief explanation of how the value of some of the assets and liabilities has been derived.

The stock figure represents the difference between materials purchased (£260 000) and those materials consumed in the sales over the six month period (£240 000). Debtors of £100 000 is the difference between the sales in the period and the cash received. The sum of £60 000 for creditors is the difference between the materials purchased (£260 000) and the cash paid at the end of the six months (£200 000). The bank overdraft is derived from the cash budget and is the balance at the end of December 19X1.

The use of worksheets, as described in earlier chapters, in the construction of the profit and loss account and the balance sheet illustrates the interrelationships between these statements. Although worksheets were not used in this example the interrelationships between these statements should still be apparent.

From a brief glance at these three budgeted statements for Sivraj, their usefulness should be apparent to you for planning. For example, it is predicted that although the company anticipates making a profit of

Table 19.3 Balance sheet as at 31 December 19X1

Fixed assets			£
Cost			24 000
Less depreciation			1 200
			22 800
Current assets		£	
Stock		20 000	
Debtors		100 000	
		120 000	
Less current			
Liabilities	£		
Creditors	60 000		
Bank Overdraft	2 000	62 000	58 000
			80 800
			£
Share capital			40 000
Profit and loss a/c			40 800
			80 800

£40 800 for the six months, which appears reasonably healthy, there will be large deficits of cash during this period. The problem for Sivraj is the pattern of cash payments and receipts. High material costs are incurred in the first two months as well as the payment for the fixed assets. In contrast, the major source of cash, sales, are higher in the later part of the period. Identifying this situation prior to trading is extremely useful as it may be possible to take action to reduce these cash deficits whilst trying to obtain some additional funding. For example, it may be possible to get receipts from sales in earlier, either by restricting the credit given to customers or by encouraging customers to pay more quickly by offering a discount for prompt payment. This would result in cash being received earlier and would thereby reduce the cash deficit each month.

By identifying cash shortages at this stage Sivraj will also be in a better position to finance any deficits. For example, the bank would look more favourably on an application for an overdraft after having some insight into the future profitability of the company. This situation can be contrasted with the negative attitude of the bank when an application for funding is made after a firm has gone into debt without any prior communication with the bank. Another possible alternative action to relieve this potentially undesirable situation could be to raise additional share capital to fund the cash deficits of the business.

In the analysis of the budgets of Sivraj our main concern has, not surprisingly, been focused on the cash deficits. It could have been the case that Sivraj had budgeted cash surpluses rather than deficits during the budget period. In these circumstances the identification of these surpluses would also be useful to the business. By identifying surpluses at this early stage the firm would be in a better position to plan the investment of such funds, e.g. in short-term deposits, to obtain the maximum amount of interest.

As previously mentioned, a number of other characteristics of the business can be analysed through the use of ratio analysis. However, in general the major benefit to budgets of this nature to an organization such as Sivraj is that events can be anticipated and action taken for the best interests of the organization.

External funding organizations will always require budgeted information from firms, similar to that produced in the case of Sivraj, before any agreement to lend money. This is particularly the case when small businesses, such as Sivraj, apply for funding from banks.

The sales and production budgets

The sales and production budgets will normally be prepared for manufacturing organizations and will reflect the respective targets for these functions in the forthcoming budget period. As previously mentioned, the summation of these budgets will be embodied within the overall profit and loss account and balance sheet. Also, as these functions will involve cash payments and receipts they will also be the source for the overall cash budget.

In Example 19.2 we shall concentrate on the sales and production budgets and subsequently determine a budgeted profit and loss account. We shall also emphasize the importance of co-ordinating these different functions within an organization, in particular the production output level necessary to support the sales volume and desired stock levels.

Example 19.2

Nadia Plc has gathered the following data about future sales and production requirements for the year 19X1.

Estimated sales.

Product	*Units*	*Price*	*Opening stock 1.1.19X1 Units*	*Desired closing stock 31.12.19X1 Units*
A	20 000	£55	8 000	10 000
B	50 000	£50	15 000	15 000
C	30 000	£65	6 000	6 000

Materials used in manufacture:

Stock no.	*Unit*	*Amount used per unit of production* A	B	C
54	Component	3	—	5
32	Metres	2	1	3
44	Kilograms	—	2	—

Estimated purchase price of materials:

Stock no.	
54	£3 per component
32	£2 per metre
44	£4 per kilogram

Stock levels of materials:

Stock no.	*Opening stock 1.1.19X1*	*Closing stock 31.12.19X1*
54	21 000 components	25 000 components
32	17 000 metres	23 000 metres
44	10 000 kilograms	8 000 kilograms

Labour requirement:

Product	*Hours per unit*	*Rate per hour*
A	4	£7
B	5	£5
C	5	£6

Production overheads are estimated at £500 000 per year. For internal management purposes Nadia adopts a marginal costing system, and therefore treats these overheads as a period charge (see Chapter 14).

In this example, we presume that the sales demand, in terms of volume, is the constraining factor. Thus the production volume will be dependent upon the sales demand.

The management of Nadia require the following budgetary information for the forthcoming budget period:

- sales budget in money terms;
- production budget in units;
- materials purchased budget in units;
- materials purchased budget in money terms;
- materials cost per unit manufactured and sold;
- the total labour hours worked during the period and the cost, plus the labour cost per unit manufactured and sold;
- the unit contribution for each product;
- the profit or loss for the budget period;
- the value of closing finished stock at the end of the budget period.

Sales budget in monetary terms

We have been given the price per unit and the volume of units that it is estimated will be sold. To calculate the total sales revenue generated from these sales we simply need to multiply these two variables:

Product	*Units × price (£)*	*Sales revenue (£000)*
A	20 000 × 55	1 100
B	50 000 × 50	2 500
C	30 000 × 65	1 950
	Total	5 550

Production budget in units

The production level during the budget period not only must satisfy the sales demand but must ensure that the stock levels are sufficient for the period. In the case of Nadia the opening and closing stock levels have been estimated, and we have been given the sales demand; from this information, and with the help of a simple equation, we shall be able to determine the production level to satisfy this demand.

The equation we shall use, sometimes referred to as the inventory formula, is as follows (measured in units):

production + opening stock = sales + closing stock

This equation states that the units produced during the budget period plus what is in stock at the beginning of this period are equal to the units to be sold plus the units required as stock at the end of the period.

For our purposes, as there is only one unknown quantity (production), we need to rearrange this formula:

sales + closing stock − opening stock = production

Applying this equation to the figures for Nadia, measured in units, we obtain the following.

Product	*Sales*	+	*Closing stock*	−	*Opening stock*	=	*Production*
A	20 000	+	10 000	−	8 000	=	22 000
B	50 000	+	14 000	−	15 000	=	49 000
C	30 000	+	6 000	−	6 000	=	30 000

The materials purchased budget measured in units

Three types of materials described by stock numbers (stock nos. 54, 32 and 44) are used in the production of A, B and C. Before determining how many units of these stocks will need to be purchased in the period we must first calculate the number of units of stock necessary to satisfy production requirements:

Product	*Units*	*Stock:* 54	32	44
A	22 000	(×3) 66 000	—	(×5)110 000
B	49 000	(×2) 98 000	(×1) 49 000	(×3)147 000
C	30 000	—	(×2) 60 000	—
Total		164 000	109 000	257 000

The figures in parentheses represent the number of units of material required for each product. For example, in the case of product A, 3 units of stock no. 54 are required to make one unit of A.

The purchase of materials required for the forthcoming budget period can now be calculated using a similar equation to that used in determining the production level:

purchases + opening stocks = production + closing stocks

Purchases etc. in this equation will be measured in terms of material units, e.g. components in the case of stock no. 54.

The equation states that the materials required for production during the period and closing stock at the end of the period will be met from the purchase of materials and the stock that is available at the beginning of the period.

From the information that is given in this example we are told the opening and closing stock requirements and we have calculated above the materials required for production. Therefore three of the four variables in the equation are known to us, and by rearranging the equation we shall be able to calculate the purchases figure.

production + closing stock − opening stock = purchases

Applying this equation to the information that has been given for the three stock numbers we obtain the following.

Stock no.	*Production*	+	*Closing stock*	−	*Opening stock*	=	*Purchases*
54	164 000	+	25 000	−	21 000	=	168 000
32	109 000	+	23 000	−	17 000	=	115 000
44	257 000	+	10 000	−	8 000	=	259 000

It should be remembered that the above purchases figures represent the units for the respective materials; thus, for example, in the case of stock no. 54 the purchases requirement will be 168 000 components.

The materials purchased in money terms

The calculation of purchases, measured in money terms, is relatively straightforward. We simply multiply the purchases in terms of units by the cost per unit which was given at the beginning of the example.

Stock no.	*Purchases (units)*		*Cost per unit* £	*Total cost* £
54	168 000	×	3	504 000
32	115 000	×	2	230 000
44	259 000	×	4	1 036 000
				1 770 000

Materials cost per unit manufactured and sold

This information may be required by management in the determination of the profitability of each of the products sold and for stock valuation purposes. All the relevant information regarding this calculation has been given and it just remains for us to perform the calculation; for each unit of product we need to multiply the cost per unit of material by the amount of the material required to manufacture each product.

Stock no.	*Cost per unit of stock (£)*	*Products*		
		A	*B*	*C*
		£	£	£
54	3	(×3) 9	—	(×5)15
32	2	(×2) 4	(×1) 2	(×3) 6
44	4	—	(×2) 8	—
Material cost per unit sold		13	10	21

The figures in parentheses represent the number of units of material required for each product.

The total labour hours worked in the period, the total cost and the cost of labour per unit of goods manufactured and sold

We begin by computing the labour cost per unit of goods manufactured and sold. This information will provide management with data that are useful to assess profitability and for stock valuation purposes. The arithmetic for the calculation is relatively simple – to obtain the total labour cost per unit we need to multiply the hours per unit by the rate per hour.

Product	*Hours per unit*	*Rate per hour* £	*Total labour cost per unit* £
A	4	7	28
B	5	5	25
C	5	6	30

For calculation of the total labour hours the production units must be multiplied by the hours per unit. If we then multiply the total labour by the rate per unit we can determine the total cost. It is important to appreciate why production units are used in these calculations rather than sales units. The reason is that the objective here is to determine how many hours were actually worked and the cost of those hours during the year. If sales units were used we would be establishing the total hours that have been consumed in producing the sales. If there are changes between the opening and closing levels of finished stocks the units produced will not equal the sales units sold. This was the case for both products A and B, as can be seen when we determined the production levels for these two products earlier. In contrast, for product C the finished stock level remained unchanged and thus the production units and the sales units were the same, i.e. 30 000 units.

Product	*Production units*	*Hours per unit*	*Total hours*	*Rate per hour* £	*Total cost* £
A	22 000	4	88 000	7	616 000
B	49 000	5	245 000	5	
C	30 000	5	150 000	6	1 225 000
			483 000		900 000
					2 741 000

The unit contribution of each product

We have used the concept of contribution in earlier chapters relating, for example, to cost behaviour and cost volume profit analysis. To remind you, the contribution per unit is equal to the sales price per unit less variable costs per unit. The only variable costs we have in this example are materials and labour. These variable costs, you will remember, have been determined earlier. Thus the contribution per unit for these three products will be as follows.

		A		*B*		C
		£		£		£
Sales price		55		50		65
Less variable costs						
Material	13		10		21	
Labour	28	41	25	35	30	51
Contribution per unit		14		15		14

The profit or loss for the budget period

We shall begin by determing the total contribution for the three products and then deduct the overhead cost, which is the convention under the marginal costing regime.

Product	*Contribution per unit*	*No. of units sold*	
	£		£
A	14	20 000	280 000
B	15	50 000	750 000
C	14	30 000	420 000
Total contribution			1 450 000
Less overheads			500 000
Profit			950 000

The value of finished stock at the end of the period

Under the marginal costing regime finished stock will be valued at marginal cost (variable cost). From the information already obtained we know the variable costs of each product and we therefore need to multiple this cost by the number of units of finished stock which was given at the beginning of this example.

Product	*Finished stock in units*	*Marginal cost*	*Value of finished stock*
		£	£
A	10 000	41	410 000
B	14 000	35	490 000
C	6 000	51	306 000
Total value of finished stock			1 206 000

The budgets prepared above will act as a source of information in the construction of the profit and loss account, balance sheet and cash budget.

The budgets constructed in this example will always be broken down further to responsible departments thus enabling the management of these departments to identify clearly the plans purely associated with their departments.

It should also be stressed that the budgets prepared for Nadia will not necessarily be common to all manufacturing organizations. The form and design of the budgetary system will depend upon the particular organization's management requirements. However, the example does illustrate the main principles in the preparation of budgets for manufacturing organizations.

In the example Nadia overheads were given as one figure, i.e. £500 000 per year. Normally, as previously mentioned in the section on the budgeting process, organizations will also prepare detailed budgets for overhead expenditure. These will represent the planned costs associated with expenses budgets associated with supporting the manufacturing function, such as machine maintenance, administration and sales. It should also be mentioned that as new technology and automation are being introduced into the manufacturing environment overhead costs are tending to grow as a proportion of the total cost of an organization's operations. Thus organizations should be placing more emphasis on planning and control of these types of costs. However, many of the systems that are in use have not been efficiently designed to cope with this phenomenon. There is considerable debate, at present, as to the methods of costing and budgeting that should be introduced to monitor overhead costs.

Summary

We began this chapter by considering the main purposes of budgets. They were described under the following headings:

- to compel planning;
- co-ordination of different functions;
- communication;
- to provide a basis for responsibility accounting;
- to provide a basis for a control mechanism;
- authorization of expenditure;
- a means to motivate employees to improve performance.

From this list it is apparent that budgets are introduced and used for a variety of reasons. Whilst it may appear initially that the introduction of budgets can only be to the advantage of the organization, they can create conflicts within the organization. For example, management may have introduced budgets for a positive reason, to motivate employees, but employees may see the budget in a negative light which has a demotivating effect. However, it will always be necessary to monitor performance.

A sequence of operations is needed to implement a planning system such as budgets effectively. This sequence of operations is known as the budget process. It is important to understand this process as it links the reasons for the implementation of the budget and the preparation of budgets. It was also stressed that the budget process and form of budgets would be dependent upon a number of contingent factors such as the type of technology employed by the organization.

The last section of the chapter focused on the preparation of budgets. Two examples were examined, both of which illustrated how the process of preparing budgets effectively co-ordinated the plans of separate functions of the organization, e.g. the sales budget and its relationship with the production and stock budgets. A number of principles, such as those underlying cash budgets, were stressed in the preparation of different budgets. It is important that you should understand these principles in order to be able to prepare budgets.

Further reading

The importance of behavioural factors in the budgeting process is well documented in *Accounting and Human Behaviour*, Chapters 3 and 4, by A. Hopwood (Prentice-Hall International, 1974).

A detailed account of variance analysis can be found in *Managerial Accounting: Method and Meaning*, by R.M. Wilson and W.F. Chua, 2nd edn (Chapman and Hall, 1992).

Organizational issues, in respect of budgeting, are well represented by *Accounting for Management Control*, Chapters 6 and 7, by C. Emmanuel, D. Otley and K. Merchant, 2nd edn (Chapman and Hall, 1990).

Review questions

1 What is a budget?
2 What are the main reasons for an organization to introduce budgets?
3 Explain why budgets may mean different things to different people within an organization, giving reasons.
4 Describe the main differences in the budgeting process for a small retail firm and a large manufacturing firm.
5 Discuss the interrelationships between the sales budget and the production budget in a manufacturing organization.
6 Explain, giving examples, the main advantages of identifying cash surpluses and deficits in a cash budget.
7 What determines the budget time period?
8 What is a master budget? Describe its role in relation to other budgets.

Problems for discussion and analysis

1 With reference to the example of Sivraj prepare a profit and loss account and balance sheet from the data using worksheets.

2 CJH Ltd is preparing its annual budget. The following data are available.

Product	*Estimated sales (units)*	*Opening stock (units)*	*Closing stock (units)*
X	18	8	10
Y	50	15	15
Z	30	6	6

Material	*Cost per unit (£)*	*Units of material used per unit of product*			*Opening stock (units)*	*Closing stock (units)*
		X	Y	Z		
A	3	3	—	5	21	25
B	2	2	1	3	17	23
C	4	—	2	1	10	15

(a) Prepare the production budget in units.
(b) Give the total budgeted cost of materials used in the production of X, Y and Z.
(c) Give the total cost of materials A, B and C purchased.

3 Faraday Ltd is a wholesaler. The management has been extremely worried about the firm's cash position over the last few years. In January 19X1 they seek your advice and ask you to prepare a cash budget for the forthcoming months of April, May and June 19X1. In addition they have asked you to write a report on the cash position over this period, and in particular on ways in which you think it could be improved.

The following data are made available to you regarding the firm's operations.

(i) Estimated sales for the six months to June 19X1:

Month	*Credit sales* £	*Cash sales* £
January	122 000	12 900
February	137 000	14 500
March	142 000	17 700
April	148 000	20 100
May	134 000	15 000
June	126 000	12 600

Cash is received immediately on cash sales. The firm allows customers one month's credit on sales other than for cash.

(ii) Purchase of goods for resale are made on credit. The firm receives two months' credit on these purchases. The purchases for the six months to June 19X1 are as follows.

Month	£
January	62 000
February	58 000
March	71 000
April	80 000
May	54 000
June	48 000

(iii) A stock check at the end of last year has revealed £45 000 of stock, valued at cost, is considered obsolete. The firm is currently negotiating the sale of this stock for £9500 and anticipates payment in May 19X1.

(iv) Faraday's manufacturing overheads are estimated to be £12 000 per month. This includes a charge for depreciation of £2000 per month. The company takes one month to pay these expenses.

(v) Selling and distribution expenses are estimated to be £50 400 a year and are incurred evenly over the year. One month's credit is taken.

(vi) The firm are currently negotiating an advertising programme with an agency. The cost will be £6300 in May and £7700 in June. Payment will be made in cash.

(vii) In June the firm anticipates paying £3880 tax to the Inland Revenue.

(viii) The firm has agreed to purchase new stock-handling equipment. The cost of £105 200 is payable in two equal instalments in April and May 19X1.

(ix) The firm expects in June to be able to take advantage of adjacent property (cost, £150 000) to expand their operation.

(x) It is estimated that the cash balance at 1 April will be £16 000.

4 Borough Equipment Plc produces two products, Main and Pain, for sale to electrical wholesalers. The following information relates to the six months ending 31 December 19X3:

Product	*Budgeted sales Units*	*Price per unit (£)*	*Budgeted stocks 1.7.19X3 (units)*	*Budgeted stocks 31.12.19X3 (units)*
Main	16 200	14.35	5 100	8 100
Pain	11 800	12.20	2 600	6 600

Components bought in and used in manufacture:

Component	*Amount used per unit of product* Main	Pain
X	5	3
Y	2	4

Component	*Price*	*Expected stocks*	*Expected stocks*
	£	*1.7.19X3*	*31.12.19X3*
X	0.68	38 000	46 000
Y	0.24	13 500	19 500

Labour:

Product	*Hours per unit*	*Rate per hour*
		£
Main	2	4.50
Pain	1	4.00

Overheads for the six months are anticipated to be £25 000. The company adopts a marginal costing system and treats overheads as a period cost.

Prepare the following:

(a) sales budget
(b) production budget
(c) purchases budget in terms of components
(d) purchases budget in pounds
(e) the total labour hours and cost for the period
(f) the contribution per unit
(g) the profit or loss for the period

Comment on the usefulness of these budgets for planning, decision making and control.

Investment decisions

20

This chapter examines the four main methods of investment appraisal within a business decision making environment: net present value, the internal rate of return, the accounting rate of return and payback methods.

Introduction

In this chapter we shall be examining how managers of businesses make long-term investment decisions *vis-à-vis* short-term decisions. The main difference between long and short-term decisions is that the benefits in the case of long-term decisions will accrue over a longer period, usually well over one year, and often much longer. This difference in time dimension has important implications in terms of the value of money. The value of money over time will be an important feature in the evaluation of the differing methods of investment appraisal available to managers, and will be considered later.

By their nature, long-term decisions tend to be strategic. This means that resources are committed for a long period of time and these decisions determine the long-term policies of the firm that are necessary to meet its objectives.

The methods of investment appraisal we will be considering are designed primarily to satisfy one objective, that is to maximize profits of the firm. The maximizing of profits can also be translated into maximizing the value of shareholders' wealth. The shareholders are the owners of the firm, to whom the management of the firm are accountable. The link between the investment decision and the finance necessary to fund the investment is that the return from an investment must adequately satisfy those providing the finance. Therefore, the criteria that are to be applied in terms of accepting or rejecting individual investment opportunities will reflect the demands of those who finance the firm.

Risk will play an important part in determining the return demanded by those funding the business. The higher the risk, the greater the return that those funding the business will demand. Differing investment opportunities have different risk profiles. The main factors that affect risk are the structure of the market and industry, changes in technology and tastes and exposure to macroeconomic variables.

It should be recognized, however, that there are other criteria than maximizing profits that a firm may adopt, in determining whether to invest. It may be that a firm's objective at a particular point in time is, for example, to maximize market share, which may be in conflict with the maximization of profits. It is likely that in such cases, the methods of investment appraisal that we will be considering would then be inappropriate.

In this chapter we will be examining and evaluating the following methods of investment appraisal.

- the accounting rate of return (ARR) method;
- the payback method;
- discounted cash flow (DCF) methods, namely:
  - the net present value (NPV) method; and
  - the internal rate of return (IRR) method.

Accounting rate of return (ARR)

A long-term investment project may be assessed by calculating its estimated accounting rate of return (ARR) and comparing it with a predetermined target ARR, the target being set by management and presumably reflecting their objectives in terms of a satisfactory return. The ARR is sometimes also referred to as return on investment (ROI). In principle these two measures are the same. There is a difference, however, between ARR and return on capital employed (ROCE). ROCE is used normally to describe the return on investment of a reporting entity as whole, for example, a company, rather than of one individual project, as in the case of ARR.

Unfortunately, and confusingly, there are several different definitions of ARR. One of the most popular is:

$$\text{ARR} = \frac{\text{Estimated average profit}}{\text{Estimated average investment}} \times 100\%$$

The other definitions include:

$$\text{ARR} = \frac{\text{Estimated total profit}}{\text{Estimated initial investment}} \times 100\%$$

and

$$\text{ARR} = \frac{\text{Estimated average profit}}{\text{Estimated initial investment}} \times 100\%$$

There are various arguments in favour of each of the above definitions. The most important point is, however, that the method adopted should be used consistently, thereby ensuring that like is compared to like.

The profit figure in this measure is the accounting profit based on accruals accounting principles and is normally taken after depreciation but before taxation. Taxation is ignored as the variation in taxes over time, which may be outside the control of the firm, can distort the measure from one period to another. This would be problematic for the appraisal of investment projects, as there would not be a consistent basis upon which to compare investments.

The use of the ARR method of appraisal involves estimating the ARR on the proposed project and comparing it with a target ARR. If the estimated rate of the proposed project exceeds the target rate, the project should be undertaken. Conversely, if the estimated return is less than the target, the proposed project should be rejected.

KEY CONCEPT 20.1
Accounting rate of return (ARR) decision rule

Compare the estimated ARR of a proposed project with the target ARR. If the estimate exceeds the target, accept the project; if it is lower, reject the project.

CASE STUDY 20.1
Hilditch Environmental Consultants Ltd

Hilditch Environmental Consultants Ltd are currently appraising an investment opportunity. The company uses the accounting rate of return for such purposes. The target ARR for the company is 20%. The following details relate to the proposed investment:

Investment – cost of the asset £80 000
Estimated life – 4 years
Estimated profit before depreciation:

	£
Year 1	20 000
Year 2	25 000
Year 3	35 000
Year 4	25 000

If the asset were to be depreciated on a straight-line basis, and the asset has a nil residual value, the annual depreciation charge will be £80 000/4 years = £20 000 per year. The annual profits after depreciation, and the mid-year net book value of the asset for each year, would be as follows.

Table 20.1

Year	*Profit after depreciation*	*Mid-year net book value*	*ARR in the year*
	£	£	%
1	0	70 000	0
2	5 000	50 000	10
3	15 000	30 000	50
4	5 000	10 000	50

The mid-year net book value in Table 20.1 is the value at the mid-point between the beginning of each year and the end of the year; for example, the value of the asset at the beginning of year 1 was £80 000 and at the end £60 000 (after deduction of depreciation of £20 000); the mid-year net book value therefore being £70 000.

From Table 20.1 it can be seen that the ARR, from a yearly perspective, is low in the early years of the project. This is partly because of low profits in year 1, but in the main it is due to the net book value of the asset being much higher in the early years. The relatively higher net book value of assets in early years is a characteristic of the straight line depreciation method which we discussed in Chapter 8.

The project does not achieve the target ARR of 20% in its first two years, but exceeds it in years 3 and 4. This begs the question whether the project should be accepted.

When the ARR from a project varies from year to year, it makes sense to take an overall view, which was implied earlier, when definitions of the method were being discussed. Using the most common definition cited earlier, that is:

$$\text{ARR} = \frac{\text{Estimated average profits}}{\text{Estimated average investment}} \times 100$$

Where:

$$\text{Estimated average profits} = \frac{\text{Total profits}}{\text{Number of years}} = \frac{\pounds 25\,000}{4} = \pounds 6250$$

Estimated average investment over the four-year period = £80 000 + 0/2 = £40 000 (the average investment being the average value of the asset at the beginning of its life, £80 000, and at the end of its life, in this case £0)

Therefore the ARR = £6250/40 000 × 100 = 15.63%

As the estimated ARR is less than the target rate of 20%, the project should be rejected.

Although, ARR adopts accounting measures which can be manipulated more easy than, say, simple inflows and outflows of cash, the measure is consistent with the way in which organizations report in their annual accounts. That is, both ARR and financial accounting information reported in the annual accounts are based on accruals accounting. Therefore, if the ARR of a project is estimated, some reasonable assessment may be made as to the effect of a proposed project on future reported profits.

The main criticism of the ARR is that it does not take account of the timing of profits generated from the investment. The model therefore assumes that the profits earned in the first year, for example, are equivalent in terms of value to profits earned in later years. That is, ignoring inflation, £1 today is assumed to be the same as £1 in 10 years' time. Intuition will lead us quickly to the conclusion that this is not so! This assumption therefore ignores the concept of the time value of money. The theme of time value of money will be considered in more detail later in this chapter when considering the methods based on discounted cash flow.

The payback method

> Payback is normally defined as the period, usually expressed in years, which it takes the cash inflows from a investment project to equal the cash outflows.
>
> **KEY CONCEPT 20.2**
> ***Definition of payback***

It should be noted that in the above definition of payback, the term 'cash flow' is used rather than accounting profit. Therefore, this method is not based on accruals accounting concepts and thus does not, for example, take account of depreciation.

Example 20.1 illustrates the use of the payback method where there are two mutually exclusive investment opportunities available to a firm; that is, where only one opportunity can be accepted.

Example 20.1

Project	*A*	*B*
	£	£
Cost of investment	50 000	50 000
Cash Inflows		
Year 1	10 000	40 000
Year 2	15 000	30 000
Year 3	20 000	10 000
Year 4	25 000	5 000
Year 5	60 000	5 000

Following the definition of pay back in Key Concept 20.2, Project A will pay back the investment after the third year. By the end of year 3, it has paid back £45 000 (£10 000 + £15 000 + £20 000) and the other £5000 will be paid back during year 4. When the actual payback occurs during a year, it is the convention to express this point in time as a fraction of a year, or in months. For example, in the case of Project A in the fourth year £25 000 is received, but only £5000 is necessary to add to previous year's cash inflows to pay back the original investment; this £5000 can then be expressed as a fraction of the total for that year – £5000/£25 000 i.e. one-fifth of the year, or in months £5000/£25 000 × 12 months = 2.4 months.

In contrast, Project B pays back the investment in 1 year and 4 months. This project therefore would normally be preferred under the payback criteria.

It should be noted that in calculating the fraction of the year or the month in which payback takes place, as in the example above, it has been assumed that the cash flows are received evenly throughout the year. Due to the inevitable uncertainty involved in long-term investment appraisal, this is a reasonable assumption. It would normally be very difficult and problematic to estimate precisely the spread of cash flows within years.

When examining two mutually exclusive projects, as in the case of Projects A and B, the usual decision is to accept the one with the shortest payback, assuming the payback period satifies some preconceived target. However, when only one investment opportunity is being examined, the payback of that opportunity will be compared with a target payback. This concept of a target payback could be employed in the case of Projects A and B above, assuming that these two projects were not mutually exclusive, that is to say, we could, if we so wished, accept both investment opportunities. For example, if our payback target was four years, Project B would be accepted because it pays back after 1 year and 4 months. Project A would also be accepted, because its payback of 3 years and 2.4 months is less than the target.

Much of the perceived risk associated with investment projects is related to uncertainty due to the time-span in which benefits in terms of cash flows are received. The longer the time period for receipt of cash, the greater the risk. Therefore, by differentiating projects in terms of the period to pay back the investment, the payback method measures this type of risk. Thus in terms of Example 20.1, Project B could be seen as less risky than Project A, because the payback period is shorter.

The method is relatively simple to understand and to calculate. Not surprisingly, the method is often used as a first screening method in the appraisal of investment opportunities, before any other of the more sophisticated methods are employed. Thus, in this context the first question to ask in assessing an investment proposal is: 'How long will it take to pay back its cost?'. The organization may, for example, have a policy that only projects that pay back within four years will be appraised using other more rigorous methods of appraisal.

There are two important criticisms of the payback method. The first is clearly fundamental and relates to the fact that cash flows after the payback period are ignored. So, it could be the case that whilst a project produces a large net cash flow (i.e. where cash inflows significantly exceed outflows), they are generated in the later part of the project and may be ignored as this is after the payback period. For example, in the case of Projects A and B in Example 20.1, Project B was preferred because of its shorter payback period, but overall Project A generates more cash inflows, totalling £130 000 as compared to only £90 000 in the case of Project B. However, Project A's cash inflows were mainly earned in the later years. The second criticism of the payback method relates to the method not taking account of the time value of money, similarly to the ARR. This criticism is not entirely valid as the method can be adapted to take account of the timing of cash inflows, which will be considered later.

Discounted cash flow (DCF)

To recap then, the ARR method of investment appraisal ignores the timing of cash flows and the opportunity cost of capital. Payback considers the time it takes to recover the original investment cost, but ignores total cash flows over a project's life.

Discounted cash flow, or DCF for short, is an investment appraisal technique which takes into account both the time value of money and also total profitability over a project's life. It is therefore often argued with much credence that DCF is a superior method to both ARR and payback as a method of investment appraisal.

From the term 'discounted cash flow', two important characteristics can be identified about the method; they are:

1 The timing of cash flows is taken into account by a process of discounting. The effect of discounting is to give a bigger value per £1 for cash flows that occur in earlier years. For example, £1 earned after one year will be worth more than £1 earned after two years, which in turn will be worth more than £1 earned after 10 years. The process of discounting involves selecting a discount rate that reflects an individual's or an organization's time value of money.
2 Cash flows are accounted for in the appraisal, rather than cost and revenues as used in the accruals accounting convention. The reason for this is that in accounting for cash flows, receipts and payments are recognized when they occur. This is not the case for the majority of costs and revenues when employing accruals accounting. For example, the cost of an investment will be accrued over the life of the investment employing a system of depreciation. In contrast, the whole of the cost of the investment when accounting for cash flows would be recognized when the payment is made. This was illustrated in Chapter 11 on Cash Flow Statements. In taking account of the time value of money it is important that the cost and benefits of an investment are recognized when they are actually paid and received, rather than when they are recognized as a debt or liability or are accrued, as in the case of capital investment expenditure, over the life of the asset.

The process of discounting

Discounting is compounding in reverse. The following example explains the relationship between discounting and compounding.

Example 20.2

Suppose that a company invests £10 000 to earn a return of 10% (compound interest). The value of the investment with the interest will accumulate as follows.

After one year £10 000 × (1.10) = £11 000
After two years £10 000 × $(1.10)^2$ = £12 100
After three years £10 000 × $(1.10)^3$ = £13 310

and so on. This is compounding. The formula for the future value of an investment including accumulated interest earned after n time-periods is:

$$FV = PV(1 + r)n$$

Where: FV is the future value of the investment with interest.
PV is the initial or present value of the investment.
r is the compound rate of return (reflecting the time value of money) per time period.
n is the number of time periods; normally measured in years.

Discounting converts future values to present values and is the reverse of compounding. For example, if a company expects to earn a (compound) rate of return of 10% on its investments, how much would it need to invest now (the present value of the future sum) to have an investment of:

£11 000 after one year? or
£12 100 after two years? or
£13 310 after three years?

The answer is £10 000 in each case, and we calculate it by discounting, as follows:

$$\text{After one year, £11 000} \times \frac{1}{1.10} = \text{£10 000}$$

$$\text{After two years, £12 000} \times \frac{1}{(1.10)^2} = \text{£10 000}$$

$$\text{After three years, £13 310} \times \frac{1}{(1.10)^3} = \text{£10 000}$$

The discounting formula to calculate the present value of a future sum of money at the end of n time periods is:

$$\text{PV} = \text{FV}\,\frac{1}{(1+r)^n}$$

KEY CONCEPT 20.3
The definition of present value

Present value can be defined as the cash equivalent now of a sum of money receivable or payable at the stated future date, discounted at a specified rate of return.

Discounting can be applied to both money receivable and also to money payable at a future date. And so by discounting all payments and receipts from a capital investment to a present value, they can be compared on a common basis at a value which takes account of when the various cash flows will take place. Example 20.3 illustrates the use of discounted cash flow method in investment appraisal.

Example 20.3

Harvey Ltd is investigating an investment opportunity which will generate £40 000 after two years and another £30 000 after three years.

Its target rate of return is 12%. The present value of these cash inflows is:

Year	*Cash flow*	*Discount factor* 12%	*Present value* £
2	40 000	$\frac{1}{(1.12)^2}$	31 880
3	30 000	$\frac{1}{(1.12)^3}$	21 360
		Total PV	53 240

The present value of the total future inflows of cash, discounted at 12%, is £53 240. This means that if Harvey Ltd can invest now to earn a return of 12% on its investments, it would have to invest £53 240 now to earn £40 000 in two years' time plus £30 000 in three years' time.

In the application of DCF to investment decisions, only future cash flows are relevant. Therefore, the principles detailed in Chapters 17 and 18 relating to decision making are also applicable to long-term investment decisions. Thus, for example, past costs are not relevant because they are sunk, whilst opportunity costs *are* relevant.

In relation to the payback method of investment appraisal, as examined earlier, the yearly cash flows can be discounted. Therefore, by discounting the cash flows the payback method would then take account of the time value of money. When discounting is applied to the payback method, the term 'discounted payback' is commonly used.

We will now consider the two main methods of using DCF to appraise investment opportunities, namely the net present value (NPV) method and the internal rate of return (IRR) method.

The net present value method

Net present value (NPV) is the value obtained by discounting all cash outflows and inflows of an investment opportunity by a chosen rate of return. It was said earlier that the rate of return was directly associated with an individual's, or in the context of business, a firm's, time value of money which will reflect a shareholder's opportunity cost. The opportunity cost in this context is the rate of return shareholders and other providers of capital forgo by investing in the firm. This opportunity cost is commonly referred to as the 'cost of capital'.

The present value of cash inflows minus the present value of the cash outflows is the NPV. Therefore, if the NPV:

- is positive, it means that the cash inflows from the investment will yield a return in excess of the cost of capital, and therefore the investment project should be undertaken. In this situation it can be seen that the business can pay its providers of capital the necessary returns and still have cash to employ in the business;
- is negative, it means that the cash inflows from the investment will

yield a return less than that required to satisfy the providers of capital, and therefore the opportunity should be rejected;
- is exactly zero, it means that the investment has generated exactly the required returns to satisfy the providers of capital, without any surplus to employ in the business.

The discount factor that was calculated using the formula $1/(1 + r)^n$ can be more conveniently determined by simply using discount tables. The discount tables for the present value of £1, for differing values of r and n, are given in the appendix at the end of this book.

Example 20.4 illustrates the use of the NPV method using present value tables.

Example 20.4

Benaud Ltd is considering a capital investment, where the estimated cash flows are:

Year	*Cash flow* £
0 (i.e. now)	(100 000)
1	60 000
2	80 000
3	40 000
4	30 000

The company's cost of capital is 15%. What is the NPV of the proposed project, and should it be undertaken?

Solution

Year	*Cash flow* £	*Discount factor at 15%*	*Present value* £
0	(100 000)	1.000	(100 000)
1	60 000	0.870	52 200
2	80 000	0.756	60 480
3	40 000	0.658	26 320
4	30 000	0.572	17 160
		NPV	56 160

The present value of cash inflows exceeds the present value of cash outflows by £56 160, which means that the project produces a DCF yield in excess of 15%. The project should therefore be undertaken.

In using DCF methods for investment appraisal, there are some important conventions to note regarding the timing of cash flows; these are:

1 A cash flow at the beginning of an investment project, described in the example above as 'now', is assumed to occur in year 0. The present value of £1 now, in year 0 is

$$\frac{1}{(1+r)^n} = \frac{1}{(1+r)^0} = £1, \text{ regardless of the value of } r.$$

Therefore, as in the example above, the discount factor to use for cash flows arising in year 0 is 1.0.

2 A cash inflow or outflow that occurs during the course of a year rather than at the year end is assumed to happen at the end of the year. For example, £2000 received half-way through the year is assumed to be received at the end of that year. This convention is adopted because of the complexity of discounting sums throughout time periods. Given the uncertainty relating to the future, it is considered that whilst the calculation does not result in an absolutely precise present value, it is a reasonable approximation of reality.

Annuities

Where there are constant cash flows arising at annual intervals for a number of years (known as annuities), time can be saved by using annuity tables, which are also in the appendix to this book. Example 20.5 illustrates the use of annuity tables as well as some of the other aspects that are pertinent to decision making using DCF techniques.

Example 20.5

Marsh plc is a manufacturing company whose management are currently appraising the production and sale of a new product. This would involve the purchase of a new machine costing £240 000 as well as using an old machine purchased for £80 000 five years ago which currently has a net book value of £60 000. There is sufficient capacity on this machine to support the production of this new product with the new machine.

Annual sales of the product would be 5000 units at a selling price of £32 per unit. Unit costs would be:

	£
Direct labour (2 hours at £4 per hour)	8
Direct materials	7
Fixed costs including depreciation	9
	24

The project would have a five-year life, after which the new machine would have a residual value of £10 000. The fixed overhead absorption rate is estimated to be £4.50 per hour, but actual expenditure would not alter should the company decide not to produce this new product.

Working capital requirements would be £10 000 at the beginning of the first year, rising to £15 000 in the second year and remaining at this level until the end of the project, when it would be recovered.

The company's cost of capital is 20%. Ignore taxation. Should the company accept this opportunity?

Solution

The NPV is calculated as follows.

Years	*Equipment*	*Working capital*	*Contribution*	*Net cash flow*	*Discount rate*	*Present value*
	£	£	£	£		£
0	(240 000)	(10 000)		(250 000)	1.000	(250 000)
1		(5 000)		(5 000)	0.833	(4 165)
1–5			85 000	85 000	2.991	254 235
5	10 000	15 000		25 000	0.402	10 050
				NPV =		10 120

Notes and commentary

1 The NPV is positive and therefore should be accepted.
2 Purchase of the new machine in Year 0 for £240 000 is an incremental cost which is therefore a relevant cost.
3 The cost of using the old machine is nil – the original cost and the current net book value are irrelevant costs as they are sunk and there appears to be no opportunity cost associated with using this machine.
4 The investment of working capital is a relevant cost because the company will forgo the possibility of being able to invest this money elsewhere for the life of the project. The amount invested as working capital is £10 000 at the beginning of the project, rising to £15 000 at the beginning of year 2. That is £5000 additional investment at the beginning of year 2, which for discounting purposes we can assume arises at the end of year 1. The full £15 000 is recoverable at the end of the projects life.
5 The contribution from the new product – 5000 units × £17(£32 – 15) = £85 000 per year. The fixed costs, because they are unavoidable and will not change whether the project is accepted or rejected, are irrelevant. This cash inflow will not change over the five-year period and therefore we can use the annuity tables in determining the present value of these cash flows.
6 The annuity discount factor can be obtained from the table – the present value of an annuity; where n is five years and r is 20%, the factor is 2.991. This discount factor is simply the sum of the individual factors for each of the five years where r is 20% from the present value tables. By multiplying the annual contribution of £85 000 per annum, we obtain the present value of this annuity.

Perpetuities

A perpetuity is an annuity which is expected to last indefinitely – for example, undated government stocks where a fixed rate of interest is received annually but where the capital is unlikely to be repaid. Often perpetuities are used to approximate perceived long time-spans, for example, for calculating the present value of anticipated returns on an investment that will be held for the foreseeable future. Another example is the revenue generated from the toll on the Dartford tunnel and bridge, which will continue for the foreseeable future.

The present value of any perpetuity is given by the annual receipt or payment, divided by the relevant discount rate. For example, the PV of £1 per annum in perpetuity at a discount rate of 10% would be £1/0.10 = £10. Similarly, the present value of £1 per annum in perpetuity at a discount rate of:

$$15\% \text{ would be } \frac{£1}{0.15} = £6.67$$

$$20\% \text{ would be } \frac{£1}{0.20} = £5$$

To apply the present value of £1 per annum in perpetuity to an investment evaluation, we simply multiply the total cash outflow or inflow by the sum of present value of £1 per annum in perpetuity. So, if it is anticipated that the revenue from the tolls at the Dartford tunnel and bridge are to generate inflows of cash of say £10 million pounds per annum for the foreseeable future at a discount rate of 15%, the present value of these streams of cash flows would be:

$$\frac{£1}{0.15} \times £10 \text{ million} = £66.7 \text{ million.}$$

Internal rate of return (IRR) method

The internal rate of return (IRR) is the second investment appraisal method based on discounted cash flow techniques. Whilst a number of the principles applicable to IRR are similar to the NPV method, there is a notable difference in the final outcome and the decision criteria. In the application of the IRR method it is necessary to calculate the exact DCF rate of return which an investment opportunity is expected to achieve, that is the rate of return at which the NPV is equal to 0, and compare this with a target rate, which should be the project's cost of capital. If the expected rate of return exceeds the target rate of return, the project should be undertaken. Conversely, if the expected rate of return is less than the target the opportunity should be rejected.

Without a computer or a programmed calculator, the calculation of the internal rate of return is made by a trial and error technique called interpolation. The first step is to calculate two present values, both as close as possible to zero. The closer to zero, the more accurate will be the end result. Ideally in applying these two rates the result should be one NPV being positive and the other negative. It is then necessary to use interpolation to establish the rate where NPV is 0. Example 20.6 illustrates the process.

Example 20.6

A company is investigating an opportunity to buy a machine for £80 000 now which, it is anticipated, will save £20 000 per annum for five years.

It is also anticipated that the machine will have a resale value of £10 000.

We begin by selecting a trial rate, say 9% (note that in this calculation we can use both the PV tables and the annuity tables):

Year	*Cash flow* £	*PV factor at 9%*	*Present value* £
0	(80 000)	1.0	(80 000)
1–5	20 000	3.890	77 800
5	10 000	0.650	6 500
		NPV	4 300

£4300 is fairly close to 0, considering the amounts we are computing. We can therefore use 9% as one of the two rates necessary for the calculation of the IRR. In addition, the NPV is positive which means that the real rate of return, where NPV is 0, is higher than 9%. We could now try, say 12%:

Year	*Cash flow* £	*PV factor at 9%*	*Present value* £
0	(80 000)	1.0	(80 000)
1–5	20 000	3.605	72 100
5	10 000	0.567	5 670
		NPV	(2 230)

This NPV is also fairly close to zero and negative. The real rate of return is therefore greater than 9% (NPV = +4300) but less than 12% (NPV = −2230).

The interpolation method assumes that the NPV rises in a linear fashion between the two NPVs. The formula to apply is:

$$\text{Rate of return} = \text{A} + \left[\frac{\text{P}}{\text{P} + \text{N}} \times (\text{B} - \text{A})\right]$$

Where A is the (lower) rate of return with a positive NPV.
B is the (higher) rate of return with a negative NPV.
P is the amount of the positive NPV.
N is the amount of the negative NPV.

Now applying this formula to the data calculated for the project we can calculate the IRR:

$$\text{IRR} = 9\% + \left[\frac{4300}{4300 + 2230} \times (12 - 9)\right]\%$$
$$= 10.\ 98\%, \text{ say } 11\%$$

If the cost of capital is, say, 10% we would accept the project because its IRR is greater; if, on the other hand, the cost of capital is 15%, we would not accept this project.

The concept of accounting for the time value of money through using the cost of capital as a discount rate is appealing from a number of perspectives. There are, however, problems in determining the correct discount rate. The cost of capital for an individual project should take account of the risk associated with the project. It is often difficult to measure precisely the risk for individual projects. A detailed discussion of the ways in which the cost of capital can be determined and in particular their problems can be found in a number of financial management texts, including Lumby (1991).

Case study 20.2 examines an investment opportunity and employs all four investment appraisal methods in determining an outcome.

It was stated earlier that the accounting rate of return (ARR) and the payback methods of investment appraisal each suffer from serious disadvantages. One ignores the timing of cash flows whilst the other does not take account of all the relevant cash flows, that is after the payback period. The DCF methods which we have examined both take account of the timing of cash flows and all the relevant cash flows.

By discounting relevant cash flows by the cost of capital and only accepting opportunities that exceed this return, both DCF methods ensure that shareholders' wealth is maximized. Research suggests that of these two DCF methods of investment appraisal, in practice IRR is favoured. The main explanation given for this preference is that managers appear to prefer to talk in relative percentage terms, rather than absolute sums of money, as in the outcome for NPV decisions. However, although in the majority of situations both the NPV and IRR methods of appraisal will give the same decision, there are occasions, namely when considering mutually exclusive projects, where the two methods are incompatible. In these circumstances the NPV should be used. A full discussion of why the NPV method is preferred can be found in *Investment Appraisal and Financing Decisions* by Lumby.

It can be argued, however, that all the methods have certain attributes, although the DCF methods are arguably the most rigorous from a theoretical perspective.

In many situations, long-term opportunities will either be accepted or rejected, based purely on financial criteria, through the employment of one or more of the methods that we have examined in this chapter. However, it will also be the case that qualitative factors, that is factors which cannot be explicitly quantified in money terms, will be influential and sometimes overriding in a situation. Examples of qualitative factors are given in Chapter 18. Although this chapter has focused on short-term decision making, the nature of the qualitative factors is likely to be similar.

CASE STUDY 20.2
Holefoods Ltd

Holefoods Ltd, an expanding catering firm, are considering tendering for a local authority contract to supply school meals. If they decide to tender and are successful, this will be their first contract in the public sector. The contract is for a period of five years.

The company has spent £2500 on a feasibility study related to this contract. From this study they have obtained the following estimates of costs, revenues and volumes.

1 The initial cost of the investment for the necessary cooking equipment will be £30 000. This sum will be payable at the beginning of the contract.
2 Selling price of meals: £1.00 per meal for the first three years, then £1.20 for years 4 and 5.
3 Cost of meals: £0.60 per meal for the first three years, then £0.70 for years 4 and 5.
4 Rent of premises is estimated to be £2000 per year.
5 Forecast of the number of meals to be sold:

Year	*No. of meals*
1	30 000
2	32 000
3	32 000
4	33 000
5	33 000

6 Transport costs: £2000 per year.
7 The company uses straight line depreciation and intends to charge £1500.
8 The company's cost of capital is 14%.
9 The company expects a payback within four years and its target accounting rate of return is 25%.

Calculate: The NPV, IRR, Payback period (undiscounted and discounted) and the ARR.

Solution

NPV

The £2500 spent on the feasibility study is considered to be irrelevant to the decision.

Years	*0*	*1*	*2*	*3*	*4*	*5*
	£	£	£	£	£	£
Cost of equipment	(30 000)					
Sales		30 000	32 000	32 000	39 600	39 600
Cost of meals		(18 000)	(19 200)	(19 200)	(23 100)	(23 100)
Transport costs		(2 000)	(2 000)	(2 000)	(2 000)	(2 000)
Rent		(2 000)	(2 000)	(2 000)	(2 000)	(2 000)
Cash flow	(30 000)	8 000	8 800	8 800	12 500	12 500
Cost of capital 14%	1.00	0.877	0.769	0.675	0.592	0.519
Net cash flow	(30 000)	7 016	6 767	5 940	7 400	6 487

Total NPV = +3610

Therefore under the NPV decision rule, accept the proposed project.

IRR

At 14% the NPV was positive £4389, therefore, the IRR, where the NPV is 0, must be greater than 14%; so lets try 20%. (Note that we only need to discount the cash flows):

	0	1	2	3	4	5
Cash flow	(30 000)	8 000	8 800	8 800	12 500	12 500
Cost of capital 20%	1.00	0.833	0.694	0.578	0.482	0.402
Net cash flow	(30 000)	6 644	6 107	5 086	6 025	5 025

Total NPV = −1113

Using interpolation the IRR =

$$14\% + \left[\frac{£3610}{£3610 + 1113} \times (20\% - 14\%)\right] = 18.59\%$$

The IRR of the project exceeds the cost of capital, therefore the project will be accepted.

Payback

Undiscounted:

Year	*Cash flows*	*Cumulative cash flow*
0	(30 000)	(30 000)
1	8 000	(22 000)
2	8 800	(13 200)
3	8 800	(4 400)
4	12 500	8 100

Therefore, the project pays back in the third year; more precisely £4440/£12 500 × 12 months = 3 years 4.2 months (assuming the cash flows arise evenly throughout the year). As this period is less than four years, the target payback period, we would accept the project.

Discounted: Using the discounted cash flow figures in the NPV calculation above based on a 14% cost of capital, the payback profile is as follows:

Year	*Cash flows*	*Cumulative cash flow*
	£	£
0	(30 000)	(30 000)
1	7 016	(22 984)
2	6 767	(16 217)
3	5 940	(10 277)
4	7 400	(2 877)
5	6 487	3 610

Therefore, the project pays back in the fifth year; more precisely £3610/£6487 × 12 months = 4 years and 6.7 months.

Accounting Rate of Return

Depreciation based on straight-line depreciation convention: £30 000/5 years = £6000 per annum; £6000 p.a. needs to be deducted from the undiscounted cash flows per annum, £30 000 (£6000 × 5 years) over the total life of the project. The sum of the undiscounted cash inflows from the project is £50 600 less £30 000 = £20 600; and the average annual returns = £20 600/5 years = £4120.

The average investment is £15 000 [(£30 000 + 0)/2]

$$\text{ARR} = \frac{£4120}{£15\,000} \times 100 = 27.5\%$$

The ARR of 27.5% is greater than the target of 25%, therefore the project is acceptable under this criterion.

Summary

In this chapter we have examined the four main financial methods of investment appraisal: accounting rate of return, payback, net present value and the internal rate of return. For each of the methods we looked at the use of the methods within a business decision making environment. The attributes of all the methods were considered. It was argued that all the methods have some use within the decision making process; this explains why a number of companies employ all four methods.

The concept of the time value of money was discussed and the processing of discounting was examined within the context of long-term decision making. Although discounted cash flow methods are relatively more theoretically rigorous, there are problems in determining the cost of capital, the discount rate.

References

Lumby, S. (1991) *Investment Appraisal and Financing Decisions*, 4th edn, Chapman and Hall.

Further reading

An interesting analysis of the use of investment appraisal methods is published by The Chartered Institute of Management Accountants in their Occasional Paper Series entitled, *Capital Budgeting for the 1990s*, by Richard Pike and Mitchell Wolfe.

Review Questions

1 Explain the main differences between DCF methods of investment appraisal and ARR.
2 Discuss the main attributes of the ARR and payback methods.
3 What is the meant by discounting cash flow? Why is it necessary to discount cash flows?
4 In the employment of DCF investment appraisal methods, explain why cash flows are used rather than accounting profits.
5 What is the effect on the value of the firm and shareholders' wealth if an investment opportunity with an NPV of £5000 is accepted?

Problems for discussion and analysis

1 The management of Boon and Border Plc are in the process of examining the company's investment opportunities. There are six

opportunities; the following details provide the relevant information regarding these opportunities.

Project A would cost £29 000 now, and would generate the following cash flows:

Year	£
1	8 000
2	12 000
3	10 000
4	6 000

The equipment included in the cost of the investment could be resold for £5000 at the start of year 5.

Project B would involve a current outlay of £44 000 on capital equipment and £20 000 on working capital. The profits from the project would be as follows:

Year	*Sales*	*Variable costs*	*Contribution*	*Fixed cost*	*Profit*
	£	£	£	£	£
1	75 000	50 000	25 000	10 000	15 000
2	90 000	60 000	30 000	10 000	20 000
3	42 000	28 000	14 000	8 000	6 000

Fixed costs include an annual charge of £4000 for depreciation; all the other fixed costs are avoidable. At the end of year 3 the working capital investment would be recovered and the equipment would be sold for £5000.

Project C would involve a current outlay of £50 000 on equipment and £15 000 on working capital. The investment in working capital would be increased to £21 000 at the end of the first year. Annual cash profits would be £18 000 per annum for five years, at the end of which the investment in working capital would be recovered.

Project D would involve an outlay of £20 000 now and a further outlay of £20 000 after one year. Cash profits thereafter would be as follows:

Year	£
2	15 000
3	12 000
4–8	8 000 p.a.

Project E is a long-term project involving an immediate outlay of £32 000 and annual cash profits of £4500 p.a. in perpetuity.

Project F is another long-term project, involving an immediate outlay of £20 000 and annual cash profits as follows:

Years	£
1–5	5 000
6–10	4 000
11 in perpetuity	3 000

The company discounts all projects of 10 years' duration or less at a cost of capital of 12%, and all longer projects at a cost of 15%.

Required:

(a) Calculate the NPV of each project, and determine which should be undertaken by the company.

(b) Calculate the IRR of projects A, C and E.

(c) Calculate the discounted and non-discounted payback periods of project A.

(d) Calculate the accounting rate of return.

2 The Waugh Electronics Company Ltd is thinking of buying, at a cost of £22 000, some new quality control equipment that is expected to save £5000 in cash operating costs. Its estimated useful life is 10 years, and it will have a zero disposal value.

Calculate:

(a) Internal rate of return.

(b) Net present value if the cost of capital is 16%.

(c) Payback period.

(d) Accounting rate of return based on initial investment and on average investment.

3 Dr Oliver has £1000 which he will decide to invest if he can be reasonably confident that his investment will earn at least 10% p.a. He is considering three projects, each of which would cost £1000 to begin:

(a) Project A would earn £1090 at the end of the first year.

(b) Project B would earn £1250 at the end of the second year.

(c) Project C would earn £700 at the end of the first year, and another £700 at the end of the second year.

Advise Dr Oliver.

Periods (n)	Interest rates (%) 1	2	3	4	5	6	7	8	9	10	11	12	13	14	15	
1	0·9901	0·9804	0·9709	0·9615	0·9524	0·9434	0·9346	0·9259	0·9174	0·9091	0·9009	0·8929	0·8850	0·8772	0·8696	1
2	0·9803	0·9612	0·9426	0·9246	0·9070	0·8900	0·8734	0·8573	0·8417	0·8264	0·8116	0·7972	0·7831	0·7895	0·7561	2
3	0·9706	0·9423	0·9151	0·8990	0·8638	0·8396	0·8163	0·7938	0·7722	0·7513	0·7312	0·7118	0·6931	0·6750	0·6575	3
4	0·9610	0·9238	0·8885	0·8548	0·8227	0·7921	0·7629	0·7350	0·7084	0·6830	0·6587	0·6355	0·6133	0·5921	0·5718	4
5	0·9515	0·9057	0·8626	0·8219	0·7835	0·7473	0·7130	0·6806	0·6499	0·6209	0·6935	0·5674	0·5428	0·5194	0·4972	5
6	0·9420	0·8880	0·8375	0·7903	0·7462	0·7050	0·6663	0·6302	0·5963	0·5645	0·5346	0·5066	0·4803	0·4556	0·4323	6
7	0·9327	0·8706	0·8131	0·7599	0·7107	0·6651	0·6227	0·5835	0·5470	0·5132	0·4817	0·4523	0·4251	0·3996	0·3759	7
8	0·9235	0·8535	0·7894	0·7307	0·6768	0·6274	0·5820	0·5403	0·5019	0·4665	0·4339	0·4039	0·3762	0·3506	0·3269	8
9	0·9143	0·8368	0·7664	0·7026	0·6446	0·5919	0·5439	0·5002	0·4604	0·4241	0·3909	0·3606	0·3329	0·3075	0·2843	9
10	0·9053	0·8203	0·7441	0·6756	0·6139	0·5584	0·5083	0·4632	0·4224	0·3855	0·3522	0·3220	0·2946	0·2697	0·2472	10
11	0·8963	0·8043	0·7224	0·6496	0·5847	0·5268	0·4751	0·4289	0·3875	0·3505	0·3173	0·2875	0·2607	0·2366	0·2149	11
12	0·8874	0·7885	0·7014	0·6246	0·5568	0·4970	0·4440	0·3971	0·3555	0·3186	0·2858	0·2567	0·2307	0·2076	0·1869	12
13	0·8787	0·7730	0·6611	0·5775	0·5051	0·4423	0·3878	0·3405	0·2992	0·2633	0·2320	0·2046	0·1807	0·1597	0·1413	14
15	0·8613	0·7430	0·6419	0·5553	0·4810	0·4173	0·3624	0·3152	0·2745	0·2394	0·2090	0·1827	0·1599	0·1401	0·1229	15
16	0·8528	0·7284	0·6232	0·5339	0·4581	0·3936	0·3387	0·2919	0·2519	0·2176	0·1883	0·1631	0·1415	0·1229	0·1069	16
17	0·8444	0·7142	0·6050	0·5134	0·4363	0·3714	0·3166	0·2703	0·2311	0·1978	0·1696	0·1456	0·1252	0·1078	0·0929	17
18	0·8360	0·7002	0·5874	0·4936	0·4155	0·3503	0·2959	0·2502	0·2120	0·1799	0·1528	0·1300	0·1108	0·0946	0·0808	18
19	0·8277	0·6864	0·5703	0·4746	0·3957	0·3305	0·2765	0·2317	0·1945	0·1635	0·1377	0·1161	0·0981	0·0829	0·0703	19
20	0·8195	0·6730	0·5537	0·4564	0·3769	0·3118	0·2584	0·2145	0·1784	0·1486	0·1240	0·1037	0·0868	0·0728	0·0611	20
25	0·7795	0·6095	0·4776	0·3751	0·2953	0·2330	0·1842	0·1460	0·1160	0·0923	0·0736	0·0588	0·0471	0·0378	0·0304	25
30	0·7419	0·5521	0·4120	0·3083	0·2314	0·1741	0·1314	0·0994	0·0754	0·0573	0·0437	0·0334	0·0256	0·0196	0·0151	30
35	0·7059	0·5000	0·3554	0·2534	0·1813	0·1301	0·0937	0·0676	0·0490	0·0356	0·0259	0·0189	0·0139	0·0102	0·0075	35
40	0·6717	0·4529	0·3066	0·2083	0·1420	0·0972	0·0668	0·0460	0·0318	0·0221	0·0154	0·0107	0·0075	0·0053	0·0037	40
45	0·6391	0·4102	0·2644	0·1407	0·1113	0·0727	0·0476	0·0313	0·0207	0·0137	0·0091	0·0061	0·0041	0·0027	0·0019	45
50	0·6080	0·3715	0·2281		0·0872	0·0543	0·0339	0·0213	0·0134	0·0085	0·0054	0·0035	0·0022	0·0014	0·0009	50

	16	17	18	19	20	21	22	23	24	25	26	27	28	29	30	
1	0·8621	0·8547	0·8475	0·8403	0·8333	0·8264	0·8197	0·8130	0·8065	0·8000	0·7937	0·7874	0·7812	0·7752	0·7692	1
2	0·7432	0·7305	0·7182	0·7062	0·6944	0·6830	0·6719	0·6610	0·6504	0·6400	0·6299	0·6200	0·6104	0·6009	0·5917	2
3	0·6407	0·6244	0·6086	0·4934	0·5787	0·5645	0·5507	0·5374	0·5245	0·5120	0·4999	0·4882	0·4768	0·4658	0·4552	3
4	0·5523	0·5337	0·5158	0·4987	0·4823	0·4665	0·4514	0·4369	0·4230	0·4096	0·3968	0·3844	0·3725	0·3611	0·3501	4
5	0·4761	0·4561	0·4371	0·4190	0·4019	0·3855	0·3700	0·3552	0·3411	0·3277	0·3149	0·3027	0·2910	0·2799	0·2693	5
6	0·4104	0·3898	0·3704	0·3521	0·3349	0·3186	0·3033	0·2888	0·2751	0·2621	0·2499	0·2383	0·2274	0·2170	0·2072	6
7	0·3538	0·3332	0·3139	0·2959	0·2791	0·2633	0·2486	0·2348	0·2218	0·2097	0·1983	0·1877	0·1776	0·1682	0·1594	7
8	0·3050	0·2848	0·2660	0·2487	0·2326	0·2176	0·2038	0·1909	0·1789	0·1678	0·1574	0·1478	0·1388	0·1304	0·1226	8
9	0·2630	0·2434	0·2255	0·2090	0·1938	0·1799	0·1670	0·1552	0·1443	0·1342	0·1249	0·1164	0·1084	0·1011	0·0943	9
10	0·2267	0·2080	0·1911	0·1756	0·1615	0·1486	0·1369	0·1262	0·1164	0·1074	0·0992	0·0916	0·0847	0·0784	0·0725	10
11	0·1954	0·1778	0·1619	0·1476	0·1346	0·1228	0·1122	0·1026	0·0938	0·0859	0·0787	0·0721	0·0662	0·0607	0·0558	11
12	0·1685	0·1520	0·1372	0·1240	0·1122	0·1015	0·0920	0·0834	0·0757	0·0687	0·0625	0·0568	0·0517	0·0471	0·0429	12
13	0·1452	0·1299	0·1163	0·1042	0·0935	0·0839	0·0754	0·0678	0·0610	0·0550	0·0496	0·0447	0·0404	0·0365	0·0330	13
14	0·1252	0·1110	0·0985	0·0876	0·0779	0·0693	0·0618	0·0551	0·0492	0·0440	0·0393	0·0352	0·0316	0·0283	0·0254	14
15	0·1079	0·0949	0·0835	0·0736	0·0649	0·0573	0·0507	0·0448	0·0397	0·0352	0·0312	0·0277	0·0247	0·0219	0·0195	15
16	0·0930	0·0811	0·0708	0·0618	0·0541	0·0474	0·0415	0·0364	0·0320	0·0281	0·0248	0·0218	0·0193	0·0170	0·0150	16
17	0·0802	0·0693	0·0600	0·0520	0·0451	0·0391	0·0340	0·0296	0·0258	0·0225	0·0197	0·0172	0·0150	0·0132	0·0116	17
18	0·0691	0·0592	0·0508	0·0437	0·0376	0·0323	0·0279	0·0241	0·0208	0·0180	0·0156	0·0135	0·0118	0·0102	0·0089	18
19	0·0596	0·0506	0·0431	0·0367	0·0313	0·0267	0·0229	0·0196	0·0168	0·0144	0·0124	0·0107	0·0092	0·0079	0·0068	19
20	0·0514	0·0433	0·0365	0·0308	0·0261	0·0221	0·0187	0·0159	0·0135	0·0115	0·0098	0·0084	0·0072	0·0061	0·0053	20
25	0·0245	0·0197	0·0160	0·0129	0·0105	0·0085	0·0069	0·0057	0·0046	0·0038	0·0031	0·0025	0·0021	0·0017	0·0014	25
30	0·0116	0·0090	0·0070	0·0054	0·0042	0·0033	0·0026	0·0020	0·0016	0·0012	0·0010	0·0008	0·0006	0·0005	0·0004	30
35	0·0055	0·0041	0·0030	0·0023	0·0017	0·0013	0·0009	0·0007	0·0005	0·0004	0·0003	0·0002	0·0002	0·0001	0·0001	35
40	0·0026	0·0019	0·0013	0·0010	0·0007	0·0005	0·0004	0·0003	0·0002	0·0001	0·0001	0·0001	0·0001	0·0000	0·0000	40
45	0·0013	0·0009	0·0006	0·0004	0·0003	0·0002	0·0001	0·0001	0·0001	0·0000	0·0000	0·0000	0·0000	0·0000	0·0000	45
50	0·0006	0·0004	0·0003	0·0002	0·0001	0·0001	0·0000	0·0000	0·0000	0·0000	0·0000	0·0000	0·0000	0·0000	0·0000	50

Amount of £1 at compound interest: $(1 + r)^n$

Periods (*n*)	Interest rates (*r*) 1	2	3	4	5	6	7	8	9	10	11	12	13	14	15	
1	1·0100	1·0200	1·0300	1·0400	1·0500	1·0600	1·0700	1·0800	1·0900	1·1000	1·1100	1·1200	1·1300	1·1400	1·1500	1
2	1·0201	1·0404	1·0609	1·0816	1·1025	1·1236	1·1449	1·1664	1·1881	1·2100	1·2321	1·2544	1·2769	1·2996	1·3225	2
3	1·0303	1·0612	1·0927	1·1249	1·1576	1·1910	1·2250	1·2597	1·2950	1·3310	1·3676	1·4049	1·4429	1·4815	1·5209	3
4	1·0406	1·0824	1·1255	1·1699	1·2155	1·2625	1·3108	1·3605	1·4116	1·4641	1·5181	1·5735	1·6305	1·6890	1·7490	4
5	1·0510	1·1041	1·1593	1·2167	1·2763	1·3382	1·4026	1·4693	1·5386	1·6105	1·6851	1·7623	1·8424	1·9254	2·0114	5
6	1·0615	1·1262	1·1941	1·2653	1·3401	1·4185	1·5007	1·5869	1·6771	1·7716	1·8704	1·9738	2·0820	2·1950	2·3131	6
7	1·0721	1·1487	1·2299	1·3159	1·4071	1·5036	1·6058	1·7138	1·8280	1·9487	2·0762	2·2107	2·3526	2·5023	2·6600	7
8	1·0829	1·1717	1·2668	1·3686	1·4775	1·5938	1·7182	1·8509	1·9926	2·1436	2·3045	2·4760	2·6584	2·8526	3·0590	8
9	1·0937	1·1951	1·3048	1·4233	1·5513	1·6895	1·8385	1·9990	2·1719	2·3579	2·5580	2·7731	3·0040	3·2519	3·5179	9
10	1·1046	1·2190	1·3439	1·4802	1·6289	1·7908	1·9672	2·1589	2·3674	2·5937	2·8394	3·1058	3·3946	3·7072	4·0456	10
11	1·1157	1·2434	1·3842	1·5395	1·7103	·8983	2·1049	2·3316	2·5804	2·8531	3·1518	3·4785	3·8359	4·2262	4·6524	11
12	1·1268	1·2682	1·4258	1·6010	1·7959	2·0122	2·2522	2·5182	2·8127	3·1384	3·4985	3·8906	4·3345	4·8179	5·3503	12
13	1·1381	1·2936	1·4685	1·6651	1·8856	2·1329	2·4098	2·7196	3·0658	3·4523	3·8833	4·3635	4·8980	5·4924	6·1528	13
14	1·1495	1·3195	1·5126	1·7317	1·9799	2·2609	2·5785	2·9372	3·3417	3·7975	4·3104	4·8871	5·5348	6·2613	7·0757	14
15	1·1610	1·3459	1·5580	1·8009	2·0789	2·3966	2·7590	3·1722	3·6425	4·1772	4·7846	5·4736	6·2543	7·1379	8·1371	15
16	1·1726	1·3728	1·6047	1·8730	2·1829	2·5404	2·9522	3·4259	3·9703	4·5950	5·3109	6·1304	7·0673	8·1372	9·3576	16
17	1·1843	1·4002	1·6528	1·9479	2·2920	2·6928	3·1588	3·7000	4·3276	5·0545	5·8951	6·8660	7·9861	9·2765	10·7613	17
18	1·1961	1·4282	1·7024	2·0258	2·4066	2·8543	3·3799	3·9960	4·7171	5·5599	6·5436	7·6900	9·0243	10·5752	12·3755	18
19	1·2081	1·4568	1·7535	2·1068	2·5270	3·0256	3·6165	4·3157	5·1417	6·1159	7·2633	8·6128	10·1974	12·0557	14·2318	19
20	1·2202	1·4859	1·8061	2·1911	2·6533	3·2071	3·8697	4·6610	5·6044	6·7275	8·0623	9·6463	11·5231	13·7435	16·3665	20
25	1·2824	1·6406	2·0938	2·6658	3·3864	4·2919	5·4274	6·8485	8·6231	10·8347	13·5855	17·0001	21·2305	26·4619	32·9190	25

	16	17	18	19	20	21	22	23	24	25	26	27	28	29	30	
1	1·1600	1·1700	1·1800	1·1900	1·2000	1·2100	1·2200	1·2300	1·2400	1·2500	1·2600	1·2700	1·2800	1·2900	1·3000	1
2	1·3456	1·3689	1·3924	1·4161	1·4400	1·4641	1·4884	1·5129	1·5376	1·5625	1·5876	1·6129	1·6384	1·6641	1·6900	2
3	1·5609	1·6016	1·6430	1·6852	1·7280	1·7716	1·8158	1·8609	1·9066	1·9531	2·0004	2·0484	2·0972	2·1467	2·1970	3
4	1·8106	1·8739	1·9388	2·0053	2·0736	2·1436	2·2153	2·2889	2·3642	2·4414	2·5205	2·6014	2·6844	2·7692	2·8561	4
5	2·1003	2·1924	2·2878	2·3864	2·4883	2·5937	2·7027	2·8153	2·9316	3·0518	3·1758	3·3038	3·4360	3·5723	3·7129	5
6	2·4364	2·5652	2·6996	2·8398	2·9860	3·1384	3·2973	3·4628	3·6352	3·8147	4·0015	4·1959	4·3980	4·6083	4·8268	6
7	2·8262	3·0012	3·1855	3·3793	3·5832	3·7975	4·0227	4·2593	4·5077	4·7684	5·0419	5·3288	5·6295	5·9447	6·2749	7
8	3·2784	3·5115	3·7589	4·0214	4·2998	4·5950	4·9077	5·2389	5·5895	5·9605	6·3528	6·7675	7·2058	7·6686	8·1573	8
9	3·8030	4·1804	4·4355	4·7854	5·1598	5·5599	5·9874	6·4439	6·9310	7·4506	8·0045	8·5946	9·2234	9·8925	10·6045	9
10	4·4114	4·8068	5·2338	5·6947	6·1917	6·7275	7·3046	7·9259	8·5944	9·3132	10·0857	10·9153	11·8059	12·7614	13·7858	10
11	5·1173	5·6240	6·1759	6·7767	7·4301	8·1403	8·9117	9·7489	10·6571	11·6415	12·7080	13·8625	15·1116	16·4622	17·9216	11
12	5·9360	6·5801	7·2876	8·0642	8·9497	10·8722	11·9912	13·2148	14·5519	16·0120	17·6053	19·3428	21·2362	23·2981	23·2981	12
13	6·8858	7·6987	8·5994	9·5964	10·6993	11·9182	13·2641	14·7491	16·3863	18·1899	20·1752	22·3588	24·7588	27·3947	30·2875	13
14	7·9875	9·0075	10·1472	11·4198	12·8392	14·4210	16·1822	18·1414	20·3191	22·7374	25·4207	28·3957	31·6913	35·3391	39·3738	14
15	9·2655	10·5387	11·9737	13·5895	15·4070	17·4494	19·7423	22·3140	25·1956	28·4217	32·0301	36·0625	40·5648	45·5875	51·1859	15
16	10·7480	12·3303	14·1290	16·1715	18·4884	21·1138	24·0856	27·4462	31·2426	35·6271	40·3579	45·7994	51·9230	58·8079	66·5417	16
17	12·4677	14·4265	16·6722	19·2441	22·1861	25·5477	29·3844	33·7588	38·7408	44·4089	50·8510	58·1652	66·4614	75·8821	86·5042	17
18	14·4625	16·8790	19·6733	22·9005	26·6233	30·9127	35·8490	41·5233	48·0386	55·5112	64·0722	73·8698	85·0706	97·8822	112·4554	18
19	16·7765	19·7484	23·2144	27·2516	31·9480	37·4043	43·7358	51·0737	59·5679	69·3889	80·7310	93·8147	108·8904	126·2422	146·1920	19
20	19·4608	23·1056	27·3930	32·4294	38·3376	45·2593	53·3576	62·8206	73·8641	86·7362	101·7211	119·1446	139·3797	162·8524	190·0496	20
25	40·8742	50·6578	62·6686	77·3881	95·3962	117·3909	144·2101	176·8593	216·5420	264·6978	323·0454	393·6344	478·9049	581·7585	705·6410	25

Periods (n)	Interest rates (%) 1	2	3	4	5	6	7	8	9	10	11	12	13	14	15	
1	0·9901	0·9804	0·9709	0·9615	0·9524	0·9434	0·9346	0·9259	0·9174	0·9091	0·9009	0·8929	0·8850	0·8772	0·8696	1
2	1·9704	1·9416	1·9135	1·8861	1·8594	1·8334	1·8080	1·7833	1·7591	1·7355	1·7125	1·6901	1·6681	1·6467	1·6257	2
3	2·9410	2·8839	2·8286	2·7751	2·7232	2·6730	2·6243	2·5771	2·5313	2·4869	2·4437	2·4018	2·3612	2·3216	2·2832	3
4	3·9020	3·8077	3·7171	3·6299	3·5460	3·4651	3·3872	3·3121	3·2397	3·1699	3·1024	3·0373	2·9745	2·9137	2·8550	4
5	4·8534	4·7135	4·5797	4·4518	4·3295	4·2124	4·1002	3·9927	3·8897	3·7908	3·6959	3·6048	3·5172	3·4331	3·3522	5
6	5·7955	5·6014	5·4172	5·2421	5·0757	4·9173	4·7665	4·6229	4·4859	4·3553	4·2305	4·1114	3·9975	3·8887	3·7845	6
7	6·7282	6·4720	6·2303	6·0021	5·7864	5·5824	5·3893	5·2064	5·0330	4·8684	4·7122	4·5638	4·4226	4·2883	4·1604	7
8	7·6517	7·3255	7·0197	6·7327	6·4632	6·2098	5·9713	5·7466	5·5348	5·3349	5·1461	4·9676	4·7988	4·6389	4·4873	8
9	8·5660	8·1622	7·7861	7·4353	7·1078	6·8017	6·5152	6·2469	5·9952	5·7590	5·5370	5·3282	5·1317	4·9464	4·7716	9
10	9·4713	8·9826	8·5302	8·1109	7·7217	7·3601	7·0236	6·7101	6·4177	6·1446	5·8892	5·6502	5·4262	5·2161	5·0188	10
11	10·3676	9·7868	9·2526	8·7605	8·3064	7·8869	7·4987	7·1390	6·8052	6·4951	6·2065	5·9377	5·6869	5·4527	5·2337	11
12	11·2551	10·5753	9·9540	9·3851	8·8633	8·3838	7·9427	7·5361	7·1607	6·8137	6·4924	6·1944	5·9176	5·6603	5·4206	12
13	12·1337	11·3484	10·6350	9·9856	9·3936	8·8527	8·3577	7·9038	7·4869	7·1034	6·7499	6·4235	6·1218	5·8424	5·5831	13
14	13·0037	12·1062	11·2961	10·5631	9·8986	9·2950	8·7455	8·2442	7·7862	7·3667	6·9819	6·6282	6·3025	6·0021	5·7245	14
15	13·8651	12·8493	11·9379	11·1184	10·3797	9·7122	9·1079	8·5595	8·0607	7·6061	7·1909	6·8109	6·4624	6·1422	5·8474	15
16	14·7179	13·5777	12·5611	11·6523	10·8378	10·1059	9·4466	8·8514	8·3126	7·8237	7·3792	6·9740	6·6039	6·2651	5·9542	16
17	15·5623	14·2919	13·1661	12·1657	11·2741	10·4773	9·7632	9·1216	8·5436	8·0216	7·5488	7·1196	6·7291	6·3729	6·0472	17
18	16·3983	14·9920	13·7535	12·6593	11·6896	10·8276	10·0591	9·3719	8·7556	8·2014	7·7016	7·2497	6·8399	6·4674	6·1280	18
19	17·2260	15·6785	14·3238	13·1339	12·0853	11·1581	10·3356	9·6036	8·9501	8·3649	7·8393	7·3658	6·9380	6·5504	6·1982	19
20	18·0456	16·3514	14·8775	13·5903	12·4622	11·4699	10·5940	9·8181	9·1285	8·5136	7·9633	7·4694	7·0248	6·6231	6·2593	20
25	22·0232	19·5235	17·4131	15·6221	14·0939	12·7834	11·6536	10·6748	9·8226	9·0770	8·4217	7·8431	7·3300	6·8729	6·4641	25
30	25·8077	22·3965	19·6004	17·2920	15·3725	13·7648	12·4090	11·2578	10·2737	9·4269	8·6938	8·0552	7·4957	7·0027	6·5660	30
35	29·4086	24·9986	21·4872	18·6646	16·3742	14·4982	12·9477	11·6546	10·5668	9·6442	8·8552	8·1755	7·5856	7·0700	6·6166	35
40	32·8347	27·3555	23·1148	19·7928	17·1591	15·0463	13·3317	11·9246	10·7574	9·7791	8·9511	8·2438	7·6344	7·1050	6·6418	40
45	36·0945	29·4902	24·5187	20·7200	17·7741	15·4558	13·6055	12·1084	10·8812	9·8628	9·0079	8·2825	7·6609	7·1232	6·6543	45
50	39·1961	31·4236	25·7298	21·4822	18·2559	15·7619	13·8007	12·2335	10·9617	9·9148	9·0417	8·3045	7·6752	7·1327	6·6605	50

	16	17	18	19	20	21	22	23	24	25	26	27	28	29	30	
1	0·8621	0·8547	8·8475	0·8403	0·8333	0·8264	0·8197	0·8130	0·8065	0·8000	0·7937	0·7874	0·7812	0·7752	0·7692	1
2	1·6052	1·5852	1·5656	1·5465	1·5278	1·5095	1·4915	1·4740	1·4568	1·4400	1·4235	1·4074	1·3916	1·3761	1·3609	2
3	2·2459	2·2096	2·1743	2·1399	2·1065	2·0739	2·0422	2·0114	1·9813	1·9520	1·9234	1·8956	1·8684	1·8420	1·8161	3
4	2·7982	2·7432	2·6901	2·6386	2·5887	2·5404	2·4936	2·4483	2·4043	2·3616	2·3202	2·2800	2·2410	2·2031	2·1662	4
5	3·2743	3·1993	3·1272	3·0576	2·9906	2·9260	2·8636	2·8035	2·7454	2·6893	2·6351	2·5827	2·5320	2·4830	2·4356	5
6	3·6847	3·5892	3·4976	3·4098	3·3255	3·2446	3·1669	3·0923	3·0205	2·9514	2·8850	2·8210	2·7594	2·7000	2·6427	6
7	4·0386	3·9224	3·8115	3·7057	3·6046	3·5079	3·4155	3·3270	3·2423	3·1611	3·0833	3·0087	2·9370	2·8682	2·8021	7
8	4·3436	4·2072	4·0776	3·9544	3·8372	3·7256	3·6193	3·5179	3·4212	3·3289	3·2407	3·1564	3·0758	2·9986	2·9247	8
9	4·6065	4·4506	4·3030	4·1633	4·0310	3·9054	3·7863	3·6731	3·5655	3·4631	3·3657	3·2728	3·1842	3·0997	3·0190	9
10	4·8332	4·6586	4·4941	4·3389	4·1925	4·0541	3·9232	3·7993	3·6819	3·5705	3·4648	3·3644	3·2689	3·1781	3·0915	10
11	5·0286	4·8364	4·6560	4·4865	4·3271	4·1769	4·0354	3·9018	3·7757	3·6564	3·5435	3·4365	3·3351	3·2388	3·1473	11
12	5·1971	4·9884	4·7932	4·6105	4·4392	4·2784	4·1274	3·9852	3·8514	3·7251	3·6059	3·4933	3·3868	3·2859	3·1903	12
13	5·3423	5·1183	4·9095	4·7147	4·5327	4·3624	4·2028	4·0530	3·9124	3·7801	3·6555	3·5381	3·4272	3·3224	3·2233	13
14	5·4675	5·2293	5·0081	4·8023	4·6106	4·4317	4·2646	4·1082	3·9616	3·8241	3·6949	3·5733	3·4587	3·3507	3·2487	14
15	5·5755	5·3242	5·0916	4·8759	4·6755	4·4890	4·3152	4·1530	4·0013	3·8593	3·7261	3·6010	3·4834	3·3726	3·2682	15
16	5·6685	5·4053	5·1624	4·9377	4·7296	4·5364	4·3567	4·1894	4·0333	3·8874	3·7509	3·6228	3·5026	3·3896	3·2832	16
17	5·7487	5·4746	5·2223	4·9897	4·7746	4·5755	4·3908	4·2190	4·0591	3·9099	3·7705	3·6400	3·5177	3·4028	3·2948	17
18	5·8178	5·5339	5·2732	5·0333	4·8122	4·6079	4·4187	4·2431	4·0799	3·9279	3·7861	3·6536	3·5294	3·4130	3·3037	18
19	5·8775	5·5845	5·3162	5·0700	4·8435	4·6346	4·4415	4·2627	4·0967	3·9424	3·7985	3·6642	3·5486	3·4210	3·3105	19
20	5·9288	5·6278	5·3527	5·1009	4·8696	4·6567	4·4603	4·2786	4·1103	3·9539	3·8083	3·6726	3·5458	3·4271	3·3158	20
24	6·0971	5·7662	5·4669	5·1951	4·9476	4·7213	4·5139	4·3232	4·1474	3·9849	3·8342	3·6943	3·5640	3·4423	3·3286	25
30	6·1772	5·8294	5·5168	5·2347	4·9789	4·7463	4·5338	4·3391	4·1601	3·9950	3·8424	3·7009	3·5693	3·4466	3·3321	30
35	6·2153	5·8582	5·5386	5·2512	4·9915	4·7559	4·5411	4·3447	4·1644	3·9984	3·8450	3·7028	3·5708	3·4478	3·3330	35
40	6·2335	5·8713	5·5482	5·2582	4·9966	4·7596	4·5439	4·3467	4·1659	3·9995	3·8458	3·7034	3·5712	3·4481	3·3332	40
45	6·2421	5·8773	5·5523	5·2611	4·9986	4·7610	4·5449	4·3474	4·1664	3·9998	3·8460	3·7036	3·5714	3·4482	3·3333	45
50	6·2463	5·8801	5·5541	5·2623	4·9995	4·7616	4·5452	4·3477	4·1666	3·9999	3·8461	3·7037	3·5714	3·4483	3·333	50

Index